MW01258388

Mechanics and Design
of Cam Mechanisms

Pergamon Titles of Related Interest

Benson & Whitehouse INTERNAL COMBUSTION ENGINES
Crouch MATRIX METHODS APPLIED TO ENGINEERING RIGID
BODY MECHANICS
Dixon FLUID MECHANICS AND THERMODYNAMICS OF
TURBOMACHINERY, 3rd Edition
Jaffee ROTOR FORGINGS FOR TURBINES
AND GENERATORS
Rao DYNAMICS OF ROTORS
Schlesinger TESTING MACHINE TOOLS, 8th Edition

Related Journals*

ENGINEERING FRACTURE MECHANICS
CIVIL ENGINEERING FOR PRACTICING AND
DESIGN ENGINEERS
INTERNATIONAL JOURNAL OF MACHINE TOOL DESIGN
AND RESEARCH
INTERNATIONAL JOURNAL OF MECHANICAL SCIENCES
MECHANISM AND MACHINE THEORY

*Free specimen copies available upon request.

Mechanics and Design of Cam Mechanisms

Fan Y. Chen

PERGAMON PRESS
New York   Oxford   Toronto   Sydney   Paris   Frankfurt

Pergamon Press Offices:

U.S.A.	Pergamon Press Inc., Maxwell House, Fairview Park, Elmsford, New York 10523, U.S.A.
U.K.	Pergamon Press Ltd., Headington Hill Hall, Oxford OX3 0BW, England
CANADA	Pergamon Press Canada Ltd., Suite 104, 150 Consumers Road, Willowdale, Ontario M2J 1P9, Canada
AUSTRALIA	Pergamon Press (Aust.) Pty. Ltd., P.O. Box 544, Potts Point, NSW 2011, Australia
FRANCE	Pergamon Press SARL, 24 rue des Ecoles, 75240 Paris, Cedex 05, France
FEDERAL REPUBLIC OF GERMANY	Pergamon Press GmbH, Hammerweg 6 6242 Kronberg/Taunus, Federal Republic of Germany

Copyright © 1982 Pergamon Press Inc.

Library of Congress Cataloging in Publication Data

Chen, Fan Y. (Fan Yu), 1931-1981
    Mechanics and design of cam mechanisms.

    Bibliography: p.
    Includes index.
1. Cams. 2. Machinery, Kinematics of.
3. Machinery, Dynamics of. I. Title.
TJ206.C484   1982   621.8′38   81-11927
ISBN 0-08-028049-8   AACR2

Printed in the United States of America

To Chi-fang

CONTENTS

FOREWORD

Before my husband became ill in November, 1981, he was waiting for the galleys on this book from Pergamon Press Inc., and had planned to complete the final proof-reading during Ohio University's winter recess. Had he known or had I known that he had only one month to live, we would have requested Pergamon Press to send the galleys earlier in the hope that he might do all the final reviewing himself in his own meticulous manner; also in the hope that he might live to see his book published for which he had worked so hard and so long.

After we learned of my husband's illness, Pergamon Press responded expediently by sending the galleys for the first thirteen chapters. He was so pleased to see them, and he struggled to sit up in his hospital bed and read page by page, but his condition deteriorated so rapidly that he was finally forced to give it up. Thus, my daughter and I picked it up, and together we tried to review the chapters for him as carefully as he would have done. During this time, we frequently had to bother him to verify some of the corrections we made. With his patient, cheerful help, we managed to read through the thirteen chapters.

We did not receive the last four chapters until after his death. With sorrow and yet with faithful determination, both of my daughters assisted me in reviewing these final chapters. Since I could no longer ask for his verification of what we corrected in these final pages, and since I did not share my husband's expertise in this field, I regret any errors that we may have overlooked.

This is my husband's first book and his last work. He would have wanted it to be presented as clearly and accurately as possible, as only he himself could have accomplished it. With this in mind, my children and I have done our best.

May I express my deep appreciation to all those who have comforted me in this time of personal loss and contributed to the completion of this book. In particular, I should like to thank Dr. Wai-Kai Chen of the University of Illinois for his kind assistance. I would ask that the readers attribute any inaccuracies in the text to me and all the worth of the book to my beloved husband who gave so many years of discipline and devotion to its writing.

Chi-fang Chen
January, 1982

ERRATA

Late in the production process it was brought to the Publisher's attention that a number of errors had made their way into the final text, despite the efforts of the author and his family during his tragic illness. Pergamon Press and Mrs. Chen are deeply grateful to Dr. George N. Sandor, P.E., Research Professor of Mechanical Engineering, University of Florida, Mr. Charles F. Reinholtz, Doctoral Candidate, Mechanical Engineering, Univeristy of Florida and Mr. Keith D. Soldner, Master of Science Candidate, Mechanical Engineering, University of Florida for undertaking a meticulous review of the text and preparing and following exhaustive Errata. Thanks also are extended to Dr. Terry E. Shoup, P.E., Professor of Mechanical Engineering and Assistant Dean of Engineering, Texas A&M University for his additional assistance in this endeavor.

ERRATA

p. 8, Fig. 1-6 title, interchange words concave and convex.

p. 21, sixth line of last paragraph, replace N^2 with N.

p. 21, last sentence, should read: The intersection of horizontally projected points on AC with vertically projected points on AB locates the necessary points for the displacement curve.

p. 26, Eq. 2-36, change $\dfrac{h\pi^2}{2\beta^3}$ to $\dfrac{h\pi^3}{2\beta^3}$.

p. 29, last sentence, replace joints with points.

p. 39, first sentence after new section heading, replace at best $p + 1$ with the first p.

p. 39, second sentence after new section heading, replace $w \geq 2p + 1$ with $w \geq 2p - 1$.

p. 39 and 40, in all equations from 3-6 to 3-8 (inclusive) the "W" terms should be the final terms in the series. For example 3-6 should be:

$$S = C_p\theta^P + C_q\theta^q + C_r\theta^r + \ldots + C_w\theta^w \tag{3-6}$$

p. 42, first sentence in part (c), change $\dfrac{h}{\beta n}$ to $\dfrac{h}{\beta^n}$.

p. 50, first equation after new section heading (9th degree polynomial) should be: $S = 126\theta^5 - 420\theta^6 + 540\theta^7 - 315\theta^8 + 70\theta^9$

p. 50, second and third equations following new section heading,

change $\dfrac{d^{4s}}{d\theta^4}$ to $\dfrac{d^4S}{d\theta^4}$

p. 51, last equation (motion No. 3) should be:
$$S = 4900\theta^5 - 29680\theta^6 + 78200\theta^7 - 112350\theta^8 + 91700\theta^9 - 40040\theta^{10} + 7280\theta^{11}.$$

p. 51, Fig. 3-7 velocity .vs. θ, exchange labels for curves 1 and 3.

p. 52, Fig. 3-8, figure incorrect, large acceleration values should be negative and occur in the second half of the cycle.

p. 53, Fig. 3-9, same note as above.

p. 60, Eq. 4-16, should be: $\bar{S} = S - S_A(1 - \bar{\theta}) - S_B\bar{\theta}$.　　　　　　(4-16)

p. 62, second term in third line of Eq. 4-21, should be:

$$\ldots \frac{d}{dX} H^{(n)}_{1i}(X_j) = \delta_{ij} \ldots$$

p. 64, last line, should be: where $f' = \dfrac{d}{dX} f$.

p. 72, Fig. 5-1 first graph, change $\dfrac{\beta}{4}$ to $\dfrac{\beta}{8}$.

p. 73, next to last equation, should be: $A = \dfrac{8\pi h'}{\beta^2}$.

p. 78, first equation, change 0.9724612 to 0.09724612.

p. 79, first and second equations, replace $(4\pi\gamma - \pi)$ with $(4\pi\gamma - 2\pi)$

p. 83, second equation should be: $\dfrac{2h_1}{\beta_1} = \dfrac{2h_2}{\beta_2} = \dfrac{2h}{\beta}$

p. 85, Fig. 5-4, first graph, change $\dfrac{\beta}{4}$ to $\dfrac{\beta}{8}$

p. 85, Fig. 5-4, second graph, the label "c" should be moved to the middle intersection of the dot-dash line with the horizontal axis.

p. 87, second to last equation should read:

$$\left[C_1 + 2h' \frac{\theta - \dfrac{\beta}{8}}{\beta} - \frac{9h'}{2\pi} \sin\left(\frac{4\pi}{3} \frac{\theta}{\beta} + \frac{\pi}{3} \right) \right] = 0 \quad \text{at } \theta = \frac{\beta}{8}$$

Errata

p. 88, third term in first equation should be: $\ldots + 2h'\left(\dfrac{\theta - \dfrac{\beta}{8}}{\beta}\right) - \ldots$

p. 93, second equation should be: $\theta_m = \theta + \dfrac{\beta}{2\pi}\left(\dfrac{\tan \delta}{\tan \gamma}\right)\sin\left(2\pi\dfrac{\theta}{\beta}\right)$

p. 93, first sentence, change $\delta = \dfrac{h}{\beta}$ to $\tan \delta = \dfrac{h}{\beta}$.

p. 95, twelfth line below INTRODUCTION should read, $\ldots$ instance, does result in a minimum acceleration, $\ldots$

p. 97, Eq. 6-3, should be: $S = \dfrac{h\theta}{\beta} - \dfrac{hm}{2\pi}\left(\sin\dfrac{2\pi\theta}{\beta} + \ldots\right.$

p. 99, between fourth and fifth line below heading 6-3, a line of print has been omitted, insert as follows: series expansion of such cam curve. Webers $\ldots$

p. 100, Fig. 6-1, replace S_i and S_f with θ_i and θ_f

p. 100, first sentence under Fig. 6-1, exchange words odd and even.

p. 101, in both occurrences change sin to cos.

p. 106, second line of second paragraph, insert the words "and described" between "Muffley" and "in", and change Qcvirk to Ocvirk.

p. 116, last sentence, change CD to H3.

p. 117, first sentence after Eq. 7-19, change CD to H3.

p. 117, next to last sentence, change DE to C4.

p. 127, Fig. 7-15, acceleration curve inverted.

p. 127, first sentence, change to: The acceleration factors for curve AC are.

p. 127, third sentence, replace with: The acceleration factor C_A of the curve FH (actually, C_D for the general MT2) should equal the deceleration factor C_D for the curve DF.

p. 129, next to last line should read $\ldots$ developed by Chen (33,34) and Chen and Shaw (36) will also $\ldots$

p. 130, first line below Eq. 8-1, replace $y(x)$ with $\ddot{y}(x)$

p. 131, first line below Eq. 8-7, delete the words up to the second order.

p. 131 and 132: The equations presented are forward difference equations. Later the text uses similar central difference equations.

p. 133, Fig. 8-2, one unit on the acceleration factor scale $= 10^{-3}$ cm.

p. 133, last line of text, change 10^3 cm to 10^{-3} cm.

p. 134, Table 8-1, all displacement and acceleration numbers have units of 10^{-3} cm, also, rightmost column should be headed Final Acceleration Factor.

p. 137, second sentence of step 2, replace stroke with station.

p. 137, fourth and fifth sentence of part 3, replace with: In Fig. 8-3, for example, the removal of one block in the third column would change $\Delta^2 S$ at 3 from 0.003 to 0.002 and would change the contribution to the lift at point M due to column 3 from 0.084 to 0.056. Similarly, the addition of one block in the second column would change the contribution to the lift at point M from column 2 from 0.058 to 0.087.

p. 138, Figure 8-4, fourth diagram, "M_3" label should be moved down one row.

p. 142, end of second paragraph, add to last sentence: . . . as a Taylor series expansion (where h is a small increment of the independent parameter Δx).

p. 142-143, Eqs. 8-11 and 8-12, replace each occurrence of Δ with δ.

p. 152, fourth line, change ordinates to coordinates.

p. 166, first equation, change $\dfrac{dF}{d\theta}$ to $\dfrac{\partial F}{\partial \theta}$

p. 166, Eq. 9-6, should be: $x = r \cos \theta \pm \dfrac{r_f}{\left[1 + \left(\dfrac{M}{N} \right)^2 \right]^{1/2}}$

p. 166, fifth equation, should be: $N = r \cos \theta + \dfrac{ds}{d\theta} \sin \theta$

p. 169, third equation, replace $\dfrac{dF}{d\theta}$ with $\dfrac{\partial F}{\partial \theta}$.

p. 170, second equation, should be: $m = -\cot \theta$

p. 170, eighth equation, replace $\dfrac{dF}{d\theta}$ with $\dfrac{\partial F}{\partial \theta}$.

p. 172, last sentence, replace $\dfrac{dF}{d\theta}$ with $\dfrac{\partial F}{\partial \theta}$.

p. 174, Table 9-1, figure references incorrect, change: (Fig. 9.5) to (Fig. 9.10), (Fig. 9.6) to (Fig. 9.11), (Fig. 9.7) to (Fig. 9.12), (Fig. 9.8) to (Fig. 9.13), (Fig. 9.9) to (Fig. 9.14), and (Fig. 9.10) to (Fig. 9.15).

p. 175, Table 9-1 for offset swinging flat faced follower, change first equations to: $x_c = x + r_c \sin \alpha$

p. 175, second equation after table 9-1, change r_c to ψ.

p. 176, second line, should be:

$$\phi = \frac{\pi}{10}\left(\frac{1}{6} - \frac{1}{2\pi} \sin \frac{\pi}{3}\right) = 0.00906 \text{ rad}$$

p. 176, third line, should be: $\dfrac{d\phi}{d\theta} = \dfrac{\pi}{10\pi}\left(1 - \cos\dfrac{\pi}{3}\right) = 0.050$

(Although π could be cancelled in the fraction $\dfrac{\pi}{10\pi}$, the author believes it is clearer this way.)

p. 180, seventh line after new section heading, change h_i to h_1.

p. 181, second equation, should be: $x = \displaystyle\int_0^{\theta_1} (r_b + h)d\theta$

p. 183, Fig. 10-4, for second curve, "h" should be measured to the base circle with radius r_{b2}.

p. 184, first and second equations should be:
$$x_1 = \int_0^{\theta_1} (r_{b1} + h)d\theta \qquad (10\text{-}6)$$

$$x_2 = \int_0^{\theta_1} (r_{b2} + h)d\theta$$

p. 185, Eq. 10-12, should be:

$$\sum M_p = 0 = (F \tan \alpha_1)\xi b - N_2 b \mp \frac{1}{2}\mu N_1 d$$

$$\pm \frac{1}{2}\mu N_2 d$$

Errata

p. 186, Eq. 10-13, should be:

$$\sum M_q = 0 = (F \tan \alpha_1)(\xi b + b) - N_1 b \mp \frac{1}{2} \mu N_1 d$$

$$\pm \frac{1}{2} \mu N_2 d$$

p. 186, Eq. 10-15, should be: $\sum F_h = Q - F \tan \alpha_1 \mp \mu_o W$

p. 186, Eqs. 10-16 and 10-17, exchange N_1 and N_2.

p. 187, Eq. 10-19 should be: $F = W = \dfrac{Q}{\tan \alpha_1 \pm \mu_o}$

p. 187, Eq. 10-20, change denominator to: $\tan \alpha_1 \pm \mu_0$

p. 188, second sentence, change . . . force Q will point . . . to . . . force Q may point . . .

p. 188, first three equations, replace P with Q.

p. 189, Eqs. 10-23 and 10-24, exchange N_1 and N_2.

p. 192, second sentence, replace F with P.

p. 192, Fig. 10-8, reverse direction of μN_1, reverse indicated direction of rotation.

p. 193, fifth line, replace μ with $\mu N_{1,2}$.

p. 194, sixth line, after the word "equations" add the text: "(which are valid for the lift position of the cycle)".

p. 194, Eq. 10-31 should read:

$$a F - \xi b N_1 + b(1 + \xi)N_2 + \mu \frac{d}{2} N_1 - \mu \frac{d}{2} N_2 = 0$$

p. 194, Eq. 10-33 and 10-34, exchange N_1 and N_2 and negate the right hand side of both equations.

p. 195, Fig. 10-10, N_1 and μN_1 should be applied to the follower by the lower left hand corner of the slide way. N_2 and μN_2 should be applied to the follower by the upper right hand corner.

p. 209, first four lines should be replaced with:

Case 1: $V_{cmin} < e < V_{cmax}$

Case 2: either $e \geq V_{cmax}$ (Fig. 10-17a)

or $e \leq V_{cmin}$ (Fig. 10-17b) .

Errata

p. 279, Eq. 12-2, lower case p should be capital P, where P is the normal load on the cam profile.

p. 284 and 286, Example 12-1, change the force on the cam nose from 650 N to 600 N and interpret this, as well as the flank force of 600 N, as the force in the follower stem at these points. Also, assume a pressure angle of 20° at the nose. P', the force per unit width on the nose, is now the same as the P' calculated for the flank.

p. 294, second line, change: $\mu = 0.03$ to $\mu = 0.3$

p. 294, Eq. 12-13, P should be P', where P' is the force on the cam per unit width.

p. 294, Eq. 12-14, σ_{max} should be σ^2_{max}.

p. 295, Figure 12-7, K has units of psi (1 MPa = 145 psi).

p. 295, Example 12-2, next to last line, change $K = 9000$ to $K = 8.30$ MPa (where 1 MPa $= 10^6$ N/m^2)

pp. 296-299, Table 12-4, K_1 should be K, and should have units of MPa.

pp. 296-299, Table 12-4, values given for B are incorrect for both the cases of pure rolling and for 9% sliding. The correct values of B can be calculated by rearranging equation (12-15) to the form: $B = (A \log_{10} K) + \log_{10} N$

To calculate B, substitute $N = 1 \times 10^8$ and substitute the values of K and A from Table 12-4. For example, for the first table entry, 1020 steel carburized, 0.045 in. in depth, 50-60 Rc, running against tool steel roll hardened to 60-62 Rc, in pure rolling:

$$B = (7.39 \log_{10} 87.6) + 8 = 22.355$$

Therefore 66.70 should be replaced by 22.355.

p. 300, Example 12-2, change 9000 to $(83.0 \times 10^6 \ N/m^2) \times (1m^2/1 \times 10^4 \ cm^2)$, and change the final result from 7090 N to 6539 N.

p. 300, five lines up from bottom, change PR to μPR.

p. 309, Example 13-1 has a number of mistakes, as follows:

p. 313 (about mid-page): change $F = 39.16 \quad \dfrac{5}{24} \leq t \leq \dfrac{1}{4}$

to $\qquad F = 78.31 \quad \dfrac{5}{24} \leq t \leq \dfrac{1}{4}$

p. 314: change $Q_1 = 2400(1 - 8t)^2 - 250 \qquad 0.074 \leq t \leq 0.089$
to $\qquad Q_1 = 2400(1 - 8t)^2 - 289.16 \qquad 0.074 \leq t \leq 0.089$

p. 314: change $Q_1 = -10.84$ $\dfrac{5}{24} \leq t \leq \dfrac{1}{4}$

to $Q_1 = 28.31$ $\dfrac{5}{24} \leq t \leq \dfrac{1}{4}$

p. 316, fourth equation from bottom: change $Q_1 = 2100 (1 - 8t)^2 + 10$ to $Q = 2100 (1 - 8t)^2 - 29.16$

p. 316, second equation from bottom: change 49.16 to 88.31

p. 323, four lines up from bottom: change $F =$ the force on the cam surface to $F =$ the force in the follower stem.

p. 326, Fig. 13-9 caption is incorrect: change to cam and reciprocating flat-faced follower.

p. 341, third line below the heading *Translational Mechanical Transformers:* insert the word mass between equivalent and at.

p. 342, equation above Eq. 14-14:

change $\quad J_3 + J_4 \left(\dfrac{n_4}{n_3} \right)^2 \quad$ to $\quad \left(\dfrac{n_2}{n_1} \right)^2 \left[J_3 + J_4 \left(\dfrac{n_4}{n_3} \right)^2 \right].$

p. 344 and 345, Example 14-1, W_t is not an actual system weight. Rather, it is the effective weight at the side load element of, first the push rod, and then the pivoted arm.

p. 354, last example, assume the plate is guided to move only in the horizontal direction.

p. 361, Eq. 14-29, change: $\tan h$ to $\tanh$ (i.e., close-up and no italics on h).

p. 362, fifth line, change, wear to at.

p. 362, equation below Eq. 14-30, change $\quad \left(\dfrac{R_e}{2} \right)^{3/2} \quad$ to $\quad \left(\dfrac{R_e}{2t_f} \right)^{3/2}$

p. 370, third line of text has an omission, should read: . . . response of an automotive valve train as shown in Fig. 14-21. Figures 14-22 to 14-24 depict . . .

p. 376, the second equation below mid-page:

change $M(h_p - r_{OG}) = M_r h_p + M_q (h_p + h_q)$
to $\quad M(h_p - r_{OG} \cos \theta) = M_r h_p + M_q (h_p + h_q),$

where θ is the angle formed by $\overline{OG}$ and the horizontal line through point 0. Assume $\cos \theta = 1$ (i.e, $\theta = 0$) for this solution.

p. 376, bottom of page: change $\quad = 0.0702$ to $= 0.1012$
and $\quad = 0.00801$ to $= 0.0299$

p. 377, Table 14-7, Region 2: change 0.00801 to 0.0299 and 0.166 to 0.188

p. 377, last line: change ... mass m in body B. to ... mass M in body B.

p. 378, third equation up from bottom:

change $= 0.234 + 0.166 + 0.0855 + 0.675$
to $\quad= 0.234 + 0.188 + 0.0855 + 0.675$

also change result from 0.585 to 0.575

p. 379, Table 14-8, Region 2 entry should read: $m_2 = M_2 = 0.188$

p. 377 and 379 headings of Tables 14-7 and 14-8 after Spring Stiffnesses: change ($\times 10^8$ N/m) to (1 unit $= 10^8$ N/m)

p. 379, first equation: change $\quad \dfrac{1}{k_{eq}} = \sum\limits_{i=1}^{6} \dfrac{1}{k_i} \quad$ to $\quad \dfrac{1}{k_{eq}} = \sum\limits_{i=1}^{4} \dfrac{1}{k_i}$

p. 379, delete the last two terms to the equation that follows the one above

(i.e., delete $\quad + \dfrac{1}{0.7186} + \dfrac{1}{1.153}$)

p. 379, last two equations: change $= 5.825 \times 10^{-8}$ to $= 3.557 \times 10^{-8}$ and change $K_{eq} = 0.1717 \times 10^8$ N/m to $K_{eq} = 2.811 \times 10^7$ N/m

p. 380, change equation to: $W_n = \sqrt{\dfrac{2.811 \times 10^7}{0.575}} = 6{,}992$ rad/sec

p. 380, second line of text, change: 5,418 to 6,992

p. 383, equation above Eq. 15-5 has a sign error, should be:

$$\ddot{X}_2 = -\omega_n^2 X_1 - 2\zeta\omega_n X_2 - \ddot{y}(t) ,$$

p. 383, Eq. 15-5: change $\begin{bmatrix} 1 & 0 \\ 0 & 1 \end{bmatrix}$ to $\begin{bmatrix} -1 & 0 \\ 0 & -1 \end{bmatrix}$

p. 384, Fig. 15-2: replace y's with x's, replace x's with z's and replace z with y.

p. 390, Fig. 15-4, displacements x, y and z should be measured from the bottom hash mark adjacent to each symbol. Also, the backlash, X_0, should be shown as the distance between the upper and lower plates.

p. 391, third line up from bottom, change δ's to Γ's

p. 398, in equations 15-27 through 15-30 the reader should assume zero offset for the follower.

Errata

p. 422, fourth line of 2nd paragraph: change simple to single

p. 465, last line: insert the word system between multiple-degree-of-freedom and coincides.

p. 475, Reference 87:   change Froce to Force.

p. 480, Reference 213:   The authors are Tesar, D. and Matthew, G.K. rather than Talbourdet, G.J.

PREFACE

The objective of this book is to provide a moderately complete and sufficiently sophisticated treatment of the kinematics, the dynamics, and the design of cam-driven mechanisms and cam-and-follower systems. The book is suitable for use not only as a reference work by design engineers, but also as a text by senior undergraduate and graduate students who are taking mechanical design courses. Faculty members of engineering departments may find this book a useful supplement to their class notes when teaching the kinematics and dynamics of machinery.

Many important contributions have been made to the subject of cam mechanisms in the past two decades. Likewise, more students and engineers are adequately prepared for the study of advanced topics in this field than was previously the case, and a greater need exists in engineering analysis and design for an understanding of such topics. As a consequence, the treatment given this subject in this book is penetrating and comprehensive, and much up-to-date material gathered from journal articles from many sources has been included. Because of the increasing use of digital computers, the computerized approach to cam mechanism analysis and synthesis is an indispensable supplement to the traditional empirical/analytical methods. The philosophy of this book is to blend various techniques involving graphical, analytical, and computer methods, with emphasis on the latter. Every attempt is made to present a book that is well-balanced as to theory, solution techniques, and actual practices of industry. Throughout the book the engineering significance of the methods and the results is strongly emphasized. Results of direct practical value in the form of design curves and tables are included. Many illustrative example problems have been integrated into the main body of the text. The Systéme International, or SI system of units, is used throughout the book since this system is intended in time to become the world-wide standard of measurement.

In addition to the introductory chapter, this book principally consists of four parts:

I. Kinematics — The kinematics of a host of cam curves is treated in Chapters 2 through 6. This includes the basic curves, the polynomial curves, the Fourier series curves, and the modified cam curves. Chapter 7 shows how to combine both basic and non-simple curves using the building block approach. In dealing with the kinematics of cam profiles, the newly developed techniques of profile synthesis are also presented in Chapter 8. The determination of profile coordinates is presented in Chapter 9.

II. Static Force Analysis — Chapter 10 deals with the important topic of force transmission, and Chapter 13 treats simple static force and torque computations.

III. Dynamics — In Chapters 14, 15, and 16 the dynamics of cams — including system modeling, formulation, solution techniques, and system responses — is given a treatment balanced between the mathematical aspects and the physical postulates.

IV. Design — The cam radius of curvature is treated in Chapter 11, and the related topics of contact stresses and wear are discussed in Chapter 12. In Chapter 17 a state-of-the-art review of the development of computer-aided designing of cam mechanisms, including synthesis and optimization, is presented.

Complete computer programs, which relate to the various important methods of analysis discussed in the text, are provided in the Appendix.

To acquaint the engineer with various sources of information (largely published journal articles) and to give him an opportunity to appreciate how knowledge of this field has grown, an extensive, but selective, list of references is provided.

The author wishes to acknowledge that he has freely consulted other books on the subject, engineering journals, etc., and that he has attempted to give specific acknowledgment where suitable and where material has been consciously used. Undoubtedly, this book owes more to the classic book by H. A. Rothbart, *Cam-Design, Dynamics, and Accuracy,* than to any other source. This book also contains some material developed from the research work of the author.

The author takes pleasure in acknowledging the support of the Ohio University Research Fellow Awards and the Baker Fund Awards Committees. Appreciation is expressed to my colleagues Drs. R. A. Lawrence and O. E. Adams, Jr. for their encouragement and support. Special thanks go to Mr. C. T. Klimko and Mr. C. T. Yu for their thorough reading of the manuscript and to Mr. N. J. Chiou for his careful typing of the manuscript.

Mechanics and Design
of Cam Mechanisms

1
Introduction

1-1. CAM MECHANISMS

A cam is a mechanical component of a machine that is used to transmit motion to another component, called the follower, through a prescribed motion program by direct contact.

A cam mechanism consists of three elements: the cam, the follower (or follower system), and the frame. The follower is in direct contact with the cam. The cam may be of various shapes. The follower system includes all of the elements to which motion is imparted by the cam. They may be connected directly to the follower, or connected through linkages and gearing. The frame of the machine supports the bearing surfaces for the cam and for the follower.

The cam mechanism is a versatile one. It can be designed to produce almost unlimited types of motion in the follower. It is used to transform a rotary motion into a translating or oscillating motion. On certain occasions, it is also used to transform one translating or oscillating motion into a different translating or oscillating motion. All translational and oscillatory input/output motions can belong to any of the following categories according to their variability in time:

• Nonuniform motion — Programmed variable speed
• Intermittent motion — Cyclic intervals of dwell
• Reversing — Cyclic change in motion direction.

Cams are used in a wide variety of automatic machines and instruments. Typical examples of their usage include textile machineries, computers, printing presses, food processing machines, internal combustion engines, and countless other automatic machines, control systems, and devices. The cam mechanism is indeed a very important component in modern mechanization.

1-2. CAMS VERSUS LINKAGES

A variety of mechanical systems is available for use by the designer to satisfy a number of motion and work function requirements. For complex motions, wheel mechanisms (such as gears) and flexible drives (such as belts and chains) cannot fulfill their purpose. In most situations, the designer must choose between a cam mechanism and a link mechanism. The inherent characteristics and the relative advantages of the two types of mechanisms have been thoroughly discussed and are summarized in Table 1-1.

Table 1-1.   Comparison Between Cams and Linkages

Cams	Linkages
Easily designed to coordinate large number of input–output motion requirements	Satisfy limited number of input–output motion requirements
Can be made small and compact	Occupy more space
Dynamic response is sensitive to the manufacturing accuracy of cam contour	Slight manufacturing inaccuracy has little effect on output response
Expensive to produce	Less expensive
Easy to obtain dynamic balance	Difficult and complicated analysis involved in dynamic balancing
Subject to surface wear	Joint wear is noncritical and quieter in operation

First, for machine operations where precise positioning requirements must be met together with phase synchronization, link mechanisms, which can satisfy a limited number of specified output conditions, can rarely meet these more complicated requirements. Cams offer flexibility in the selection of working periods, dwells, and other items; their use permits a better timing of interfacing movements in a machine.

Secondly, it is very important to consider the compactness of design. A cam system is generally much more compact than its counterpart linkage system. This can best be illustrated by an example. Consider the design of a mechanism for operating the valves on an internal combustion engine. A mechanism must be used that will convert rotation to translation. The valves must remain closed during the compression and firing strokes of the engine, and the velocity of the valves must be zero (dwell) during the intake and exhaust strokes of the engine. One seeks a "dwell linkage" that has a translational rise–dwell–return–dwell output motion event when input motion is uniform rotation. One might propose a modified Scotch–yoke mechanism consisting of a partially curved slot, but such a mechanism would be cumbersome and impractical. Alternatively, a six–bar linkage, such as the one shown in Fig. 1-1a, would be a better linkage design so far as force transmission and the control of velocity and acceleration are concerned. Fig. 1-1b shows the schematic of a cam–and–follower system design. Fig. 1-2a shows the standard valve operating mechanism for an overhead valve engine. In this design, the camshaft is housed in the lower part of the engine. This shaft transmits the valve lift movement by means of a tappet, a push rod, and a rocker arm. Other schemes of design are shown in Fig. 1-2b, c, d. Scheme b shows an overhead camshaft that activates valves by means of intermediary rockers. Scheme c shows an overhead camshaft that activates valves by intermediary valve levers, which also have an oscillating motion. Scheme d shows twin overhead camshafts that directly activate two rows of valves arranged in a V–pattern. It is therefore apparent that linkage is a poor choice in this case because it occupies too much space. For a given input speed, inertia forces are proportional to the masses of the links; these forces might be greater at higher speeds in dwell linkages than in the cams. In addition, it is relatively simple to balance dynamically a camshaft. On the contrary, it is difficult and complicated to balance a linkage system.

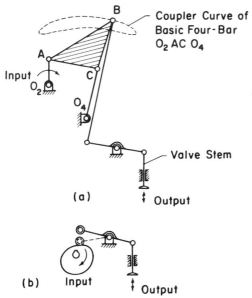

Fig. 1-1. (a) Six–bar dwell linkage, (b) Schematic of cam–and–follower system for over–head valve operating mechanism.

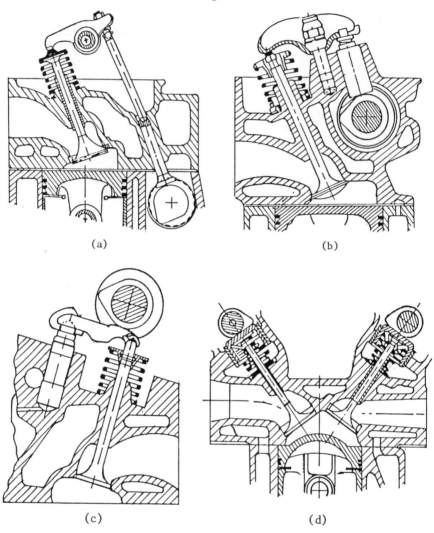

(a)   (b)

(c)   (d)

Fig. 1-2. Standard over–head valve operating mechanism.

To keep the comparison in proper perspective, however, the advantages of linkages must also be kept in mind. Linkages are usually cheaper and easier to manufacture because the dynamic performance of a linkage is not as sensitive to manaufacturing errors as is that of a cam. A small error on a cam profile can cause severe vibration in the response of the follower. Also, the connected joints in linkages are less subject to wear than are the surfaces of cams and followers.

In this day and age, the design of mechanical linkages is a highly developed science; one often hears the opinion that the operation of high–speed machinery can be made quieter and smoother by replacing cams with a link system designed or synthesized to give approximately the same output motion. As the state–of–knowledge of cam design advances to produce cams that are quieter and smoother, the reported advantages of linkages in this respect may become less significant.

1-3. CLASSIFICATION OF CAM MECHANISMS

We can classify cam mechanisms according to the modes of input/output motion, the configuration and the arrangement of the follower, and the shape of the cam. We can also classify cams according to the different types of motion events of the follower and by means of a great variety of the motion characteristics of the cam profile.

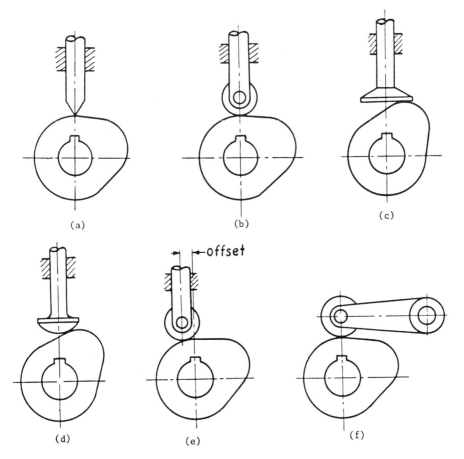

Fig. 1-3.

Modes of Input/Output Motion

(a) Rotating cam–translating follower (Fig. 1-3a, b, c, d, e)
(b) Rotating follower (Fig. 1-3f)
     The follower arm swings or oscillates in a circular arc with respect to the follower pivot.
(c) Translating cam–translating follower (Fig. 1-4)
(d) Stationary cam–translating follower
(e) Stationary cam–rotating follower
     The follower system revolves with respect to the center line of the vertical shaft.

Follower Configuration

(a) Knife–edge follower (Fig. 1-3a)
(b) Roller follower (Fig. 1-3b, e, f)
(c) Flat–faced follower (Fig. 1-3c)
(d) Oblique flat–faced follower
(e) Spherical–faced follower (Fig. 1-3d)
     A spherical face compensates for misalignment. It is used for applications where the cam profile is a steep curve. It is also used as a secondary follower.

Follower Arrangement

(a) In–line follower
     The center line of the follower passes through the center line of the cam shaft.

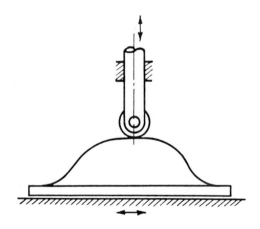

Fig. 1-4. Translating cam–translating follower.

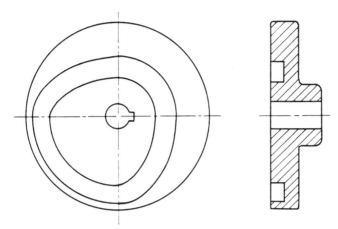

Fig. 1-5. Grooved cam.

(b) Offset follower
The center line of the follower does not pass through the center line of the cam shaft. The amount of offset is the distance between these two center lines. The offset causes a reduction of the side thrust present in a roller follower.

Cam Shape

(a) Plate cam or disc cam
The follower moves in a plane perpendicular to the axis of rotation of the camshaft. A translating or a swinging arm follower must be constrained to maintain contact with the cam profile.
(b) Grooved cam or closed cam (Fig. 1-5)
This is a plate cam with the follower riding in a groove in the face of the cam.
(c) Cylindrical cam or barrel cam (Fig. 1-6a)
The roller follower operates in a groove cut on the periphery of a cylinder. The follower may translate or oscillate. If the cylindrical surface is replaced by a conical one, a conical cam results.
(d) Globoidal cam (Fig. 1-6b, c)
The cam is either convex or concave. Rotating about its axis, the cam has a circumferential contour cut into a surface of revolution. It may be utilized for indexing an intermittent rotating follower.
(e) End cam (Fig. 1-6e, f)
This cam has a rotating portion of a cylinder, a cone, or a sphere, which oscillates a follower having its axis perpendicular to the cam axis. The follower translates or oscillates, whereas the cam usually rotates. The end cam

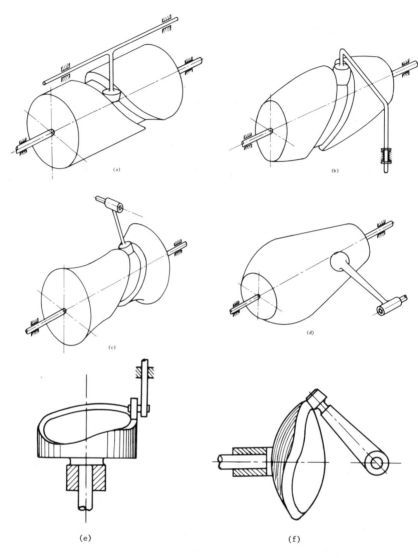

Fig. 1-6. (a) Cylindrical cam, (b) Globoidal cam (concave), (c) Globoidal cam (convex), (d) Camoid cam, (e) End cam, (f) End cam.

is rarely used because of the cost and the difficulty in cutting its contour.

(f) Camoid cam (Fig. 1-6d)

This is a three–dimensional cam having a curved face, rotated about the longitudinal axis, and moved relative to the follower along this axis. Thus the position of the translating follower is dependent upon these two variables: the cam angular and the translational positions.

There are numerous other special–purpose cams used in various kinds of machinery. However, it is not the purpose of this text to provide a description of all of them. Excellent compilations of special cams and their applications are given by Rothbart (193).

In all cases the follower must be constrained to follow the cam. This may be done by means of a

• Gravity constraint — The weight of the follower system is sufficient to maintain contact.

• Spring constraint — The spring must be properly designed to maintain contact.

• Positive mechanical constraint — A groove maintains positive action.

In Fig. 1-7 the follower has two rollers, separated by a fixed distance, which act as the constraint; the mating cam in such an arrangement is often called a constant–diameter cam. A mechanical constraint can also be introduced by employing dual or conjugate cams in an arrangement similar to Fig. 1-8. Each cam then has its own roller, but the rollers are mounted on the same reciprocating or oscillating follower.

Cam Indexing Mechanisms

Driving cams have a barrel–like shape with a groove or a rib to engage rollers that are attached to the driver wheel.

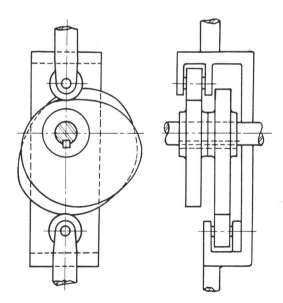

Fig. 1-7. Conjugate cam (translational).

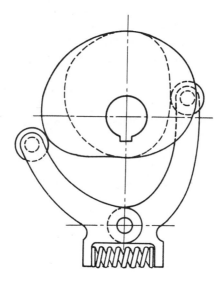

Fig. 1-8. Conjugate cam (swinging).

A grooved barrel cam (Fig. 1-9) permits a backlash during the indexing period. The existence of backlash is due to the difference between the groove width and the roller diameter. It is difficult to maintain high precision locking during the dwell.

A barrel cam with a rib (Fig. 1-10), sometimes called a roller gear drive or a Ferguson drive, permits the use of conjugate cam followers riding on both sides of the rib. It has wide applications in indexing dials, turrets, tables, or heavy rotary machine bases, etc. because of the following decided advantages it possesses over other indexing mechanisms:

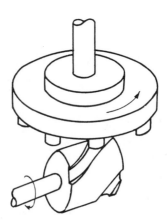

Fig. 1-9. Grooved barrel cam used for indexing machine.

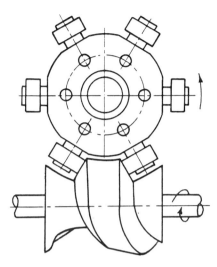

Fig. 1-10. Ferguson drive for indexing machine.

1. The rollers are always in contact with the rib without backlash.
2. The preload is easily adjustable to compensate for minute misalignment due to assembly or to wear.
3. The roller gear can be locked as soon as it stops moving, so that no time lag exists for the locking operation in dial feeds.

1-4. CAM NOMENCLATURE

We shall give a few definitions here to which the reader may refer as the need arises. Fig. 1-11 illustrates the cam nomenclature defined in the following:

The trace point. A theoretical point on the follower; it corresponds to the point of fictitious knife–edge follower and is used to generate the pitch curve. In case of a roller follower, the trace point is at the center of the roller.

The pitch curve. The path generated by the trace point as the follower is rotated about a stationary cam.

The pitch point. The point on the cam pitch curve that has the largest pressure angle.

The working curve. The working surface of a cam in contact with the follower. For the knife–edge follower of the plate cam, the pitch curve and the working curves coincide. In a closed or grooved cam there is an inner profile and an outer working curve.

The pitch circle. A circle from the cam center through the pitch point. The pitch circle radius is used to calculate a cam of minimum size for a given pressure angle.

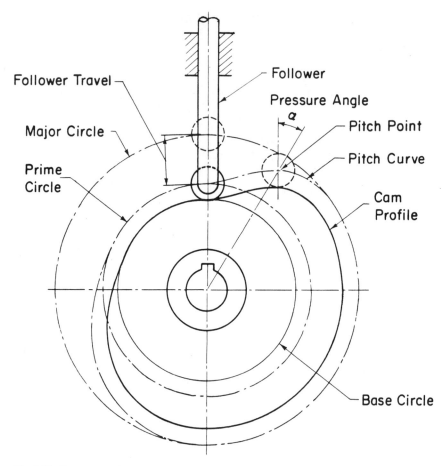

Fig. 1-11. Cam nomenclature.

The prime circle. The smallest circle from the cam center through the pitch curve.

The major circle. The largest circle from the cam center to the pitch curve.

The base circle. The smallest circle from the cam center that can be drawn tangent to the pitch curve.

The stroke or throw. The greatest distance through which the follower moves.

The follower displacement. The position of the follower from a specific zero or rest position in relation to time, measured in seconds, or some fraction of the machine cycle (cam displacement), measured either in degrees or in centimeters.

The pressure angle. The angle at any point between the normal to the pitch curve and the instantaneous direction of the follower motion. This angle is important in cam design because it represents the steepness of the cam profile.

The radius of curvature. At any point on the pitch curve is the radius of a circle known as the "osculating circle," tangent to the curve, whose "curvature" is the same as that of the pitch curve at that point. Here, we define the curvature as a measure of the rate of change of the angle of inclination of the tangent with respect to the arc length.

The transition point. The position of maximum velocity where acceleration changes from positive to negative (force on the follower changes direction). In a closed cam this is sometimes referred to as the crossover point, where, due to the reversing acceleration, the follower roller leaves one cam profile and crosses over to the opposite (or conjugate) cam profile.

1-5. DESIGN CONSIDERATION

In any cam mechanism the first decision always relates to motion specifications. It is necessary to develop a complete timing diagram for the machine, showing the displacement of the mechanism and its proper spacing and place in the time cycle, as well as its relation to the motion specifications of other mechanisms. If these displacements are sequential and bear no close relationship to one another, it is usually possible to select a simple, optimum cam profile. Basically, a good cam profile is one that has the lowest maximum acceleration; unfortunately, there are other considerations to be met, and a compromise must be made with other optimizing parameters. On the other hand, if two or more mechanisms must be synchronized and have their motions closely coordinated, it may be necessary to use a less than optimum cam profile for at least part of the total displacement. This brings about the need for careful boundary matching and the blending together of composite profiles. The choice of optimum profiles for each type depends, to a considerable extent, on the corresponding dynamic performance of the profile.

Besides motion considerations, a primary concern of the designer must be the type and the magnitude of loading to be resisted by the cam and the roller surfaces. The forces may be of several types including:
• Working loads
• Inertia forces
• Impact forces
• Friction forces

Working loads represent the useful work done by the mechanism. Their application may augment or reduce the other forces in the system.

Moving machine parts are subject to acceleration. The inertia or D'Alembert forces are a product of the mass and the acceleration of the follower system. For low speeds, the inertia load is low and will cause no appreciable deflection of components. The output motion will largely accord with the kinematically determined performance. At high speeds, however, the inertia load will increase. The cam mechanism, loaded by the increasing inertia forces, is prone to deflection and creates vibrations, which produce vibratory stresses in the follower system and remain after the cam rise is completed. These stresses may magnify the basic stresses caused by the accelerating forces generated by the cam profile, and will account for fatigue between cam and roller.

The magnitude of these forces is influenced by the acceleration characteristics, the elasticity, and the damping of the follower mechanism. In general, friction forces may or may not oppose inertia forces, but they do dampen the vibratory forces somewhat.

Impact forces are caused by separation, due to clearance and/or vibration, between the cam and the roller surfaces. This effect is sometimes called crossover shock.

A mechanism that is vibrating excessively will not only exhibit undesirable deviation from its intended ideal kinematic or geometric performance, but also will increase the potential for structural damage.

From the above discussion, we can see that in the analysis and the design of cam–driven mechanisms, there are always two basic problems, kinematics and dynamics, the two of which (each involving many parameters) are intrinsically and complicatedly related.

Kinematics (geometry of motion) will be treated in Chapters 2 through 9 and in Chapter 11. Static forces will be treated in Chapters 10 and 13. After an introduction of the dynamic modeling of systems in Chapter 14, the vibratory responses of the cam–and–follower system will be treated in Chapters 15 and 16. In addition, the problems of contact stresses and surface wear will be treated in Chapter 12. Finally, in Chapter 17 we will give an overview of the current development of computer–aided design and optimization of cam–driven mechanisms.

2
Cam Motion-Basic Curves

2-1. MOTION EVENTS

When the cam turns through one motion cycle, the follower executes a series of events consisting of rises, dwells, and returns. Rise is the motion of the follower away from the cam center; dwell is the motion during which the follower is at rest; and return is the motion of the follower toward the cam center. The three common events of a follower's motion are designated in abbreviated form as follows:

DRD   (dwell–rise–dwell) This is the most fundamental type of motion event. It has a dwell at the beginning and the end of the rise. We could just as well think of DRD as meaning dwell–return–dwell; the significance is the same.

DRRD (dwell–rise–return–dwell) There is no dwell between the rise and the return in this case. We could just as well think of DRRD as meaning dwell–return–rise–dwell, that is, with the dwell at the "top" of the stroke.

RRR   (rise–return–rise) In this case, there is no dwell. This sequence of motion is better adapted to an eccentric or a linkage.

These three types of motion events are shown schematically in Fig. 2-1.

There are many follower motions that can be used for the rises and the returns. In this Chapter we shall describe a number of so called "basic curves" of DRD type and derive their kinematic equations.

Basic curves belong primarily to two classes: simple algebraic polynomial and trigonometric. The simple algebraic polynomial curves include the con-

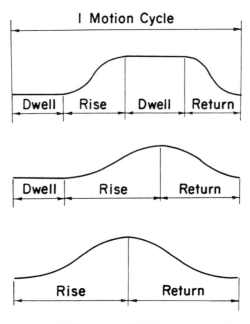

Fig. 2-1. Cam motion events: (a) DRD event; (b) DRRD event; and (c) RRR event.

stant velocity or the straight line, the constant acceleration or the parabolic, and the modified constant velocity curves. Higher degree polynomial curves will be treated in Chapter 3. The trigonometric curves include the simple harmonic, the cycloidal, and the elliptical curves. The attenuated harmonic and the modified trigonometric curves will be treated separately in Chapters 5 and 6.

2-2. CONSTANT VELOCITY MOTION

Let us begin with the simplest form of algebraic polynomial or a straight–line equation

$$S = C_0 + C_1\theta , \tag{2-1}$$

where S is the follower displacement. C_0 and C_1 are constants, and θ is the cam angle.

Starting from the zero position and designating the total rise as h during cam rotation β gives

$$C_0 = 0$$

$$h = C_1\beta$$

or

$$C_1 = \frac{h}{\beta} \ .$$

Substitution into Equation (2-1) gives

$$S(\theta) = \frac{h}{\beta} \theta \ . \tag{2-2}$$

Thus

$$V(\theta) = \frac{dS}{d\theta} = \frac{h}{\beta} \tag{2-3}$$

$$A(\theta) = \frac{d^2S}{d\theta^2} = 0 \ . \tag{2-4}$$

Fig. 2-2 shows that the displacement diagram for constant velocity of uniform motion is a straight line with a uniform slope. Thus the velocity of the follower during the motion is constant, and the acceleration is zero except at the beginning and the end of rise, where the acceleration reaches infinity instantaneously.

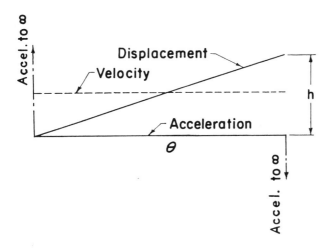

Fig. 2-2. Constant velocity motion.

2-3. MODIFIED CONSTANT VELOCITY MOTION WITH CIRCULAR ARCS

The constant velocity curve is never used in its entirety in a cam mechanism. It is used only in a modified form in combination with other curves. One such modification is made by using a circular arc tangent to the dwells. This is shown in Fig. 2-3.

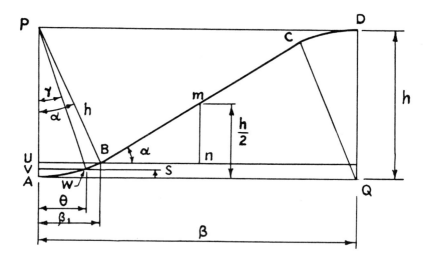

Fig. 2-3. Modified constant velocity motion with blended circular arcs.

The displacement can be derived from the geometry of Fig. 2-3 as

$$\overline{UB} = h \sin \alpha$$

$$\overline{UA} = h \left(1 - \cos \alpha\right)$$

$$\overline{mn} = \frac{h}{2} - \overline{UA} = \frac{h}{2} \left(2 \cos \alpha - 1\right)$$

$$\overline{Bn} = \frac{\overline{mn}}{\tan \alpha} = \frac{\left(2 \cos \alpha - 1\right)}{2 \tan \alpha} h \, .$$

A general expression for follower displacement within the range of circular motion is

$$S = \overline{AV} = h \left(1 - \cos \gamma\right) \, .$$

In the meantime, from triangle VWP we can write

$$\theta = h \sin \gamma \ .$$

Thus

$$S(\theta) = h \left(1 - \sqrt{1 - \frac{\theta^2}{h^2}} \right) . \qquad (2\text{-}5)$$

This leads to

$$V(\theta) = \frac{dS}{d\theta} = \frac{\theta}{(h^2 - \theta^2)^{1/2}} , \qquad (2\text{-}6)$$

and

$$A(\theta) = \frac{h^2}{(h^2 - \theta^2)^{3/2}} . \qquad (2\text{-}7)$$

The velocity and the acceleration diagrams of this case are given in Fig. 2-4.

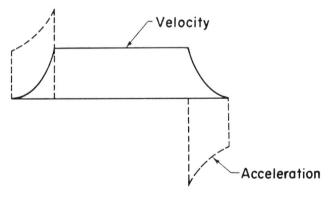

Fig. 2-4. Velocity and acceleration relations for modified constant velocity with blended circular arcs.

2-4. CONSTANT ACCELERATION MOTION

This curve, also known as the parabolic or the gravity curve, has constant positive and negative accelerations. The displacement equation for the first half of the motion can be written

$$S = C\theta^2 .$$

(2-8)

This equation is valid only between the initial point and the point of inflection of the curve. If the inflection point occurs midway through the rise stroke, i.e., when $\theta = \dfrac{\beta}{2}$, and $S = \dfrac{h}{2}$, then the constant C can be evaluated using this as a boundary condition. Thus

$$C = \frac{2h}{\beta^2} ,$$

so that when $0 \leq \theta \leq \dfrac{\beta}{2}$,

$$S(\theta) = \frac{2h}{\beta^2} \theta^2$$

(2-9)

$$V(\theta) = \frac{4h}{\beta^2} \theta .$$

(2-10)

The maximum velocity occurs at the inflection point where $\theta = \dfrac{\beta}{2}$. Its value is

$$V_{max}(\theta) = \frac{2h}{\beta}$$

(2-11)

$$A(\theta) = \frac{4h}{\beta^2} = \text{constant} .$$

(2-12)

The derivative of the acceleration or the jerk is

$$J(\theta) = 0 ,$$

(2-13)

except where changes in acceleration occur, in which case the jerk is infinite.

The part of the curve between the inflection point and the maximum displacement can be written as

$$S = C_1 + C_2\theta + C_3\theta^2 .$$

(2-14)

Using the following three boundary conditions,

$\theta = \beta \qquad S = h$

$\theta = \dfrac{\beta}{2} \qquad V_{max} = \dfrac{2h}{\beta}$

$\theta = \beta \qquad V = 0 \, ,$

values for the constants C_1 , C_2 , and C_3 can be determined to be

$C_1 = h \qquad C_2 = \dfrac{4h}{\beta} \qquad C_3 = -\dfrac{2h}{\beta^2} \, .$

When these constants are substituted into Eq. (2-14), the displacement equation for $\dfrac{\beta}{2} \le \theta \le \beta$ is found to be

$$S(\theta) = h - \frac{2h}{\beta^2}(\beta - \theta)^2 . \tag{2-15}$$

This leads to

$$V(\theta) = \frac{4h}{\beta}\left(1 - \frac{\theta}{\beta}\right) \tag{2-16}$$

$$A(\theta) = -\frac{4h}{\beta^2} . \tag{2-17}$$

Finally the jerk is given by

$$J(\theta) = 0 , \tag{2-18}$$

except at changes in acceleration, where the jerk is infinite.

Construction of the typical half displacement diagram is shown in Fig. 2-5. Line AB represents the number of degrees through which the cam rotates to produce follower displacement $h/2$. It is divided into the desired number (N) of equal parts. Here, it is shown with N = 4. Line AC represents to scale the displacement of the follower. Any line AD is drawn and divided into N^2 parts in units 1, 4, 9, and 16. Lines parallel to CD are drawn intersecting line AC. The intersection of horizontally projected points on AB locates the necessary points for the displacement curve.

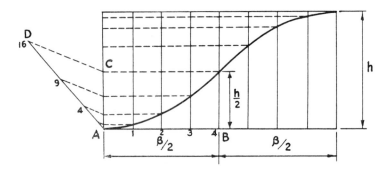

Fig. 2-5. Construction of the displacement diagram of constant acceleration motion.

The motion diagram for constant acceleration is shown in Fig. 2-6. Constant acceleration provides the lowest acceleration of all curves for a given motion. However, it has an abrupt change of acceleration at the terminals and at the transition point, thus making it undesirable for applications at high speeds.

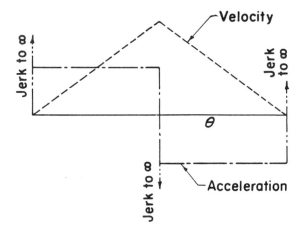

Fig. 2-6. Velocity, acceleration, and jerk relations for constant acceleration motion.

2-5. SKEWED CONSTANT ACCELERATION MOTION

If the point of inflection is not located at the midpoint of the follower's motion range, the kinematic equations are derived as follows:

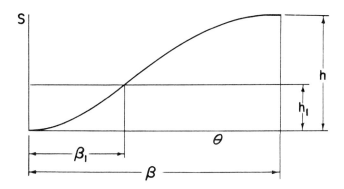

Fig. 2-7. Displacement diagram of the skewed constant acceleration motion.

Referring to Fig. (2-7) we can write

for the concave
parabola $\qquad S_1 = C_1 \theta^2$ $\qquad (0 < \theta \le \beta_1)$ $\quad$ (2-19)

for the convex
parabola $\qquad h - S_2 = C_2 (\beta - \theta)^2$ $\qquad (\beta_1 \le \theta \le \beta)$ $\quad$ (2-20)

where C_1 and C_2 are constants to be determined by boundary conditions. Denoting the ratio $\dfrac{\beta}{\beta_1}$ by r and using the boundary condition at the junction, which is located at the inflection point, we obtain

$$h_1 = C_1 \left(\frac{\beta}{r} \right)^2 \qquad (2\text{-}21)$$

$$h - h_1 = C_2 \left(\beta - \frac{\beta}{r} \right)^2 . \qquad (2\text{-}22)$$

Eliminating h_1 from Eqs. (2-21) and (2-22) gives

$$C_1 \left(\frac{\beta}{r} \right)^2 + C_2 \left(\frac{r - 1}{r} \right)^2 \beta^2 = h . \qquad (2\text{-}23)$$

Since the velocities at the point of inflection should be equal, we differentiate Eqs. (2-19) and (2-20) and equate them to obtain

$$C_1 = C_2 (r - 1) . \qquad (2\text{-}24)$$

Solving Eqs. (2-23) and (2-24) gives

$$C_1 = \frac{rh}{\beta^2} \qquad C_2 = \frac{rh}{(r-1)\,\beta^2} \;.$$
(2-25)

The kinematic equations of the skewed constant acceleration motion are then

for $0 < \theta \le \beta_1$

$$S_1\,(\theta) = \frac{rh}{\beta^2}\,\theta^2$$
(2-26)

$$V_1\,(\theta) = \frac{2rh}{\beta^2}\,\theta$$
(2-27)

$$A_1\,(\theta) = \frac{2rh}{\beta^2}$$
(2-28)

for $\beta_1 \le \theta \le \beta$

$$S_2\,(\theta) = h - \frac{rh}{(r-1)\,\beta^2}\,(\beta - \theta)^2$$
(2-29)

$$V_2\,(\theta) = \frac{2rh}{(r-1)\,\beta^2}\,(\beta - \theta)$$
(2-30)

$$A_2\,(\theta) = -\,\frac{2rh}{(r-1)\,\beta^2}$$
(2-31)

Fig. 2-8 shows the velocity and the acceleration diagrams of this version.

2-6. SIMPLE HARMONIC MOTION

Simple harmonic motion is characterized by having its acceleration proportional to its displacement and in the opposite direction of its displacement. As illustrated in Fig. 2-9, a point Q, the projection of point P, moves vertically along the diameter of the circle with simple harmonic motion as P rotates uniformly around the circumference of a circle of radius R. Choosing one end

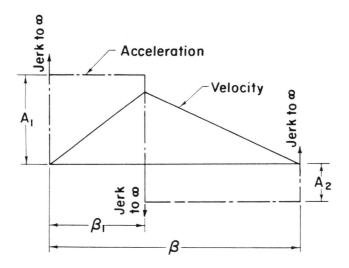

Fig. 2.8. Velocity, acceleration, and jerk diagram of skewed constant acceleration motion.

of the diameter as a reference, the general expression for the movement of point Q is

$$S = R (1 - \cos \phi) . \tag{2-32}$$

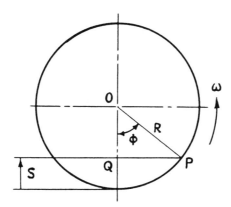

Fig. 2-9. Simple harmonic motion.

Therefore, to construct the displacement diagram, a semicircle with radius equal to one–half the follower's displacement is drawn, as shown in Fig. 2-10, and is divided into as many equal parts as the horizontal axis has been divided. The intersection of the horizontally projected points of the semicircle with the vertically projected points on AB locates the necessary points for the displacement curve.

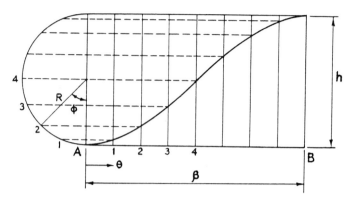

Fig. 2-10. Construction of the displacement diagram of simple harmonic motion.

The relationship between angle ϕ of the generating circle and the cam angle θ is

$$\frac{\phi}{\theta} = \frac{\pi}{\beta} \, .$$

Substituting this into Eq. (2-32) yields the displacement equation

$$S(\theta) = \frac{h}{2} \left(1 - \cos \frac{\pi\theta}{\beta} \right), \tag{2-33}$$

from which we can obtain

$$V(\theta) = \frac{h\pi}{2\beta} \sin \frac{\pi\theta}{\beta} \tag{2-34}$$

$$A(\theta) = \frac{h\pi^2}{2\beta^2} \cos \frac{\pi\theta}{\beta} \tag{2-35}$$

$$J(\theta) = -\frac{h\pi^2}{2\beta^3} \sin \frac{\pi\theta}{\beta} \, . \tag{2-36}$$

The velocity, the acceleration, and the jerk diagrams of this motion are displayed in Fig. 2-11. Simple harmonic motion has a smooth, continuous acceleration but has a sudden change at the dwell ends. As a consequence, the jerk becomes infinite at the ends.

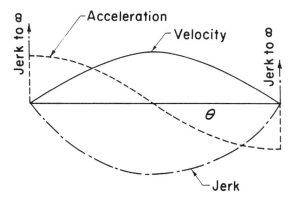

Fig. 2-11. Velocity, acceleration, and jerk relations for simple harmonic motion.

2-7. CYCLOIDAL MOTION

Cycloidal motion is obtained by rolling a circle on the ordinate AC. This is shown in Fig. 2-12 by dashed lines. The circumference of this circle is equal to the follower rise h. The graphical construction shown in solid lines in Fig. 2-12, however, is more convenient for obtaining the displacement curve. Use point A as the center and draw a circle with radius R equal to $\dfrac{h}{2\pi}$. Divide this circle into the same number of parts as are to be used for the horizontal axis AB. From the projection of these points on the ordinate, draw lines that are parallel to the diagonal AD and that intersect the vertical projections of the divisions of the abscissa. These intersections locate the necessary points for the displacement curve.

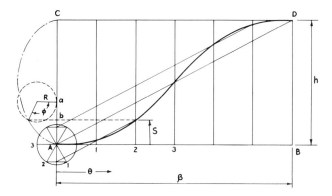

Fig. 2-12. Construction of the displacement diagram of cycloidal motion.

From the generating principle involved, the equation for the displacement can be written

$$S = \overline{Aa} - \overline{ab}$$

$$S = R\phi - R\sin\phi, \tag{2-37}$$

but

$$\frac{\theta}{\beta} = \frac{\phi}{2\pi},$$

and

$$2\pi R = h.$$

Using these two identities in Eq. (2-37) leads to the following kinematic equations:

$$S(\theta) = h\left(\frac{\theta}{\beta} - \frac{1}{2\pi}\sin\frac{2\pi\theta}{\beta}\right) \tag{2-38}$$

$$V(\theta) = \frac{h}{\beta}\left(1 - \cos\frac{2\pi\theta}{\beta}\right) \tag{2-39}$$

$$A(\theta) = \frac{2h\pi}{\beta^2}\sin\frac{2\pi\theta}{\beta} \tag{2-40}$$

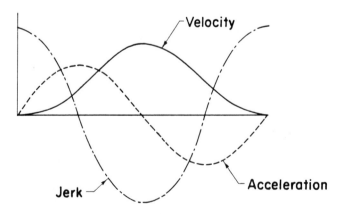

Fig. 2-13. Velocity, acceleration, and jerk relations of cycloidal motion.

$$J(\theta) = \frac{4h\pi^2}{\beta^3}\cos\frac{2\pi\theta}{\beta} \ . \tag{2-41}$$

The corresponding diagrams for velocity, acceleration, and jerk are shown in Fig. 2-13. As there is no sudden change in acceleration at the dwell ends, the cycloidal cam has the smoothest motion among all of the basic curves, and is therefore suitable for high-speed applications.

2-8. ELLIPTICAL MOTION

From descriptive geometry we know that the basic equation for the ellipse is

$$\frac{x^2}{a^2} + \frac{y^2}{b^2} = 1 \ , \tag{2-42}$$

where a and b are the semi-major and the semi-minor axes of the ellipse, respectively.

As shown in Fig. 2-14, to construct an elliptical curve begin by laying out the ordinate with the follower's rise equal to the minor axis of the ellipse. Next, draw two imaginary concentric semicircles with their radii equal to the semi-major and the semi-minor axes of the ellipse, respectively, to establish the semi-ellipse. Finally, divide the arc of these imaginary semicircles and the abscissa into the same number of equal parts and project these intercepts of the ellipse to their respective cam angle divisions. Then connect the joints to yield the curve.

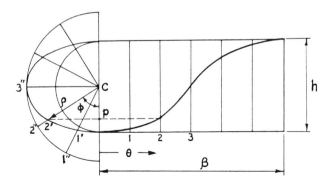

Fig. 2-14. Construction of the displacement diagram of elliptical motion.

One sees from Fig. 2-14 that when $\theta = 0$, $\phi = 0$, and when $\theta = \beta$, $\phi = \pi$; therefore,

$$\phi = \frac{\pi}{\beta} \theta .$$ (2-43)

Using Eq. (2-42), the polar coordinates of the ellipse may be expressed as

$$\rho^2 = x^2 + y^2$$

$$= b^2 + \frac{a^2 - b^2}{a^2} x^2 .$$

Referring to the triangle $Cp2'$ in Fig. 2-14 and using Eq. (2-43), we obtain

$$\rho^2 = b^2 + \frac{a^2 - b^2}{a^2} \rho^2 \sin^2 \frac{\pi\theta}{\beta}$$

or

$$\rho^2 \left(1 - \frac{a^2 - b^2}{a^2} \sin^2 \frac{\pi\theta}{\beta} \right) = b^2 .$$

Therefore,

$$\rho = \frac{b}{\sqrt{1 - \alpha \sin^2 \frac{\pi\theta}{\beta}}} ,$$ (2-44)

where

$$\alpha = \frac{a^2 - b^2}{a^2} = \frac{n^2 - 1}{n^2} .$$

Here n is the semi–major to the semi–minor axes ratio. Since b is equal to half of h, it follows from the geometry of Fig. 2-14 that the displacement equation is

$$S(\theta) = \frac{h}{2} - \rho \cos \phi$$

or

$$S(\theta) = \frac{h}{2}\left(1 - \frac{\cos\dfrac{\pi\theta}{\beta}}{\sqrt{1 - \alpha\sin^2\dfrac{\pi\theta}{\beta}}}\right).$$ (2-45)

Differentiating Eq. (2-45) with respect to θ gives the velocity equation

$$V(\theta) = \frac{\pi h}{2\beta}\ \frac{\sin\dfrac{\pi\theta}{\beta}}{n^2\left(1 - \alpha\sin^2\dfrac{\pi\theta}{\beta}\right)^{3/2}}.$$ (2-46)

Differentiating Eq. (2-46) with respect to θ again gives the acceleration equation

$$A(\theta) = \frac{\pi^2 h}{2\beta^2}\cos\frac{\pi\theta}{\beta}\ \frac{1 + 2\alpha\sin^2\dfrac{\pi\theta}{\beta}}{n^2\left(1 - \alpha\sin^2\dfrac{\pi\theta}{\beta}\right)^{5/2}}.$$ (2-47)

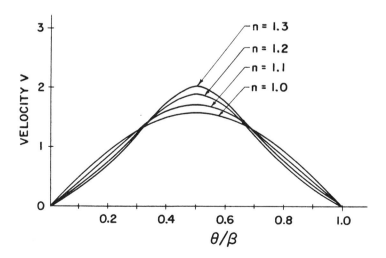

Fig. 2-15. Velocity diagram of elliptical motion.

One might note that when n is equal to 1, α becomes zero, and the above three equations describing the displacement, the velocity, and the acceleration of elliptical motion degenerate to become equations for simple harmonic motion.

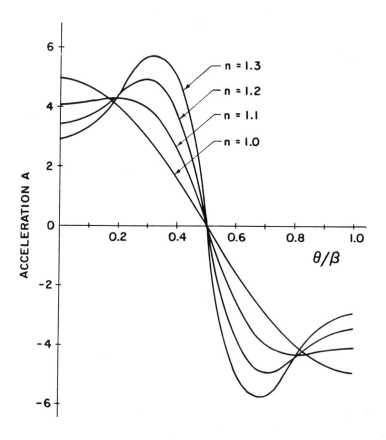

Fig. 2-16. Acceleration diagram of elliptical motion.

Fig. 2-15 and Fig. 2-16 show the velocity and the acceleration curves for ratios $n = 1.0$, 1.2, and 1.3. Further increases in the ratio n are not practical, since the velocity at the mid–transition point and the accelerations at the beginning and the end of the stroke increase when the ratio n increases.

Therefore, the profile of the elliptical curve and its kinematic characteristics depend upon the assumed proportions of the major and the minor axes of the ellipse. Proper proportions in the ratio between major and minor axes produce cams of acceptable performance at moderate speeds.

2-9. BASIC CURVE FACTORS

To simplify determination of the cam profile and the velocity and the acceleration of the follower, point–by–point factors have been calculated from the equations for the characteristics of simple harmonic and cycloidal curves. These factors are given in Tables A-1 and A-2 in Appendix A. The tabulated values are dimensionless, the cam angle factor going from 0° to 120° and the displacement factor K going from 0 to 1.

To determine increments on a cam, the given values of θ must be multiplied by the ratio $\beta/120$. For example, if β is 60°, the increment is $60/120 = 1/2$°. If every other point is used, then the increments would be $2(60)/120 = 1$°. Every fourth point would yield increments of $4(60)/120 = 2$°.

To determine the actual values of follower displacement, velocity, and the acceleration using these factors, the following equations should be used:

Displacement $\qquad S = Kh$

Velocity $\qquad V = C_v h \left(\dfrac{6N}{\beta} \right)$

Acceleration $\qquad A = C_a h \left(\dfrac{6N}{\beta} \right)^2 ,$

where K, C_v, and C_a are the displacement factor, the velocity factor, and the acceleration factor, respectively, and N is the camshaft speed in rpm.

3
Polynomial Cam Curves

3-1. POLYNOMIAL CURVES

The basic curves that we have studied in Chapter 2 may be inadequate on some occasions, especially in high–speed applications. An alternative, versatile manner of motion specification is to use a polynomial function. The use of algebraic polynomials for cam curves is based upon Dudley's polydyne method (72). The name "polydyne" is a neologism that is derived from the words "polynomial" and "dynamic" because the differential equations of motion connecting the follower motion with the cam displacement are solved by means of polynomial equations. We shall not treat dynamics until later but will now concentrate on the "poly" part of the name polydyne.

The nth degree polynomial equation is of the form

$$S = C_0 + C_1\theta + C_2\theta^2 + C_3\theta^3 + \ldots + C_n\theta^n, \tag{3-1}$$

where S and θ are the cam follower displacement and the cam angle, as before. The C's are constant coefficients chosen so that S and certain of its derivatives satisfy the prescribed boundary conditions of the motion event. Eq. (3-1) is used by defining as many boundary conditions as the situation demands. As many successive terms of different powers are used as there are conditions needed to define the action of the mechanism. This technique can be used to generate a smooth and aesthetically acceptable profile that will fulfill the design requirements, although the mathematical manipulations involved may sometimes be quite cumbersome.

For convenience of representation we shall normalize both the rise and the cam angle, i.e., the maximum rise and the maximum cam angle will both be set equal to unity.

3-2. CONSTANT VELOCITY POLYNOMIAL AND 2–3 POLYNOMIAL

The simplest case of the cam profile is the constant curve $S(\theta) = \dfrac{h}{\beta}\,\theta$ derived in Chapter 2. The normalized form is

$$S = \theta .$$ (3-2)

The boundary conditions used in this case are when $\theta = 0, S = 0$; and when $\theta = 1, S = 1$. They control only the position at the ends. It is apparent that this cam is kinematically primitive. Nevertheless, it is the lowly antecedent of all polynomial curves. For the 2–3 polynomial, the four boundary conditions to be satisfied are

when $\theta = 0, \quad S = 0, \quad V = 0$

when $\theta = 1, \quad S = 1, \quad V = 0 .$

The cubic polynomial

$$S = C_0 + C_1\theta + C_2\theta^2 + C_3\theta^3$$

is used. The first and second derivatives with respect to θ are

$$V = C_1 + 2C_2\theta + 3C_3\theta^2 .$$

Substituting the four boundary conditions into the polynomial equation and solving these equations, we obtain the coefficients

$C_0 = 0$

$C_1 = 0$

$C_2 = 3$

$C_3 = -2 .$

Therefore, the resulting polynomial has the form

$$S = 3\theta^2 - 2\theta^3 \tag{3-3}$$

$$V = 6\theta - 6\theta^2$$

$$A = 6 - 12\theta$$

$$J = -12 .$$

These are plotted in Fig. 3-1. Note that the jerk is infinite at the end points of the curve. This is undesirable.

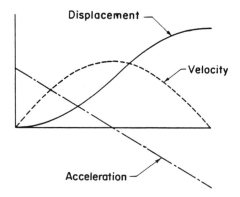

Fig. 3-1. Displacement, velocity, and acceleration for 2–3 polynomial motion.

3-3. THE 3–4–5 POLYNOMIAL

In addition to the control of displacement and velocity, we impose the condition that the acceleration must be zero at the terminals. The boundary conditions are

when $\theta = 0$, $S = 0$, $V = 0$, $A = 0$

when $\theta = 1$, $S = 1$, $V = 0$, $A = 0$.

The required polynomial, which must accommodate six conditions, becomes

$$S = C_0 + C_1\theta + C_2\theta^2 + C_3\theta^3 + C_4\theta^4 + C_5\theta^5 .$$

The velocity and the acceleration equations required for determination of the coefficients can be obtained by simple differentiation.

$$V = C_1 + 2C_2\theta + 3C_3\theta^2 + 4C_4\theta^3 + 5C_5\theta^4$$

$$A = 2C_2 + 6C_3\theta + 12C_4\theta^2 + 20C_5\theta^3 .$$

Substituting in the boundary conditions and solving the simultaneous equations yields

$$C_0 = C_1 = C_2 = 0$$

$$C_3 = 10$$

$$C_4 = -15$$

$$C_5 = 6 .$$

This results in the following polynomial and its derivatives:

$$S = 10\theta^3 - 15\theta^4 + 6\theta^5 \tag{3-4}$$

$$V = 30\theta^2 - 60\theta^3 + 30\theta^4$$

$$A = 60\theta - 180\theta^2 + 120\theta^3$$

$$J = 60 - 360\theta + 360\theta^2 .$$

See Fig. 3-2 for the plots. This polynomial compares favorably with the cycloidal cam.

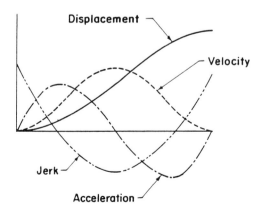

Fig. 3-2. Displacement, velocity, acceleration, and jerk for 3–4–5 polynomial motion.

3-4. THE 4–5–6–7 POLYNOMIAL

Successive derivative control can be extended into the equations to produce zero jerk at the ends. That is

when $\theta = 0$, $S = 0$, $V = 0$, $A = 0$, $J = 0$

when $\theta = 1$, $S = 1$, $V = 0$, $A = 0$, $J = 0$.

These eight conditions establish the general polynomial

$$S = C_0 + C_1\theta + C_2\theta^2 + C_3\theta^3 + C_4\theta^4 + C_5\theta^5 + C_6\theta^6 + C_7\theta^7 .$$

In dealing with high–degree polynomials, simplifications can be made if we realize that when $\theta = 0$, $\dfrac{d^n S}{d\theta^n} = 0$. Subsequently, the coefficient for that derivative is $C_n = 0$. This truth is well-recognized and is summarized in the following table for polynomials thus far derived, including the 4–5–6–7 polynomial.

Powers in General Polynomials	Zero Derivatives (at $\theta = 0$)	Powers in Remaining Terms
0 and 1		1
0 to 3	V	2, 3
0 to 5	V, A	3, 4, 5
0 to 7	V, A, J	4, 5, 6, 7

For the 4–5–6–7 polynomial, $C_0 = C_1 = C_2 = C_3 = 0$. The remaining conditions at $\theta = 1$ give the following four equations:

$$C_4 + C_5 + C_6 + C_7 = 0$$

$$4C_4 + 5C_5 + 6C_6 + 7C_7 = 0$$

$$12C_4 + 20C_5 + 30C_6 + 42C_7 = 0$$

$$24C_4 + 60C_5 + 120C_6 + 210C_7 = 0 .$$

Solving these simultaneously yields the displacement equation for the 4–5–6–7 polynomial curve and its derivatives

$$S = 35\theta^4 - 84\theta^5 + 70\theta^6 - 20\theta^7 \tag{3-5}$$

$$V = 140\theta^3 - 420\theta^4 + 420\theta^5 - 140\theta^6$$

$$A = 420\theta^2 - 1680\theta^3 + 2100\theta^4 - 840\theta^5$$

$$J = 840\theta - 5040\theta^2 + 8400\theta^3 - 4200\theta^4 .$$

Fig. 3-3 shows a plot of these curves.

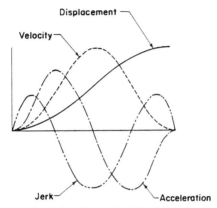

Fig. 3-3. Displacement, velocity, acceleration, and jerk for 4-5-6-7 polynomial motion.

3-5. GENERAL DERIVATION OF DRD POLYNOMIAL CURVES

This way of successive derivative control for a DRD event can be generalized by directly writing the polynomial as

$$S = C_p\theta^p + C_q\theta^q + C_r\theta^r + C_w\theta^w + \ldots \tag{3-6}$$

in which we have eliminated at best $p + 1$ zero coefficients because of the initial boundary conditions. The exponents p, q, r, and w in Eq. (3-6) are integers such that $p < q < r < w$, and $w \geq 2p + 1$. With $\theta = 1$, the following set of linear equations for the evaluation of coefficients can be written:

$$C_p + C_q + C_r + C_w + \ldots = 1$$

$$pC_p + qC_q + rC_r + wC_w + \ldots = 0$$

$$p(p-1)C_p + q(q-1)C_q + r(r-1)C_r + w(w-1)C_w + \ldots = 0$$

$$p(p-1)(p-2)C_p + q(q-1)(q-2)C_q + r(r-1)(r-2)C_r$$

$$+ w(w-1)(w-2)C_w + \ldots = 0 .$$

This system of equations can be represented in matrix notation as

$$[A]\{C\} = \{B\} ,$$
(3-7)

where $[A]$ is a square matrix,

$$
\begin{bmatrix}
1 & 1 & 1 & 1 \\
p & q & r & w \\
p(p-1) & q(q-1) & r(r-1) & w(w-1) \\
p(p-1)(p-2) & q(q-1)(q-2) & r(r-1)(r-2) & w(w-1)(w-2) \\
\cdot & \cdot & \cdot & \cdot \\
\cdot & \cdot & \cdot & \cdot \\
\cdot & \cdot & \cdot & \cdot
\end{bmatrix}
$$

$\{C\}$ is the solution vector whose components are $\{C_p, C_q, C_r, C_w \ldots\}$, and $\{B\}$ is the column vector $\{1, 0, 0, 0 \ldots\}$.

With the use of some algebra, the solution of Eq. (3-7) can be found (209) to be

$$C_p = \frac{qrw \ldots}{(q-p)\ (r-p)\ (w-p)\ \ldots}$$
(3-8)

$$C_q = \frac{prw \ldots}{(p-q)\ (r-q)\ (w-q)\ \ldots}$$

$$C_r = \frac{pqw \ldots}{(p-r)\ (q-r)\ (w-r)\ \ldots}$$

$$C_w = \frac{pqr \ldots}{(p-w)\ (q-w)\ (r-w)\ \ldots} .$$

Note that in Eq. (3-8) the subscript i of C_i does not appear as an element of the numerator and is always the last term in each of the factors of the denominator. These formulas form a systematic pattern and are easy to use.

The evaluation of coefficients for symmetric polynomials can also be accomplished by a simple systematic triangularization process (238).

Example 3-1

(a) Find the coefficient of the 3–4–5 polynomial curve of a normalized DRD cam by using Eq. (3-8).
(b) Determine the maximum velocity and acceleration of the 3-4-5–polynomial curve.
(c) Find the particular displacement, velocity, and acceleration equations for the follower, using the 3–4–5 polynomial, if the actual rise is 1.5 cm in 60° of cam rotation.

Solutions to Example 3-1

(a) Using Eq. (3-8),

$$C_3 = \frac{(4)(5)}{(4-3)(5-3)} = 10$$

$$C_4 = \frac{(3)(5)}{(3-4)(5-4)} = -15$$

$$C_5 = \frac{(3)(4)}{(3-5)(4-5)} = 6 .$$

Thus

$$S = 10\theta^3 - 15\theta^4 + 6\theta^5 ,$$

which gives the same results obtained in Eq. (3-4).

(b) To obtain the maximum velocity, the acceleration is set equal to zero. Thus

$$60\theta - 180\theta^2 + 120\theta^3 = 0$$

or $$\theta(2\theta^2 - 3\theta + 1) = 0$$

$$\theta = 0, 0.5, \text{ and } 1.$$

The maximum velocity occurs when $\theta = 0.5$. Substituting this value for θ in the expression of velocity gives

$$V_{max} = 30(0.5)^2 - 60(0.5)^3 + 30(0.5)^4$$

$$= 1.875 .$$

The maximum acceleration occurs when the jerk is zero.

Thus

$$60 - 360\theta + 360\theta^2 = 0$$

or $6\theta^2 - 6\theta + 1 = 0$

$$0 = 0.2113 \text{ and } 0.7887 .$$

Therefore, the maximum positive acceleration occurs at $\theta = 0.2113$ ($\theta = 0.7887$ gives the same maximum, but the acceleration is negative) and is

$$A_{max} = 60\,[0.2113 - 3(0.2113)^2 + 2(0.2113)^3]$$

$$= 5.780 .$$

(c) In general, if β is the total cam angle and h is the corresponding total rise of the follower, it can be shown that the conversion to actual conditions is accomplished by multiplying each term of the polynomial $C_n\theta^n$ by the

ratio $\dfrac{h}{\beta n}$, giving $hC_n\left(\dfrac{\theta}{\beta}\right)^n$. Therefore, if we multiply each term of the

3-4-5 polynomial equation by $\dfrac{1.5}{60^n}$, we obtain

$$S = \frac{20}{3}\left(\frac{\theta}{60}\right)^3 - 10\left(\frac{\theta}{60}\right)^4 + 4\left(\frac{\theta}{60}\right)^5 .$$

Differentiating gives

$$V = \frac{1}{3}\left(\frac{\theta}{60}\right)^2 - \frac{2}{3}\left(\frac{\theta}{60}\right)^3 + \frac{1}{3}\left(\frac{\theta}{60}\right)^4$$

$$A = \frac{1}{90}\left(\frac{\theta}{60}\right) - \frac{1}{30}\left(\frac{\theta}{60}\right)^2 + \frac{1}{45}\left(\frac{\theta}{60}\right)^3 ,$$

Where θ is in degrees.

3-6. MODES OF CONTROL

In addition to assigning zero to one or more displacement derivatives at the boundary, we can also impose the following three modes of control:
• No control.
• Assignment of finite quantities to one or more displacement derivatives at the initial or the terminal point.
• Interior or local control.

We shall use a DRRD cam motion event to demonstrate the use of these three different modes of control.

No Control

At the ends of a symmetrical DRRD event (Fig. 3-4), suppose that we require the displacement, the velocity, and the acceleration to be zero. However, at the midstation, displacement, of course, is 1, velocity is zero, and acceleration is left loose (no control). In addition, for continuous acceleration at the midstation, there must be zero jerk at that point. Thus the boundary conditions for the rise portion of the motion event are

when $\theta = 0$, $S = 0$, $V = 0$, $A = 0$;

when $\theta = 1$ (midstation), $S = 1$, $V = 0$, $A =$ no control, and $J = 0$.

A polynomial

$$S = C_0 + C_1\theta + C_2\theta^2 + C_3\theta^3 + C_4\theta^4 + C_5\theta^5$$

is first assumed. Upon the substitution of the first three boundary conditions, it reduces to

$$S = C_3\theta^3 + C_4\theta^4 + C_5\theta^5 .$$

Substituting with the other end conditions (midstation) yields

$$C_3 + C_4 + C_5 = 1$$

$$3C_3 + 4C_4 + 5C_5 = 0$$

$$6C_3 + 24C_4 + 60C_5 = 0 .$$

Solving these equations as usual gives

$$S = \frac{20}{3} \theta^3 - \frac{25}{3} \theta^4 + \frac{8}{3} \theta^5 \qquad\qquad (3\text{-}9)$$

$$V = 20\theta^2 - \frac{100}{3} \theta^3 + \frac{40}{3} \theta^4$$

$$A = 40\theta - 100\theta^2 + \frac{160}{3} \theta^3 .$$

The return portion would be symmetric to this curve, as shown in Fig. 3-4.

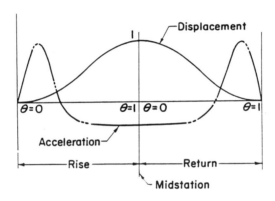

Fig. 3-4. Fifth–degree polynomial curve for DRRD cam.

Assignment of Finite Quantities to One or More Displacement Derivatives at Terminal Points

If the dynamics of the cam form obtained above are to be closely controlled, we cannot leave the acceleration at the midevent independent. Instead, we must assign a finite quantity to the acceleration at that point. This is illustrated by an example.

Example 3-2

Consider a dwell–rise–return–dwell cam with a maximum follower displacement h. The angular displacement for the rise portion is β_1 and for the return portion is β_2. Determine the polynomial equations if the following boundary conditions are to be satisfied:

rise portion

$$\theta = 0, \quad S = 0, \quad V = 0, \quad A = 0$$

$$\theta = \beta_1, \quad S = h, \quad V = 0, \quad A = -a .$$

return portion (based on a new coordinate system obtained by shifting the ordinate β_1 units to the right)

$$\theta = 0, \quad S = h, \quad V = 0, \quad A = -a$$

$$\theta = \beta_2, \quad S = 0, \quad V = 0, \quad A = 0 .$$

In addition, to assure the continuity of acceleration curves at the juncture, we require that the jerk at $\theta = \beta_1$ on the rise portion be equal to the jerk at $\theta = 0$ on the return portion.

The polynomial to be used is of the form

$$S = C_0 + C_1\theta + C_2\theta^2 + C_3\theta^3 + C_4\theta^4 + C_5\theta^5 .$$

During the rise period, using the first three boundary conditions gives

$$C_0 = C_1 = C_2 = 0 .$$

The remaining conditions give

$$C_3\beta_1^3 + C_4\beta_1^4 + C_5\beta_1^5 = h$$

$$3C_3\beta_1^2 + 4C_4\beta_1^3 + 5C_5\beta_1^4 = 0$$

$$6C_3\beta_1 + 12C_4\beta_1^2 + 20C_5\beta_1^3 = -a .$$

Solving these three linear equations yields

$$C_3 = \frac{1}{\beta_1^3}\left(10h - \frac{a}{2}\beta_1^2\right)$$

$$C_4 = -\frac{1}{\beta_1^4}(15h - a\beta_1^2)$$

$$C_5 = -\frac{1}{\beta_1^5}\left(6h - \frac{a}{2}\beta_1^2\right) .$$

Similarly, during the return period, substituting in the boundary conditions gives

$$C_0 = h$$

$$C_1 = 0$$

$$C_2 = -\frac{a}{2}$$

$$C_3 = -\frac{1}{\beta_2{}^3}\left(10h - \frac{3}{2}a\beta_2{}^2\right)$$

$$C_4 = \frac{1}{\beta_2{}^4}\left(15h - \frac{3}{2}a\beta_2{}^2\right)$$

$$C_5 = -\frac{1}{\beta_2{}^5}\left(6h - \frac{a}{2}\beta_2{}^2\right).$$

Note that all of the coefficients obtained are dependent on the finite value of acceleration a, which, in turn, is a function of the proportion $\dfrac{\beta_1}{\beta_2}$. The relationship between a and $\dfrac{\beta_1}{\beta_2}$ can be established by applying the jerk condition at the juncture. That is

$$(J) \text{ at } \theta = \beta_1 \text{ rise} = (J) \text{ at } \theta = 0 \text{ return}$$

$$(6C_3 + 24C_4\theta + 60C_5\theta^2) \text{ at } \theta = \beta_1 \text{ rise} = (6C_3 + 24C_4\theta$$

$$+ 60C_5\theta^2) \text{ at } \theta = 0 \text{ return}.$$

Substituting the appropriate coefficients into this equation yields

$$\frac{6}{\beta_1{}^3}\left(10h - \frac{a}{2}\beta_1{}^2\right) - \frac{24}{\beta_1{}^3}(15h - a\beta_1{}^2) + \frac{60}{\beta_1{}^3}\left(6h - \frac{a}{2}\beta_1{}^2\right)$$

$$= -\frac{6}{\beta_2{}^3}\left(10h - \frac{3}{2}a\beta_2{}^2\right)$$

$$\frac{60h}{\beta_1^{3}} - \frac{9a}{\beta_1} = -\frac{60h}{\beta_2^{3}} + \frac{9a}{\beta_2}$$

$$a = \frac{20h}{3\beta_1^{2}\beta_2^{2}} \left(\frac{\beta_1^{3} + \beta_2^{3}}{\beta_1 + \beta_2} \right)$$

or

$$a = \frac{20h}{3\beta_1^{2}} \left(\frac{r^{3} + 1}{r + 1} \right) = \frac{20h}{3\beta_2^{2}} \left[\frac{\left(\dfrac{1}{r}\right)^{3} + 1}{1 + \dfrac{1}{r}} \right],$$

where $r = \dfrac{\beta_1}{\beta_2}$. For a specified value of r, say $r = \dfrac{3}{2}$,

$$a = \frac{35h}{3\beta_1^{2}} = \frac{140h}{27\beta_2^{2}} \quad .$$

The polynomial equations for the rise portion are

$$S = \frac{h}{6} \left(25\tau_1^{3} - 20\tau_1^{4} + \tau_1^{5} \right)$$

$$V = \frac{5h}{6\beta_1} \left(15\tau_1^{2} - 16\tau_1^{3} + \tau_1^{4} \right)$$

$$A = \frac{5h}{3\beta_1^{2}} \left(15\tau_1 - 24\tau_1^{2} + 2\tau_1^{3} \right)$$

$$J = \frac{5h}{\beta_1^{3}} \left(5 - 16\tau_1 + 2\tau_1^{2} \right),$$

where $\tau_1 = \dfrac{\theta}{\beta_1}$.

The equations for the return portion are (with $\tau_2 = \dfrac{\theta}{\beta_2}$)

$$S = h\left[1 - \frac{1}{9}\left(\frac{70}{3}\tau_2^{\,2} - 20\tau_2^{\,3} - 65\tau_2^{\,4} - \frac{92}{3}\tau_2^{\,5}\right)\right]$$

$$V = \frac{20h}{27\beta_2}(-7\tau_2 - 9\tau_2^{\,2} + 39\tau_2^{\,3} - 23\tau_2^{\,4})$$

$$A = \frac{20h}{27\beta_2^{\,2}}(-7 - 18\tau_2 + 117\tau_2^{\,2} - 92\tau_2^{\,3})$$

$$J = \frac{40h}{9\beta_2^{\,3}}(-3 + 39\tau_2 - 46\tau_2^{\,2}).$$

Fig. 3-5 shows the plots.

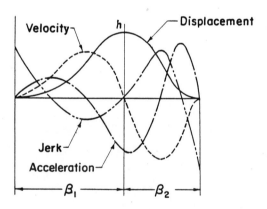

Fig. 3-5.

A special case of interest occurs when $\beta_1 = \beta_2 = \beta$. Then $a = \dfrac{20h}{3\beta^2}$, and the jerk becomes zero at the point $\theta = \beta$. The displacement and acceleration curves are symmetrical with respect to the midstation, and the velocity and jerk curves are anti–symmetric with respect to that station. This is shown in Fig. 3-6.

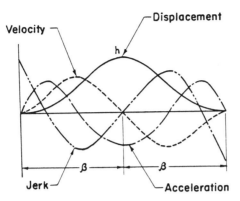

Fig. 3-6.

The corresponding kinematic equations for this case are:

for the rise,

$$S = \frac{h}{3} (20\tau^3 - 25\tau^4 + 8\tau^5)$$

$$V = \frac{20h}{3\beta} (3\tau^2 - 5\tau^3 + 2\tau^4)$$

$$A = \frac{20h}{3\beta^2} (6\tau - 15\tau^2 + 8^3)$$

$$J = \frac{40h}{\beta^3} (1 - 5\tau + 4\tau^2)$$

and for the return,

$$S = h \left(1 - \frac{10}{3} \tau^2 + 5\tau^4 - \frac{8}{3} \tau^5 \right)$$

$$V = \frac{h}{\beta} \left(- \frac{20}{3} \tau + 20\tau^3 - \frac{40}{3} \tau^4 \right)$$

$$A = \frac{20h}{3\beta^2} (-1 + 9\tau^2 - 8\tau^3)$$

$$J = \frac{40h}{\beta^3} (3\tau - 4\tau^2) ,$$

with $\tau = \dfrac{\theta}{\beta}$.

Interior or Local Control

When only considering the beginning and the terminal conditions, there is a tendency to have the acceleration curve skewed to the midstation, where the acceleration changes sign. Interior motion control can eliminate this situation. Let us consider a 9th–degree polynomial

$$S = 126\theta^5 - 420\theta^6 + 540\theta^7 + 315\theta^8 + 70\theta^9$$

that satisfies the boundary conditions

$$\theta = 0, \quad S = 0, \quad V = 0, \quad A = 0, \quad J = 0, \quad \frac{d^{4s}}{d\theta^4} = 0$$

$$\theta = 1, \quad S = 1, \quad V = 0, \quad A = 0, \quad J = 0, \quad \frac{d^{4s}}{d\theta^4} = 0 .$$

We need not verify the polynomial here. With the material covered thus far in this chapter, the reader should be able to carry out the routines of verification if he desires to do so. Let us designate this given motion as Motion No. 1 and just note that Motion No. 1 gives a peak velocity of 2.46 and a peak acceleration of 9.37.

Suppose a designer wants to impose the symmetrical displacement condition

$$\theta = \frac{1}{2}, \quad S = \frac{1}{2}$$

$$\theta = \frac{1}{2}, \quad V = \text{no control} .$$

Altogether there are 12 conditions. The polynomial specification is extended to include the 11th power. The resulting motion, to be designated as Motion No. 2, is

$$S = 336\theta^5 - 1890\theta^6 + 4740\theta^7 - 6615\theta^8 + 5320\theta^9 - 2310\theta^{10} + 420\theta^{11} .$$

Motion No. 2 has a peak velocity of 2.05 and a peak acceleration of 7.91. Next, suppose another designer requires the additional velocity control

$$\theta = \frac{1}{2}, \quad S = \frac{1}{2}$$

$$\theta = \frac{1}{2}, \quad V = 1.75 .$$

The resulting motion, No. 3, is

$$S = 490\theta^5 - 2968\theta^6 + 7820\theta^7 - 11235\theta^8 - 4004\theta^{10} + 728\theta^{11} .$$

The subsequent Motion No. 3 has a peak acceleration of 8.4.

The velocities and accelerations of all three of these motions are shown superimposed in Fig. 3-7.

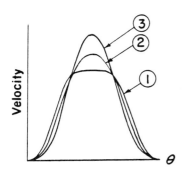
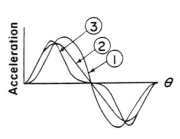

Fig. 3-7. Comparison of velocity and acceleration characteristics among three polynomial motions:
(1) 9th – degree polynomial
(2) 11th – degree symmetric polynomial
(3) 11th – degree polynomial with midpoint velocity control.

Therefore, the classical role of the polynomial technique may be extended in this way to create new polynomials capable of satisfying almost any motion requirement and offering the designer some flexibility in the final motion choice. Matthew (155) has demonstrated, by using 7th–degree polynomials, the usefulness of this technique for minimizing the cam pressure angles, the surface force, and the driving torque, as well as the magnitude of the jerk, and has compared the characteristics of those modified polynomial curves with those of the modified sine curve (see Chapter 5). The results show some trade–offs between the various criteria and the specifications. For example, the use of a modified polynomial curve makes it possible to reduce the maximum total static force on the cam by about 13% (with respect to that of the modified sine curve), but it entails a 50 percent increase in maximum initial jerk, which is normally regarded as a factor linked to the vibratory response of the follower. A combination of specifications that will come close to simultaneously optimizing all criteria does not appear likely.

3-7. EXPONENT MANIPULATION

A certain degree of curve shape adjustment can be accomplished by manipulating the exponents of the polynomial. This is not as precisely predictable as might be desired. There are no exact rules available for this curve–manipulating process. With experience, the number of trials needed to obtain a desired result may be reduced. The arithmetic involved is so complicated that computer implementation is almost a practical necessity. For example, the fifth–order polynomial family could have the power 3–4–5, 3–5–7, 3–6–9, etc.

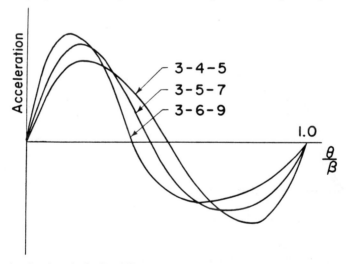

Fig. 3-8. Acceleration of a family of fifth–order polynomial curves.

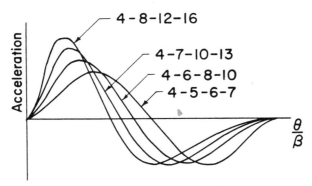

Fig. 3-9. Acceleration of a family of seventh–order polynomial curves.

The seventh–order polynomial family could have the powers 4–5–6–7, 4–6–8–10, 4–7–10–13, etc. A demonstration of progressive changes in the powers of these two basic sets of curves is given by Figs. 3-8 and 3-9. The following observations of the influence of higher powers on the topological nature of acceleration can be made.

- To obtain anti–symmetry in the acceleration curves with respect to the mid-station of the interval, choose sequential values for the higher exponents (i.e., 3–4–5, 4–5–6–7, etc.).
- To produce a skewed effect in the acceleration curves, space the higher exponents by 2, 3, . . . (i.e., 3–5–7, 4–6–8–10 (spaced by 2), and 3–6–9, 4–7–10–13 (spaced by 3), etc.).
- The higher the powers, the greater is the area under the displacement curve, and the greater are the maximum acceleration and the maximum jerk, which both shift toward the start of the rise.

Polynomial curves having exponents as high as 50 have been successfully adapted (215) to automotive cams. Fig. 3-10 shows a family of such high–order DRRD polynomials. The corresponding conditions for the rise portion of each of these curves are

$$\text{when} \quad \theta = 0, \quad S = 0, \quad V = 0, \quad A = 0, \quad J = 0, \quad \frac{d^4S}{d\theta^4} = 0$$

$$\theta = 1, \quad S = 0.350, \quad V = 0, \quad A = 0, \quad J = 0 .$$

The general polynomial equation is of the form

$$S = C_0\theta^2 + C_p\theta^p + C_q\theta^q + C_r\theta^r + C_w\theta^w ,$$

wherein the exponents p, q, r, and w may have values such that $8 \leq p < q < r < w \leq 50$.

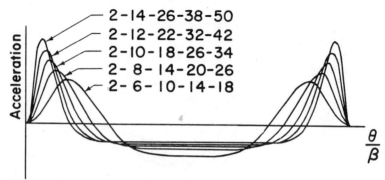

Fig. 3-10. A family of high-order DRRD polynomial curves.

A solution is first found that satisfies the boundary conditions and has a minimum acceptable value of valve lift. Then, with this initial set of exponents known, the valve lift boundary value is increased in discrete steps, with modifications to the exponents as required, until the optimum design is found. The exponent manipulation involves the whole spectrum of possible combinations of exponents that satisfy the design criteria. Sometimes, a possible exponent mapping, such as the one shown in Fig. 3-11, is helpful in keeping track of the systematics involved in the exponent manipulating process. Experience will aid in minimizing the number of trials necessary to obtain a final desired result.

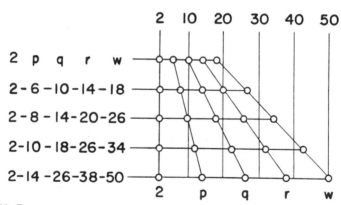

Fig. 3-11. Exponent mapping.

4
Motion Specifications by Other Polynomials*

The principal advantages in using the simple algebraic polynomial equation for approximating a function are
- The resulting equation represents the simplest type of function of sufficient flexibility.
- The solution of the subsequent set of linear algebraic equations associated with the process appears to be fairly straightforward and requires very little knowledge of mathematics.

However, this latter advantage is not strictly true. For low–order power polynomials, the solutions may be obtained quite easily. However, as the conditions of control become complex, the order of the polynomial increases, and one runs into numerical difficulties.

As we know, polynomials are usually the most convenient functions for the approximation of a continuous function when the desired interval of approximation is finite. We will first present the orthogonal polynomial here. We will then consider the interpolation of a function by the osculating polynomial.

---

*The material in this chapter assumes higher ability in mathematics than that in other chapters. It may be skipped without a loss of continuity.

4-1. REPRESENTATION OF CAM PROFILES BY ORTHOGONAL POLYNOMIALS

An orthogonal polynomial is represented in the following form:

$$S = a_0 P_0(\theta) + a_1 P_1(\theta) + a_2 P_2(\theta) + \ldots + a_m P_m(\theta) , \qquad (4\text{-}1)$$

in which $a_0, a_1, \ldots, a_m$ are constant coefficients of the equation up to the mth order, and $P_0(\theta)$, $P_1(\theta), \ldots, P_m(\theta)$ are themselves polynomial equations. Polynomials $P_0(\theta)$, $P_1(\theta), \ldots, P_m(\theta)$ are said to be "orthogonal" because they possess the property that the products of any two polynomials of jth and k^{th} orders, e.g., $P_j(\theta)$ and $P_k(\theta)$, are zero when summed over the data range except in the cases where $j = k$. Mathematically, this is represented as follows:

$$\gamma_{jk} = \sum_{i=1}^{N} P_j(\theta_i) P_k(\theta_i) = 0 \quad \text{for } j \neq k , \qquad (4\text{-}2)$$

and

$$\gamma_{jk} = \sum_{i=1}^{N} [P_j(\theta_i)]^2 \neq 0 \quad \text{for } j = k ,$$

where N equals the number of data $\theta_1, \theta_2, \ldots, \theta_N$ over which the polynomials are orthogonal. For example, if we wish to fit a second–order polynomial to 5 points, then the orthogonal property would entail the summations over the range of the 5 points to give

$$\sum_{i=1}^{5} P_0(\theta) P_1(\theta) = \sum_{i=1}^{5} P_0(\theta) P_2(\theta) = \sum_{i=1}^{5} P_1(\theta) P_2(\theta) = 0 ,$$

while values are available for only the following summations:

$$\sum_{i=1}^{5} [P_0(\theta)]^2 , \ \sum_{i=1}^{5} [P_1(\theta)]^2 , \ \text{and} \ \sum_{i=1}^{5} [P_2(\theta)]^2 .$$

An error, ϵ_i, may be defined at each point as

$$\epsilon_i = \left| S_i - \sum_{j=0}^{m} a_j P_j(\theta_i) \right|^2 , \qquad (4\text{-}3)$$

and the summation $\Gamma^2 = \sum_{i=1}^{N} \epsilon_i^2$ is to be minimized based on the least–square
error. If $\Gamma^2 = 0$, the fit of the orthogonal polynomial is not an approximation
but exact.

Letting

$$\delta_j = \sum_{i=1}^{N} S_i P_j(\theta_i) \tag{4-4}$$

$$\gamma_{jk} = \sum_{i=1}^{N} P_j(\theta_i) P_k(\theta_i) ,$$

the condition that Γ^2 be a minimum leads to

$$\frac{\delta\Gamma^2}{\delta a_j} = 0 \quad \text{with } j=0, 1, 2, \ldots, m$$

or

$$2 \sum_{i=1}^{N} \left\{ \left[S_i - \sum_{j=0}^{m} a_j P_j(\theta_i) \right] P_j(\theta_i) \right\} = 0 . \tag{4-5}$$

That is

$$\delta_j = \sum_{k=0}^{m} a_k \gamma_{jk} . \tag{4-6}$$

In expanded form, this is equivalent to

$$\delta_1 = \gamma_{00} a_0 + \gamma_{01} a_1 + \ldots + \gamma_{0m} a_m \tag{4-7}$$

$$\delta_2 = \gamma_{10} a_0 + \gamma_{11} a_1 + \ldots + \gamma_{1m} a_m$$

. . . .

$$\delta_m = \gamma_{m0} a_0 + \gamma_{m1} a_1 + \ldots + \gamma_{mm} a_m .$$

There are now $m+1$ simultaneous equations and $m+1$ unknowns. At this
point the orthogonality condition is introduced to simplify solutions.

Using the orthogonality condition, we obtain an equivalent set of equations that contains only one term on the right–hand side of each equation, viz.

$$\delta_0 = \gamma_{00} a_0 \tag{4-8}$$

$$\delta_1 = \gamma_{11} a_1$$

$$\delta_2 = \gamma_{22} a_2$$

$$\delta_m = \gamma_{mm} a_m .$$

This gives

$$a_i = \frac{\delta_i}{\gamma_{ii}} . \tag{4-9}$$

As we can see, the major advantages of this approach are that no coefficient is dependent on another and that it is not necessary to solve a set of linear equations. The need to solve such a set of equations is the main cause of ill–conditioning in the power polynomial. An additional benefit is the saving of computing time, since the a_i's are independent of the degree of fit m.

The next step is to select suitable orthogonal polynomials that will fulfill our requirements. A number of techniques have been used to generate the needed orthogonal polynomials, e.g., the one developed by Hays and Vickers (97). However, the most useful of these methods is the one Forsythe (81) developed in 1957.

In Forsythe's approach the orthogonal polynomials are generated by the use of a three–term recurrence relation in which three polynomials of different orders (j, $j-1$, and $j-2$) are linked by the following formula:

$$P_j(\theta) = (\theta - \alpha_j) P_{j-1}(\theta) - \beta_{j-1} P_{j-2}(\theta) , \tag{4-10}$$

where α_j and β_{j-1} are constants, and j is a typical order. In general, this relation allows us to evaluate the highest order of the three polynomials from a knowledge of the two immediate lower orders, e.g., the third order is generated from the second and first orders. Forsythe chose $P_0(\theta)$ to be unity. Ignoring all of the polynomials with orders less than $P_0(\theta)$, we find that the polynomials up to the mth order can be generated from the following equations:

$$P_0(\theta) = 1 \tag{4-11}$$

$$P_1(\theta) = \theta P_0(\theta) - \alpha_1 P_0(\theta)$$

$$P_2(\theta) = \theta P_1(\theta) - \alpha_2 P_1(\theta) - \beta_1 P_0(\theta)$$

$$\cdots\cdots$$

$$P_j(\theta) = \theta P_{j-1}(\theta) - \alpha_j P_{j-1}(\theta) - \beta_{j-1} P_{j-2}(\theta) \ ,$$

where the α_j and β_j must be chosen in such a way as to satisfy the orthogonality property

$$\sum_{i=1}^{N} P_j(\theta_i) P_k(\theta_i) = 0 \ , \quad j \neq k \ .$$

α_j is computed by multiplying the recurrence relations $P_j(\theta_i)$ by $P_{j-1}(\theta_i)$ and summing over the N data points

$$\sum_{i=1}^{N} P_j(\theta_i) P_{j-1}(\theta_i) = \sum_{i=1}^{N} \theta_i \, [P_{j-1}(\theta_i)]^2 - \alpha_j \sum_{i=1}^{N} [P_{j-1}(\theta_i)]^2$$

$$- \beta_{j-1} \sum_{i-1}^{N} P_{j-1}(\theta_i) P_{j-2}(\theta_i) \ .$$

For $P_j P_{j-1}$ and $P_{j-1} P_{j-2}$ to be orthogonal with respect to the summation it must follow that

$$\alpha_j = \frac{\displaystyle\sum_{i=1}^{N} \theta_i \, [P_{j-1}(\theta_i)]^2}{\displaystyle\sum_{i=1}^{N} [P_{j-1}(\theta_i)]^2} \ . \tag{4-12}$$

For a similar argument

$$\beta_j = \frac{\displaystyle\sum_{i=1}^{N} [P_j(\theta_i)]^2}{\displaystyle\sum_{i=1}^{N} [P_{j-1}(\theta_i)]^2} \ . \tag{4-13}$$

The coefficients a_0 , a_1 ,... , a_m of the equation are evaluated from

$$a_m = \frac{\sum_{i=1}^{N} S_i P_m(\theta_i)}{\sum_{i=1}^{N} [P_m(\theta_i)]^2} . \qquad (4\text{-}14)$$

For further details about this method, the reader is referred to the work of Forsythe.

For an orthogonal polynomial to be useful in applications, it is necessary to build boundary conditions into its solution. We shall refer to the technique developed by Clenshaw and Hayes (50). Essentially, the approach used by Clenshaw and Hayes is an extension of the Forsythe method with the major difference between the two techniques being that Forsythe assumes the first orthogonal polynomial to be unity, $P_0(\theta) = 1$, while Clenshaw and Hayes allow $P_0(\theta)$ to be a function that incorporates the boundary conditions. All of the other steps for generating the higher order polynomials are exactly the same.

To fit a set of data through the use of an orthogonal polynomial that requires the curve to pass exactly through the terminal points $A(\theta_A, S_A)$ and $B(\theta_B, S_B)$, we normalize the abscissa θ so that it is zero at A and unity at B, or

$$\bar{\theta} = \frac{\theta - \theta_A}{\theta_B - \theta_A} , \qquad (4\text{-}15)$$

and we transform the dependent variable S by using the following relation:

$$\bar{S} - S - S_A(1 - \bar{\theta}) - S_B\bar{\theta} . \qquad (4\text{-}16)$$

This relation is derived from the boundary requirements imposed, and its validity can be readily checked in this manner:

At $\theta = \theta_A$ or $\bar{\theta} = 0$, $\bar{S} = S - S_A$ or $S = S_A + \bar{S}$

At $\theta = \theta_B$ or $\bar{\theta} = 1$, $\bar{S} = S - S_B$ or $S = S_B + \bar{S}$.

The boundary requirements are automatically satisfied if the transformed ordinates $\bar{S}$ are also zero at the locations $\theta = \theta_A$ and $\theta = \theta_B$. These conditions can be achieved by incorporating the factor $\bar{\theta}(1 - \bar{\theta})$ into the $\bar{S}$ function. Since the function $\bar{S}$ is the orthogonal polynomial

$$\bar{S} = C_0 P_0(\bar{\theta}) + C_1 P_1(\bar{\theta}) + \ldots + C_m P_m(\bar{\theta}) , \qquad (4\text{-}17)$$

the simplest method to include the factor $\bar{\theta}(1 - \bar{\theta})$ is to start the recurrence relation by letting $P_0(\bar{\theta}) = \bar{\theta}(1 - \bar{\theta})$ instead of unity, i.e.,

$$P_0(\bar{\theta}) = \bar{\theta}(1 - \bar{\theta}) \tag{4-18}$$

$$P_1(\bar{\theta}) = \bar{\theta}P_0(\bar{\theta}) - \alpha_1 P_0(\bar{\theta})$$

$$\ldots$$

$$P_m(\bar{\theta}) = \bar{\theta}P_{m-1}(\bar{\theta}) - \alpha_m P_{m-1}(\bar{\theta}) - \beta_{m-1}P_{m-2}(\bar{\theta}) \, .$$

This allows us to have this factor built into the solution to give $S = S_A$ at $\theta = \theta_A$ and $S = S_B$ at $\theta = \theta_B$.

In a similar manner, if we specify that the slope (velocity) at point A should be zero, then our transformed function becomes

$$\overline{S} = S - S_A(1 - \bar{\theta}^2) - S_B\bar{\theta}^2 \, , \tag{4-19}$$

and the factor used to begin our recurrence relation is now $\bar{\theta}^2(1 - \bar{\theta})$. If we specify that the acceleration at point A should be zero, then the transformed function becomes

$$\overline{S} = S - S_A(1 - \bar{\theta}^3) - S_B\bar{\theta}^3 \, , \tag{4-20}$$

and the factor used for initiating the recurrence relation is $\bar{\theta}^3(1 - \bar{\theta})$.

While this method is a most versatile approach for least squares curve fitting, it is less easily applied to practical problems than is the ordinary power polynomial because of the form of the equation. To achieve the best of both worlds — the use of the orthogonal polynomial for obtaining the solution and the simple algebraic polynomial for the final representation of cam profile — a computer subroutine can be written whereby a given set of data may be solved by orthogonal polynomials using the Clenshaw–Hayes approach and then transformed back to simple algebraic polynomials by the use of a matrix. The combination of these two steps has been found to be most useful in cam profile design.

4-2. REPRESENTATION OF CAM PROFILES BY OSCULATING POLYNOMIALS

Osculating polynomials interpolate a function $f(X)$ whose values are given at discrete stations. According to Falk (239), these polynomials $H_{ki}^{(m)}(x)$ have the following properties:

$$H_{oi}^{(n)}(X_j) = \delta_{ij} \; ; \quad \frac{d}{dX} H_{oi}^{(n)}(X_j) = 0 \; ; \quad \frac{d^2}{dX^2} H_{oi}^{(n)}(X_j) = 0 \; ; \quad (4\text{-}21)$$

$$\ldots\ldots \qquad \frac{d^n}{dX^n} H_{oi}^{(n)}(X_j) = 0$$

$$H_{1i}^{(n)}(X_j) = 0 \; ; \quad \frac{d}{dX} H_{1i}^{(n)}(X_j) = 0 \; ; \quad \frac{d^2}{dX^2} H_{1i}^{(n)}(X_j) = 0 \; ;$$

$$\ldots\ldots \qquad \frac{d^n}{dX^n} H_{1i}^{(n)}(X_j) = 0$$

$$\ldots\ldots$$
$$\ldots\ldots$$

$$H_{ni}^{(n)}(X_j) = 0 \; ; \quad \frac{d}{dX} H_{ni}^{(n)}(X_j) = 0 \; ; \quad \frac{d^2}{dX^2} H_{ni}^{(n)}(X_j) = 0 \; ;$$

$$\ldots\ldots \qquad \frac{d^n}{dX^n} H_{ni}^{(n)}(X_j) = \delta_{ij} \, ,$$

where n is the number of derivatives that the set can interpolate, and X_j is specific values of the argument X of the polynomial. For example, if $n=0$; $i, j = 1, 2$; and $X_1 = 0, X_2 = a$; the requirements become

$$H_{01}^{(0)}(0) = 1 \; ; \quad H_{01}^{(0)}(a) = 0$$

$$H_{02}^{(0)}(0) = 0 \; ; \quad H_{02}^{(0)}(a) = 1 \, .$$

A pair of polynomials $H_{01}^{(0)}(X)$ having these properties is

$$H_{01}^{(0)}(X) \;=\; \frac{X - X_2}{X_1 - X_2} \;=\; \frac{-(X - a)}{a}$$

$$H_{02}^{(0)}(X) \;=\; \frac{X - X_1}{X_2 - X_1} \;=\; \frac{X}{a} \, .$$

These are known as Lagrange interpolation formulas. We will call them oscula-tory polynomials of zero order. They are shown in Fig. 4-1. They can be used to interpolate a function $f(X)$ at the two points $X_1 = 0$ and $X_2 = a$, given the val-ues $f(0)$ and $f(a)$ are such that

$$f(X) = H_{01}^{(0)}(X)f(0) + H_{02}^{(0)}(X)f(a) .$$ (4-22)

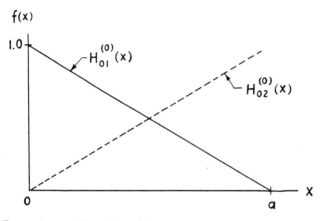

Fig. 4.1. Zero–order osculating polynomials.

These interpolation formulas can be generated for any number of points and for as many derivatives as are desired. For instance, if we set $n = 1$; $i, j = 1, 2$; and $X_1 = 0$, $X_2 = a$ in Eq. (4-21), the requirements are

$$H_{01}^{(1)}(0) = 1 ; \frac{d}{dX} H_{01}^{(1)}(0) = 0 ; H_{01}^{(1)}(a) = 0 ; \frac{d}{dX} H_{01}^{(1)}(a) = 0$$

$$H_{02}^{(1)}(0) = 0 ; \frac{d}{dX} H_{02}^{(1)}(0) = 0 ; H_{02}^{(1)}(a) = 1 ; \frac{d}{dX} H_{02}^{(1)}(a) = 0$$

$$H_{11}^{(1)}(0) = 0 ; \frac{d}{dX} H_{11}^{(1)}(0) = 1 ; H_{11}^{(1)}(a) = 0 ; \frac{d}{dX} H_{11}^{(1)}(a) = 0$$

$$H_{12}^{(1)}(0) = 0 ; \frac{d}{dX} H_{12}^{(1)}(0) = 0 ; H_{12}^{(1)}(a) = 0 ; \frac{d}{dX} H_{12}^{(1)}(a) = 1 .$$

A set of polynomials having these properties is

$$H_{01}^{(1)}(X) = \left[1 - 2\left(\frac{X - X_1}{X_1 - X_2}\right)\right]\left(\frac{X - X_2}{X_1 - X_2}\right)^2 \qquad\qquad (4\text{-}23)$$

$$= \frac{1}{a^3}(2X^3 - 3aX^2 + a^3)$$

$$H_{02}^{(1)}(X) = \left[1 - 2\left(\frac{X - X_2}{X_2 - X_1}\right)\right]\left(\frac{X - X_1}{X_2 - X_1}\right)^2$$

$$= \frac{1}{a^3}(-2X^3 + 3aX^2)$$

$$H_{11}^{(1)}(X) = (X - X_1)\left(\frac{X - X_2}{X_1 - X_2}\right)^2$$

$$= \frac{1}{a^2}(X^3 - 2aX^2 + a^2X)$$

$$H_{12}^{(1)}(X) = (X - X_2)\left(\frac{X - X_1}{X_2 - X_1}\right)^2$$

$$= \frac{1}{a^2}(X^3 - aX^2).$$

These are recognizable as Lagrange interpolation formulas. We will call them osculatory polynomials of first order. They are shown in Fig. 4-2. The values of the osculatory polynomials, as well as the first derivatives at the discrete stations ($X=0$ and $X=a$ here), coincide with the corresponding values of the function $f(X)$. Thus

$$f(X) = H_{01}^{(1)}(X)f(0) = H_{02}^{(1)}(X)f(a) + H_{11}^{(1)}(X)f'(0) \qquad\qquad (4\text{-}24)$$

$$+ H_{12}^{(1)}(X)f'(a),$$

where $f' = \dfrac{d}{dX}$.

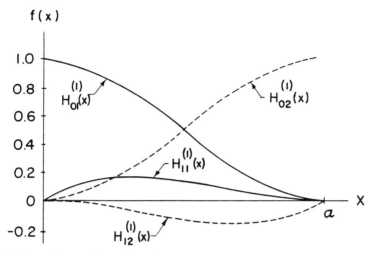

Fig. 4-2. First–order osculating polynomials.

In this fashion, higher order osculating polynomials can be generated. The second– and third–order osculating polynomials are given in the following. The second–order osculating polynomial is shown in Fig. 4-3.

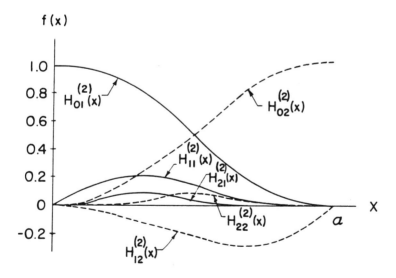

Fig. 4-3. Second–order osculating polynomials.

Second–order osculating polynomial — interpolate up to the second derivatives of the function

$$f(X) = H^{(2)}_{01}(X)f(0) + H^{(2)}_{02}(X)f(a) + H^{(2)}_{11}(X)f'(0) \tag{4-25}$$

$$+ H^{(2)}_{12}(X)f'(a) + H^{(2)}_{21}(X)f''(0) + H^{(2)}_{22}(X)f''(a) ,$$

where

$$H^{(2)}_{01}(X) = \frac{1}{a^5} (a^2 - 10a^2X^3 + 15aX^4 - 6X^5) \tag{4-26}$$

$$H^{(2)}_{02}(X) = \frac{1}{a^5} (10a^2X^3 - 15aX^4 + 6X^5)$$

$$H^{(2)}_{11}(X) = \frac{1}{a^4} (a^4X - 6a^2X^3 + 8aX^4 - 3X^5)$$

$$H^{(2)}_{12}(X) = \frac{1}{a^4} (-4a^2X^3 + 7aX^4 - 3X^5)$$

$$H^{(2)}_{22}(X) = \frac{1}{2a^3} (a^3X^2 - 3a^2X^3 + 3aX^4 - X^5)$$

$$H^{(2)}_{22}(X) = \frac{1}{2a^3} (a^2X^3 - 2aX^4 + X^5) .$$

Third–order osculating polynomial — interpolate up to the third derivatives of the function

$$f(X) = H^{(3)}_{01}(X)f(0) + H^{(3)}_{02}(X)f(a) + H^{(3)}_{11}(X)f'(0) \tag{4-27}$$

$$+ H^{(3)}_{12}(X)f'(a) + H^{(3)}_{21}(X)f''(0) + H^{(3)}_{22}(X)f''(a)$$

$$+ H^{(3)}_{31}(X)f'''(0) + H^{(3)}_{32}(X)f'''(a) ,$$

where

$$H_{01}^{(3)}(X) = \frac{1}{a^7} (a^7 - 35a^3 X^4 + 84a^2 X^5 - 70aX^6 + 20X^7)$$

$$H_{02}^{(3)}(X) = \frac{1}{a^7} (35a^3 X^4 - 84a^2 X^5 + 70aX^6 - 20X^7)$$

$$H_{11}^{(3)}(X) = \frac{1}{a^6} (a^6 X - 20a^3 X^4 + 45a^2 X^5 - 36aX^6 + 10X^7)$$

$$H_{12}^{(3)}(X) = \frac{1}{a^6} (-15a^3 X^4 + 39a^2 X^5 - 34aX^6 + 10X^7)$$

$$H_{21}^{(3)}(X) = \frac{1}{2a^5} (a^5 X^2 - 10a^3 X^4 + 20a^2 X^5 - 15aX^6 + 4X^7)$$

$$H_{22}^{(3)}(X) = \frac{1}{2a^5} (5a^3 X^4 - 14a^2 X^5 + 13aX^6 - 4X^7)$$

$$H_{31}^{(3)}(X) = \frac{1}{6a^4} (a^4 X^3 - 4a^3 X^4 + 6a^2 X^5 - 4aX^6 + X^7)$$

$$H_{32}^{(3)}(X) = \frac{1}{6a^4} (-a^3 X^4 + 3a^2 X^5 - 3aX^6 + X^7) .$$

A typical cam profile of a DRD motion event can be represented by osculating polynomials. To show this we consider the following examples:

Example 4-1   A continuous DRD cam profile represented by a third–order osculating polynomial.

If a third–order osculating polynomial represents the cam profile, there are eight unknown coefficients in the equations. If continuity at the boundary up to the first derivative is assumed, there are four boundary conditions (two each at $\theta = 0$ and $\theta = \beta$).

There are four conditions for the four remaining unknowns. A first–order osculating polynomial that has terms up to the third power and that satisfies the boundary conditions up to the first derivative can be used as the cam profile.

The boundary conditions are

$$y(0) = 0 \qquad y(\beta) = h$$

$$\dot{y}(0) = 0 \qquad \dot{y}(\beta) = 0 \ .$$

The expression for y satisfying these conditions is

$$y(\theta) = H_{01}^{(1)}(\theta)y(0) + H_{02}^{(1)}(\theta)y(\beta) + H_{11}^{(1)}(\theta)\dot{y}(0)$$

$$+ \ H_{12}^{(1)}(\theta)\dot{y}(\beta) \qquad (0 \leq \theta \leq \beta) \ .$$

Substituting the boundary conditions into the above equation gives

$$y(\theta) = H_{02}^{(1)}h$$

$$= h \frac{1}{\beta^3} (3\beta\theta^2 - 2\theta^3)$$

or

$$y(\tau) = h(3\tau^2 - 2\tau^3) , \qquad 0 \leq \tau \leq 1 \ ,$$

where the nondimensional ratio is $\tau = \dfrac{\theta}{\beta}$.

This is exactly the same as the 2–3 polynomial cam.

Example 4-2   A continuous DRD cam profile represented by a fifth–order osculating polynomial.

If a fifth–order polynomial represents the curve, there are twelve unknown coefficients in the equations. If continuity up to the second derivatives is assumed, there are six boundary conditions (three each at $\theta = 0$ and $\theta = \beta$).

There are six conditions for the six remaining unknowns. A second–order osculating polynomial that has terms up to the fifth power and that satisfies the boundary conditions up to the second derivative can be used as the cam profile. The boundary conditions are

$$y(0) = 0, \quad \dot{y}(0) = 0, \quad \ddot{y}(0) = 0$$

$$y(\beta) = h, \quad \dot{y}(\beta) = 0, \quad \ddot{y}(\beta) = 0.$$

The expression for y satisfying these conditions is

$$y(\theta) = H_{01}^{(2)}(\theta)y(0) + H_{02}^{(2)}(\theta)y(\beta)$$

$$+ H_{11}^{(2)}(\theta)\dot{y}(0) + H_{12}^{(2)}(\theta)\dot{y}(\beta)$$

$$+ H_{21}^{(2)}(\theta)\ddot{y}(0) + H_{22}^{(2)}(\theta)\ddot{y}(\beta), \quad 0 \le \theta \le \beta.$$

Substituting the boundary conditions into the above equation gives

$$y(\theta) = H_{02}^{(2)} h$$

$$= h \frac{1}{\beta^5} (10\beta^2\theta^3 - 15\beta\theta^4 + 6\theta^5)$$

or

$$y(\tau) = h(10\tau^3 - 15\tau^4 + 6\tau^5), \quad 0 \le \tau \le 1.$$

This is exactly the same as the 3–4–5 polynomial cam.

Example 4-3   A continuous DRD cam profile represented by a seventh–order osculating polynomial.

If a seventh–order polynomial represents the curve, there are sixteen unknown coefficients in the equations. If continuity up to the third derivatives is assumed, there are eight boundary conditions (four each at $\theta = 0$ and $\theta = \beta$).

There are eight conditions for the eight remaining unknowns. A third–order osculating polynomial that has terms up to the seventh power and that satisfies the boundary conditions up to the third derivatives can be used as the cam profile.

The boundary conditions are

$$y(0) = 0 \qquad \dot{y}(0) = 0 \qquad \ddot{y}(0) = 0 \qquad \dddot{y}(0) = 0$$

$$y(\beta) = 0 \qquad \dot{y}(\beta) = 0 \qquad \ddot{y}(\beta) = 0 \qquad \dddot{y}(\beta) = 0 .$$

The expression for y satisfying these conditions is

$$y(\theta) = H_{01}^{(3)}(\theta)y(0) + H_{02}^{(3)}(\theta)y(\beta)$$

$$+ H_{11}^{(3)}(\theta)\dot{y}(0) + H_{12}^{(3)}(\theta)\dot{y}(\beta)$$

$$+ H_{21}^{(3)}(\theta)\ddot{y}(0) + H_{22}^{(3)}(\theta)\ddot{y}(\beta)$$

$$+ H_{31}^{(3)}(\theta)\dddot{y}(0) + H_{32}^{(3)}(\theta)\dddot{y}(\beta) , \qquad 0 \le \theta \le \beta .$$

Substituting the boundary conditions into the above equation gives

$$y(\theta) = H_{02}^{(3)}(\theta)y(\beta)$$

$$= h\,[\,H_{02}^{(3)}(\theta)\,]$$

$$= h\left[\frac{1}{\beta^7}\,(35\beta^3\theta^4 - 84\beta^2\theta^5 + 70\beta\theta^6 - 20\theta^7)\right]$$

or

$$y(\tau) = h(35\tau^4 - 84\tau^5 + 70\tau^6 - 20\tau^7) , \qquad 0 \le \tau \le 1 .$$

This is exactly the same as the 4–5–6–7 polynomial cam.

5
Modified Cam Curves

In an effort to incorporate the better features of the basic curves into one optimum curve, designers have tried many combinations of these basic curves. The aim has always been to produce a cam with the lowest possible maximum acceleration and to produce smooth acceleration curves with bounded jerk at any point in the curve.

One of the early composite curves was the "trapezoid," so called because the acceleration curve is made up of a pair of isosceles trapezoids. The displacement curve is a series of subsegments that are alternately cubic and parabolic. Neklutin (172) was probably the first to appreciate that the trapezoidal acceleration curve is an improvement over the parabolic curve, and that it offers good dynamic response characteristics under high–speed operation. To date, however, these characteristics have not proved better than those of the cycloidal curve.

5-1. THE MODIFIED TRAPEZOIDAL CURVE

A combination cam that has been used in lieu of the trapezoidal acceleration cam is the modified trapezoidal type (172). In the modified trapezoid the cubic equation has been replaced by the cycloid in the first, the third, the fourth, and the sixth segments of the curve. The reason for this is to reduce the maximum acceleration at the expense of a somewhat higher jerk at the start and the end of the curve.

In Fig. 5-1 we see the basic cycloidal curve from which the combination curve is developed. This figure also shows the displacement and the acceleration diagrams of the modified trapezoid. The variables pertaining to the cycloidal curve will be denoted by the primed symbols in the drawing. Let us first divide one-half of the rise into its three segments: from A to B the follower is accelerated according to a quarter sine wave: from B to C the acceleration is constant; and from C to D the acceleration decreases to zero according to a quarter sine wave. After D, the follower is decelerated in the same way that it was accelerated.

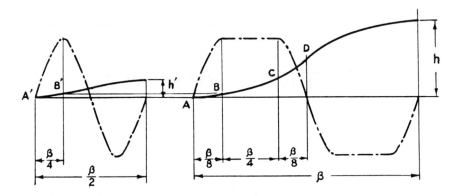

Fig. 5-1. Symmetrical modified trapezoidal curve.

The equations of the curve from A to B are

$$S = h' \left(\frac{2\theta}{\beta} - \frac{1}{2\pi} \sin 4\pi \frac{\theta}{\beta} \right) \qquad (5\text{-}1)$$

$$S' = \frac{h'}{\beta} \left(2 - 2 \cos 4\pi \frac{\theta}{\beta} \right)$$

$$S'' = \frac{8\pi h'}{\beta^2} \sin 4\pi \frac{\theta}{\beta} .$$

When point B is reached, $\theta = \dfrac{\beta}{8}$. Substituting this value of θ into Eq. (5-1), the displacement, the velocity, and the acceleration equations at point B become

$$S_1 = h' \left(\frac{1}{4} - \frac{1}{2\pi} \right)$$

$$S_1' = \frac{2h'}{\beta}$$

$$S_1'' = \frac{8\pi h'}{\beta^2} \ .$$

The general equations of the curve from B to C are

$$S = S_1 + V_0 \left(\theta - \frac{\beta}{8} \right) + \frac{1}{2} A \left(\theta - \frac{\beta}{8} \right)^2$$

$$S' = V_0 + A \left(\theta - \frac{\beta}{8} \right)$$

$$S'' = A \ .$$

To get displacement, velocity, and acceleration to match at the junction B, it is necessary to have

$$V_0 = \frac{2h'}{\beta}$$

$$A = \frac{8\pi h'}{\beta_2} \ .$$

Therefore, the equations of the curve from B to C become

$$S = h' \left(\frac{1}{4} - \frac{1}{2\pi} \right) + \frac{2h'}{\beta} \left(\theta - \frac{\beta}{8} \right) + \frac{4\pi h'}{\beta^2} \left(\theta - \frac{\beta}{8} \right)^2 \quad (5\text{-}2)$$

$$S' = \frac{2h'}{\beta} + \frac{8\pi h'}{\beta^2} \left(\theta - \frac{\beta}{8}\right)$$

$$S'' = \frac{8\pi h'}{\beta^2} \ .$$

When point C is reached, $\theta = \frac{3}{8}\beta$. Substituting this into the last two terms on the right hand side in Eq. (5-2), we obtain

$$S_2 = \frac{h'}{2} + \frac{\pi h'}{4} \ .$$

Realizing that the cycloidal displacement is the sum of a constant velocity displacement and a harmonic displacement, we write, without a loss of generality, the displacement equations of the curve from C to D as

$$S = S_1 + S_2 + C_1 + C_2 \ \frac{\theta - \frac{3}{8}\beta}{\beta} + C_3 \sin\left(4\pi \ \frac{\theta - \frac{\beta}{4}}{\beta}\right).$$

Hence,

$$S' = \frac{C_2}{\beta} + C_3 \ \frac{4\pi}{\beta} \cos 4\pi \ \frac{\theta - \frac{\beta}{4}}{\beta} \tag{5-3}$$

$$S'' = -C_3 \ \frac{16\pi^2}{\beta^2} \sin 4\pi \ \frac{\theta - \frac{\beta}{4}}{\beta} \ ,$$

where C_1, C_2, and C_3 are undetermined coefficients that can be obtained in the following manner:

An acceleration match at point C $\left(\text{when } \theta = \frac{3}{8}\beta\right)$ requires

$$\frac{8\pi h'}{\beta^2} = \left[-C_3 \frac{16\pi^2}{\beta^2} \sin 4\pi \frac{\theta - \frac{\beta}{4}}{\beta} \right]_{at\ \theta = \frac{3}{8}\beta},$$

thus giving

$$C_3 = -\frac{h'}{2\pi}.$$

A velocity match at point C requires

$$\left[\frac{2h'}{\beta} + \frac{8\pi h'}{\beta^2} \left(\theta - \frac{\beta}{8} \right) \right]_{\theta = \frac{3\beta}{8}}$$

$$= \left[\frac{C_2}{\beta} - \frac{h'}{2\pi} \frac{4\pi}{\beta} \cos 4\pi \frac{\theta - \frac{\beta}{4}}{\beta} \right]_{\theta = \frac{3}{8}\beta},$$

from which we obtain

$$C_2 = 2h'(1 + \pi).$$

In addition, the total displacement at point C is

$$S = S_1 + S_2$$

or equivalently

$$\left[C_1 + 2h'(1 + \pi) \frac{\theta - \frac{3}{8}\beta}{\beta} \right.$$

$$\left. - \frac{h'}{2\pi} \sin 4\pi \frac{\theta - \frac{\beta}{4}}{\beta} \right]_{\theta = \frac{3}{8}\beta} = 0,$$

from which C_1 can be obtained

$$C_1 = \frac{h'}{2\pi} \, .$$

Knowing the values of C_1, C_2, and C_3 and substituting them into the displacement equation gives the curve from C to D

$$S = \left(\frac{h'}{4} - \frac{h'}{2\pi} \right) + \left(\frac{h'}{2} + \frac{\pi h'}{4} \right) + \frac{h'}{2\pi}$$

$$+ \, 2h'(1 + \pi) \, \frac{\theta - \dfrac{3}{8}\beta}{\beta} - \frac{h'}{2\pi} \sin 4\pi \, \frac{\theta - \dfrac{\beta}{4}}{\beta}$$

or

$$S = h' \left[-\frac{\pi}{2} + 2(1 + \pi) \frac{\theta}{\beta} - \frac{1}{2\pi} \sin 4\pi \, \frac{\theta - \dfrac{\beta}{4}}{\beta} \right] . \qquad (5\text{-}4)$$

At point D $\left(\text{i.e., when } \theta = \dfrac{\beta}{2} \right)$ the total displacement can be found from this equation to be

$$S = h' \left(1 + \frac{\pi}{2} \right) .$$

Having already obtained the expressions for displacements S_1 and S_2, we can easily find the displacement of the final segment S_3 to be

$$S_3 = S - S_1 - S_2$$

or

$$S_3 = h' \left(\frac{1}{4} + \frac{\pi}{4} + \frac{1}{2\pi} \right) .$$

Finally, from the relationship

$$S_1 + S_2 + S_3 = \frac{h}{2} ,$$

we establish the relationship between h' and h

$$h' = \frac{h}{2 + \pi} . \tag{5-5}$$

Therefore, the displacement equations of the first three segments of the modified trapezoidal motion are

$$S = \frac{h}{2 + \pi} \left(\frac{2\theta}{\beta} - \frac{1}{2\pi} \sin 4\pi \frac{\theta}{\beta} \right) \qquad 0 \le \theta \le \frac{\beta}{8} \tag{5-6}$$

$$S = \frac{h}{2 + \pi} \left[\frac{1}{4} - \frac{1}{2\pi} + \frac{2}{\beta} \left(\theta - \frac{\beta}{8} \right) \right.$$

$$\left. + \frac{4\pi}{\beta^2} \left(\theta - \frac{\beta}{8} \right)^2 \right] \qquad \frac{\beta}{8} \le \theta \le \frac{3}{8} \beta$$

$$S = \frac{h}{2 + \pi} \left[-\frac{\pi}{2} + 2(1 + \pi) \frac{\theta}{\beta} \right.$$

$$\left. -\frac{1}{2\pi} \sin 4\pi \frac{\theta - \frac{\beta}{4}}{\beta} \right] \qquad \frac{3}{8} \beta \le \theta \le \frac{\beta}{2} .$$

Evaluating all constants and denoting the ratio $\frac{\theta}{\beta}$ by γ, the displacement, the velocity, the acceleration, and the jerk equations of the symmetrical, modified trapezoidal cam curve can be described as follows:

for $0 \le \gamma \le \dfrac{1}{8}$,   (5-7)

$$S = 0.9724612h\left(4\gamma - \frac{1}{\pi}\sin 4\pi\gamma\right)$$

$$V = 0.3889845\,\frac{h}{\beta}\,(1 - \cos 4\pi\gamma)$$

$$A = 4.888124\,\frac{h}{\beta^2}\,(\sin 4\pi\gamma)$$

$$J = 61.425769\,\frac{h}{\beta^3}\cos 4\pi\gamma$$

for $\dfrac{1}{8} \le \gamma \le \dfrac{3}{8}$,

$$S = h(2.44406184\gamma^2 - 0.22203097\gamma + 0.00723407)$$

$$V = \frac{h}{\beta}\,(4.888124\gamma - 0.222031)$$

$$A = \frac{h}{\beta^2}\,(4.888124)$$

$$J = 0$$

for $\dfrac{3}{8} \le \gamma \le \dfrac{1}{2}$,

$$S = h(1.6110154\gamma - 0.0309544\sin(4\pi\gamma - \pi) - 0.3055077)$$

$$V = \frac{h}{\beta}\,(1.6110154 - 0.3889845\cos(4\pi\gamma - \pi))$$

$$A = \frac{h}{\beta^2}\,(4.888124\sin(4\pi\gamma - \pi))$$

$$J = 61.425769\,\frac{h}{\beta^3}\cos(4\pi\gamma - \pi)$$

for $\dfrac{1}{2} \leq \gamma \leq \dfrac{5}{8}$,

$$S = h(1.6110154\gamma + 0.0309544 \sin (4\pi\gamma - \pi) - 0.3055077)$$

$$V = \dfrac{h}{\beta} (1.6110154 + 0.3889845 \cos (4\pi\gamma - \pi))$$

$$A = \dfrac{h}{\beta^2} (-4.888124 \sin (4\pi\gamma - 2\pi))$$

$$J = -61.425769 \dfrac{h}{\beta^3} (4\pi\gamma - 2\pi)$$

for $\dfrac{5}{8} \leq \gamma \leq \dfrac{7}{8}$,

$$S = h(4.6660917\gamma - 2.44406184\gamma^2 - 1.2292648)$$

$$V = \dfrac{h}{\beta} (4.6660917 - 4.888124\gamma)$$

$$A = \dfrac{h}{\beta^2} (-4.888124)$$

$$J = 0$$

for $\dfrac{7}{8} \leq \gamma \leq 1$,

$$S = h(0.6110154 + 0.3889845\gamma + 0.0309544 \sin (4\pi\gamma - 3\pi))$$

$$V = \dfrac{h}{\beta} (0.3889845 + 0.3889845 \cos (4\pi\gamma - 3\pi))$$

$$A = \dfrac{h}{\beta^2} (-4.888124 \sin (4\pi\gamma - 3\pi))$$

$$J = -61.425769 \dfrac{h}{\beta^3} \cos (4\pi\gamma - 3\pi) .$$

The modified trapezoidal curve has the following peak value:

$$V_{max} = 2\,\frac{h}{\beta} \tag{5-8}$$

$$A_{max} = 4.888\,\frac{h}{\beta^2}$$

$$J_{max} = 61.43\,\frac{h}{\beta^3}\quad.$$

The non–dimensional factors of the displacement, the velocity, and the acceleration of this curve are given in Table A-3 in Appendix A.

Example 5-1

A cam is to be designed for the feed slide of a punch press. A modified trapezoidal cam profile is selected. The feed is to occur in 120°, and the follower's travel is to be 8 cm. We also assume that the base circle radius is 16 cm. If the machine is to operate at 180 rpm, determine the cam displacement profile and calculate the maximum velocity and the acceleration.

With reference to Table A-3 in Appendix A, if every third point in that table is used, increments on the cam are $\dfrac{3(120)}{120} = 3°$.

The calculations are shown in skeleton form in Table 5-1.

Table 5-1   Calculation for the Example Problem 5–1

θ (Degrees)	K	Kh (cm)	$R_b + Kh$ (cm)
0	0.00000	0.0000	16.0000
15	0.01767	0.1414	16.1414
30	0.10451	0.8361	16.8361
45	0.26767	2.1414	18.1414
60	0.50000	4.0000	20.0000
75	0.73233	5.8586	21.8586
90	0.89549	7.1639	23.1639
105	0.98233	7.8586	23.8586
120	1.00000	8.0000	24.0000

The maximum velocity in this example occurs at the midpoint. Thus

$$V = C_v h \left(\frac{6N}{\beta} \right)$$

$$= 2.0(8) \left(\frac{6 \times 180}{120} \right)$$

$$= 144 \ \frac{cm}{sec} \ .$$

The maximum acceleration in this example is constant from $\theta = 15°$ to $45°$.

$$A = C_a h \left(\frac{6N}{\beta} \right)^2$$

$$= 4.8881(8) \left(\frac{6 \times 180}{120} \right)^2$$

$$= 3167.5 \ \frac{cm}{sec^2} \ .$$

The maximum deceleration in this example is constant from $75°$ to $105°$ and

equals $-3167.5 \ \dfrac{cm}{sec^2}$.

In modified trapezoidal motion, the fraction of the total rise angle through which the cam has turned when the cycloidal curve becomes tangent to the parabolic curve (Fig. 5-1) is known as the "b–value" for the motion. We used $b = \dfrac{1}{8}$ in the derivation. Note that if $b = 0$, the motion is parabolic; if $b = 1$, the motion becomes cycloidal. Practice indicates that $b = \dfrac{1}{8}$ gives the most satisfactory follower performance. Wolford and Kersten (234) have verified that $b = \dfrac{1}{8}$ is the optimal choice.

5-2. THE SKEWED MODIFIED TRAPEZOIDAL CURVE

The situation may arise that the follower requires a particular velocity and acceleration at some critical points in the motion. This can be accomplished by skewing the acceleration profile as seen in Fig. 5-2. We are interested in determining the effect of a change in the cam angular displacement allotted for a stroke on the change in magnitude of the acceleration and of the velocity. Neklutin (173) has treated the modified trapezoidal curve with unequal periods of acceleration and deceleration and has presented his results in tabular form for designers who require quick, practical solutions. Ragsdell and Gilkey (184) have related the skewed acceleration to a correspondingly symmetrical one. Usually, the cam design has progressed to an advanced stage before skewing is considered. Therefore, cam throw h and angle β have been determined and will be considered as constants. Since h and β are constant, this fixes V_{max} and the maximum acceleration for symmetrical curve A_{sym} .

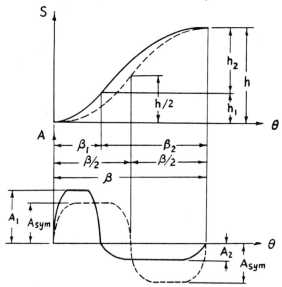

Fig. 5-2. S–θ and A–θ relationship for a skewed modified trapezoidal curve.

Let β_1 and β_2 be the periods during acceleration and deceleration, respectively, and let $p = \dfrac{\beta_1}{\beta_2}$ be the skew ratio. The other symbols are as labeled in Fig. 5-2. Then

$$\beta_1 + \beta_2 = \beta$$

$$h_1 + h_2 = h .$$

The velocity match at the transition point requires that

$$(V_{max})_1 = (V_{max})_2$$

or

$$\frac{2h_1}{\beta_1} = \frac{2h_2}{\beta_2} = \frac{h}{\beta} \; .$$

Therefore,

$$\beta_1 = \frac{p}{1+p} \beta \qquad\qquad (5\text{-}9)$$

$$h_1 = \frac{p}{1+p} h$$

and

$$\beta_2 = \frac{1}{1+p} \beta \qquad\qquad (5\text{-}10)$$

$$h_2 = \frac{1}{1+p} h \; .$$

The relationship between the skewed acceleration and the corresponding symmetrical one can be established as follows:

since $\quad A_{sym} = \dfrac{kh}{\beta^2}$

$$A_1 = k \frac{2h_1}{(2\beta_1)^2} \qquad\qquad A_2 = k \frac{2h_2}{(2\beta_2)^2}$$

$$A_1 = \frac{\beta^2}{h} A_{sym} \frac{2h_1}{(2\beta_1)^2} = \left(\frac{\beta_1 + \beta_2}{2\beta_1}\right)^2 \left(\frac{2p}{1+p}\right) A_{sym}$$

$$= \left(\frac{1+p}{2p}\right)^2 \left(\frac{2p}{1+p}\right) A_{sym} \; .$$

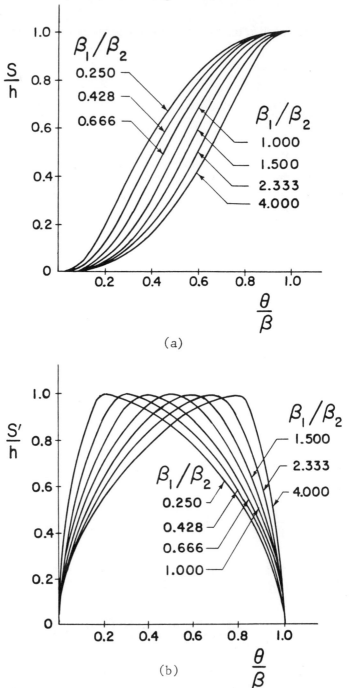

Fig. 5-3. (a) Normalized displacement for different skew ratio, (b) Normalized velocity for different skew ratio.

Thus

$$A_1 = \left(\frac{1+p}{2p}\right) A_{sym} .$$ (5-11)

Similarly,

$$A_2 = \left(\frac{1+p}{2}\right) A_{sym} .$$ (5-12)

Fig. 5-3a shows the effect of the shape of the chosen cam profile for a range of skew ratio p. Fig. 5-3b shows the normalized velocity–displacement plot for the same range of skew ratio p.

The modified trapezoidal curve has gained popularity in industry. However, it has one objectionable characteristic; the torque goes from positive maximum to negative maximum in one–fifth of the travel time. If dynamic forces represent the major part of the load on the cam, this comparatively sudden release of energy may be detrimental. Much better torque characteristics can be obtained with the modified sine curve and the modified cycloidal curve.

5-3. THE MODIFIED SINE CURVE

This curve is a combination of cycloidal and harmonic quadrants occupying different parts of the working period. The change from positive to negative torque occurs in 0.42 of the travel time, which makes it attractive for indexing large mass dials or turrets.

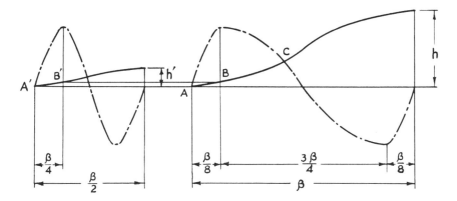

Fig. 5-4. Modified sine curve.

Fig. 5-4 shows the basic cycloidal curve from which the combination curve is developed. This figure also shows the displacement and the acceleration diagram of the modified sine curve. The primed symbols used in the drawing refer to the basic cycloidal curve. Let us first divide one–half of the rise into two segments: the follower is accelerated from A to B $\left(\text{from } \theta = 0 \text{ to } \theta = \dfrac{\beta}{8}\right)$ according to a quarter sine wave, and the acceleration decreases to zero from B to C $\left(\text{from } \theta = \dfrac{\beta}{8} \text{ to } \theta = \dfrac{\beta}{2}\right)$, again according to a quarter sine wave.

The equations of cycloidal motion from A to B are

$$S = h'\left(\frac{2\theta}{\beta} - \frac{1}{2\pi}\sin 4\pi\,\frac{\theta}{\beta}\right) \tag{5-13}$$

$$S' = \frac{h'}{\beta}\left(2 - 2\cos 4\pi\,\frac{\theta}{\beta}\right)$$

$$S'' = \frac{8\pi h'}{\beta^2}\sin 4\pi\,\frac{\theta}{\beta}\ .$$

At the end of the first segment $\theta = \dfrac{\beta}{8}$, so the kinematic equations at point B are

$$S_1 = h'\left(\frac{1}{4} - \frac{1}{2\pi}\right)$$

$$S_1' = \frac{2h'}{\beta}$$

$$S_1'' = \frac{8\pi h'}{\beta^2}\ .$$

The general displacement equation of the sine curve from B to C is

$$S = S_1 + C_1 + C_2\,\frac{\theta - \dfrac{\beta}{8}}{\beta} + C_3\sin\left(\frac{4\pi\theta}{3\beta} + \frac{\pi}{3}\right). \tag{5-14}$$

Then

$$S' = \frac{C_2}{\beta} + C_3 \frac{4\pi}{3\beta} \cos\left(\frac{4\pi\theta}{3\beta} + \frac{\pi}{3}\right)$$

$$S'' = -C_3 \frac{16\pi^2}{9\beta^2} \sin\left(\frac{4\pi}{3} \frac{\theta}{\beta} + \frac{\pi}{3}\right).$$

where the coefficients C_1, C_2, and C_3 can be determined by the match of boundary conditions at point B.

The acceleration match requires that

$$\frac{8\pi h'}{\beta^2} = \left[-C_3 \frac{16\pi^2}{9\beta^2} \sin\left(\frac{4\pi}{3} \frac{\theta}{\beta} + \frac{\pi}{3}\right) \right]_{\theta = \frac{\beta}{8}}$$

$$C_3 = -\frac{9h'}{2\pi}.$$

The velocity match requires that

$$\frac{2h'}{\beta} = \left[\frac{C_2}{\beta} - \frac{9h'}{2\pi} \cos\left(\frac{4\pi}{3} \frac{\theta}{\beta} + \frac{\pi}{3}\right) \right]_{\text{at } \theta = \frac{\beta}{8}}$$

$$C_2 = 2h'.$$

When $\theta = \frac{\beta}{8}$, $S = S_1$ or

$$\left[C_1 + 2h' \frac{\beta - \frac{\beta}{8}}{\beta} - \frac{9h'}{2\pi} \sin\left(\frac{4}{3} \frac{\theta}{\beta} + \frac{\pi}{3}\right) \right]_{\text{at } \theta = \frac{\beta}{8}} = 0,$$

from which $C_1 = \frac{9h'}{2\pi}.$

Then

$$S = \left(\frac{h'}{4} - \frac{h'}{2\pi} \right) + \frac{9h'}{2\pi} + 2h' \left(\frac{\beta - \frac{\beta}{8}}{\beta} \right) \tag{5-15}$$

$$- \frac{9h'}{2\pi} \sin \left(\frac{4\pi}{3} \frac{\theta}{\beta} + \frac{\pi}{3} \right)$$

$$= h' \left[\frac{4}{\pi} + 2 \frac{\theta}{\beta} - \frac{9}{2\pi} \sin \left(\frac{4\pi}{3} \frac{\theta}{\beta} + \frac{\pi}{3} \right) \right].$$

When $\theta = \dfrac{\beta}{2}$, the total half rise is

$$S = h' \left(1 + \frac{4}{\pi} \right).$$

Hence,

$$S_2 = S - S_1 = \left(\frac{3}{4} - \frac{9}{2\pi} \right) h'.$$

Finally, from the relationship

$$S = S_1 + S_2 = \frac{h}{2}$$

we obtain $h' = \dfrac{\pi}{2(\pi + 4)} h$.

Therefore, the displacement equations of the modified sine curve are

$$S = h\left[\frac{\pi}{4+\pi}\,\frac{\theta}{\beta} - \frac{1}{4(4+\pi)}\sin\left(4\pi\,\frac{\theta}{\beta}\right)\right] \qquad 0 \le \theta \le \frac{\beta}{8} \qquad (5\text{-}16)$$

$$S = h\left[\frac{2}{4+\pi} + \frac{\pi}{4+\pi}\,\frac{\theta}{\beta} - \frac{9}{4(4+\pi)}\right.$$

$$\left.\sin\left(\frac{4\pi}{3}\,\frac{\theta}{\beta} + \frac{\pi}{3}\right)\right] \qquad\qquad \frac{\beta}{8} \le \theta \le \frac{7}{8}\beta$$

$$S = h\left[\frac{4}{4+\pi} + \frac{\pi}{4+\pi}\,\frac{\theta}{\beta} - \frac{1}{4(4+\pi)}\right.$$

$$\left.\sin\left(4\pi\,\frac{\theta}{\beta}\right)\right] \qquad\qquad \frac{7}{8}\beta \le \theta \le \beta.$$

Evaluating all constants and denoting the ratio $\dfrac{\theta}{\beta}$ by γ, the displacement, the velocity, the acceleration, and the jerk equations of the modified sine curve are

for $0 \le \gamma \le \dfrac{1}{8}$

$$S = h(0.43989\,\gamma - 0.035014 \sin 4\pi\gamma)$$

$$V = 0.43989\,\frac{h}{\beta}\,(1 - \cos 4\pi\gamma)$$

$$A = 5.52794\,\frac{h}{\beta^2}\,\sin 4\pi\gamma$$

$$J = 69.4659\,\frac{h}{\beta^3}\,\cos 4\pi\gamma.$$

for $\dfrac{1}{8} \le \gamma \le \dfrac{7}{8}$

$$S = h\left[0.28005 + 0.43989\,\gamma - 0.315055 \cos\left(\frac{4\pi}{3}\gamma - \frac{\pi}{6} \right) \right]$$

$$V = \frac{h}{\beta}\left[0.43989 + 1.31967 \sin\left(\frac{4\pi}{3}\gamma - \frac{\pi}{6} \right) \right]$$

$$A = 5.52794\,\frac{h}{\beta^2}\cos\left(\frac{4\pi}{3}\gamma - \frac{\pi}{6} \right)$$

$$J = -23.1553\,\frac{h}{\beta^3}\sin\left(\frac{4\pi}{3}\gamma - \frac{\pi}{6} \right).$$

for $\dfrac{7}{8} \le \gamma \le 1$

$$S = h\left[0.56010 + 0.43989\,\gamma - 0.035014 \sin 2\pi(2\gamma - 1) \right]$$

$$V = \frac{h}{\beta}\left[0.43989\,(1 - \cos 2\pi(2\gamma - 1)) \right]$$

$$A = 5.52794\,\frac{h}{\beta^2}\sin 2\pi(2\gamma - 1)$$

$$J = 69.4659\,\frac{h}{\beta^3}\cos 2\pi(2\gamma - 1). \tag{5-17}$$

The maximum velocity of the modified sine curve is $V_{max} = 1.760\,\dfrac{h}{\beta}$, the maximum acceleration is $A_{max} = 5.528\,\dfrac{h}{\beta^2}$, and the maximum jerk is $J_{max} = 69.47\,\dfrac{h}{\beta^3}$. The non-dimensionalized displacement, velocity, and acceleration factors are given in Table A-4, Appendix A.

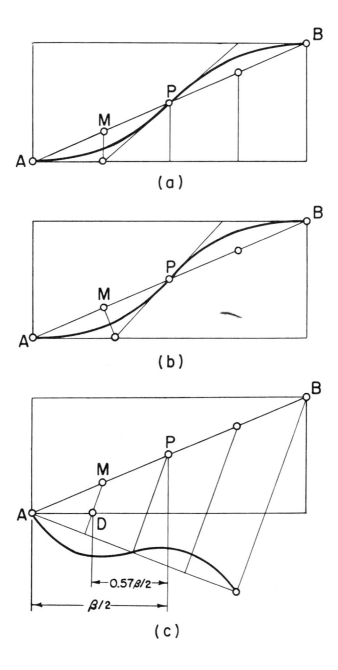

Fig. 5-5. (a) Pure cycloidal motion, (b) Alt modified cycloidal motion, (c) Wildt modified cycloidal motion.

5-4. THE MODIFIED CYCLOIDAL CURVE

From Chapter 2, we know that a standard cycloidal curve can be used in a DRD cam to produce a smooth acceleration characteristic. A cycloidal curve may be viewed here as the combination of a sine curve and a constant–velocity line with a slope equal and opposite to the terminal slope of the sine curve. Fig. 5-5a depicts a pure cycloidal curve used in a typical DRD motion event. Point A is the beginning of motion, and point B is the end of motion. P is the mid-stroke transition point, and APB is the constant–velocity line. M is the midstation between A and P. The sine amplitudes are to be added to the constant–velocity line in this true cycloidal case in a direction perpendicular to the base of dwell. An early attempt was made by Alt (2) to modify the true cycloid in such a manner that the sine amplitudes are made perpendicular to the constant–velocity line instead of perpendicular to the base line of dwell. This is portrayed in Fig. 5-5b. Such modification resulted in a somewhat lower value in peak velocity, but a higher peak acceleration than that of the true cycloidal. Wildt tried, with his modified cycloidal curve (232), to obtain an optimum orientation of the amplitude for the superimposed sine wave. Wildt's modification is supported by the geometric construction shown in Fig 5-5c. In this figure, a point D equal to 0.57 the distance $\dfrac{\beta}{2}$ is the first chosen, and then is joined to DM by a straight line. The base of the sine curve is then constructed perpendicular to DM. This procedure results in a maximum acceleration of 5.88 $\dfrac{h}{\beta^2}$, which is comparable to that of the modified trapezoidal curve, whereas the standard cycloidal curve has a maximum acceleration of 6.28 $\dfrac{h}{\beta^2}$. There is a 6.8% reduction in acceleration. Fig. 5-6 shows the comparison of the three acceleration curves.

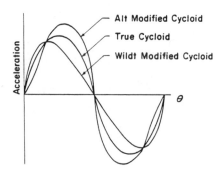

Fig. 5-6. Comparison of acceleration curves.

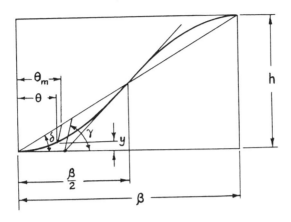

Fig. 5-7.

Based on Fig. 5-7, the displacement equation of the modified cycloidal motion is

$$S = h \left[\frac{\theta_m}{\beta} - \frac{1}{2\pi} \sin \left(2\pi \frac{\theta_m}{\beta} \right) \right],$$ (5-18)

where

$$\theta_m = 0 + \frac{\beta}{2\pi} \left(\frac{\tan \delta}{\tan \gamma} \right) \sin \left(2\pi \frac{\theta}{\beta} \right)$$

where $\delta = \dfrac{h}{\beta}$ and γ governs the direction of the amplitude for the super-imposed sine wave, i.e., the angle of "distortion" of the cycloid. For a pure cycloidal curve $\gamma = 90°$ and therefore $\theta_m = \theta$, the velocity and acceleration equations are

$$V = \frac{h}{\beta} \left[\frac{1 - \cos 2\pi \frac{\theta}{\beta}}{1 - K \cos 2\pi \frac{\theta}{\beta}} \right]$$ (5-19)

$$A = \frac{h}{\beta^2} \ \frac{2\pi(1 - K)\sin 2\pi \dfrac{\theta}{\beta}}{\left[1 - K\cos\left(2\pi \dfrac{\theta}{\beta}\right)\right]^3} \ , \tag{5-20}$$

where $K = \dfrac{\tan \delta}{\tan \gamma}$.

The optimum value of K, which will give the lowest peak acceleration,

$$A_{max} = 5.89 \ \frac{h}{\beta^2} \ , \text{ is}$$

$$K = 1 - \frac{1}{2} \ \sqrt{3} \ = 0.134 \ .$$

Further detailed discussion of the modified cycloidal motion and the geometry involved can be found in the book by Jensen (113).

6
Fourier Series Curves

6-1. INTRODUCTION

We discussed in Chapter 2 the use of basic, parabolic sinusoidal, and cycloidal curves for cam profiles of the DRD type. We also demonstrated in Chapter 5 how these basic curve segments may be combined together to form a variety of cam profiles.

Basically, there are two main objectives in the selection and designing of cam profiles. These are

1. To produce a minimum acceleration of (and hence a minimum dynamic load on) the follower.

2. To avoid excessive vibratory response in the follower caused by having high "harmonic contents" in the profile.

These two profile objectives are not compatible. The parabolic profile, for instance, does not result in minimum acceleration, but has a high harmonic content, since the Fourier expansion for a parabolic curve has an infinite number of terms. Because each term is associated with a certain forcing frequency, it is likely to induce resonance vibrations in the follower at some of those frequencies. The cycloidal cam, on the other hand, having but a fundamental frequency in the acceleration, has minimum harmonic content. The cycloidal profile is the least likely to excite vibration in the follower, but this is at the expense of high acceleration. It causes 57% higher acceleration in the follower than does the parabolic profile. Any good general–purpose cam can be optimized with a curve–intermediate between the parabolic and the cycloidal, but with the fewest and lowest possible harmonics.

95

6-2. HARMONIC CURVES FOR DRD MOTION

Based on the rationale stated above, a number of harmonic curves of the DRD motion event have been proposed. The kinematic equations of some representative harmonic curves are given below:

Gutman 1–3 Harmonic Curve (90)

$$S = h\left[\frac{\theta}{\beta} - \frac{15}{32\pi} \sin \frac{2\pi\theta}{\beta} - \frac{1}{96\pi} \sin \frac{6\pi\theta}{\beta} \right] \tag{6-1}$$

$$V = \frac{h}{\beta}\left[1 - \frac{15}{16} \cos \frac{2\pi\theta}{\beta} - \frac{1}{16} \cos \frac{6\pi\theta}{\beta} \right]$$

$$A = \frac{h\pi}{8\beta^2}\left[15 \sin \frac{2\pi\theta}{\beta} + 3 \sin \frac{6\pi\theta}{\beta} \right]$$

$$J = \frac{h\pi^2}{4\beta^3}\left[15 \cos \frac{2\pi\theta}{\beta} + 9 \cos \frac{6\pi\theta}{\beta} \right].$$

Gutman's 1–3 harmonic curve can be obtained from the Fourier series expansion of the displacement of the parabolic curve by retaining the first two terms of the series. The resulting curve has a harmonic content triple the frequency of the cycloidal curve and has a maximum acceleration of 5.15 $\frac{h}{\beta^2}$, which is 129% of the acceleration of the parabolic curve, or 82% of the maximum acceleration of the cycloidal curve.

In a similar manner, if we retain up to and including the first three terms in the Fourier series expansion of the displacement of the parabolic curve, the equation of Gutman's fifth–order harmonic curve can be obtained.

We must also note that for a DRD motion event, the Fourier series used must be an odd harmonic curve, which has polar symmetry with respect to the midpoint of the curve.

Freudenstein Harmonic Curve (84)

Freudenstein's 1-3 harmonic curve

$$S = \frac{h\theta}{\beta} - \frac{h}{2\pi}\left(\frac{27}{28}\sin\frac{2\pi\theta}{\beta} + \frac{1}{84}\sin\frac{6\pi\theta}{\beta}\right) \tag{6-2}$$

$$V = \frac{h}{\beta}\left(1 - \frac{27}{28}\cos\frac{2\pi\theta}{\beta} - \frac{1}{28}\cos\frac{6\pi\theta}{\beta}\right)$$

$$A = \frac{2\pi h}{\beta^2}\left(\frac{27}{28}\sin\frac{2\pi\theta}{\beta} + \frac{3}{28}\sin\frac{6\pi\theta}{\beta}\right)$$

$$J = \frac{4\pi^2 h}{\beta^3}\left(\frac{27}{28}\cos\frac{2\pi\theta}{\beta} + \frac{9}{28}\cos\frac{6\pi\theta}{\beta}\right)$$

In agreement with the rationale stated above, Freudenstein's 1–3 harmonic curve is supported on the basis of minimizing the dynamic acceleration factor (which is the product of the cam acceleration factor and the dynamic amplification factor of the system). The resulting curve has a maximum acceleration of 5.39 $\frac{h}{\beta^2}$, which is 135% of the acceleration of the parabolic curve, or 86% of the acceleration of the cycloidal curve.

The equations of Freudenstein's 1-3-5 harmonic curve are

$$S = \frac{h}{\beta} - \frac{hm}{2\pi}\left(\sin\frac{2\pi\theta}{\beta} + \frac{1}{54}\sin\frac{6\pi\theta}{\beta}\right. \tag{6-3}$$

$$\left. + \frac{1}{1250}\sin\frac{10\pi\theta}{\beta}\right)$$

$$m = \frac{1125}{1192}$$

$$V = \frac{h}{\beta} \left[1 - m \left(\cos \frac{2\pi\theta}{\beta} + \frac{1}{18} \cos \frac{6\pi\theta}{\beta} \right.\right.$$

$$\left.\left. + \frac{1}{250} \cos \frac{10\pi\theta}{\beta} \right) \right]$$

$$A = \frac{2\pi h}{\beta^2} m \left(\sin \frac{2\pi\theta}{\beta} + \frac{1}{6} \sin \frac{6\pi\theta}{\beta} + \frac{1}{50} \sin \frac{10\pi\theta}{\beta} \right)$$

$$J = \frac{4\pi^2 h}{\beta^3} m \left(\cos \frac{2\pi\theta}{\beta} + \frac{1}{2} \cos \frac{6\pi\theta}{\beta} + \frac{1}{10} \cos \frac{10\pi\theta}{\beta} \right).$$

This curve has a maximum acceleration of 5.06 $\frac{h}{\beta^2}$, which is 126% of the acceleration of the parabolic curve, or 81% of the acceleration of the cycloidal curve.

In this way, other higher order multiple harmonic curves can be generated. Baranyi (9) has derived and tabulated the Fourier coefficients up to and including the seventeenth harmonic of the profile groups for the DRD cam. Unfortunately, these high–order harmonic curves do not generally produce satisfactory dynamic response of the follower. This has been verified in a recent study of cam dynamics by Chen (45). Therefore, if the conditions for a good general–purpose cam rise between two dwells are the minimization of peak acceleration as well as of harmonic content, a seemingly obvious solution is to expand the parabolic rise into a Fourier series and truncate it at a certain harmonic. Freudenstein suggested that, as a rule of thumb, a cam curve whose highest harmonic is not greater than 10% of the order of the resonant harmonic should be selected.

The attenuated trigonometric series scheme has another serious drawback, which is associated with the truncation process of the Fourier series because of the nature of its nonuniform convergence, commonly known as "Gibbs phenomenon." When a truncated Fourier series of n–terms is used for the approximation of a given motion curve (such as the parabolic curve), it produces a least–squares deviation from the given motion. As the value of n becomes large, the peak value of the approximating curve approaches not that of the original motion, but a value about 15% in excess of the original motion (18% in the case of the parabolic motion). In this situation, the designer must either correct the discrepancy or completely ignore it. Correction is not an easy matter, because the terms of the approximating series are not orthogonal, and all coefficients of the approximating series must be altered every time when a correctional term is introduced into the truncation process. Ignoring this deviation, on the other hand, causes undesirable discontinuities at the dwell boundaries.

Despite all of this, there is a definite advantage of using a harmonic series for cam motion specifications. This advantage is the direct knowledge of the harmonic content of the forcing function applied to the cam–and–follower system. With this knowledge, the designer can adjust his system parameters to avoid the resonance at certain harmonics.

6-3. HARMONIC CURVES WITH FINITE TERMINAL VELOCITY

So far, we have covered a wide variety of dwell-to-dwell transitional curves. These DRD curves are cumbersome to use for cam applications that require transitions between end points with finite terminal velocities. An approximate method suggested by Weber (227) enables the user to generate easily Fourier eber's method is based on the superposition principle in which simple curves are combined to develop a complex curve. A curve is considered to be the composite of two elements; a chord (constant velocity line) connecting the end–points of the curve, and a Fourier sine series having terminal slopes equal and opposite to the chordal slope discontinuities such that the composite curve is slope-continuous. If we denote m_i and m_f as the initial and final slopes, respectively, and m_c as the chordal slope, then with reference to Fig. 6-1, the equation of follower displacement can be written

$$S = S_i + (\theta - \theta_i)m_c - P \sum_{j=1}^{N} a_j \frac{\Delta\theta}{2\pi j} \sin\left(2\pi j \frac{\theta - \theta_i}{\Delta\theta}\right) \tag{6-4}$$

$$- Q \sum_{k=1}^{M} a_k \frac{\Delta\theta}{(2k-1)\pi} \sin\left[(2k-1)\pi \frac{\theta - \theta_i}{\Delta\theta}\right],$$

where

$$P = m_c - \frac{m_i + m_f}{2}$$

$$Q = \frac{m_f - m_i}{2}$$

$$\sum_{j=1}^{N} a_j = 1$$

$$\sum_{k=1}^{M} a_k = 1 \, .$$

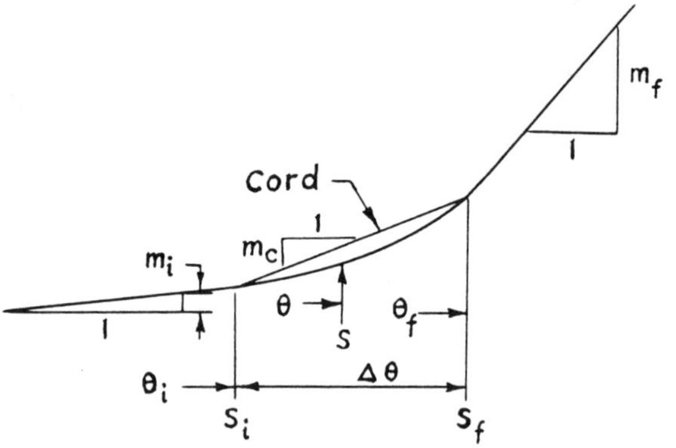

Fig. 6-1. Harmonic curves with finite terminal velocity.

In Eq. (6-4) the first term represents the chord of the segment, the second term represents the sum of N terms of the Fourier odd series, and the third term represents the sum of M terms of the Fourier even series. The velocity, the acceleration, and the jerk may be determined as follows:

$$V = m_c - P \sum_{j=1}^{N} a_j \cos\left(2\pi j \frac{\theta - \theta_i}{\Delta \theta}\right) \tag{6-5}$$

$$- Q \sum_{k=1}^{M} a_k \cos\left[(2k - 1)\pi \frac{\theta - \theta_i}{\Delta \theta}\right]$$

$$A = P \sum_{j=1}^{N} a_j \frac{2\pi j}{\Delta \theta} \sin\left(2\pi j \frac{\theta - \theta_i}{\Delta \theta}\right)$$

$$+ Q \sum_{k=1}^{M} a_k \frac{(2k - 1)\pi}{\Delta \theta} \sin\left[(2k - 1)\pi \frac{\theta - \theta_i}{\Delta \theta}\right]$$

$$J = P \sum_{j=1}^{N} a_j \left(\frac{2 \pi j}{\Delta \theta} \right)^2 \sin \left(2 \pi j \frac{\theta - \theta_i}{\Delta \theta} + \frac{1}{2} \pi \right)$$

$$+ Q \sum_{k=1}^{M} a_k \left[\frac{(2k - 1) \pi}{\Delta \theta} \right]^2 \sin \left[(2k - 1) \pi \frac{\theta - \theta_i}{\Delta \theta} + \pi \right].$$

7
Combination of Cam Curves

7-1. FUNDAMENTAL CONDITIONS OF COMBINATION OF MOTIONS

In Chapter 2, the characteristics of the basic curves, such as the parabolic, the simple harmonic, and the cycloidal, were introduced. These functional, symmetrical curves are used because of their simplicity of construction and ease of analysis. In situations where these simple curves are inadequate, such as the requiring of specific velocities, intermediate displacements or accelerations, and motion specification for unsymmetrical rise and fall, combinations of motions are frequently used. The modified constant velocity motion is the simplest example. The modified trapezoidal motion and modified sine motion described earlier in Chapter 5 are other examples.

We will now outline the fundamental conditions for combining curves and will illustrate some of the more typical combinations of simple curves. It is not possible to show all combinations, but it should be noted that any combination of basic curves may be utilized to fulfill the requirements of the fundamental conditions. The conditions to be satisfied usually are

1. The sum of the displacements during each of the various motions is equal to the total stroke, h or L*.

$$S_1 + S_2 + \ldots = h .$$

---

*The symbols h and L are used interchangeably throughout this chapter.

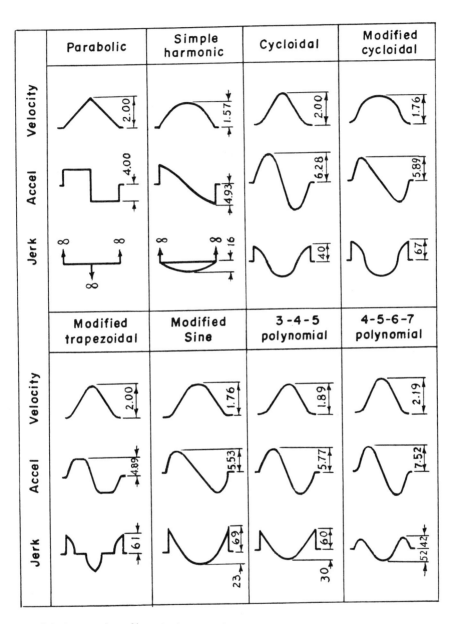

Fig. 7-1. A comparison of important cam curves.

2. The sum of the angles turned through by the cam during each of the various motions is equal to the total cam angle, or

$$\beta_1 + \beta_2 + \ldots = \beta .$$

3. It is necessary that the velocities of all curves at the junction be equal.
4. An advanced condition for high–speed action requires that the accelerations of all curves at the junction be equal.

For the convenience of quick reference we have presented Fig. 7-1, which gives a comparison of cam curves of importance. Note that the velocity, the

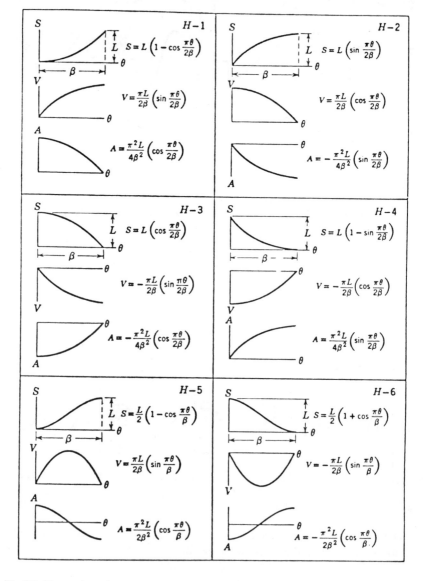

Fig. 7-2. Harmonic motion characteristics.

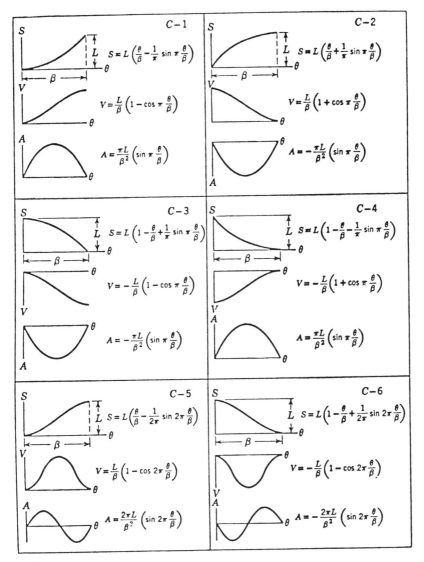

Fig. 7-3. Cycloidal motion characteristics.

acceleration, and the jerk curves presented in this figure are all normalized, i.e., they all have a unit total displacement h in a unit cam angular displacement β.

7-2. BUILDING-BLOCK APPROACH

Based on the fundamental conditions of combining cam curves, a customized cam can be developed with predesigned "building block" cam curve segments,

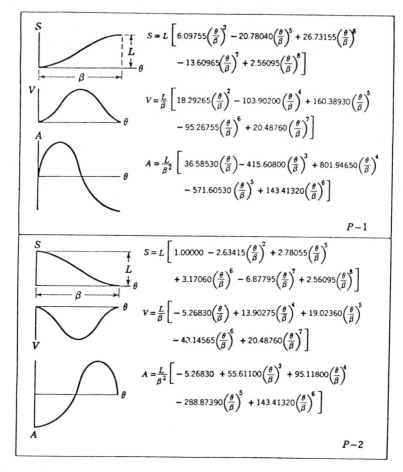

$$S = L\left[6.09755\left(\frac{\theta}{\beta}\right)^3 - 20.78040\left(\frac{\theta}{\beta}\right)^5 + 26.73155\left(\frac{\theta}{\beta}\right)^6\right.$$
$$\left. - 13.60965\left(\frac{\theta}{\beta}\right)^7 + 2.56095\left(\frac{\theta}{\beta}\right)^8\right]$$

$$V = \frac{L}{\beta}\left[18.29265\left(\frac{\theta}{\beta}\right)^2 - 103.90200\left(\frac{\theta}{\beta}\right)^4 + 160.38930\left(\frac{\theta}{\beta}\right)^5\right.$$
$$\left. - 95.26755\left(\frac{\theta}{\beta}\right)^6 + 20.48760\left(\frac{\theta}{\beta}\right)^7\right]$$

$$A = \frac{L}{\beta^2}\left[36.58530\left(\frac{\theta}{\beta}\right) - 415.60800\left(\frac{\theta}{\beta}\right)^3 + 801.94650\left(\frac{\theta}{\beta}\right)^4\right.$$
$$\left. - 571.60530\left(\frac{\theta}{\beta}\right)^5 + 143.41320\left(\frac{\theta}{\beta}\right)^6\right]$$

P−1

$$S = L\left[1.00000 - 2.63415\left(\frac{\theta}{\beta}\right)^2 + 2.78055\left(\frac{\theta}{\beta}\right)^5\right.$$
$$\left. + 3.17060\left(\frac{\theta}{\beta}\right)^6 - 6.87795\left(\frac{\theta}{\beta}\right)^7 + 2.56095\left(\frac{\theta}{\beta}\right)^8\right]$$

$$V = \frac{L}{\beta}\left[-5.26830\left(\frac{\theta}{\beta}\right) + 13.90275\left(\frac{\theta}{\beta}\right)^4 + 19.02360\left(\frac{\theta}{\beta}\right)^5\right.$$
$$\left. - 43.14565\left(\frac{\theta}{\beta}\right)^6 + 20.48760\left(\frac{\theta}{\beta}\right)^7\right]$$

$$A = \frac{L}{\beta^2}\left[-5.26830 + 55.61100\left(\frac{\theta}{\beta}\right)^3 + 95.11800\left(\frac{\theta}{\beta}\right)^4\right.$$
$$\left. - 288.87390\left(\frac{\theta}{\beta}\right)^5 + 143.41320\left(\frac{\theta}{\beta}\right)^6\right]$$

P−2

Fig. 7-4. Eighth-degree polynomial motion characteristics.

and then assembled to produce the required motion specifications.

Among the basic curves, the constant velocity and the parabolic motion curves should not be used by themselves, except at very low speeds. The infinite jerk that occurs in three places in the parabolic motion makes it a poor selection in high-speed applications.

As a means of avoiding infinite jerk, a building-block approach has been suggested by Kloomok and Muffley in Mabie and Qcvirk (147) that utilizes the following three analytic functions:
• Cycloidal
• Harmonic
• Eighth-degree polynomial

The usefulness of these curves may be further expanded by combining them with half-curve segments to make a single contour. Figs. 7-2, 7-3, and 7-4 display the displacement, the velocity, and the acceleration characteristics of these curve segments.

Used singly or in combination, these three curves offer effective solutions for the majority of functional situations encountered in cam design. The curves all have continuous derivatives at all intermediate points; thus acceleration changes gradually, and jerk is finite. Infinite jerk is avoided at the end points by matching accelerations. For example, when a rise follows a dwell, the zero acceleration at the end of the dwell is matched by selecting a curve having zero acceleration at the start of the rise. The acceleration required at the end of the rise is determined by the succeeding condition. If a fall follows immediately, the rise can end in a fairly high value of deceleration, because this can be matched precisely by a curve having the same deceleration for the start of the fall. This technique of selecting and sizing the basic blocks and matching the velocity, the acceleration, or both is just like playing with tinker toys. Table 7-1 offers a guideline for curve selections. The selection of profiles to suit particular requirements is made according to the following criteria:

(1) The full cycloidal curve, having zero acceleration at both ends of the motion, is particularly well-suited to the DRD event. Because the pressure angle is relatively high $(c_v = 2.00)$ and the acceleration returns to zero unnecessarily, two full cycloids should not be coupled together.

(2) Of the three curves, the harmonic provides the lowest peak acceleration $\left(C_A = \dfrac{\pi^2}{2}\right)$ and pressure angle $\left(C_v = \dfrac{\pi}{2}\right)$ for a given rise. Therefore, it is preferred when the acceleration at both the start and the finish can be matched to the end acceleration of the adjacent profiles. Because the acceleration at the midpoint is zero, the half-harmonic curve can often be used where a constant-velocity rise follows an acceleration. Alternately, the half-harmonic could be coupled to a half-cycloid or to a half-polynomial.

(3) The eighth-degree polynomial provides a peak acceleration and a pressure angle intermediate between the harmonic and the cycloidal curves. Its non-symmetrical acceleration characteristics can be very useful. For example, the zero acceleration at the start of a rise or at the conclusion of a fall can be coupled to a dwell. Similarly, the finite acceleration at the end of the rise permits coupling to a harmonic curve or to the start of a polynomial fall.

The following situations are typical:

Cycloidal–Constant Velocity Coupling

This combination is used when the design requires a fixed velocity at some section of the cam's profile. It is also advantageous when fixed cam dimensions

Table 7-1. A Guideline for Selection of Cam Curves

	Displacement Curve	Required Boundary Conditions	Recommended Type of Motion
D-R-D		Acceleration at *A, B* = 0 Velocity at *A, B* = 0	Cycloidal Modified Sine Modified Trapezoidal
DR-CV-RD		Acceleration at *A, B, C, D* = 0 Velocity at *B* = Vel. at *C* Velocity at *A, D* = 0	Half Cycloid-*CV*-Half Cycloid Polynomial-*CV*-Polynomial
D-R-R-D		Acceleration at *A, C* = 0 Acceleration match at *B* Velocity at *A, B, C* = 0	Cycloid-Harmonic
R-R-R		Acceleration match at *A, B* Velocity at *A,B* = 0	Harmonic
Combination		Acceleration at *A, B, C, E* = 0 Acceleration match at *D*	Harmonic Modified Trapezoidal Modified Sine Polynomial

result in a greater pressure angle than desired if a full cycloidal curve is used.

In Fig. 7-5 the segment AB is half–cycloidal (curve C1, Fig. 7-3), and the segment BC is constant velocity.

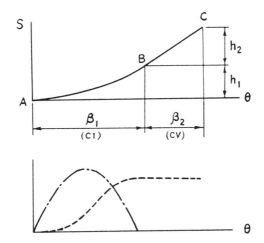

Fig. 7-5. Cycloid–constant velocity coupling.

The velocity equation of curve C1 is

$$V_{C_1} = \frac{h}{\beta} \left(1 - \cos \frac{\pi\theta}{\beta} \right) .$$

At point B,

$$V_B = \frac{h_1}{\beta_1} \left(1 - \cos \frac{\pi\beta_1}{\beta_1} \right) = \frac{2h_1}{\beta_1} .$$

The velocity at the same point B for constant–velocity motion is

$$V_B = \frac{h_2}{\beta_2} .$$

Therefore, for velocity matching, it is necessary to have

$$\frac{2h_1}{h_2} = \frac{\beta_1}{\beta_2} . \tag{7-1}$$

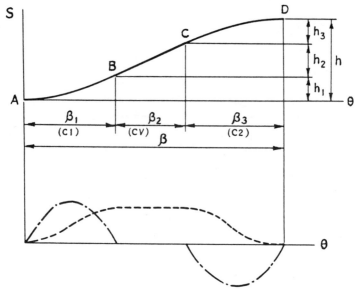

Fig. 7-6. Cycloid–constant velocity–cycloid in DRD event.

Modified Constant–Velocity Motion with Cycloidal Curve Segments in DRD Events

As shown in Fig. 7-6, the displacement curve ABCD represents a typical DRD event. A constant–velocity motion is preceded by a half–cycloid, curve C1, and followed by another half–cycloid, curve C2. The symbols are as labeled in the diagram.

We know that a velocity match at point B requires

$$\frac{2h_1}{h_2} = \frac{\beta_1}{\beta_2} \; . \tag{7-2}$$

The velocity equation of curve C2 is

$$V_{C2} = \frac{h}{\beta}\left(1 + \cos\frac{\pi\theta}{\beta}\right) \; .$$

At point C, $\theta = 0$, and

$$V_C = \frac{2h_3}{\beta_3} \; .$$

Realizing that the velocity at C is the same as the velocity at B, we make a velocity match at point C to give

$$\frac{2h_3}{\beta_3} = \frac{h_2}{\beta_2} = \frac{2h_1}{\beta_1}$$

or

$$\frac{h_1}{h_3} = \frac{\beta_1}{\beta_3} \, . \tag{7-3}$$

Combining Eqs. (7-2) and (7-3) and using the relationships

$$\beta_1 + \beta_2 + \beta_3 = \beta \tag{7-4}$$

$$h_1 + h_2 + h_3 = h \, , \tag{7-5}$$

we obtain

$$h\beta_1 = h_1(\beta + \beta_2) \, . \tag{7-6}$$

In Eqs. (7-2), (7-4), (7-5), and (7-6), if the total cam angle and the total rise h are specified together with any other two additional parameters, we can solve the equations for the rest of them.

Example 7-1

A cam is to have a 0.6–cm cycloidal rise coupled to a constant velocity curve that acts through 45° and which in turn is coupled to a cycloidal curve. The total displacement of the follower is to be 2.5 cm and is to occur in 120°.

Here $h = 2.5$ cm, $\beta = 120°$, $h_1 = 0.6$ cm, and $\beta_2 = 45°$.

From Eq. (7-6)

$$\beta_1 = \frac{h_1}{h} (\beta + \beta_2)$$

$$= \frac{0.6(120 + 45)}{2.5} = 39.6° \, .$$

From Eq. (7-4)

$$\beta_3 = \beta - \beta_1 - \beta_2 = 120° - 39.6° - 45° = 35.4° .$$

From Eq. (7-2)

$$h_2 = 2h_1 \frac{\beta_2}{\beta_1} = 2(0.6) \frac{45}{39.6} = 1.364 \text{ cm.}$$

And finally, from Eq. (7-5)

$$h_3 = h - h_1 - h_2 = 2.5 - 0.6 - 1.364 = 0.536 \text{ cm.}$$

Cycloidal–Harmonic Coupling

Consider the schematic diagram Fig. 7-7, in which the segment AB is half–cycloid (curve C1, Fig. 7-3) and the segment BC is half–harmonic (curve H2, Fig. 7-2).

The velocity equation of segment C1 of the curve is

$$V_{C1} = \frac{h}{\beta} \left(1 - \cos \frac{\pi\theta}{\beta} \right) .$$

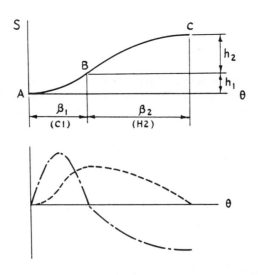

Fig. 7-7. Cycloid–harmonic coupling.

At the end point B, $\theta = \beta_1$, and the velocity is

$$V_B = \frac{h_1}{\beta_1} \left(1 - \cos \frac{\pi \beta_1}{\beta_1} \right) = \frac{2h_1}{\beta_1} \; .$$

Likewise, the velocity equation of the second segment H2 of the curve is

$$V_{H2} = \frac{\pi h}{2\beta} \cos \left(\frac{\pi \theta}{2\beta} \right) .$$

At the beginning point B, $\theta = 0$, and the velocity is

$$V_B = \frac{\pi h_2}{2\beta_2} \cos \frac{\pi (0)}{\beta} = \frac{\pi h_2}{2\beta_2} \; .$$

A continuity of velocity at point B requires

$$\frac{2h_1}{\beta_1} = \frac{\pi h_2}{2\beta_2}$$

or

$$\frac{4h_1}{\pi h_2} = \frac{\beta_1}{\beta_2} \; . \tag{7-7}$$

Eq. (7-7) shows the necessary relations between the linear and angular displacements for proper cycloidal–harmonic curve coupling.

Cycloidal–Harmonic Coupling in DRRD Events

A typical symmetrical displacement diagram of DRRD motion using cycloidal–harmonic curve blending is shown in Fig. 7-8. The curve segments used are:

AB — half-cycloid C1, rise
BC — half-harmonic H2, rise
CB′ — half-harmonic H3, return
B′A′ — half-cycloid C4, return.

Let p be the ratio between the deceleration period and the acceleration period; thus $\beta_2 = p\beta_1$.

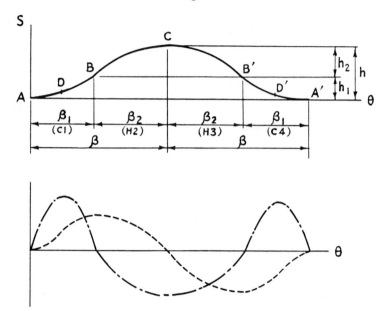

Fig. 7-8. Cycloid–harmonic coupling in DRRD event (symmetrical case).

During the rise, a velocity match of curves C1 and H2 at point B requires

$$\frac{\beta_2}{\beta_1} = \frac{\pi h_2}{4 h_1} .$$

But

$$h_1 + h_2 = h.$$

Solving these two equations and using the definition of p gives

$$h_1 = \frac{\pi}{4p + \pi} h , \tag{7-8}$$

and

$$h_2 = \frac{4p}{\pi + 4p} h . \tag{7-9}$$

The maximum velocity at point B is

$$V_B = \frac{2 h_1}{\beta_1} = \frac{\pi h_2}{2 \beta_2} .$$

Using either Eq. (7-8) or Eq. (7-9) and the relations

$$\beta_1 = \frac{1}{p + 1} \beta$$

$$\beta_2 = \frac{p}{p + 1} \beta ,$$

we obtain

$$V_B = \frac{2\pi(p + 1)}{(\pi + 4p)} \frac{h}{\beta} . \qquad (7\text{-}10)$$

The maximum positive acceleration at D is

$$A_D = \frac{\pi h_1}{\beta_1^2} = \frac{\pi^2(p + 1)^2}{(4p + \pi)} \frac{h}{\beta^2} . \qquad (7\text{-}11)$$

The maximum negative acceleration at C is

$$A_C = -\frac{\pi^2 h_2}{4\beta_2^2} = -\frac{\pi^2(p + 1)^2}{p(4p + \pi)} \frac{h}{\beta^2} . \qquad (7\text{-}12)$$

As a special case, when $p = 1$, Eqs. (7-8) through (7-12) become

$$h_1 = 0.4399h \qquad (7\text{-}13)$$

$$h_2 = 0.5601h \qquad (7\text{-}14)$$

$$V_B = 1.759 \frac{h}{\beta} \qquad (7\text{-}15)$$

$$A_D = 5.528 \frac{h}{\beta^2} \qquad (7\text{-}16)$$

$$A_C = -5.528 \frac{h}{\beta^2} . \qquad (7\text{-}17)$$

Fig. 7-9 depicts the case where the working periods between the rise and the return are not equal. One stroke has a longer working period, which may be called a "slow" stroke, and the other has a shorter working period, so it may be

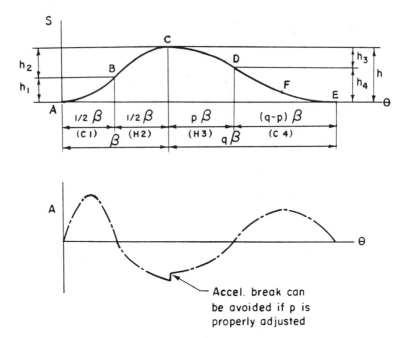

Fig. 7-9. Cycloid–harmonic coupling in DRRD event (unsymmetrical case).

called a "fast" stroke. Let q be the ratio of the period of the slow stroke to that of the fast stroke.

The curve segments are:

AB — half-cycloid C1, rise
BC — half-harmonic H2, rise
CD — half-harmonic H3, return
DE — half-cycloid C4, return .

Let the period of AB and BC be equal, so that Eqs. (7-13) through (7-17) derived above are directly applicable for the rise portion of the motion. The periods of CD and DE are not equal. So let p represent the ratio of the periods of CD to AB.

Schmidt (202) was the first to recognize that unless the ratio p is properly adjusted, there will be an instantaneous change in the magnitude of the acceleration at point C. Our problem is to show how the proper value of p can be found so that the acceleration discontinuity can be avoided.

The acceleration equation of curve CD is

$$A_{H3} = -\frac{\pi^2 h}{4\beta^2} \cos \frac{\pi\theta}{2\beta} .$$

At point C, $\theta = 0$, thus

$$A_C = -\frac{\pi^2 h_3}{4p^2\beta^2} \, .$$

This needs to be matched with the acceleration at the end point of curve BC, which is governed by Eq. (7-17). Thus

$$-\frac{\pi^2 h_3}{4p^2\beta^2} = -5.528 \frac{h}{\beta^2} \, .$$

Therefore,

$$h_3 = \frac{22.112}{\pi^2} p^2 h \qquad\qquad (7\text{-}18)$$

and

$$h_4 = \left(1 - \frac{22.112}{\pi^2} p^2\right) h \, . \qquad\qquad (7\text{-}19)$$

The velocity equation of curve CD is

$$V_{H3} = -\frac{\pi h}{2\beta} \sin \frac{\pi\theta}{2\beta} \, .$$

At point D, $\theta = p\beta$, thus

$$V_D = -\frac{\pi h_3}{2(p\beta)} \sin \frac{\pi p\beta}{2p\beta} = -\frac{\pi h_3}{2p\beta} \, .$$

The velocity equation of curve DE is

$$V_{C4} = -\frac{h}{\beta}\left(1 + \cos \frac{\pi\theta}{\beta}\right) \, .$$

At point D, $\theta = 0$, thus

$$V_D = -\frac{2h_4}{(q-p)\beta} \, .$$

A velocity match at point D necessitates

$$- \frac{\pi h_3}{2p\beta} = - \frac{2h_4}{(q-p)\beta} \; .$$

Combining Eqs. (7-18) and (7-19) results in a quadratic equation in p

$$\left(\frac{44.224}{\pi^2} - \frac{22.112}{2\pi} \right) p^2 + \frac{22.112}{2\pi} qp - 2 = 0$$

or

$$p^2 + 3.6597qp - 2.0799 = 0 \; ,$$

the positive root of which is

$$p = - 1.8299q + \frac{1}{2} \sqrt{13.393q^2 + 8.3196} \; . \tag{7-20}$$

Knowing p, we can work backwards to find the maximum velocity

$$V_D = 3.5192 \frac{h}{\beta} \; . \tag{7-21}$$

The maximum positive acceleration at point F can be determined from the equation

$$A_{C4} = \frac{\pi h}{\beta^2} \sin \frac{\pi \theta}{\beta} \; .$$

Replacing h by h_4, β by $(q-p)\beta$, and setting θ equal to $\frac{1}{2}(q-p)\beta$ gives

$$A_F = \frac{\pi h_4}{(q-p)^2 \beta^2}$$

or

$$A_F = \frac{\pi(1 - 2.240p^2)}{(q-p)^2} \frac{h}{\beta^2} \; . \tag{7-22}$$

The maximum negative acceleration at point C given by this equation is the same as in Eq. (7-17).

Harmonic to Eighth–Degree Polynomial Coupling

Let us first consider a harmonic curve H5, which is to match with an eighth–degree polynomial curve P2 at point B, as shown in Fig. 7-10. The velocities at the end of the curve H5 and at the beginning of the curve P2 are already matched, since they both are zero. The accelerations need to be matched.

The equation of acceleration for the curve H5 is

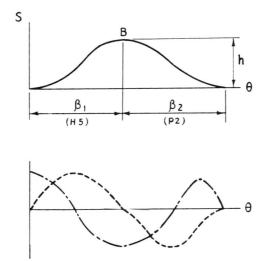

Fig. 7-10. Harmonic (H5) and eighth–degree polynomial coupling.

$$A_{H5} = \frac{\pi^2 h}{2\beta^2} \cos \frac{\pi \theta}{\beta}.$$

Thus

$$A_B = A_{H5}\bigg|_{\theta = \beta_1} = -\frac{\pi^2 h}{2\beta_1^2}.$$

The equation of acceleration for the curve P2 is

$$A_{P2} = \frac{h}{\beta^2}\left[-5.2683 + 55.6110 \left(\frac{\theta}{\beta}\right)^3 + 95.1180 \left(\frac{\theta}{\beta}\right)^4 \right.$$

$$\left. -288.8739 \left(\frac{\theta}{\beta}\right)^5 + 143.4132 \left(\frac{\theta}{\beta}\right)^6 \right].$$

Thus

$$A_B = A_{P2}\Big|_{\theta=0} = -5.2683\,\frac{h}{\beta_2^{\,2}}\,.$$

A continuity of acceleration requires

$$-\frac{\pi^2 h}{2\beta_1^{\,2}} = -5.2683\,\frac{h}{\beta_2^{\,2}}$$

or

$$\left(\frac{\beta_2}{\beta_1}\right)^2 = \frac{10.54}{\pi^2}\,. \tag{7-23}$$

In a similar manner, we can show that the harmonic curve H2 can be coupled together with the eighth–degree polynomial curve P2 (Fig. 7-11). The relationship of linear and angular displacements for the combination is

$$\left(\frac{\beta_2}{\beta_1}\right)^2 = \frac{21.08}{\pi^2}\,. \tag{7-24}$$

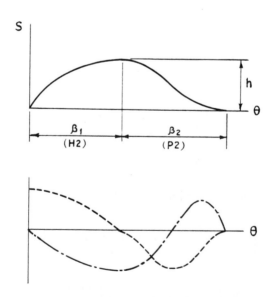

Fig. 7-11. Harmonic (H2) and eighth–degree polynomial coupling.

By the same token, we can match the curve segments P1 with H6 and P1 with H3.

Example 7-2

A cam–driven mechanism for use as an IBM card picker is to be designed using composite profiles. As shown in the schematic of Fig. 7-12, the picker knife initially accelerates along curve AB to the peripheral velocity of the feed rolls, then moves along path BC with constant velocity for a specified length of time until the feed rolls pick up the card. The picker knife then decelerates along CD and finally returns along DE toward the initial position.

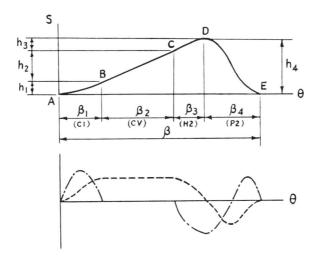

Fig. 7-12. Motion characteristics of IBM card picker.

To show that trigonometric curves and polynomial curves can be blended together for practical purposes, we will choose the composition of the curve segments as follows:

    AB — half–cycloid C1, rise
    BC — constant velocity, rise
    CD — half-harmonic H2, rise
    DE — eighth–degree polynomial P2, return.

The calculations include

$$h_1 + h_2 + h_3 = h_4$$

$$\beta_1 + \beta_2 + \beta_3 + \beta_4 = \beta .$$

Constant-velocity portion requires

$$V_{CV} = \frac{h_2}{\beta_2} \ .$$

To match velocity at point B, Eq. (7-1) gives

$$\frac{2h_1}{h_2} = \frac{\beta_1}{\beta_2} \ .$$

Similarly, a velocity match at point C requires

$$\frac{2h_2}{\pi h_3} = \frac{\beta_2}{\beta_3}$$

To match accelerations of the half–harmonic curve H2 with the eighth–degree polynomial at point D requires, from Eq. (7-24),

$$\frac{21.08}{\pi^2} \ \frac{h_4}{h_3} = \left(\frac{\beta_4}{\beta_3}\right)^2 \ .$$

All h's and V_{CV} are known; thus all of the angle β's can be calculated. The displacement equations, as a function of θ with respect to the zero position, are

$$S = h_1 \left(\frac{\theta_1}{\beta_1} - \frac{1}{\pi} \ \sin \frac{\pi\theta}{\beta_1} \right) \qquad \text{for } 0 \le \theta \le \beta_1$$

$$S = h_1 + \frac{h_2}{\beta_2} \ (\theta - \beta_1) \qquad \text{for } \beta_1 \le \theta \le (\beta_1 + \beta_2)$$

$$S = h_4 - h_3 \ \sin \frac{\pi(\beta_1 + \beta_2 + \beta_3 - \theta)}{2\beta_3} \quad \begin{aligned} &\text{for } \beta_1 + \beta_2 \le \theta \le \beta_1 \\ &\qquad\qquad + \beta_2 + \beta_3 \end{aligned}$$

$$S = h_4 - h_4 \ (1.0 - 2.63415\tau^2 + 2.78055\tau^5 + 3.17060\tau^6$$
$$- 6.87795\tau^7 + 2.56095\tau^8)$$

$$\text{with} \quad \tau = \frac{\theta - (\beta_1 + \beta_2 + \beta_3)}{\beta_4} \qquad \text{for } \beta_1 + \beta_2 + \beta_3 \le \theta \le \beta \ .$$

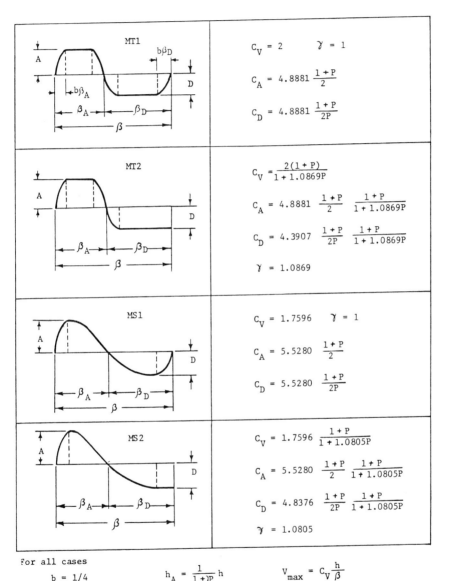

For all cases

$b = 1/4$

$\beta_A = \dfrac{1}{1+P}\,\beta$

$\beta_D = \dfrac{P}{1+P}\,\beta$

$h_A = \dfrac{1}{1+P}\,h$

$h_D = \dfrac{P}{1+P}\,h$

$P = \beta_D\,/\,\beta_A$

$V_{max} = C_V \dfrac{h}{\beta}$

$A_{max} = C_A \dfrac{h}{\beta^2}\;;\quad D_{max} = C_D \dfrac{h}{\beta^2}$

(P = 1 for symmetric case)

Fig. 7-13. Modified trapezoidal and modified sine characteristics.

7-3. COMBINATION OF NON-SIMPLE CURVES — AN EXTENSION OF THE BUILDING-BLOCK APPROACH

The building-block approach may be expanded to include other types of curves and modified functions in addition to those previously discussed. The key considerations in determining which curves to use are the magnitude of the acceleration and of the velocity factors, the jerk characteristics, and the torque characteristics, as well as the complexity and the amount of work involved in matching the curves.

Fig. 7-13 presents two different types of acceleration diagrams; each of them is developed for both DRD and DRRD motion events. The two types are based on the modified trapezoidal curve and the modified sine curve developed in Chapter 5.

As we recall, the modified trapezoidal motion is itself a combination of sine curve quadrants and uniform acceleration. The modified trapezoidal motion is preferred when a lower acceleration is important or when a higher C_V factor is desirable, but it is not so ideal for moving a heavy load. The modified sine motion is itself a combination of sine quadrants occupying different parts of the working period. It is preferred for a high output torque.

Without a loss of generality, we can list nonsymmetric motion cases in Fig. 7-13. A ratio P, which is defined as

$$P = \frac{time\ for\ the\ deceleration\ period}{time\ for\ the\ acceleration\ period},$$

is employed. Symmetrical motion configuration may be viewed as a special case with $P = 1$. The velocity factor C_V and the acceleration factor C_A are a function of P.

The following two examples illustrate how to apply this group of building blocks. Further information can be found in the work by Neklutin (173).

Example 7-3

A cam, which transmits a heavy load, moves a stroke of $h = 6$ cm and immediately returns towards its initial position without a dwell. Each stroke takes place during a cam rotation of $\beta = 120°$. Assume $P = \dfrac{3}{2}$ for both the forward and the return strokes.

The relevent motion diagram is shown in Fig. 7-14. Using the modified sine curve MS2 from Fig. 7-13, we can calculate the forward motion stroke

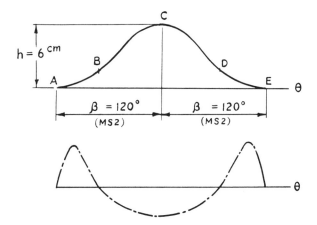

Fig. 7-14.

$$h = 6 \text{ cm}, \quad \beta = 120°, \quad P = \frac{3}{2}$$

$$\beta_1 = \frac{1}{1 + P} \beta = 48°$$

$$\beta_2 = \frac{P}{1 + p} \beta = 72°$$

$$h_1 = \frac{h}{1 + 1.0805 P} = 2.2894 \text{ cm}$$

$$h_2 = \frac{1.0805 P}{1 + 1.0805 P} h = 3.7106 \text{ cm.}$$

The velocity factor is

$$C_V = 1.7596 \frac{1 + P}{1 + 1.0805 P} = 1.7 .$$

The acceleration factors are

$$C_A = 5.528 \frac{(1 + P)^2}{2(1 + 1.0805 P)} = 6.592 \text{ for the accelerating period, and}$$

$$C_D = 4.8376 \ \frac{(1 + P)^2}{2P(1 + 1.0805P)} = 3.846 \text{ for the decelerating period.}$$

Because of the symmetry between the forward and the return strokes, the displacement, the velocity, and the acceleration of the return stroke are mirror images of the displacement, the velocity, and the acceleration of the forward stroke, e.g., the deceleration of the forward stroke is the same as the acceleration of the return stroke.

The actual point-to-point displacement can be calculated by a computer using the equations associated with the modified sine curves (Chapter 5). The labor involved may be tremendous unless complete normalized tables of values are at hand.

Example 7-4

Consider an application in which the required cam output stroke of 7 cm, in 200° of rotation is to be accomplished between dwells. The program specifications are

ABC	0° ~ 30°	rise 2 cm with MT1
CD	30° ~ 50°	dwell
DFH	50° ~200°	rise 5 cm with MT2
		and return 7 cm with MT2
after H	200° ~ 360°	dwell.

Note that for the first DRD rise stroke a modified trapezoidal curve of MT1 type from Fig. 7-13 is used. For the subsequent DRRD movement, which consists of the second step of the rise stroke and the return stroke, a modified trapezoidal curve of MT2 type is used. Assume $P = \dfrac{2}{3}$ for each of the modified trapezoidal rise or fall strokes.

As shown in Fig. 7-15, we can compute the following for the DRD movement along path ABC:

$$h_{AB} = \frac{1}{1 + P} \ h_1 = \frac{3}{5} \ (2) = 1.2 \text{ cm}$$

$$h_{BC} = h_1 - h_{AB} = 2 - 1.2 = 0.8 \text{ cm}$$

$$\beta_{AB} = \frac{1}{1 + P} \ \beta_{AC} = \frac{3}{5} \ (30°) = 18°$$

$$\beta_{BC} = 30° - \beta_{AB} = 12°.$$

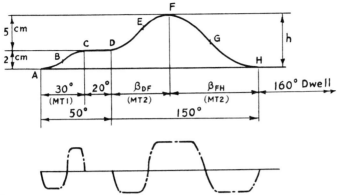

Fig. 7-15.

The acceleration factors are

$$C_A = 4.888 \; \frac{1 + P}{2} = 4.075$$

$$C_D = 4.888 \; \frac{1 + P}{2P} = 6.11.$$

For the subsequent DRRD movement along the DEFGH path, an acceleration match at this point F requires

$$(C_D)_{DF} \; \frac{h_2}{\beta_{DF}^2} = (C_A)_{FH} \; \frac{h}{\beta_{FH}^2} \; .$$

The acceleration factor C_A of the curve FH should equal the deceleration factor C_D of the curve DF. This leads to

$$\frac{\beta_{FH}}{\beta_{DF}} = \sqrt{\frac{h}{h_2}} = \sqrt{\frac{7}{5}} = 1.1832.$$

But

$$\beta_{DF} + \beta_{FH} = 150°.$$

Solving for β_{DF} and β_{FH}, we obtain

$$\beta_{DF} = 68.71°$$

$$\beta_{FH} = 81.29°.$$

The acceleration factors are

$$C_A = 4.3907 \ \frac{(1 + P)^2}{2P(1 + 1.0869P)} = 5.30 \ (\text{FG portion})$$

$$C_D = 4.8881 \ \frac{(1 + P)^2}{2(1 + 1.0869P)} = 3.94 \ (\text{GH portion}).$$

8
Profile Synthesis By Numerical Methods

8-1. INTRODUCTION

Many basic cam curves and combinations of these curves can be used to develop cam profiles. However, when these theoretical curves are calculated and the displacements are rounded to the manufacturing tolerance of the nearest two hundredth of a milimeter, the resultant displacement curve has an unsatisfactory degree of variance from the original curve. Thus the actual acceleration pattern fluctuates and diverges from the theoretical pattern. A common practice to deal with this situation is to smooth out the "irregularities" in the acceleration curve without greatly altering the general shape of the lift curve. This is generally known as the "curve adjustment" or the "curve smoothing" process.

In this chapter, after a brief introduction of the finite differences, we will first describe Johnson's finite–difference method (116) for curve smoothing and the modification of Johnson's method. Other numerical algorithms using finite mathematics to synthesize cam profiles developed by Chen (33, 34, 36) will also be described.

8-2. FINITE DIFFERENCES

If a function $y = y(x)$ and its derivatives are continuous, we may use a Taylor series expansion to write

$$y(x + \Delta x) = y(x) + (\Delta x)\dot{y}(x) + \frac{(\Delta x)^2}{2!} \ddot{y}(x) \tag{8-1}$$

$$+ \frac{(\Delta x)^3}{3!} \dddot{y}(x) + \ldots,$$

where the dots represent differentiation with respect to x. If $y(x)$ and higher terms are not included in the expansion, then the approximation is said to be valid up to the second order. The more terms that are included, the more accurate is the approximation.

As shown in Fig. 8-1, h is a small equally spaced increment Δx. The particular independent variable under consideration is designated by x_i, where i is a dummy index, and the corresponding dependent variable is y_i; the neighboring points on the abscissa to the left of x_i are designated by $x_{i-1}, x_{i-2}, \ldots$, etc., and those to the right of x_i are designated by $x_{i+1}, x_{i+2}, \ldots$, etc. The corresponding ordinates are denoted by $y_{i-1}, y_{i-2}, \ldots$, and $y_{i+1}, y_{i+2}, \ldots$, respectively. With this notation, Eq. (8-1) can be written in the form

$$y_{i+1} = y_i + h\dot{y}_i + \frac{h^2}{2!} \ddot{y}_i + \ldots \tag{8-2}$$

Similarly,

$$y_{i-1} = y_i - h\dot{y}_i + \frac{h^2}{2!} \ddot{y}_i - \ldots, \tag{8-3}$$

where the higher order terms of the series expansion have been ignored. Combining Eqs. (8-2) and (8-3) gives

$$\dot{y}_i = \frac{1}{2h} y_i' \tag{8-4}$$

$$\ddot{y}_i = \frac{1}{h^2} y_i'', \tag{8-5}$$

where

$$y_i' = y_{i+1} - y_{i-1}, \tag{8-6}$$

and

$$y_i'' = y_{i-1} - 2y_i + y_{i+1} . \tag{8-7}$$

Eqs. (8-4) and (8-5) are the central–difference approximations up to the second order for the first derivative (velocity) and second derivative (acceleration) of the function represented by a set of discrete data. We will call y_i' the velocity factor and y_i'' the acceleration factor.

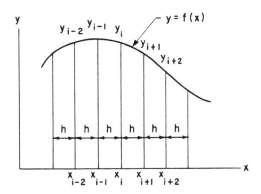

Fig. 8-1. Central–difference approximation of a function.

Given an equally spaced discrete function, we can construct a difference table as follows

x_0	y_0			
		Δy_0		
x_1	y_1		$\Delta^2 y_0$	
		Δy_1		$\Delta^3 y_0$
x_2	y_2		$\Delta^2 y_1$		$\Delta^4 y_0$
		Δy_2		$\Delta^3 y_1$
x_3	y_3		$\Delta^2 y_2$	
		Δy_3		
x_4	y_4			

The diagonal pattern makes each entry the difference of its two nearest neighbors to the left, except for the x_k, y_k. The differences of the y_k values are denoted

$$\Delta y_k = y_{k+1} - y_k$$

and are called first differences. The differences of these first differences are denoted $\Delta^2 y_k = \Delta(\Delta y_k) = \Delta y_{k+1} - \Delta y_k = y_{k+2} - 2y_{k+1} + y_k$ and are called second differences. In general,

$$\Delta^n y_k = \Delta^{n-1} y_{k+1} - \Delta^{n-1} y_k$$

defines the nth differences. Each difference proves to be a combination of the y values in column two. A simple example is $\Delta^3 y_0 = y_3 - 3y_2 + 3y_1 - y_0$. The general result is

$$\Delta^k y_0 = \sum_{j=0}^{k} (-1)^j \binom{k}{j} y_{k-j},$$

where $\binom{k}{j}$ is a binomial coefficient.

8-3. JOHNSON'S METHOD OF CAM CURVE SMOOTHING

This method is a trial–and–error procedure of adjusting the initial displacement to obtain a smoothly varying acceleration pattern. The rationale and the process of Johnson's method (116) are described below.

In the design of cams, once an initial displacement of the follower has been determined, the acceleration factor y_i'' of Eq. (8-7) can be calculated at each discrete point, and a plot of these acceleration values versus the cam angle can be obtained. Often, excessive fluctuations occur in the acceleration plot, which is sometimes so erratic that the general shape is beyond recognition.

Generally, the acceleration curve is the one requiring modification. When modifying this curve, the displacement of the point whose acceleration factor deviates the most from a smooth curve must be adjusted. For each displacement adjusted, the associated acceleration factors must be corrected. Note that the adjustment of the displacement for any point results in a correction of the acceleration factors for three points. For the point whose displacement has been adjusted (the central point), the change in the acceleration factor equals -2 times the displacement adjustment. For each of the two adjacent points, the acceleration factor changes $+1$ times the displacement adjustment.

Next, we need to traverse the points in a sequential manner, adjusting the displacement by considering the effect that each adjustment has on the acceleration factors. By so doing, the variation of the acceleration factor can readily be made to have any characteristic desired. In general, several traverses are necessary to obtain the desired characteristics. In any particular traverse, care should be exercised so that the adjusted displacements do not diverge too far from the initial displacement. Otherwise, a large acceleration factor will result

at the end of the traverse, and many more traverses will be necessary for a satisfactory development.

Example 8-1

A cam has a rise of 0.726 cm during 70° of cam rotation. Using five–degree
intervals, modify the cam acceleration curve by Johnson's method.

The intent is to smooth out the irregularities of the acceleration curve and to
equalize the peak magnitudes of acceleration during both the accelerating and
the decelerating periods. The displacement values are first tabulated in Table
8-1 for each 5° increment angle. Using Eq. (8-7), the acceleration factor is
calculated, tabulated, and plotted in Fig. 8-2.

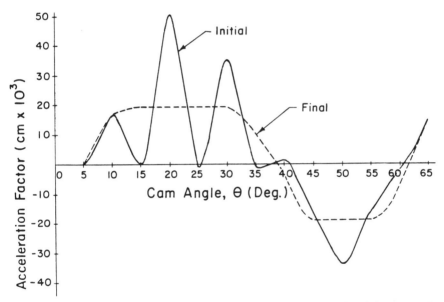

Fig. 8-2. Smoothing of acceleration factor resulting from adjustment in displacement of
example 8–1.

To show a typical calculation step, let us consider the data for the 20° point.
If the displacement of this point is first adjusted by $+17$, its acceleration factor
changes by $-2(17) = -34$. Hence, its corrected acceleration factor becomes
$+51 - 34 = 17$. In the meantime, increasing the displacement of the 20° point
by $+17$ also changes the acceleration factor of the 15° point by an amount of
$+17(0 + 17 = 17)$ and that of the 25° point by $+16(-1 + 17 = +16)$. At the
end of the first trial step, the displacements of the 15° and the 25° points have
remained unchanged from their initial values, whereas the displacement of the
20° point is now $34 + 17 = +51 \times 10^3$ cm. The process is repeated for the subse-

Table 8-1. Repeated Cam Curve Adjustments

θ (°)	Initial Displacement (cm × 10³)	Initial Acceleration Factor × 10³	Displacement Adjustment			Modification to			Final Displacement (cm × 10³)	Final Acceleration
			1	2	3	1	2	3		
0	0	0							0	0
5	0	0							0	0
10	0	+17							0	+17
15	17	0							17	+19
20	34	+51	+17	+2		~~+17~~	+19	+18	53	+18
25	102	−1		+4	+1	~~+17~~	~~+13~~ ~~+17~~	+19	108	+19
30	169	+35	+9	+2		~~+16~~ +25	~~+17~~ ~~+19~~ +21	+18	180	+18
35	271	−1				+8	~~+21~~ ~~+17~~ +10		271	+10
40	372	+1				−8	~~−3~~	−4	372	−4
45	474	−17		−4	−1	−26	~~−17~~ −21	−19	469	−19
50	559	−34	−8	−4		−18	−22 −14 −18	−19	547	−19
55	610	−16		−4	−1	−24	~~−28~~ −20	−18	605	−18
60	645	−2							645	−7
65	678	+15					−6	−7	678	−7
70	726								726	

quent trials. In every trial step, the old value of the acceleration factor is discarded, and a new value is substituted. Three trial steps were used in this example. The number of trial steps used and the amount of adjustment in each step depend upon the nature of the problem encountered and the experience of the designer in using this method.

8-4. A MODIFICATION OF JOHNSON'S METHOD — THE AREA–MOMENT OR INFLUENCE–COEFFICIENT METHOD

Attempts to establish more guidelines for and a more systematic approach to Johnson's curve smoothing process have been made by a number of investigators. Lenz (141) has suggested the use of a bar chart or stacked blocks in keeping account of the shift in the acceleration pattern. Crossley (53) has identified some typical modes of pattern change and has established the "moment" analogy. Fox (82) has formalized these concepts and put them into a systematic procedure that is suitable for machine computation. Before describing this procedure, let us first clarify the terms "area–moment" and "influence–coefficient".

The "area–moment" used in the modified Johnson's method is similar to the area–moment method used for determining the deflection of beams in the study of mechanics of materials. When a beam is treated as a continuum, the flexibility influence function $a(x, \xi)$ is defined as the deflection at any point x along the beam due to a unit load at a point ξ. It follows that the increment of deflection, du, due to the load $f(\xi)d\xi$ is

$$du(x, \xi) = a(x, \xi)f(\xi)d\xi \, ,$$

where $f(\xi)$ is a distributed loading function. The total deflection at x is obtained by integrating over the length L of the beam

$$u(x) = \int_0^L a(x, \xi)f(\xi)d\xi \, .$$

The effectiveness of this method for determining the deflections of a continuous beam depends, to a considerable extent, on the ease of evaluating the integral. When the loading function is approximated by rectangles, the influence function $a(x, \xi)$ in the integral transformation indicated above represents the same concept as the influence coefficient a_{ij} in the linear transformation. Therefore, the influence coefficient a_{ij} in this situation, may be defined as the deflection at point $x = x_i$ due to a concentrated unit load applied at point $x = x_j$.

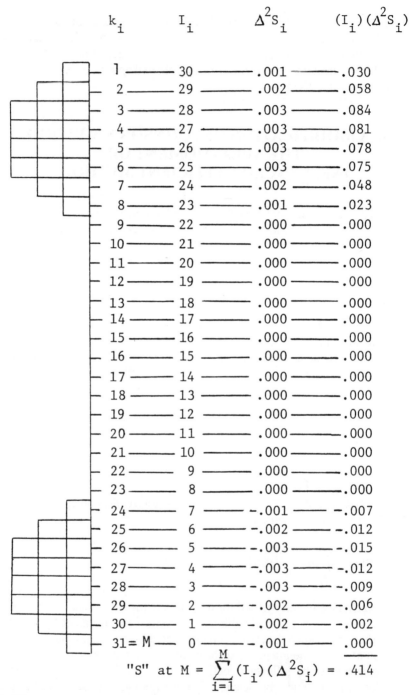

k_i	I_i	$\Delta^2 s_i$	$(I_i)(\Delta^2 s_i)$
1	30	.001	.030
2	29	.002	.058
3	28	.003	.084
4	27	.003	.081
5	26	.003	.078
6	25	.003	.075
7	24	.002	.048
8	23	.001	.023
9	22	.000	.000
10	21	.000	.000
11	20	.000	.000
12	19	.000	.000
13	18	.000	.000
14	17	.000	.000
15	16	.000	.000
16	15	.000	.000
17	14	.000	.000
18	13	.000	.000
19	12	.000	.000
20	11	.000	.000
21	10	.000	.000
22	9	.000	.000
23	8	.000	.000
24	7	-.001	-.007
25	6	-.002	-.012
26	5	-.003	-.015
27	4	-.003	-.012
28	3	-.003	-.009
29	2	-.002	-.006
30	1	-.002	-.002
31 = M	0	-.001	.000

$$\text{"S" at } M = \sum_{i=1}^{M} (I_i)(\Delta^2 s_i) = .414$$

Fig. 8-3.

The beam deflection increases proportionally with the load, so we have the relation

$$\delta_{ij} = a_{ij} F_j,$$

where δ represents the deflection, and F represents the unit load. The total deflection at $x = x_i$, denoted δ_i, is obtained by

$$\delta_i = \sum_{j=1}^{n} \delta_{ij} = \sum_{j=1}^{n} a_{ij} F_j, \quad (i = 1, 2, \dots, n),$$

where j is a dummy index and n is the number of rectangular strips used for the approximation of loading function.

When this concept is applied to cams, we can write by analogy

$$S = \sum_{i=1}^{M} (I_i)(\Delta^2 S_i),$$

where S is the displacement at point M (see Fig. 8-3) $\Delta^2 S_i$ is the second difference of equally spaced discrete values of the displacement S_i, and I_i is a numbering system used to identify the location of the discrete stations measured from point M. Here I_i is called the "influence coefficient."

Having defined the influence coefficient, we may outline the modified Johnson's method of cam curve smoothing as follows:
1. Compute and plot the acceleration factors corresponding to the available initial displacement curve as before.
2. This acceleration factor curve is approximated by a series of step functions, which for ease of manipulation has influence numbers assigned to each step function column. The influence numbers represent the moment arms about the midpoint of the cam motion stroke "M" for the incremental areas under the acceleration curve. The step function columns are in turn broken down into stacked blocks as shown in Fig. 8-3.
3. Compute the lift at point M using the methods of the area–moment. If the lift at M is not equal to the desired lift, shuffle the blocks in the $\Delta^2 S$ until the desired lift is achieved. The lift value at M may be changed by adding or subtracting blocks from the appropriate columns. In Fig. 8-3, for example, the removal of block 1 would change $\Delta^2 S$ at 13 from 0.003 to 0.002 and would change the contribution to lift at point M due to column 13 from 0.039 to 0.026. Similarly, the removal of block 2 would change the contribution to the lift at point M from column 10 from 0.030 to 0.020.
4. Develop the point–by–point values of the displacement curve using the scheme illustrated in Fig. 8-4 for any value of M. This procedure is suitable for computer programming.

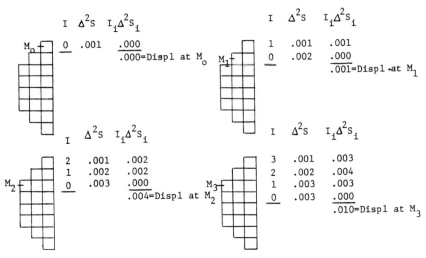

Fig. 8-4.

In manipulating these blocks several observations can be made.

- The greater the number of acceleration blocks used, the higher is the maximum velocity. This result is obvious because the velocity is directly proportional to the number of acceleration blocks.
- To reduce the peak velocity, the bulk of the acceleration blocks should be placed as far from point M as possible. Obviously, one block in a column with the influence number of 14 contributes as much to the lift at M as two blocks in a column with an influence number of 7 or as one block in each of a set of columns with influence numbers 6, 4, 3, and 1.
- If the initial and final slopes of the cam are to be zero, the final block pattern must have equal numbers of positive and negative $\Delta^2 S$ blocks.

This approach has the further advantage of permitting intermediate control points in the cam lift where displacements, velocities, or both can be controlled at discrete points by means of a routine manipulation.

8-5. NUMERICAL ALGORITHMS FOR SYNTHESIZING CAM DISPLACEMENT FROM A PRESCRIBED ACCELERATION CURVE

Graphical integration, which has been used in the past and appears in almost every textbook on kinematics, often lacks the desired accuracy and is very time-consuming. The methods to be described below are approximate in nature, but they are highly accurate and do not require trial-and-error procedures.

Finite–Difference Algorithms by Mathematical Induction

Suppose that the designer has touched up an acceleration curve for a cam, its values being described discretely. The problem is to find directly the corresponding cam displacement values that satisfy, in advance, the appropriate end conditions of the motion. Chen (33) has developed an algorithm based on the following derivation.

Multiplying both sides of the acceleration factor, Eq. (8-7), by $(N-i)$, where $i = 1, 2, \ldots, (N-1)$, N being the final station of the finite nodal point, and summing up, we obtain

$$\sum_{i=1}^{N-1} (N - i) y_i'' = \sum_{i=1}^{N-1} (N - i)(y_{i-1} - 2y_i + y_{i+1}) .$$

The right–hand side of this equation may be expanded as follows:

$$\sum_{i=1}^{N-1} (N - i)(y_{i-1} - 2y_i + y_{i+1})$$

$$= \sum_{i=1}^{N-1} (N - i) y_{i-1} - 2 \sum_{i=1}^{N-1} (N - i) y_i + \sum_{i=1}^{N-1} (N - i) y_{i+1}$$

$$= (N - 1) y_0 + (N - 2) y_1 + (N - 3) y_2 + \ldots + y_{N-2}$$

$$- 2 [(N - 1) y_1 + (N - 2) y_2 + \ldots + 2 y_{N-2} + y_{N-1}]$$

$$+ (N - 1) y_2 + (N - 2) y_3 + \ldots + 2 y_{N-1} + y_N$$

$$= (N - 1) y_0 - N y_1 + y_N$$

or

$$y_1 = \frac{N y_0 + h}{N} - \frac{1}{N} \sum_{i=1}^{N-1} (N - i) y_i'', \qquad (8\text{-}8)$$

where y_0 is the initial reading of the ordinate, y_N is the final reading of the ordinate, and h is the total lift.

Knowing y_1 from Eq. (8-8), we can use Eq. (8-7) to find, in a sequential order,

$$y_2 = -y_0 + 2y_1 + y_1''$$

$$y_3 = y_2'' - y_1 + 2y_2 = -2y_0 + 3y_1 + (2y_1'' + y_1'')$$

$$y_4 = y_3'' - y_2 + 2y_3 = -3y_0 + 4y_1 + (3y_1'' + 2y_2'' + y_3'')$$

$$y_5 = y_4'' - y_3 + 2y_4 = -4y_0 + 5y_1 + (4y_1'' + 3y_2'' + 2y_3'' + y_4'')$$

. . . .

. . . .

Thus, by mathematical induction, we can write

$$y_n = (1 - n)y_0 + ny_1 + \sum_{i=1}^{n-1}(n - i)y_i'' \qquad (8\text{-}9)$$

for $n = 2, 3, 4, \ldots, (N - 1)$.

Eqs. (8-8) and (8-9) form the basis of the synthesis equations. To test the efficiency and the accuracy of the algorithm, we will illustrate its use with an example.

Example 8-2

A cam, which rotates at a uniform speed of 100 rpm, imparts motion to the follower. For the sake of simplicity, let us consider a simple harmonic motion. Corresponding to 30° of cam shaft rotation, the follower moves one unit outward from its starting position. For the purpose of demonstrating the accuracy of this method, the kinematic characteristics of simple harmonic motion are computed by using Eqs. (8-8) and (8-9) above and are then compared with the results obtained in the exact solution. The exact solution, of course, calls for knowing the equations that give displacement and acceleration for simple harmonic motion. These equations are well–known to be

$$y = \frac{h}{2}\left(1 - \cos\frac{\pi\theta}{\beta}\right)$$

$$\ddot{y} = \frac{h}{2}\left(\frac{\pi\dot{\theta}}{\beta}\right)^2 \cos\frac{\pi\theta}{\beta} \quad ,$$

where θ and $\dot{\theta}$ are, respectively, the angular displacement and velocity of the cam shaft, and β is the total angular travel of the cam.

Table 8-2 exhibits the results of the computations. Values of follower displacement $y(\theta)$ and acceleration $\ddot{y}$, as computed from the theoretically exact formulas of simple harmonic motion, are given for the values of θ_i that increase from 0° to 30° by increments of 1°. The third column in the Table represents the theoretically computed values of simple harmonic displacement y_i. The fourth column contains the results of the synthesized displacements that are calculated from Eqs. (8-8) and (8-9) using known values of acceleration from column 2.

Comparing the numerical data obtained under columns (3) and (4) in Table 8-2, we see that the error in the synthesized values of $y_{ic}(\theta)$ is on no occasion greater than 0.00009.

Table 8-2. Computer Printout for Example 8-2

(1)	(2)	(3)	(4)	(5)
Angle θ (°)	Acceleration $\ddot{y}$ Unit/sec^2	Exact Displacement y_i	Approx. Displacement y_{ic}	Error
0	1973.93	0.00000	0.00000	0.00000
1	1963.11	0.00273	0.00271	0.00002
2	1930.79	0.01092	0.01087	0.00005
3	1877.32	0.02447	0.02440	0.00006
4	1803.27	0.04322	0.04314	0.00008
5	1709.47	0.06698	0.06689	0.00009
6	1596.94	0.09549	0.09539	0.00009
7	1466.91	0.12842	0.12833	0.00009
8	1320.81	0.16543	0.16534	0.00009
9	1160.24	0.20610	0.20602	0.00008
10	986.96	0.25000	0.24992	0.00007
11	802.87	0.29663	0.29656	0.00007
12	609.98	0.34549	0.34544	0.00004
13	410.40	0.39604	0.39601	0.00003
14	206.33	0.44773	0.44772	0.00001
15	0.00	0.50000	0.50000	0.00000
16	− 206.33	0.55226	− .55228	− 0.00001
17	− 410.40	0.60395	0.60399	− 0.00003
18	− 609.98	0.65451	0.65456	− 0.00005
19	− 802.87	0.70336	0.70343	− 0.00006
20	− 986.96	0.75000	0.75007	− 0.00007
21	− 1160.24	0.79389	0.79398	− 0.00008
22	− 1320.81	0.83456	0.83466	− 0.00009
23	− 1466.91	0.87157	0.87167	− 0.00009
24	− 1596.94	0.90450	0.90460	− 0.00009
25	− 1709.47	0.93301	0.93301	− 0.00009
26	− 1803.27	0.95677	0.95685	− 0.00008
27	− 1877.32	0.97552	0.97559	− 0.00006
28	− 1930.79	0.98907	0.98912	− 0.00005
29	− 1963.11	0.99726	0.99728	− 0.00002
30	− 1973.93	1.00000	1.00000	0.00000

A FORTRAN program of this method, FDSYN1, has been developed by Chen (33) and is listed in Appendix B.

Refinement of Finite–Difference Synthesis of Cam Profiles with Data Interpolation

An extension of the preceding algorithm for upgrading the numerical accuracy of the synthesized cam profile can be calculated by an appropriate modification of the values of the proposed acceleration pattern. Specifically, the technique is to differentiate the Stirling interpolation formula for the refinement of the initial data so that they will be correct to differences of high order.

We must realize that the well–known second–order central–difference equation, Eq. (8-5),

$$a_i = \ddot{y}_i = \frac{1}{h^2} (y_{i-1} - 2y_i + y_{i+1})$$

is only a one–term approximation of

$$y_{i-1} - 2y_i + y_{i+1} = 2 \left(\frac{h^2}{2!} a_i + \frac{h^4}{4!} a_i^{(2)} + \frac{h^6}{6!} a_i^{(4)} \right. \tag{8-10}$$

$$\left. + \frac{h^8}{8!} a_i^{(6)} + \frac{h^{10}}{10!} a_i^{(8)} + \ldots \right),$$

which can be written as a Taylor series expansion.

If the acceleration pattern is given in discrete form, the derivatives on the right side of Eq. (8-10) may be replaced by their approximate expressions in finite differences. For instance, we can write

$$\tag{8-11}$$

$$a_i^{(2)} = \frac{1}{h^2} \left(\Delta^2 - \frac{1}{12} \Delta^4 + \frac{1}{90} \Delta^6 - \frac{1}{560} \Delta^8 + \frac{1}{3150} \Delta^{10} - \ldots \right) a_i$$

$$a_i^{(4)} = \frac{1}{h^4} \left(\Delta^4 - \frac{1}{6} \Delta^6 + \frac{7}{240} \Delta^8 - \frac{41}{7560} \Delta^{10} + \ldots \right) a_i$$

$$a_i^{(6)} = \frac{1}{h^6} \left(\Delta^6 - \frac{1}{4} \Delta^8 + \frac{13}{240} \Delta^{10} - \ldots \right) a_i$$

$$a_i^{(8)} = \frac{1}{h^8} \left(\Delta^8 - \frac{1}{3} \Delta^{10} + \ldots \right) a_i$$

$$a_i^{(10)} = \frac{1}{h^{10}} \left(\Delta^{10} - \ldots \right) a_i$$

using the central difference notation, correctly to differences of the tenth order. Eq. (8-11) can be derived by successively differentiating the Stirling interpolation formula. More details about this process can be obtained from Reference (34).

Substituting Eq. (8-11) into Eq. (8-10), we obtain

$$y_{i-1} - 2y_i + y_{i+1} = h^2 a_i + 2h^2 \left(\frac{1}{4!} \Delta^2 - \frac{3}{2 \cdot 6!} \Delta^4 \right. \tag{8-12}$$

$$\left. + \frac{31}{3 \cdot 8!} \Delta^6 - \frac{289}{2 \cdot 10!} \Delta^8 + \frac{6657}{2 \cdot 12!} \Delta^{10} \right) a_i.$$

The equation is correct to differences of the tenth order. Clearly, the first term on the right side of Eq. (8-12) is given directly as the function to be integrated. The remaining terms are the even differences, which must be obtained from a table of finite differences drawn up for a_i. In Eq. (8-12) any number of terms can be retained on the right–hand side. The accuracy attainable by the formula depends upon the order to which differences can be calculated, and upon the rate of decrease in magnitude of the successive differences.

After the initially proposed values of acceleration are refined in accordance with Eq. (8-12), the synthesis Eqs. (8-8) and (8-9) are again used for computing the cam displacement.

To show the detailed procedures involved in the computations and to test the accuracy of the method, we will give an illustrative example.

Example 8-3

A cam that rotates at a uniform speed of 100 rpm imparts cycloidal motion to the follower. Corresponding to 10° of cam rotation, the follower is to lift one unit from rest. Cycloidal motion is described by the equations

$$y(\theta) = \left(\frac{\theta}{\beta} - \frac{1}{2\pi} \sin \frac{2\pi}{\beta} \theta \right) h$$

$$V(\theta) = \dot{y}(\theta) = \frac{h}{\beta} \left(1 - \cos \frac{2\pi}{\beta} \theta \right)$$

$$a(\theta) = \ddot{y}(\theta) = \frac{2\pi h}{\beta^2} \sin \frac{2\pi}{\beta} \theta ,$$

where y is the displacement of the follower, and θ is the angular displacement of the cam at any time. β and h represent, respectively, the total angular displacement of the cam and the overall stroke of the follower. Dots signify differentiation with respect to time.

Table 8-3 exhibits the results of computations. Values of follower displacement $y(\theta)$, and acceleration $a(\theta)$, as computed from the theoretically exact formulas above, are given for values of θ_i that increase from zero to ten by increments of one degree. The third column in the table represents the theoretically computed values of cycloidal displacement of the follower y_i. The fourth column contains the results of the synthesized displacements that are computed from Eqs. (8-8) and (8-9) using the known values of acceleration from column 2. These are compared with the results listed in column 6, which are obtained by using Eq. (8-8) and (8-9) with refinement of the acceleration data in accordance with Eq. (8-12).

In using Eq. (8-12), the central differences of the initial values of acceleration are first calculated. These are tabulated separately in Table 8-4. The modified values of $a(\theta)$ are computed as shown in Table 8-5. Note that most of the correction is contributed by the second differences.

Comparing data obtained in column 4 and column 6 with the exact values listed in column 3 in Table 8-3, we see that the errors in $y(\theta)$ range from about 0.003 to 0.005 in cam profile synthesis without initial data refinement, and that the maximum error is no greater than 0.00002 in profile synthesis with initial data refinement.

A FORTRAN program FDSYN2, using the refined finite–difference synthesis algorithm has been written by the author (34) and is given in Appendix B.

The Finite–Integration Method for Synthesizing Cam Profile

When the finite–integration method is used to solve differential equations, the differential equation is regarded as an integral equation in the highest derivative of the dependent variable. This integral equation is subsequently discretized by a number of algebraic equations, one for each point in the range of the independent variable x. With the aid of a specially formulated integrating matrix, the solution of the differential equation is then reduced to the solution of a matrix equation with boundary conditions. The latter equation is

Table 8-3. Numerical Results of Computation for Example 8-3

θ (deg)	$\dfrac{d^2y}{d\theta^2}$	$y(\theta)$ Exact	$y(\theta)$ without refinement	$\dfrac{d^2y}{d\theta^2}$ refined	$y(\theta)$ with refinement	Error without refinement	Error with refinement
0.0	0.000000	0.000000	0.000000	0.000000	0.000000	0.000000	0.000000
1.0	0.036931	0.006451	0.003313	0.035755	0.006431	0.003139	0.000020
2.0	0.059756	0.048634	0.043557	0.057817	0.046818	0.005079	0.000016
3.0	0.059756	0.148634	0.143557	0.057815	0.148623	0.005079	0.000011
4.0	0.036931	0.306451	0.303313	0.035731	0.306445	0.003139	0.000006
5.0	0.000000	0.500000	0.500000	0.000000	0.500000	0.000000	0.000000
6.0	−0.036931	0.693549	0.696687	−0.035731	0.693555	−0.003139	−0.000006
7.0	−0.059756	0.851365	0.856443	−0.057815	0.851377	−0.005079	−0.000011
8.0	−0.059756	0.951365	0.956443	−0.057817	0.951382	−0.005079	−0.000016
9.0	−0.036931	0.993548	0.996687	−0.035755	0.993569	−0.003139	−0.000020
10.0	0.000000	1.000000	1.000000	0.000000	1.000000	0.000000	0.000000

Table 8-4. Central–Difference Table of the Initial Acceleration Used in Example 8-3

$a(\theta)$	δa	$\delta^2 a$	$\delta^3 a$	$\delta^4 a$	$\delta^5 a$	$\delta^6 a$	$\delta^7 a$	$\delta^8 a$	$\delta^9 a$	$\delta^{10} a$
0.000000										
	0.036931									
0.036931		−0.014105								
	0.022825		−0.008719							
0.059756		−0.022825		0.008719						
	0.000000		0.000000		0.000000					
0.059756		−0.022825		0.008719		−0.003332				
	−0.022825		0.008719		−0.003332		0.001277			
0.036931		−0.014105		0.005386		−0.002054		0.000777		
	−0.036931		0.014105		−0.005386		0.002054		−0.000777	
0.000000		0.000000		0.000000		0.000000		0.000000		0.000000
	−0.036931		0.014105		−0.005386		0.002054		−0.000777	
−0.036931		0.014105		−0.005386		0.002054		−0.000777		
	−0.022825		0.008719		−0.003332		0.001277			
−0.059756		0.022825		−0.008719		0.003332				
	0.000000		0.000000		0.000000					
−0.059756		0.022825		−0.008719						
	0.022825		−0.008719							
−0.036931		0.014105								
	0.036931									
0.000000										

146

Table 8-5. Modified Values of Initial Acceleration Used in Example 8–3

Refined‡ $a(\theta)$	$a(\theta)$	$\dfrac{1}{12}\delta^2 a$	$-\dfrac{1}{240}\delta^4 a$	$\dfrac{62}{3\cdot 8!}\delta^6 a$	$-\dfrac{289}{10!}\delta^8 a$	$\dfrac{6657}{12!}\delta^{10} a$
0.000000	0.000000					
0.035755	0.036931	−0.001175				
0.057817	0.059756	−0.001902	−0.000036			
0.057815	0.059756	−0.001902	−0.000036	−0.000001		
0.035731	0.036931	−0.001175	−0.000022	−0.000001	0.000000	
0.000000	0.000000	0.000000	0.000000	0.000000	0.000000	0.000000
−0.035731	−0.036931	0.001175	0.000022	0.000001	0.000000	
−0.057815	−0.059756	0.001902	0.000036	0.000001		
−0.057817	−0.059756	0.001902	0.000036			
−0.035755	0.036931	0.001175				
0.000000	0.000000					

‡Refined values of $a(\theta)$ are computed according to Equation (8-12).

easily solved on a digital computer. We will show how to apply the one–sided integration formulas for the construction of an integrating matrix and how they are applied to the synthesis of cam profiles.

In the study of motion characteristics, with time as an independent variable, the velocity integral $V(t)$ is

$$V_i(t) = \int_0^{ih} a(t)dt + C_1 \, , \qquad (8\text{-}13)$$

where C_1 is an integration constant dependent upon the boundary condition. For a DRD motion event, the boundary condition $V(0) = 0$ causes C_1 to vanish. Then the definite integral can be approximated by the matrix equation

$$\{V\} = \frac{h}{12} \, [B] \, \{a\} \, , \qquad (8\text{-}14)$$

where $\{V\}$ and $\{a\}$ represent the velocity column matrix $(V_0, V_1, V_2, \ldots, V_n)^T$ and the acceleration column matrix $(a_0, a_1, a_2, \ldots, a_n)^T$, respectively, with the superscript T representing the transpose. $[B]$ is a $(n+1)^{th}$–order square matrix of the form

$$[B] = \begin{bmatrix} 0 & 0 & 0 & 0 & 0 & 0 & 0 & \ldots & 0 \\ 5 & 8 & -1 & 0 & 0 & 0 & 0 & \ldots & 0 \\ 4 & 16 & 4 & 0 & 0 & 0 & 0 & \ldots & 0 \\ 4 & 16 & 9 & 8 & -1 & 0 & 0 & \ldots & 0 \\ 4 & 16 & 8 & 16 & 9 & 8 & -1 & \ldots & 0 \\ 4 & 16 & 8 & 16 & 8 & 16 & 4 & \ldots & 0 \end{bmatrix}. \qquad (8\text{-}15)$$

The elements of this matrix can be generated systematically as follows: the first row is trivially zero; the second row elements, 5, 8, and -1, and the third row elements, 4, 16, and 4, are recognizable as the weighting factors in the integration formulas

$$I_{13}(i) = \frac{h}{12} \, (5y_i + 8y_{i+1} - y_{i+2}) \qquad (8\text{-}16)$$

$$I_{23}(i) = \frac{h}{12} \, (4y_{i+1} + 16y_{i+1} + 4y_{i+2}) \, , \qquad (8\text{-}17)$$

where $I_{nm}(i)$ represents the integral of $y(t)$ from $t=t_i$ to $t=t_{i+n}$, using m terms in approximation in a Taylor series Eqs. (8-16) and (8-17) are one–sided integration formulas of the integral of function $y(t)$, which can be obtained either by integrating its Taylor series expansion term by term or by integrating Newton's interpolation formula, as normally done in textbooks on numerical analysis (99). These basic row elements are utilized as building blocks in the construction of the integrating matrix. It can be readily seen in Fig. 8-5 that the subsequent rows are generated by a progressive, systematic march of time and superposition using these basic row elements.

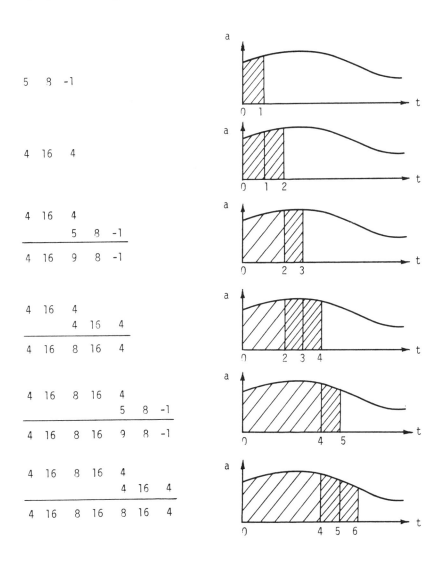

Fig. 8-5. Modified Values of Initial Acceleration Used in Example 8–3.

The displacement $y(t)$ may be obtained by integrating the velocity $V(t)$. Thus

$$y_i(t) = \int_0^{ih} dt \int_0^t a(\xi)\, d\xi + C_2 , \qquad (8\text{-}18)$$

where C_2 is a constant of integration. For a DRD event, the boundary condition is $y(0) = 0$. This causes the integration constant C_2 to vanish. Therefore, the double integration can be represented by

$$\{y\} = \frac{h^2}{144}\, [B]^2\, \{a\} . \qquad (8\text{-}19)$$

Eq. (8-19) is the synthesis formula for an arbitrarily prescribed acceleration form.

Table 8-6. Numerical Results of Computation for Example 8–4

θ (°)	$y(\theta)$ Exact	$\dfrac{d^2 y}{d\theta^2}$	$y(\theta)$ Finite Integration	Error
0.0	0.000000	0.000000	0.000000	0.000000
2.0	0.001781	0.002589	0.001783	−0.000002
4.0	0.013718	0.004581	0.013718	0.000000
6.0	0.043673	0.005668	0.043670	0.000003
8.0	0.095978	0.005789	0.095969	−0.000009
10.0	0.171155	0.005052	0.171137	0.000012
12.0	0.266324	0.003665	0.266295	0.000029
14.0	0.376026	0.001887	0.375985	0.000041
16.0	0.493237	−0.000019	0.493180	0.000057
18.0	0.610404	−0.001827	0.610332	0.000072
20.0	0.720354	−0.003362	0.720268	0.000086
22.0	0.816979	−0.004523	0.816881	0.000098
24.0	0.895645	−0.005282	0.895538	0.000107
26.0	0.953298	−0.005686	0.953188	0.000110
28.0	0.988298	−0.005833	0.988178	0.000120
30.0	0.999999	−0.005853	0.999879	0.000119

Example 8-4

To show that the finite–integration method can be used for cam profile synthesis involving a large number of nodal points without affecting its degree of accuracy, we will consider an eighth–degree polynomial, the displacement and the acceleration equations of which are given in Fig. 7-4 in Chapter 7. A tabulation of the displacement factors of this polynomial motion corresponding to the range of a cam rotational angle of 60° with 1° increments has also been made available by Kloomok and Muffley, see reference (36), and its results are reproduced for every 2° in column 2 of Table 8-6. The data listed in column 4 of this table represent the computer printout of the displacement factors based on this scheme. Glancing through the last column, we notice that the absolute error is never greater than 0.000120, based on unity lift.

The computer program for this example, FINTG, using the finite–integration method has been written by the author (36) and is given in Appendix B.

Other numerical algorithms in synthesizing cam profiles for a prescribed acceleration pattern and a jerk pattern have been made available by Di Benedetto (64, 65, 66, 67). We cannot introduce them here because of space limitation.

9
Determination of Cam Profile Coordinates

9-1. GRAPHICAL METHOD OF DETERMINING CAM PROFILES

Certain cam motion curves are easily laid out by graphical procedures. Graphical methods have inherent accuracy limitations and should therefore be used only for relatively low–speed cams. When a high degree of accuracy is important, as at high speeds, the ordinates of the curve must be calculated by computer, and the accuracy of manufacture must be correspondingly adequate. However, the graphical construction provides a clear geometrical visualization of the formation process involved, based on the principle of "inversion," while the analytical method makes this visualization difficult because everything is buried under its algebraic complexity.

To graphically determine a cam profile, we will consider an inversion of a cam–follower mechanism in which the cam is considered the fixed member. The follower is then located in its proper position relative to the cam, corresponding to a number of different cam rotation angles. Kinematic inversion will not affect the relative motion between the cam and the follower. The cam profile is the envelope of the follower profiles, as the follower moves around the cam. As a part of the inversion process, the matter of rotation is very important. To preserve the correct sequence of events, the direction of inverted rotation of the follower must be the reverse of the prescribed direction of cam rotation.

The examples that follow represent typical layout procedures in graphical cam design. Variants of the layout procedures used will be found in most books on the kinematics of machinery. The construction procedures are illustrated by well-executed drawings taken from Kepler (241).

Radial Cam with Roller Follower

For the cam–and–follower arrangement shown in Fig. 9-1, draw the cam profile based on the displacement diagram shown in the upper right corner.

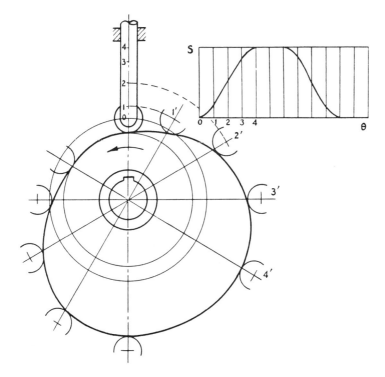

Fig. 9-1. Radial cam with roller follower.

Procedure.
1. Draw the base circle.
2. Draw the follower in its home positive (0° position), tangent to the base circle.
3. Draw the reference circle through the center of the follower in its 0° position.

4. Draw radial lines from the center of the cam, corresponding to the vertical lines in the displacement diagram.
5. Transfer displacements s_1, s_2, s_3, etc. from the displacement diagram to the appropriate radial lines, measuring from the reference circle.
6. Draw in the follower outline on the various radial lines.
7. Draw a smooth curve tangent to these follower outlines.

To draw a smooth curve, it may be necessary to transfer additional intermediate points from the displacement diagram.

Cam with Offset Roller Follower

For the cam–and–follower arrangement shown in Fig. 9-2, draw the cam profile based on the displacement diagram shown in the upper right corner.

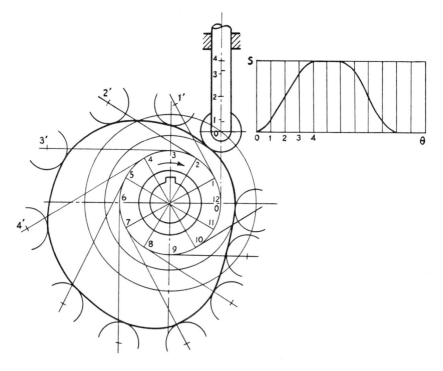

Fig. 9-2. Cam with offset roller follower.

Procedure.

1. Draw the base circle.
2. Draw the follower in its home position (0° position), tangent to the base circle.

3. Draw the reference circle through the center of the follower in its home position.
4. Draw the offset circle tangent to the follower center line.
5. Divide the offset circle into a number of divisions corresponding to the divisions in the displacement diagram, and number accordingly.
6. Draw tangents to the offset circle at each number.
7. Lay off the various displacements s_1, s_2, s_3, etc. along the appropriate tangent lines, measuring from the reference circle.
8. Draw in the follower outlines on the various tangent lines.
9. Draw a smooth curve tangent to these follower outlines.

Cam with Swinging Roller Follower

For the cam–and–follower arrangement shown in Fig. 9-3, draw the cam profile based on the same displacement diagram used in the earlier examples.

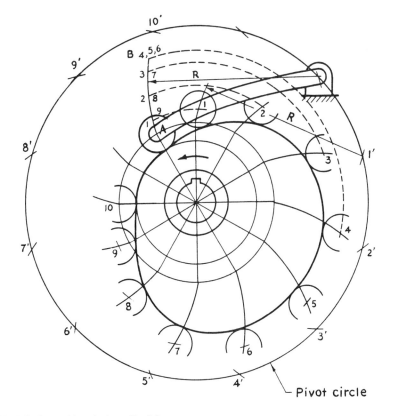

Fig. 9-3. Cam with swinging roller follower.

Procedure.

 1. Draw the base circle.
 2. Draw the follower in its home position, tangent to the base circle.
 3. Draw the reference circle through the center of the follower.
 4. Locate points around the reference circle corresponding to the divisions in the displacement diagram, and number accordingly.
 5. Draw a pivot circle through the follower pivot.
 6. Locate the pivot points around the pivot circle corresponding to each point on the reference circle, and number accordingly.
 7. From each of the pivot points, draw an arc whose radius is equal to the length of the follower arm.
 8. At the zero position, draw the two extreme positions of the follower lever by laying off the arc AB equal to the maximum displacement.
 9. Lay off the various displacement s_1, s_2, s_3, etc. along this arc.
10. Rotate each of the points on arc AB to its proper position around the cam profile.
11. Draw in the follower outline at each of the points just located.
12. Draw a smooth curve tangent to the follower outlines.

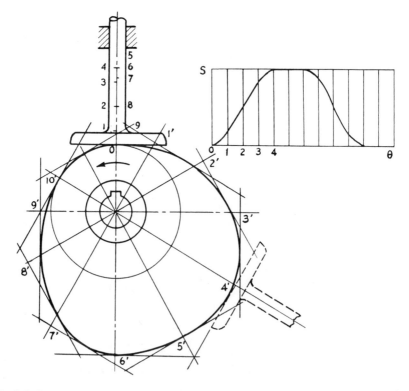

Fig. 9-4. Cam with translating flat–faced follower.

Cam with Translational Flat–Faced Follower

For the cam–and–follower arrangement shown in Fig. 9-4, draw the cam profile based on the displacement diagram shown in the upper right corner.

Procedure.
1. Draw the base circle, which in this case also serves as the reference circle.
2. Draw the follower in its home position, tangent to the base circle.
3. Draw radial lines corresponding to the divisions in the displacement diagram, and number accordingly.
4. Draw in the follower outline on the various radial lines by laying off the appropriate displacements and drawing lines perpendicular to the radial lines.
5. Draw a smooth curve tangent to the follower outlines.

Notice in the figure that the tangent points usually fall at the midpoints of the inner sides of the small triangles that are formed around the periphery of the cam.

Cam with Swinging Flat–Faced Follower

For the cam–and–follower arrangement shown in Fig. 9-5, draw the cam profile based on the same displacement diagram as is used in the previous case.

Procedure.
1. Draw the base circle, which in this case also serves as the reference circle.
2. Draw the follower in its home position, tangent to the base circle.
3. Draw radial lines corresponding to the divisions in the displacement diagram, and number accordingly.
4. Draw a pivot circle through the follower pivot.
5. Locate the pivot points around the pivot circle, and number accordingly.
6. Locate the trace point on the flat face at an arbitrary radius R from the pivoted point at zero position.
7. At the zero position, draw the two extreme positions of the follower lever by laying off the arc AB equal to the maximum displacement.
8. Lay off the various displacements s_1, s_2, s_3, etc. along this arc.
9. Locate the trace point $1''$ relative to the cam at the intersection of the arc of radius R, centered at $1'$, and the arc of radius 01, centered at 0. Establish points $2''$, $3''$, etc. in a similar manner.
10. The first position of the flat follower face, relative to the cam, is the straight line through point $1''$ that is tangent to the small circle of radius r_f, centered at point $1'$. Construct the successive positions of the follower face in a similar manner.

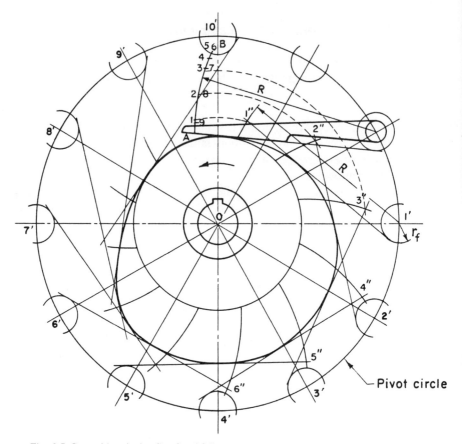

Fig. 9-5 Cam with swinging flat–faced follower.

11. Draw a smooth curve tangent to the family of straight lines representing the follower face.

9-2. THE ANALYTICAL METHOD OF DETERMINING CAM PROFILES

For high speed machines, the method by which points on the pitch curve are determined by graphical layout is not adequate, especially when the cam is manufactured by an incremental cutting process or by a numerically controlled milling machine. To develop equations for cam profile coordinates, the relative geometry of the cam and the follower must be described at both the lowest follower position and at some displaced follower position consistent with the rotational direction of the cam. Because of the voluminous calculations required in conjunction with its complicated geometry, the analytical method of determining cam profiles and cutter coordinates was subordinated to graphical techniques. With the widespread use of digital computers and programmable calculators, these calculations need no longer to be a deterrent.

The following coordinate systems have been used for deriving cam profiles:

- Polar coordinates.
- Rectangular coordinates (relative to the cam shaft center).
- Rectangular coordinates in which the ordinate or the Y–axis is represented by a line drawn from the cam shaft center to the center of the cam roll at its outer–most position, and the abscissa, or the X–axis, is normal to the Y–axis.

The third coordinate system, used by Cram (52), is not as commonly utilized as the first two types of coordinates.

Even if the choice of coordinates is the same, the form of the derived equation may be different, but their end results should agree. Variants of the equations representing the profile coordinates depend upon the approach used in derivation. Churchill and Hanson (49) employed the theory of envelopes, Davidson (55) suggested a method using instant centers, and others merely used brute force. We will introduce the method using the theory of envelopes to determine the cam profile and cutter–coordinate equations for the six major types of cam–follower arrangements. These major types are

Radial cams with roller followers
Translating cams with offset roller followers
Swinging cams with roller followers
Radial cams with flat–faced followers
Cams with swinging centric flat–faced followers
Cams with swinging eccentric flat–faced followers.

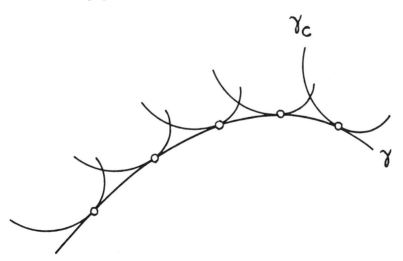

Fig. 9-6. Envelope of a family of curves depending on a parameter.

Envelope of a One–Parameter Family of Curves

Suppose $S\{\gamma_c\}$ is a family of smooth curves on a surface, depending on a parameter c. A smooth curve γ is called an envelope of the family S if
(1) for every point of the curve γ it is possible to give a curve γ_c of the family that is tangent to the curve γ at this point,
(2) for every curve γ_c of the family it is possible to give a point on the curve γ at which the curve γ_c is tangent to γ, and
(3) no curve of the family has a segment in common with the curve γ.

See Fig. 9-6 for this definition.

  Now let us introduce a theorem.

Theorem: Suppose the curves γ_c of a family S are given by the equation $F(x, y, c) = 0$, where F is continuous and continuously differentiable for all its arguments in a neighborhood of the point (x_0, y_0, c_0). At the point (x_0, y_0, c_0) let the following relations hold:

$$F(x_0, y_0, c_0) = 0 \tag{9-1}$$

$$\frac{\partial F}{\partial c}(x_0, y_0, c_0) = 0 \tag{9-2}$$

$$\begin{vmatrix} \dfrac{\partial F}{\partial x} & \dfrac{\partial F}{\partial y} \\[2ex] \dfrac{\partial^2 F}{\partial c \partial x} & \dfrac{\partial^2 F}{\partial c \partial y} \end{vmatrix} \neq 0, \quad \frac{\partial^2 F}{\partial c^2} = 0. \tag{9-3}$$

Then in a certain neighborhood u of the point (x_0, y_0), and for c from a definite neighborhood V of the point c_0, there exists an envelope of the family $F(x, y, c) = 0$.
  In general, we may obtain the equation of the envelope from the equations

$$F(x, y, c) = 0 \tag{9-4}$$

$$\frac{\partial F}{\partial c}(x, y, c) = 0 \tag{9-5}$$

by expressing x and y as a function of the parameter c or by expressing c as a function of the variables x, y and substituting for c into Eq. (9-4)

$$F(x, y, c(x, y)) = 0 ,$$

i.e., by elimination of the parameter c from Eq. (9-4).

Example 9-1

Consider the equation $F(x, y, c) = 0$ as

$$y - cx - \frac{4}{c} = 0 .$$

Then $\dfrac{\partial F}{\partial c} = -x + \dfrac{4}{c^2} = 0 .$

Eliminating c from the above two equations yields

$$y^2 = 16x ,$$

which is the envelope (Fig. 9-7).

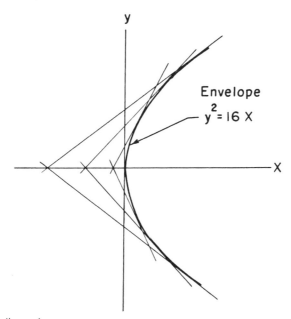

Fig. 9-7. Parabolic envelope.

Example 9-2

Consider the equation $F(x, y, c) = 0$ as

$$[x^2 + (y - c)^2]^2 - b^2 [x^2 - (y - c)^2] = 0 .$$

This represents a lemniscate of width $2b$ with its center located at $x = 0$, $y = c$. As c is varied, a series of lemniscates translated along the y-axis is determined.

Eq. (9-5), $\dfrac{\partial F}{\partial c} = 0$, requires

$$(y - c)[2x^2 + 2(y - c)^2 - b^2] = 0 .$$

A solution of this equation is $y = c$.

Substituting this solution into the equation $F(x, y, c) = 0$ yields

$$x^2(x^2 - b^2) = 0$$

or

$$x = 0, +b, -b .$$

The two lines $x = \pm b$ are envelopes, but $x = 0$ is not an envelope. $x = 0$ consists of nodal points of the curves of the family (Fig. 9-8). Note also that nothing new is obtained from the solution $y \neq c$.

It is important to note that in the general theorem stated above, the conditions in Eq. (9-3) are sufficient but not necessary for the existence of the envelope in the neighborhood of the point (x_0, y_0). If conditions in Eq. (9-3) are not fulfilled, Eqs. (9-4) and (9-5) need not define the envelope. An additional example is used here to illustrate this.

Example 9-3

Consider a family of curve $F(x, y, c) = 0$ as

$$(y - c)^2 - (x - c)^3 = 0 .$$

From Eq. (9-5) it follows that

$$\frac{\partial F}{\partial c} = 0 = - 2(y - c) + 3(x - c)^2$$

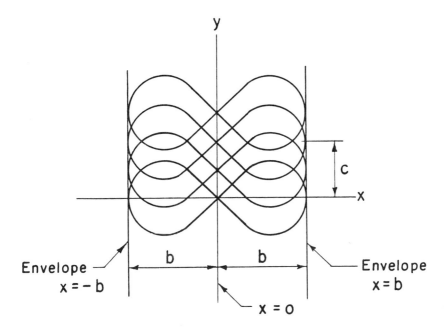

Fig. 9-8. Linearly translating lemniscates.

or

$$y - c = \frac{3}{2}(x - c)^2.$$

Substituting this into $F(x, y, c) = 0$ gives

$$\frac{9}{4}(x - c)^3\left(x - c - \frac{4}{9}\right) = 0.$$

Hence, the solutions are

case 1 $x = c,$ $y = c$ (or $y = x$)

case 2 $x = c + \dfrac{4}{9},$ $y = c + \dfrac{8}{27}$ $\left(\text{or } y = x - \dfrac{4}{27}\right).$

Conditions (9-3) in the general theorem are

$$\Delta \;=\; \begin{vmatrix} \dfrac{\partial F}{\partial x} & \dfrac{\partial F}{\partial y} \\[1.2em] \dfrac{\partial^{2} F}{\partial c\, \partial x} & \dfrac{\partial^{2} F}{\partial c\, \partial y} \end{vmatrix} \;=\; \begin{vmatrix} -\,3(x-c)^{2} & 2(y-c) \\[1em] =\,6(x-c) & -\,2 \end{vmatrix}$$

$$= 6(x-c)\,[\,(x-c) - 2(y-c)\,]$$

$$\frac{\partial^{2} F}{\partial c^{2}} = 2 - 6(x-c)\,.$$

The solution of case 2 is a straight–line envelope because $\Delta = -\dfrac{32}{81} \neq 0$ and $\dfrac{\partial^{2} F}{\partial c^{2}} = -\dfrac{2}{3} \neq 0$ when we use $x = c + \dfrac{4}{9}$ and $y = c + \dfrac{8}{27}$. The solution of case 1 is evidently not an envelope since $\Delta = 0$ and $\dfrac{\partial^{2} F}{\partial c^{2}} = 2 \neq 0$ when we use $x = c,\ y = c$. It is merely a straight–line locus of cuspidal points. Fig. 9-9 shows the situation.

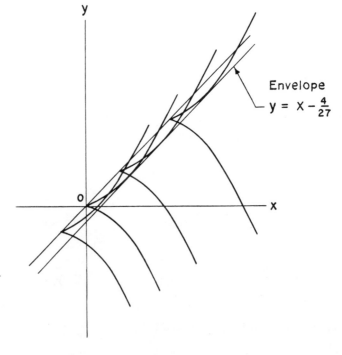

Envelope
$y = x - \frac{4}{27}$

Fig. 9-9.

The envelope theory will now be applied to determine the cam working profile coordinates. For roller–follower cams, two envelopes (Fig. 9-10) — one inner envelope and one outer envelope — are obtained. Both envelopes are applicable for grooved cams. Only the inner envelope is used with plate cams.

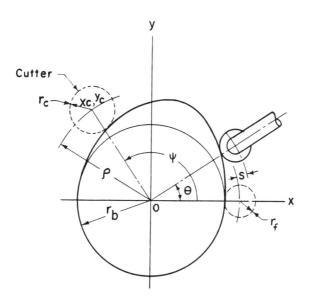

Fig. 9-10. Radial cam with roller follower.

Radial Cams with Roller Followers. Referring to Fig. 9-10, the radial distance r to the center of the follower is

$$r = r_b + r_f + s,$$

where

r_b is the base circle radius,

r_f is the roller radius, and

s is the cam rise, which is a function of cam angular displacement θ.

The general equation of the envelope is

$$F(x, y, \theta) = (x - r \cos \theta)^2 + (y - r \sin \theta)^2 - r_f^2 = 0 .$$

It is now differentiated with respect to θ :

$$\frac{dF}{d\theta} = 2r \sin \theta (x - r \cos \theta) - 2r \cos \theta (y - r \sin \theta) = 0 .$$

The rectangular coordinates of a point on the cam profile corresponding to a specific angle of cam rotation θ are obtained by solving these two equations simultaneously. The coordinates are

$$x = r \cos \theta + \frac{r_f}{\left[1 + \left(\dfrac{M}{N} \right)^2 \right]^{1/2}} \tag{9-6}$$

$$y = \frac{xM + r \dfrac{ds}{d\theta}}{N} , \tag{9-7}$$

where

$$M = r \sin \theta - \frac{ds}{d\theta} \cos \theta$$

$$N = r \cos \theta - \frac{ds}{d\theta} \sin \theta ,$$

and

$$\frac{ds}{d\theta} = \frac{dr}{d\theta} .$$

Here the proper sign choice may be determined by examining $\theta = 0$ when $x = r_b$. At this point

$$r = r_b + r_f$$

$$\frac{dr}{d\theta} = \frac{ds}{d\theta} = 0 ,$$

and

$$x = r_f + r_b \pm r_f .$$

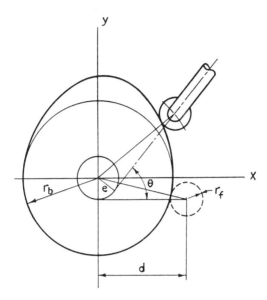

Fig. 9-11. Translating cam with offset roller follower.

Only the lower sign is justified in the above equation; thus the negative sign should be used to establish the inner envelope. The outer envelope is not required unless a grooved cam is used.

Translating Cams with Offset Roller Followers. The roller follower of this type of cam, Fig. 9-11, moves radially along a line that is offset from the cam center by an amount e.

The general equation of the envelope is

$$F(x, y, \theta) = [\, x - e \sin \theta - (d + s) \cos \theta \,]^2$$
$$+ [\, y + e \cos \theta - (d + s) \sin \theta \,]^2 - r_f^2 = 0 \,,$$

where

$$d = [\, (r_b + r_f)^2 - e^2 \,]^{1/2}.$$

Differentiating F with respect to θ, setting the result equal to zero, and solving for x and y, we obtain the profile coordinates

$$x = e \sin \theta + (d + s) \cos \theta \pm \frac{r_f}{\left[\, 1 + \left(\dfrac{U}{V}\right)^2 \,\right]^{1/2}} \qquad (9\text{-}8)$$

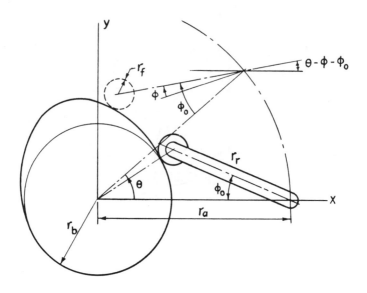

Fig. 9-12. Swinging roller–follower cam.

$$y = \frac{xU + (d + s)\dfrac{ds}{d\theta}}{V} \ , \tag{9-9}$$

where

$$U = (d + s) \sin \theta - \left|e + \frac{ds}{d\theta}\right| \cos \theta$$

$$V = (d + s) \cos \theta + \left|e + \frac{ds}{d\theta}\right| \sin \theta \ .$$

Again, the lower sign is associated with the inner envelope.

Swinging Cams with Roller Followers. As shown by the geometry of Fig. 9-12, the initial position of the follower before lift starts is designated by ϕ_0

$$\phi_0 = \cos^{-1} \frac{r_r^2 + r_a^2 - (r_b + r_r)^2}{2r_a r_r} \ ,$$

where r_r is the length of the roller–follower arm, and r_a is the distance between the pivot point of the swinging follower and the center of the cam.

The implicit equation of the family is

$$F(x, y, \theta) = (x - r_a \cos \theta + r_r \cos \alpha)^2$$
$$+ (y - r_a \sin \theta + r_r \sin \alpha)^2 - r_f^2 = 0 ,$$

where

$$\alpha = \theta - \phi - \phi_0 .$$

Then

$$\frac{dF}{d\theta} = 2(x - r_a \cos \theta + r_r \cos \alpha) \left[r_a \sin \theta - r_r \sin \alpha \left(1 - \frac{d\phi}{d\theta}\right) \right]$$

$$+ 2(y - r_a \sin \theta + r_r \sin \alpha) \left[-r_a \cos \theta + r_r \cos \alpha \left(1 - \frac{d\phi}{d\theta}\right) \right]$$

$$= 0 .$$

Solving these two equations simultaneously gives the profile coordinates

$$x = r_a \cos \theta - r_r \cos \alpha \pm \frac{r_f}{\left[1 + \left(\dfrac{P}{Q}\right)^2 \right]^{1/2}} \tag{9-10}$$

$$y = \frac{xP}{Q} , \tag{9-11}$$

where

$$p = r_a \sin \theta - r_r \left(1 - \frac{d\phi}{d\theta}\right) \sin \alpha$$

$$Q = r_a \cos \theta - r_r \left(1 - \frac{d\phi}{d\theta}\right) \cos \alpha .$$

The negative sign gives the inner cam profile.

Translating Cams with Flat–Face Followers. Fig. 9-13 shows a translating cam with a flat–face follower. The general equation of the family of lines forming the envelope is governed by a straight line

$$y = mx + b,$$

where m is the slope, and b is the y–intercept. In this case

$$m = \cos \theta$$

$$b = \frac{(r_b + s)}{\sin \theta} .$$

Also

$$x = (r_b + s) \cos \theta$$

$$y = (r_b + s) \sin \theta .$$

Hence,

$$y = \frac{r_b + s - x \cos \theta}{\sin \theta} .$$

Therefore,

$$F(x, y, \theta) = y \sin \theta + x \cos \theta - (r_b + s) = 0$$

$$\frac{dF}{d\theta} = y \cos \theta - x \sin \theta - \frac{ds}{d\theta} = 0 .$$

Solving these two equations yields the profile coordinates

$$x = (r_b + s) \cos \theta - \frac{ds}{d\theta} \sin \theta \qquad (9\text{-}12)$$

$$y = (r_b + s) \sin \theta + \frac{ds}{d\theta} \cos \theta . \qquad (9\text{-}13)$$

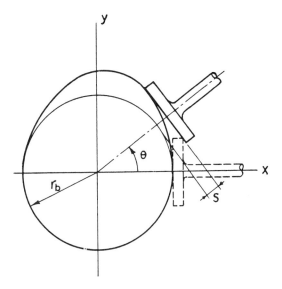

Fig. 9-13. Radial cam with flat–faced follower.

Cams with Flat–Face Centric Swinging Followers. The flat–face swinging–follower cams (Fig. 9-14) are of the centric type if the face, when extended, passes through the follower pivot.

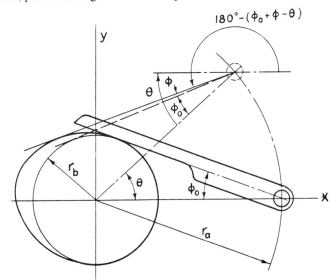

Fig. 9-14. Cam with swinging centric flat-faced follower.

The initial position of the follower before lift starts is

$$\phi_0 = \sin^{-1} \frac{r_b}{r_a} \ .$$

The general form of the equation of the family is the straight line

$$y = mx + b \ ,$$

where the slope is

$$m = - \tan (\phi - \theta + \phi_o),$$

and the y–axis intercept is

$$b = r_a [\sin \theta + \cos \theta \tan (\phi - \theta + \phi_o)] \ ,$$

in which we have used the relationships $x = r_a \cos \theta$ and $y = r_a \sin \theta$. Therefore,

$$F(x, y, \theta) = y + \tan (\phi - \theta + \phi_o)(x - r_a \cos \theta) - r_a \sin \theta = 0.$$

Setting $\dfrac{dF}{d\theta} = 0$ and solving simultaneously in the usual manner, we obtain

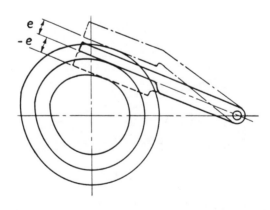

Fig. 9-15. Cam with swinging eccentric flat–faced follower.

$$x = r_a(\cos \theta + A \cos \beta) \tag{9-14}$$

$$y = r_a(\sin \theta + A \sin \beta), \tag{9-15}$$

where

$$A = \frac{\cos (\theta + \beta)}{\dfrac{d\phi}{d\theta} - 1}$$

$$\beta = \phi_o + \phi - \theta.$$

Cams with Flat–Face Eccentric Swinging Followers. A swinging flat–face follower of the eccentric type is shown in Fig. 9-15. The amount of eccentricity (or offset) e is the distance between a line through the cam pivot and the follower face. The distance e is considered positive or negative, depending on whether the effect of e is to increase or to decrease the size of the in–line follower cam. The profile coordinates are

$$x = r_a(\cos \theta + A \cos \beta) + e \sin \beta \tag{9-16}$$

$$y = r_a(\sin \theta + A \sin \beta) + e \cos \beta, \tag{9-17}$$

where

$$A = \frac{\cos (\theta + \beta)}{\dfrac{d\phi}{d\theta} - 1}$$

$$\beta = \phi_o + \phi - \theta.$$

Note that when $e = 0$, Eqs. (9-16) and (9-17) degenerate to become Eqs. (9-14) and (9-15).

9-3. CUTTER COORDINATES

For cam manufacture, the location of the milling cutter or of the grinding wheel, i.e., the trace of the cutter or the grinder path, should be known in order to produce the right cam profile.

If the milling cutter size is different from that of the follower, the geometry required to describe the cutter center is a circle representing the cutter and the polar coordinates ρ and ψ locating the cutter center from point O. As shown in Fig. 9-10, the circle is tangent to the cam profile and has radius r_c. To locate the cutter center in the x–y coordinate system, we must first determine the projections of ρ on the x-axis and on the y-axis. These projectional components are designated as x_c and y_c. The mathematical expressions of x_c and y_c for various types of cam–follower arrangements are given in Table 9-1.

Table 9-1   Summary of Cutter–Center Equations for Various Types of Cam and Follower

Translating Roller	In-Line (Fig. 9-5)	$x_c = x + \dfrac{r_c}{r_f}(r \cos \theta - x)$ $y_c = y + \dfrac{r_c}{r_f}(r \sin \theta - y)$
	Offset (Fig. 9-6)	$x_c = x + \dfrac{r_c}{r_f}(x_f - x)$ $y_c = y + \dfrac{r_c}{r_f}(y_f - y)$ $x_f = e \sin \theta + (d+s) \cos \theta$ $y_f = -e \cos \theta + (d+s) \sin \theta$ $d = [(r_b + r_f)^2 - e^2]^{1/2}$
Swinging Roller	(Fig. 9-7)	$x_c = x + \dfrac{r_c}{r_f}(x_f - x)$ $y_c = y + \dfrac{r_c}{r_f}(y_f - y)$ $x_f = r_a \cos \theta - r_r \cos \alpha$ $y_f = r_a \sin \theta - r_r \sin \alpha$ $\alpha = \theta - \phi - \phi_o$
Translating Flat-Face	(Fig. 9-8)	$x_c = x + r_c \cos \theta$ $y_c = y + r_c \sin \theta$

Table 9-1   Cont'd.

Swinging Flat-Face	In-line (Fig. 9-9)	$x_c = x + r_c \sin \alpha$ $y_c = y + r_c \cos \alpha$ $\alpha = \phi - \theta + \phi_o$
	Offset (Fig. 9-10)	$x_c = x + x_c \sin \alpha$ $y_c = y + r_c \cos \alpha$ $\alpha = \phi - \theta + \phi_o$

Using the following coordinate conversions

$$\rho = (x_c^2 + y_c^2)^{1/2}$$

$$r_c = \tan^{-1}\left(\frac{y_c}{x_c}\right),$$

polar coordinate equations of the cutter center can also be obtained.

Example 9-4

Consider a swinging flat–face follower with $r_a = 7$, $e = 0.5$, (assumed positive), and $r_b = 2$. When the cam rotates 180° clockwise, the follower is to swing 18° by cycloidal motion. Determine the cam profile coordinates for a sample position, say, $\theta = 30°$.

The equation for cycloidal motion is

$$\phi = h\left(\frac{\theta}{\beta} - \frac{1}{2\pi} \sin \frac{2\pi\theta}{\beta}\right).$$

Hence,

$$\frac{d\phi}{d\theta} = \frac{h}{\beta}\left(1 - \cos \frac{2\pi\theta}{\beta}\right),$$

where $h = \dfrac{\pi}{10}$ rad, $\beta = \pi$. For $\theta = \dfrac{\pi}{6}$ rad we have

$$\phi = \frac{\pi}{10}\left(1 - \frac{1}{2\pi}\sin\frac{\pi}{3}\right) = 0.00906 \text{ rad}$$

$$\frac{d\phi}{d\theta} = \frac{\pi}{10\pi}\left(1 - \cos\frac{\pi}{3}\right) - 0.050 .$$

The initial angle is

$$\phi_o = \sin^{-1}\left(\frac{e + r_b}{r_a}\right) = \sin^{-1}\left(\frac{0.5 + 2}{7}\right) = 0.365 \text{ rad.}$$

To solve the example, first compute the value of β and A for $\theta = \dfrac{\pi}{6}$ rad

$$\beta = \phi_o + \phi - \theta$$

$$= 0.365 + \frac{\pi}{10} - \frac{\pi}{3}$$

$$= 0.1556 \text{ rad}$$

$$A = \frac{\cos(\theta + \beta)}{\dfrac{d\phi}{d\theta} - 1} = \frac{\cos\left(\dfrac{\pi}{6} + 0.1556\right)}{0.050 - 1} = -0.8191 .$$

Then substitute these into Eqs. (9-16) and (9-17),

$$x = r_a(\cos\theta + A\cos\beta) + e\sin\beta$$

$$= 7\left[\cos\frac{\pi}{6} - 0.8191\cos(0.1556)\right] + 0.5\sin(0.1556)$$

$$= 0.4758$$

$$y = r_a(\sin\theta + A\sin\beta) + e\cos\beta$$

$$= 7\left[\sin\frac{\pi}{3} - 0.8191\sin(0.1556)\right] + 0.5\cos(0.1556)$$

$$= 3.1050 \ .$$

10
Pressure Angle and
Transmission of Forces

10-1. INTRODUCTION

Selection of cam dimensional parameters such as the base circle radius and the follower offset is normally made at an early stage of cam design to satisfy one or more of the following conditions:
- To limit the pressure angle to prevent jamming between the follower stem and its guide, and to obtain as little side thrust against the follower as possible.
- To limit the minimum value of the cam profile radius of curvature to avoid undercutting, which results in incorrect follower movement and causes large contact stresses between the cam and the follower.

In general, the pressure angle decreases and the radius of curvature increases when the base circle radius of the cam increases. However, a minimum size of the base circle is desirable for saving space, reducing weight, decreasing the inertia effects, shortening the path of follower movement, and as a result reducing wear.

In the past, cam designers utilized the empirical method of constructing cams. Using this method, the pressure angle and the radius of curvature are observed visually from repeated graphical layouts of the cam for a series of consecutive positions until an acceptable design is obtained. This trial–and–error

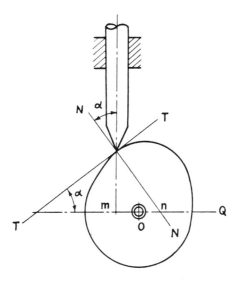

10-1. Pressure angle.

procedure is very time–consuming. In this chapter, we will present an analytical treatment for determing the cam size for proper follower action. Mathematical derivations of the pressure angle of cams are presented.

10-2. PRESSURE ANGLE

The pressure angle of a cam is the angle between the line of motion of the follower and the normal to the cam surface at the point of contact between the cam and the follower. This is represented by angle α in Fig. 10-1. In the absence of friction, the follower may be viewed as a free–body, as shown in Fig. 10-2a. The force R exerted on the follower by the cam is along the common normal line NN. We can resolve R into two components. The component $R \cos \alpha$ is the force that must be applied to the cam to overcome the loads on the cam. The other component $R \sin \alpha$ is the normal reaction. It is apparent that the pressure angle α should not be large. A large pressure angle causes the follower to jam against its guides, which results in bending of the follower stem. An excessive pressure angle also causes rough running and rapid wear on the cam, the roller, and the supporting bearing.

If the frictional resistance is taken into account, as shown in Fig. 10-2b, force R is shifted toward the right side of NN, making an angle τ, the angle of friction, if the cam is set to rotate counterclockwise. The effective pressure angle thus becomes $\alpha + \tau$. This is equivalent to having an increase in the pressure angle. Conversely, if the cam rotates clockwise, as shown in Fig. 10-2c, the

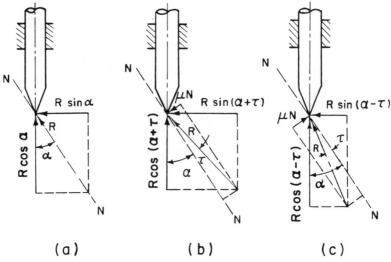

(a)   (b)   (c)

Fig. 10-2.

effective pressure angle becomes $\alpha - \tau$, which is equivalent to having a decrease in pressure angle.

Now let us refer to the location of points n and m in Fig. 10-1. Point n is the intersecting point between the common normal and line OQ, and point m is the intersecting point between the center line of the follower and line OQ. To have the pressure angle as small as possible, the cam should rotate clockwise if point n is to the right of point m. Conversely, the cam should rotate counterclockwise if point n is to the left of point m.

10-3. VARIATION OF PRESSURE ANGLE

The pressure angle α measured on an actual radial cam (Fig. 10-3a) is not the same as the pressure angle ϕ measured from a cam displacement diagram, as shown in Fig. 10-3b. In Fig. 10-3b a typical dwell–rise–dwell motion event of a cam is represented in the displacement diagram by the pitch curve ABC for a total rise h in a travel of arc distance x_h, which corresponds to the cam angle of rotation, β. Let point B be the point of inflection of the displacement curve, at which $s = h_i$, and let point P be any point on the displacement curve with its pressure angle indicated by ϕ. We will find the relationship between α and ϕ using the following derivations:

With reference to Fig. 10-3c we can write

$$\tan \alpha = \frac{dR}{R \, d\theta} .$$
        (10-1)

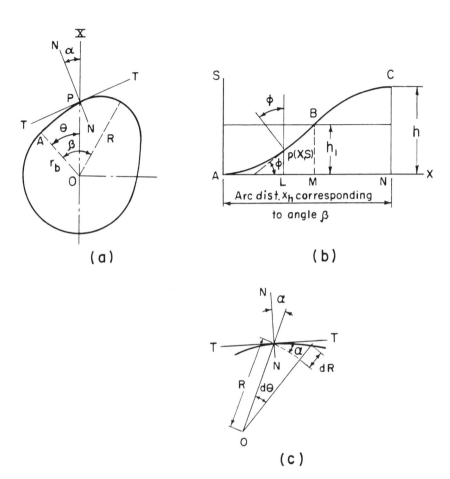

Fig. 10-3.

Since $R = r_b + s$ with r_b being the base circle radius,

$$\frac{dR}{d\theta} = \frac{dR}{dx}\frac{dx}{d\theta} = \frac{ds}{dx}\frac{dx}{d\theta} = \frac{dx}{d\theta}\tan\phi \ . \qquad (10\text{-}2)$$

At point B, the relationship between x and θ is

$$x = (r_b + h_1)\,\theta \ .$$

Hence, $\dfrac{dx}{d\theta} = r_b + h_1$.

Substituting this into Eq. (10-2) gives

$$\frac{dR}{d\theta} = (r_b + h_1) \tan \phi .$$

Therefore, from Eq. (10-1) we have

$$\tan \alpha = \frac{r_b + h_1}{r_b + s} \tan \phi . \tag{10-3}$$

$$\text{If } s < h_1 , \frac{r_b + h_1}{r_b + s} > 1, \tan \alpha > \tan \phi, \text{ or } \alpha > \phi . \tag{10-4}$$

$$\text{If } s = h_1 , \frac{r_b + h_1}{r_b + s} = 1, \tan \alpha_{max} = \tan \phi_{max} , \text{ or } \alpha_{max} = \phi_{max} .$$

$$\text{If } s > h_1 , \frac{r_b + h_1}{r_b + s} < 1, \tan \alpha < \tan \phi, \text{ or } \alpha < \phi .$$

Therefore, the pressure angle is a maximum, α_{max}, at the point of inflection. At this point the pressure angle α measured on an actual radial cam is equal to the pressure angle ϕ measured from the displacement diagram. The value of α is larger than ϕ below the point of inflection and is smaller than ϕ above the point of inflection.

10-4. PRESSURE ANGLE VERSUS CAM SIZE

It is well-known that the pressure angle can be reduced by increasing the pitch circle radius and hence the cam size. This is a fact that is stated in almost every kinematics textbook without proof. Of course, one can always verify this statement by means of a graphical layout. We will attempt to verify this analytically here.

In Fig. 10-4 a typical cam with DRD motion is represented by the curve $A_1B_1C_1$ for a total cam rise h from a base circle with radius r_{b1}, which corresponds to the cam angular displacement, β. Let point B_1 be the point of inflection of the displacement curve. The follower displacement at this point is $s = h_1$. Superimposed in the figure is a second curve $A_2B_2C_2$, which has the

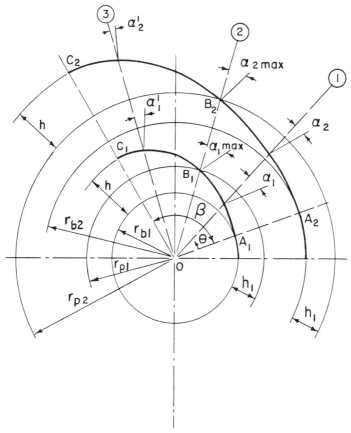

Fig. 10-4. Cam size effect to pressure angle.

same motion characteristics and motion specifications as the first displacement curve, i.e., the same type of motion and the same total lift h to cover the same cam angular displacement β. The only difference between the two is that the base circle radius of the latter is r_{b2}.

Based on the geometry of Fig. 10-4 and using a method similar to that used for deriving Eq. (10-2) in section 10-3, we can write

$$\tan \phi_1 = \frac{ds}{dx_1} = \frac{ds}{d\theta}\frac{d\theta}{dx_1} \tag{10-5}$$

$$\tan \phi_2 = \frac{ds}{dx_2} = \frac{ds}{d\theta}\frac{d\theta}{dx_2} ,$$

where ϕ_1 and ϕ_2 are the pressure angles at points B_1 and B_2, measured from the displacement diagram of curve $A_1B_1C_1$ and $A_2B_2C_2$, respectively. This term x_1 and x_2 are defined as

$$x_1 = (r_{b1} + h_1)\, \theta \tag{10-6}$$

$$x_2 = (r_{b2} + h_1)\, \theta \,.$$

It follows that

$$\tan \phi_1 = \frac{1}{r_{b1} + h_1} \frac{ds}{d\theta} \tag{10-7}$$

$$\tan \phi_2 = \frac{1}{r_{b2} + h_1} \frac{ds}{d\theta}$$

or

$$\frac{\tan \phi_1}{\tan \phi_2} = \frac{r_{b2} + h_1}{r_{b1} + h_1} \,. \tag{10-8}$$

From Eq. (10-3) we can write

$$\frac{\tan \alpha_1}{\tan \alpha_2} = \frac{r_{b1} + h_1}{r_{b1} + s} \frac{r_{b2} + s}{r_{b2} + h_1} \frac{\tan \phi_1}{\tan \phi_2} \,. \tag{10-9}$$

Using Eq. (10-8) gives

$$\frac{\tan \alpha_1}{\tan \alpha_2} = \frac{r_{b2} + s}{r_{b1} + s} \,. \tag{10-10}$$

Since $r_{b2} > r_{b1}$, we come to the conclusion that

$$\tan \alpha_1 > \tan \alpha_2 \,,$$

hence, $\alpha_1 > \alpha_2$.

That is to say, the pressure angle increases as the cam size decreases.

10-5. PRESSURE ANGLE AND STATIC FORCE TRANSMISSION

Translating Cam with Reciprocating Follower

Let us first consider the forces acting on the translating follower of a translating cam, shown in Fig. 10-5a. The forces acting on the cam, which moves to the right, are shown in Fig. 10-5b.

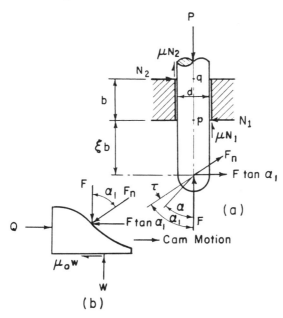

Fig. 10-5. Force transmission of translating cam with reciprocating roller follower.

Realizing that the two bodies in Fig. 10-5 are in equilibrium, five equations of static equilibrium can be written: three for the follower and two for the cam. These are

for the follower

$$\sum F_y = 0 = F - P \mp \mu(N_1 + N_2) \qquad (10\text{-}11)$$

$$\sum M_p = 0 = (F \tan \alpha_1)\xi b - N_1 b \mp \frac{1}{2} \mu N_1 d \qquad (10\text{-}12)$$

$$\pm \frac{1}{2} \mu N_2 d$$

$$\sum M_q = 0 = (F \tan \alpha_1)(\xi b + b) - N_2 b \mp \frac{1}{2} \mu N_1 d \qquad (10\text{-}13)$$

$$\pm \frac{1}{2} \mu N_2 d$$

and for the cam

$$\sum F_v = 0 = -F + W \qquad (10\text{-}14)$$

$$\sum F_h = 0 = \pm Q - F \tan \alpha_1 \mp \mu_o W, \qquad (10\text{-}15)$$

where the upper sign and the lower sign in the above equations refer to the follower rise period and the follower fall period, respectively. The notations are

μ	= the coefficient of friction between the follower stem and its guide bearing
μ_o	= the coefficient of friction between the translational cam and its guide
μ_1	= the coefficient of friction between cam and follower in the case of a sliding follower
N, N_2	= the force normal to the follower stem
F	= the force parallel to the follower stem
F_n	= the force normal to the cam profile
P	= the total external load on the follower, including static weight, spring force, inertia, etc
α	= the pressure angle
α_1	= the effective pressure angle, i.e., $\alpha_1 = \alpha + \tan^{-1} \mu_1$
b	= the follower guide length
ξ	= the ratio of follower overhang to guide length
d	= the guide width or diameter.

Solving first for N_1 and N_2 from Eqs. (10-12) and (10-13), after neglecting the minute difference between the frictional moments of $\frac{1}{2} \mu N_1 d$ and $\frac{1}{2} \mu N_2 d$, yields

$$N_2 = (F \tan \alpha_1)(1 + \xi) \qquad (10\text{-}16)$$

$$N_1 = (F \tan \alpha_1)\xi. \qquad (10\text{-}17)$$

Adding Eqs. (10-16) and (10-17), substituting into Eq. (10-11), and solving for F gives

$$F = \frac{P}{1 \mp \mu(1 + 2\xi)\tan\alpha_1} \quad . \tag{10-18}$$

From Eqs. (10-14) and (10-15) we have

$$F = W = \frac{\pm Q}{\tan\alpha_1 \mp \mu_o} \quad . \tag{10-19}$$

Combining Eqs. (10-18) and (10-19) gives the relationship between P and Q

$$P = \frac{[1 \mp \mu\tan\alpha_1(1 + 2\xi)]Q}{\tan\alpha_1 \mp \mu_o} \quad . \tag{10-20}$$

The follower will jam in its guide when the numerator of Eq. (10-20) becomes zero. Therefore, if we set

$$1 - \mu\tan\alpha_1(1 + 2\xi) = 0 \ ,$$

we can obtain

$$\alpha_1 = \tan^{-1}\left[\frac{1}{\mu(1 + 2\xi)}\right]$$

and

$$\alpha = \tan^{-1}\left[\frac{1}{\mu(1 + 2\xi)}\right] - \tan^{-1}\mu_1 \tag{10-21}$$

for the maximum pressure angle without causing follower jamming.

By way of illustration, if we assume $\mu = \mu_1 = 0.1$ and $\xi = 2$, the follower jam occurs at $\alpha = 57.72°$. Under this situation, regardless of the amount of force Q we apply to the cam, we can not raise the follower. When the ratio ξ is reduced to 1 with the same values of μ and μ_1, the angle at which jamming occurs is increased to 67.59°. A reduction in the coefficients of friction also increases the jamming angle.

When $\alpha = 30°$, Eq. (10-20) gives $Q = 0.966\ P$. This indicates that for the same load P, the force required to actuate the follower becomes tremendous when the value α is large. This situation is obviously undersirable. During the fall, the force Q will point to the left if the cam is the driver, and the friction forces will be reversed as indicated by the lower sign in the derivations. Again for $\mu = \mu_1 = 0.1$ and $\xi = 2$, when

$$\alpha = 11.92°, \quad P = 0$$
$$\alpha < 11.92°, \quad P \text{ is directed to the left (the cam drives the follower)}$$
$$\alpha > 11.92°, \quad P \text{ is directed to the right (the follower drives the cam).}$$

In any case the follower cannot jam in its guides during the fall period. For this reason, a designer of cams is usually concerned about the magnitude of the pressure angle only during the rise of the follower. By keeping the follower overhang as small as possible and by using a roller at the end of the follower, rolling action is substituted for wedging action, and jamming of the follower can be avoided in most practical cases.

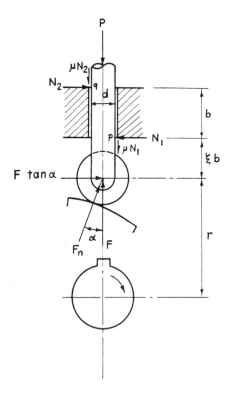

Fig. 10-6. Force transmission of radial cam with reciprocating roller follower.

Radial Cam with Reciprocating Roller Follower

We learned from the previous section that the problem of follower jamming can be lessened if we use a roller at the end of the follower. Fig. 10-6 shows a typical radial cam with a reciprocating roller follower. Since a roller is used, we may neglect the friction between the roller and the cam; that is to say, the effect of μ is negligible in this case.

Based on the free–body diagram of the follower, static equilibrium expressed by one force equation,

$$\sum F_v = 0 \,,$$

and two moment equations,

$$\sum M_p = 0$$

and

$$\sum M_q = 0 \,,$$

gives the same set of equations as Eqs. (10-11), (10-12), and (10-13), except that α_1 is now α. We will not reproduce these equations here. The solutions for the resulting three equations are

$$F = \frac{P}{1 \mp \mu(2\xi + 1)\tan\alpha} \tag{10-22}$$

$$N_1 = \frac{\xi b P}{\mu(b + 2\xi b) - b\cot\alpha} = \frac{\xi P}{\mu(1 + 2\xi) - \cot\alpha} \tag{10-23}$$

$$N_2 = \frac{-(\xi b + b)P}{\mu(b + 2\xi b) - b\cot\alpha} = \frac{-(1 + \xi)P}{\mu(1 + 2\xi) - \cot\alpha} \,. \tag{10-24}$$

In Eq. (10-22) the term $\mu(2\xi + 1) \cdot \tan\alpha$ is called the friction factor. Denoting the friction factor by f, we can rewrite Eq. (10-22) in the form

$$F = \frac{P}{1 \mp f} \,. \tag{10-25}$$

Based on an averaged value of $\mu = 0.1$, the magnitude of f for some sampled values of ξ and μ is tabulated below:

α \ ξ	0.25	0.5	1.0	2.0
10°	0.026	0.035	0.053	0.088
20°	0.055	0.073	0.109	0.182
30°	0.087	0.115	0.173	0.288
40°	0.126	0.168	0.252	0.419

The normal force F_n, which is essential in determining the contact stress between the cam and the roller, is

$$F_n = \frac{F}{\cos\alpha} = \frac{P}{(1 \mp f)\cos\alpha} , \tag{10-26}$$

and the torque on the cam shaft is

$$T = rF \tan \alpha , \tag{10-27}$$

where r is the radius measured from the cam shaft to the reference point. The maximum torque determines the cam shaft load, the power necessary to drive the system. Note that the normal force becomes infinity when the denominator of Eq. (10-26) equals zero. Therefore, we can find the maximum pressure angle α_m by setting

$$\cos \alpha_m \mp \mu(2\xi + 1) \sin \alpha_m = 0$$

or

$$1 \mp \mu(2\xi + 1) \tan \alpha_m = 0 ,$$

which leads to

$$\alpha_m = \tan^{-1}\left[\frac{\pm 1}{\mu(2\xi + 1)}\right] . \tag{10-28}$$

Eq. (10-28) will generally give higher values for the pressure angle than are usually selected. For example, if $\xi = 2$ and the values for the coefficient of friction of bronze on steel are $\mu(\text{kinetic}) = 0.10$, and $\mu(\text{static}) = 0.15$, then from Eq. (10-28) the maximum pressure angle for each condition is:

kinetic $\quad \alpha_m = \tan^{-1} \dfrac{1}{0.10(5)} = 63.43°$

static $\quad \alpha_m = \tan^{-1} \dfrac{1}{0.15(5)} = 53.13°$.

The value of μ could momentarily rise to as much as 0.4, say under a combination of a high load, a low speed, and an excessive amount of clearance (backlash) between stem and stem bearing. These circumstances, together with poor lubrication, could easily arise when starting the machine.

The values of μ, ξ, and the bearing clearance should be kept as small as possible, and the bearing length b should be kept as large as possible. Ball bearings for the linear moving stem are commercially available to give very low friction and backlash. In addition, the follower stem should be made rigid. Fulfilling these requirements will give the largest pressure angle and the smoothest follower action possible.

We can also visualize the follower jamming condition by a graphical layout. Sometimes graphical interpretation gives more insight into the problem. The set of forces that act on the follower as it is lifted by the cam is shown in Fig. 10-7a. In this Figure the reaction R_1 is the vector sum of N_1 and μN_1. Similarly, the reaction R_2 is the vector sum of N_2 and μN_2. Forces R_1 and R_2 intersect at point I. The relationship between the contact force F_n and the external load P from the follower may be obtained by taking the moment about point I. Thus

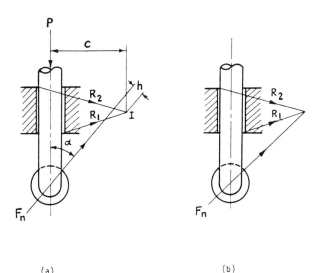

(a)   (b)

Fig. 10-7.

$$F_n h = Pc .$$

As α increases, the amount of offset h decreases, and the value of h may become as small as zero. When this occurs, F becomes equal to zero, and the follower has jammed. Since the follower must, when jammed, be under the equilibrium of only three forces, these three forces must pass through a common point. If this condition did not hold, two of the forces would pass through a common point, and the third would have a moment about that point, contradicting the assumed condition of equilibrium. Consequently, we can draw a diagram as shown in Fig. 10-7b. The reactions R_1 and R_2 at the guides are drawn at the assumed friction angles, meeting in a point. A line through this point from the follower position gives the direction of F_n in which jamming occurs. The corresponding measurement of angle α is the maximum pressure angle.

If the external load P is not applied at an angle, follower jamming of a radial cam without offset is only of concern when the follower moves in a direction opposite to that of the load. If we now refer to Fig. 10-6, jamming occurs during the rise only. During the fall, the equations derived in this section hold if we refer to the lower sign in the equations. In the investigation of follower jamming during the fall it is now F_n that must be zero. It follows immediately that P is an axial force, which can never pass through the intersection of the guide reactions during the fall. Therefore, jamming cannot occur.

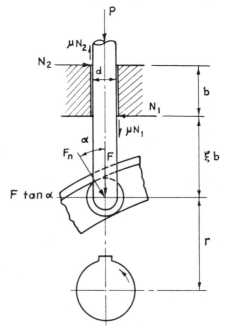

Fig. 10-8. Force diagram of a closed cam.

The typical force diagram of a closed or a grooved cam that does not use a spring during deceleration of the load is shown in Fig. 10-8. The analysis in this section is valid if we realize that the direction of force F may be downward during the fall in this case; the contact then being between the outer profile of the cam and the roller. As a consequence, the signs of F and μ are both changed during the fall.

As may be seen in Fig. 10-6, the greater the pressure angle, the greater the magnitude of the side thrust on the follower. During action, the side thrust varies continuously, depending upon the cam curve used. It is interesting to compare cam curves on the basis of the magnitudes of the side thrust that they produce. Fig. 10-9 presents such a comparison for a number of cam curves. For a meaningful comparison we must place all cams under the same conditions, i.e., equal base circle size, equal range of cam rotation β, and equal loading condition. In addition, let us assume that all cams have unity lift and unity follower weight.

For convenience, the maximum side thrust of the parabolic curve is normalized and is made to serve as a basis of comparison with the side thrust of other curves.

From Fig. 10-9 it is apparent that the trigonometric function and the modified trigonometric function curves (d), (e), and (i) are superior to the others, and that the trapezoidal, the modified trapezoidal, and the 4–5–6–7 polynomial curves produce about the same magnitude of side thrust. Among all curves, the cubic No. 1 curve and the circular–arc–tangent curve give the greatest amount of side thrust.

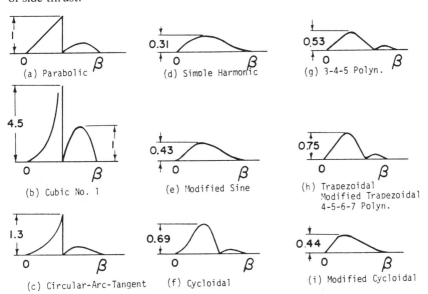

Fig. 10-9. Comparison of side thrust of some typical cam curves.

Radial Cam with Reciprocating Flat–Faced Follower

The side thrust or jamming effect on flat–faced followers is inconsequential compared to roller followers, because the pressure angle is zero. A flat–faced follower is shown in Fig. 10-10 with normal forces N_1 and N_2. The directions of N_1 and N_2 vary depending on whether the eccentricity a is to the right or to the left of the cam centerline. The equilibria of horizontal forces, vertical forces, and moments about the point q give the following equations:

$$- \mu_o F + N_1 - N_2 = 0 \tag{10-29}$$

$$F - \mu N_1 - \mu N_2 = P \tag{10-30}$$

$$aF - b(1 + \xi)N_1 + \xi b N_2 + \mu \frac{d}{2} N_1 - \mu \frac{d}{2} N_2 = 0 , \tag{10-31}$$

where μ_o is the coefficient of friction at the contact between the cam and the follower. The other symbols are the same as defined previously.

Assuming that the difference between $\mu \dfrac{d}{2} N_1$ and $\mu \dfrac{d}{2} N_2$ is negligible, the solutions of the above three equations are

$$F = \frac{bP}{\Gamma} \tag{10-32}$$

$$N_1 = \frac{(a - \mu_o \xi b)P}{\Gamma} \tag{10-33}$$

$$N_2 = \frac{[a - \mu_o b(1 + \xi)]P}{\Gamma} , \tag{10-34}$$

with $\Gamma = b - 2a\mu + \mu\mu_o b(1 + 2\xi)$.

The jamming condition of the follower in this case can be found by setting P equal to zero. Therefore, to avoid follower jamming we must have

$$a < \frac{b}{2\mu} + \frac{\mu_o(1 + \xi)}{2} , \tag{10-35}$$

For best performance, the values of ξ, μ, and a should be kept small, and the rigidity of the follower stem should be as great as possible.

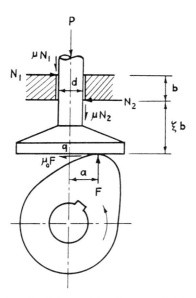

Fig. 10-10. Force transmission of radial cam with reciprocating flat-face follower.

Radial Cam with Swinging Roller Follower

As shown in Fig. 10-11, the forces acting on a swinging arm are the normal reaction at the cam F_n and the bearing reactions Q_a and Q_t at the pivoted point Q of the swinging arm. Static force balance requires

$$F_n \sin \alpha - Q_a = 0 \qquad (10\text{-}36)$$

$$F_n \cos \alpha - Q_t = 0 \qquad (10\text{-}37)$$

$$F_n \ell \cos \alpha - T = 0 , \qquad (10\text{-}38)$$

where T is the total torque of the follower with respect to point Q. This includes the torques due to the effects of springs, inertia, etc. The solutions of Eqs. (10-36), (10-37), and (10-38) are

$$F_n = \frac{T}{\ell \cos \alpha} \qquad (10\text{-}39)$$

$$Q_a = \frac{T}{\ell} \tan \alpha \qquad (10\text{-}40)$$

$$Q_l = \frac{T}{\ell} .$$

                                                                    (10-41)

Eqs. (10-39), (10-40), and (10-41) are applicable during the fall motion period as well. In the case of a closed cam, the only thing required is a change in the sign of F_n in Eq. (10-39).

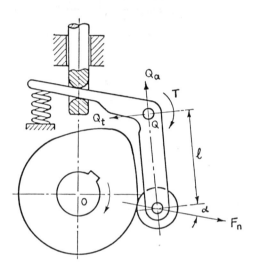

Fig. 10-11. Force transmission of radial cam with swinging roller follower.

   With the proper location of the swinging arm pivot, it becomes virtually impossible to jam the follower of this type of arrangement. Therefore, the swinging roller follower is an improvement over the flat–faced follower in that the distribution of forces allows a much larger limiting pressure angle for satisfactory performance.

10-6. PRESSURE ANGLE AND CAM GEOMETRIC PARAMETERS

Radial Cam with Reciprocating Roller Follower

In this section we will discuss the relationship between the size of the cam, the pressure angle, and the type of curve needed in the case of a reciprocating offset roller follower. Let

r_o = the prime circle radius.
s = the displacement of the follower.
e = the amount of offset.
ω_c = the angular velocity of the cam.
θ = the cam angle of rotation for displacement s.
V_f = the velocity of the follower.
t = time.

Based on the geometry of Fig. 10-12,

$$d = \sqrt{r_o^2 - e^2} \ .$$ (10-42)

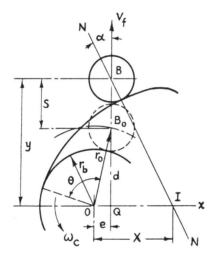

Fig. 10-12.

Also, the common normal NN cuts the line of centers $0x$ at I, which is the pole location between the cam and the follower. Therefore, letting $OI = X$, we can write

$$X\omega_c = V_f$$

or

$$X = \frac{V_f}{\omega_c} = \frac{\dfrac{ds}{dt}}{\dfrac{d\theta}{dt}} = \frac{ds}{d\theta} \ .$$ (10-43)

Therefore, X or $\overline{OI}$ represents the converted velocity $\dfrac{V_f}{\omega_c}$ of the follower. The pressure angle for the offset follower is

$$\tan \alpha = \frac{\overline{OI} - e}{y} \, .$$

Using Eqs. (10-42) and (10-43), the pressure angle becomes

$$\tan \alpha = \frac{\dfrac{ds}{d\theta} - e}{s + \sqrt{r_o^2 - e^2}} \, . \tag{10-44}$$

Note that if the offset e equals zero,

$$\tan \alpha = \frac{\dfrac{ds}{d\theta}}{s + r_o} \, . \tag{10-45}$$

In Eqs. (10-44) or (10-45) s and $\dfrac{ds}{d\theta}$ depend upon the type of motion curve.

Effect of Offset. From Eqs. (10-44) and (10-45) we can see that as long as s is increasing, $\dfrac{ds}{d\theta}$ will be positive, and provided that e is not excessive, the effect of offsetting the follower is to reduce the pressure angle. Conversely, when s is decreasing, $\dfrac{ds}{d\theta}$ will be negative, and an offset will increase the pressure angle. Since jamming of the follower can occur only when s is increasing (i.e., during the lift), offsetting is usually advantageous. The following example shows the effect of offsetting on the pressure angle of a cam.

Example 10-1

A plate cam, which rotates at 400 rpm, imparts motion to a reciprocating roller follower. The follower lifts 3.25 cm with simple–harmonic motion during 150° of cam rotation. If the prime circle diameter is 10 cm, determine the value of the pressure angle when $\theta = 30°$ for (a) a radial follower (zero offset) and (b) a follower with offset $e = 1$ cm opposite to the cam rotation.

The displacement and the velocity equations for simple harmonic motion are

$$s = \frac{h}{2} \left(1 - \cos \frac{\pi\theta}{\beta} \right),$$

and

$$V_f = \frac{h\pi\omega}{2\beta} \sin \frac{\pi\theta}{\beta},$$

where, in this case, $\theta = 30°$ (0.524 rad), $\beta = 150°$ (2.618 rad), $\dfrac{\theta}{\beta} = \dfrac{1}{5}$,

$h = 3.25$ cm, and $\omega_c = 400 \times \dfrac{2\pi}{60} = 41.89$ rad/sec. Substituting these values into the above equations gives

$$s = 0.3108 \text{ cm}$$

$$V_f = 48.05 \text{ cm/sec.}$$

(a) Radial follower ($e = 0$)

Using Eq. (10-45),

$$\tan \alpha = \frac{\dfrac{ds}{d\theta}}{s + r_o},$$

where $\dfrac{ds}{d\theta} = \dfrac{V_f}{\omega_c} = \dfrac{48.05}{41.89} = 1.147;$ then

$$\tan \alpha = \frac{1.147}{0.3108 + 5} = 0.2160$$

$$\alpha = 12.19°.$$

(b) Follower offset ($e = 1$ cm)

Using Eq. (10-44),

$$\tan \alpha = \frac{\dfrac{ds}{d\theta} - e}{s + \sqrt{r_o^2 - e^2}}$$

$$\alpha = \tan^{-1}\left[\frac{1.147 - 1}{0.3108 + \sqrt{(5)^2 - (1)^2}}\right] = \tan^{-1}(0.0282) = 1.62°.$$

Maximum Pressure Angle and Cam Size — Radial Cam with Radial Roller Follower. In many problems the maximum pressure angle is a controlling factor because it dictates the size of the cam necessary to meet the given requirements of motion. Therefore, we are particularly interested in finding the magnitude of the maximum pressure angle and the location where this maximum occurs. For cams with reciprocating offset followers and for cams with oscillating roller followers, the process of finding the maximum pressure angle and its corresponding location involves the solution of a complicated transcendental equation. This can normally be accomplished by a mathematical search for the maximum through computer programming. However, in the case of a cam with a radial follower, we can derive an exact expression for finding the maximum pressure angle. This is given as follows.

Differentiating the pressure angle α in Eq. (10-45) with respect to time t and setting the result equal to zero give

$$\sec^2 \alpha \frac{d\alpha}{dt} = \frac{d}{dt}\left(\frac{1}{r_o + s}\right)\frac{ds}{d\theta}$$

or

$$\frac{d\alpha}{dt} = \omega \cos^2 \alpha \left[\frac{1}{r_o + s}\frac{d^2s}{d\theta^2} - \frac{\left(\dfrac{ds}{d\theta}\right)^2}{(r_o + s)^2}\right] = 0. \tag{10-46}$$

Let

$R_p =$ the radius of the pitch curve in contact with the reference point of the follower.

θ_p = the cam angle in radians through which the cam turns while the follower rises from rest to where the pressure angle is a maximum.

α_m = the maximum pressure angle.

ω = the constant angular velocity of the cam.

Dividing Eq. (10-46) by $\omega \cos^2 \alpha$, which cannot be equal to zero, and realizing that $R_p = r_o + s$ on the basis of the definition of R_p, we obtain

$$R_p = \frac{\left(\dfrac{ds}{d\theta}\right)^2_p}{\left(\dfrac{d^2 s}{d\theta^2}\right)_p} \,, \tag{10-47}$$

where the subscript p refers to the pitch point value. Using Eq. (10-45) again, the maximum pressure angle can be expressed as

$$\tan \alpha_m = \frac{1}{R_p} \left(\frac{ds}{d\theta}\right)_p$$

or

$$\tan \alpha_m = \frac{\left(\dfrac{d^2 s}{d\theta^2}\right)_p}{\left(\dfrac{ds}{d\theta}\right)_p} \,. \tag{10-48}$$

Since $\dfrac{ds}{d\theta} = \dfrac{1}{\omega}\dfrac{ds}{dt}$ and $\dfrac{d^2 s}{d\theta^2} = \dfrac{1}{\omega^2}\dfrac{d^2 s}{dt^2}$ by use of the derivative chain rule, Eqs. (10-47) and (10-48) may also be expressed using time as an independent variable,

$$R_p = \frac{\left(\dfrac{ds}{dt}\right)^2_p}{\left(\dfrac{d^2 s}{dt^2}\right)_p} \,, \tag{10-49}$$

and

$$\tan \alpha_m = \frac{\left(\dfrac{d^2s}{dt^2}\right)_p}{\omega \left(\dfrac{ds}{dt}\right)_p}. \tag{10-50}$$

With these two equations we can, if they are solvable in closed forms, construct the smallest radial cam with a prescribed pressure angle. Unfortunately, the closed form solutions exist only for some simple basic motion curves. For example, in the case of parabolic motion,

$$\frac{ds}{dt} = \frac{4h\theta\omega}{\beta^2}$$

$$\frac{d^2s}{dt^2} = \frac{4h\omega^2}{\beta^2},$$

which give

$$R_p = \frac{4h}{\beta^2}\,\theta_p^2 = 2s_p \tag{10-51}$$

$$\tan \alpha_m = \frac{1}{\theta_p}. \tag{10-52}$$

Eq. (10-51) shows that R_p equals exactly twice the travel s_p of the follower from rest provided that the constant acceleration persists through θ_p. What happens if the initial constant acceleration is shorter than θ_p? The acceleration will then be either negative or zero for the ensuing period, since α will decrease when the acceleration is negative. Therefore, α_m is the value attained at the end of the lifting period.

A second example is simple-harmonic motion, with the following velocity and acceleration characteristics

$$\frac{ds}{dt} = \frac{h\pi\omega}{2\beta}\sin\frac{\pi\theta}{\beta}$$

$$\frac{d^2s}{dt^2} = \frac{h}{2}\left(\frac{\pi\omega}{b}\right)^2\cos\frac{\pi\theta}{b},$$

which give

$$R_p = \frac{h \sin^2 \dfrac{\pi \theta_p}{\beta}}{2 \cos \dfrac{\pi \theta_p}{\beta}} \qquad (10\text{-}53)$$

$$\tan \alpha_m = \frac{\pi}{\beta} \cot \frac{\pi \theta_p}{\beta} \; . \qquad (10\text{-}54)$$

In the two types of motion indicated above, the pitch circle radius R_p and the angle θ_p for a prescribed value of maximum pressure angle α_m can be determined explicitly. For other types of motion (cycloidal motion, for instance) the exact location of θ_p corresponding to α_m cannot be determined explicitly. A transcendental equation must be solved to obtain this information.

If there are several rises on the same cam, R_p must be calculated separately for each one and the largest value chosen.

Nomogram for Maximum Pressure Angle — Radial Cam with Radial Roller Follower. As we can see from the previous section, certain steps are usually required to obtain the maximum pressure angle in design calculations. First, the maximum must be located by differentiating α with respect to θ and then setting the resulting expression equal to zero. This may or may not lead to an explicit solution for θ_p, depending upon the type of motion function. For the majority of motions, this process involves the solution of a cumbersome transcendental equation. The value of θ_p so obtained is substituted back into the general pressure angle equation to find α_m. If α_m is not satisfactory, the parameters must be changed and the entire process of maximization repeated.

This procedure is too time–consuming for design purposes. The designer needs a precalculated maximum pressure angle corresponding to the value of h, r_o, and β in the problem. Nomograms have been prepared that simplify the necessary design calculations. Fig. 10-13 shows a circular nomogram made available by the Barber–Colman Company (125). Fig. 10-14 shows another version of combined nomograms* proposed by Koumans (136). The use of these charts eliminates the necessity for either a graphical or a mathematical solution to the problem. For more details on nomogram construction, the reader is referred to Reference (247).

---

*Providing information for both maximum pressure angle and minimum radius of curvature. For the treatment of the radius of curvature, refer to Chapter 11.

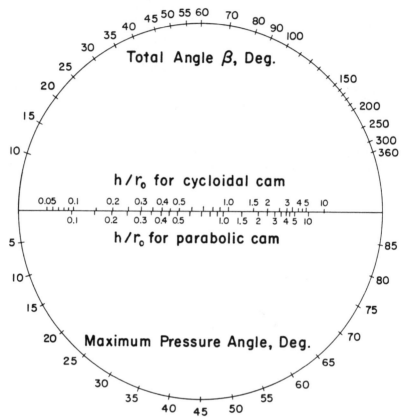

Fig. 10-13. Circular nomogram for maximum pressure angle, radial cam with reciprocating roller follower.

Example 10-2

Design a cycloidal cam for a dwell–rise–dwell motion event with $h = 1.6$ cm and $\beta = 30°$.

First solution: Assume $r_o = 3.8$ cm; then $\dfrac{h}{r_o} = 0.42$. From Fig. 10-13, we obtain $\alpha_m = 54°$, which is somewhat large.

Second solution: For the given value of h and β we must increase the value of r_o to 10.67 cm to make $\alpha_m = 30°$. This is not an economical design. We do not want to make the cam excessively large. Therefore, if we go back and change β to 70° for $\alpha_m = 30°$, we have a better design. Consequently, the cam runs faster to maintain the lift time at a constant value.

Determination of Minimum Base Circle by Graphical Method — Radial Cam with Reciprocating Offset Roller Follower. Eq. (10-44) does not lend itself

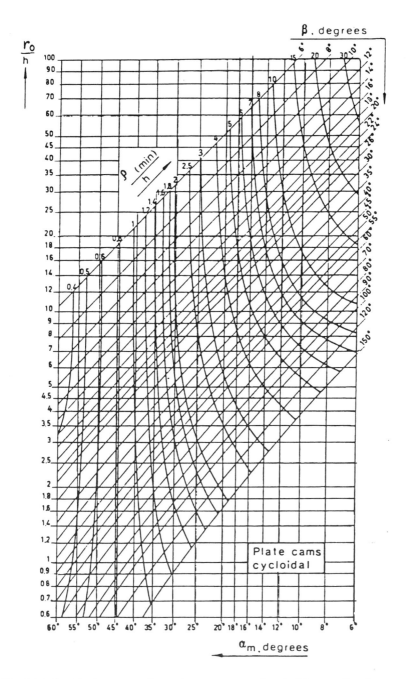

Fig. 10-14. Combined nomogram for maximum pressure angle and minimum radius of curvature (Koumans).

readily to the determination of the minimum base circle radius for a pre-scribed value of α_{max} because s and $\dfrac{ds}{d\theta}$, corresponding to α_{max}, are unknowns. A graphical technique suggested by Hirschhorn (101) overcomes this situation.

As shown in Fig. 10-15, we first plot $\dfrac{ds}{d\theta}$ (that is, V_c) versus the s curve by placing the s–axis parallel to the line of the follower stroke passing through the cam center O, and by placing the V_c–axis perpendicular to the line of the fol-lower stroke passing through the lowest position of the follower roller center B. Then the line drawn from Q to any given point on the V_c versus s curve will make an angle with respect to the line of the follower stroke equal to the appro-priate pressure angle α. The line drawn from Q tangent to the curve will define the maximum pressure angle α_m.

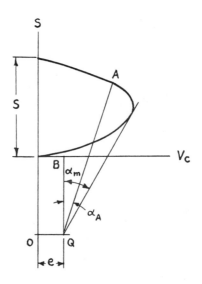

Fig. 10-15.

Conversely, the tangent drawn to a given V_c versus s curve with a prescribed value of α_m and offset e will intersect the line of stroke at point Q, thus locating the position of O. The length OB is the required minimum dwell radius r_o. The corresponding minimum base radius of the cam is

$$r_b = r_o - r_f ,$$

where r_f is the radius of the follower roller.

Example 10-3

A disc cam rotating counterclockwise at 400 rpm actuates a reciprocating roller follower whose center line is offset 0.65 cm to the right of the camshaft center. The follower motion is cycloidal, and its stroke s of 3.0 cm is accomplished in a cam rotation of 90°. The roller radius is 1.3 cm, and the maximum pressure angle α_m is 30°. Determine the minimum base radius r_b.

For cycloidal motion

$$s(\theta) = h\left(\frac{\theta}{\beta} - \frac{1}{2\pi}\sin 2\pi \frac{\theta}{\beta}\right), \text{ and}$$

$$V(\theta) = \frac{h}{\beta}\left(1 - \cos \frac{2\pi\theta}{\beta}\right).$$

Then

$$V_c = \frac{V(t)}{\omega} = \frac{\omega V(\theta)}{\omega} = V(\theta).$$

To establish the maximum pressure angle, it is not necessary to plot the complete V_c versus s curve, but it is sufficient to draw a small part of the curve just below $(V_c)_{\max}$. Realizing that $(V_c)_{\max}$ occurs at midstroke, when $\frac{\theta}{\beta} = 0.5$, we need to compute the following few points:

$$\frac{\theta}{\beta} = 0.40, \quad s = 1.220 \text{ cm}, \quad V_c = 3.46 \text{ cm}$$

$$\frac{\theta}{\beta} = 0.45, \quad s = 1.35 \text{ cm}, \quad V_c = 3.73 \text{ cm}$$

$$\frac{\theta}{\beta} = 0.50, \quad s = 1.5 \text{ cm}, \quad V_c = 3.82 \text{ cm}.$$

The construction, Fig. 10-16, shows that $OB = 4.15$ cm, thus giving $(r_b)_{\min} = 4.15 - 1.30 = 2.85$ cm.

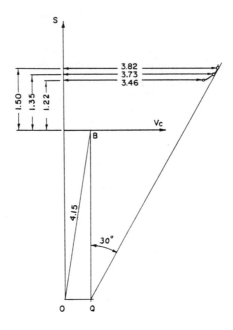

Fig. 10-16.

Determination of Optimum Cam Geometric Parameters. Smooth and noise-less motion is an important objective of cam design. To achieve this, the designer must create a minimum–sized cam and yet avoid follower jamming due to excessive pressure angles and minimize the frequency of side–thrust reversal. The problem is solved by selecting the proper follower offset for the smallest possible cam. Fenton (78) proposed a method based on the following rationale.

In section 10-6, with reference to Fig. 10-12, we have derived the pressure angle expression Eq. (10-44). Let us reproduce it here

$$\tan \alpha = \frac{V_c - e}{s + \sqrt{r_o^2 - e^2}} \ . \tag{10-44}$$

Both the follower velocity V and the converted follower velocity V_c are positive if directed away from the rotating cam. The follower offset is positive if dis-placed in a direction opposite to the cam rotation. Since the denominator of Eq. (10-44) is always positive as the cam rotates, the sign of $\tan \alpha$ is governed by the sign of $(V_c - e)$.

Fig. 10-17 shows the plot of V_c versus the s curve. Let us consider the follow-ing two cases:

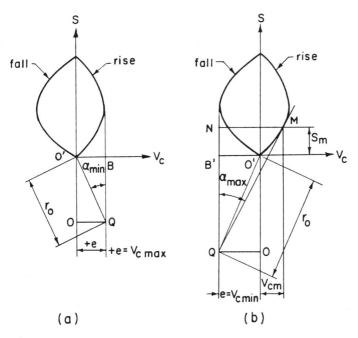

Fig. 10-17.

Case 1: either $e < V_{c\text{max}}$ (Fig. 10-17a)

   or $e < V_{c\text{min}}$ (Fig. 10-17b)

Case 2: either $e < V_{c\text{max}}$ (Fig. 10-17a)

   or $e > V_{c\text{min}}$ (Fig. 10-17b) .

The quantity $(V_c - e)$ will change signs during cam rotation in case 1, but it will not change signs in case 2. However, the cam size r_o becomes unnecessarily large in the second case. Therefore, it seems logical to say that for the smallest possible cam that causes the least side–thrust reversal, and hence the quietest operational cam,

$$V_{c\text{max}} = e \tag{10-55}$$

or

$$V_{c\text{min}} = e , \tag{10-56}$$

whichever results in a smaller cam size.

The remaining problem is to find the minimum cam size corresponding to a prescribed value for the maximum pressure angle without causing the follower to jam in its guide. Let

s_m = the instantaneous follower displacement at the maximum pressure angle.

V_{cm} = the instantaneous value of the converted follower velocity at the maximum pressure angle.

α_c = the permissible pressure angle.

Consider the following two separate conditions:

(a) Negative Pressure Angle Condition

From triangle $O'BQ$ in Fig. 10-17a,

$$\sin \alpha_{min} = \frac{e}{r_o}$$

for negative pressure angles. Limiting α_{min} to α_c and using Eq. (10-55) give

$$r_o = \frac{V_{c\,max}}{\sin \alpha_c} \tag{10-57}$$

(b) Positive Pressure Angle Condition

When $e = V_{c\,min}$, the pressure angle is always positive. The maximum value of the positive pressure angle may be found by differentiating Eq. (10-44) with respect to s, then setting the derivative equal to zero. If $\dfrac{d}{ds} (\tan \alpha) = 0$, then $\alpha = \alpha_m$, $s = s_m$, and $V_c = V_{cm}$. Thus

$$\tan \alpha_m = \frac{dV_c}{ds} = \frac{V_{cm} - V_{c\,min}}{s_m + d} \, ,$$

where d is the initial displacement of the follower.

If α_m is limited to α_c, then

$$\tan \alpha_c = \frac{dV_c}{ds} = \frac{V_{cm} - V_{c\,min}}{s_m + d} \, .$$

From triangle QMN of Fig. 10-17b,

$$QN = \frac{V_{cm} - V_{c\min}}{\tan \alpha_m}$$

$$QB' = QN - s_m .$$

If α_m is limited to α_c, then

$$QB' = \frac{V_{cm} - V_{c\min}}{\tan \alpha_c} - s_m .$$

Therefore, triangle $QB'O'$ gives

$$r_o = \left[\left(\frac{V_{cm} - V_{c\min}}{\tan \alpha_c} - s_m \right)^2 + (V_{c\min})^2 \right]^{1/2} . \qquad (10\text{-}58)$$

Eqs. (10-57) and (10-58) are used to determine which value of the follower offset produces the smaller cam size.

Example 10-4

A disc cam imparts motion to a reciprocating roller follower. The follower motion is simple–harmonic, and its stroke s is 1.5 cm. The lift period occurs over 120° of cam rotation and the fall period over 150°. The roller radius is 1.0 cm, and the maximum allowable pressure angle is 30°. Determine the follower offset and the minimum cam size for quiet and smooth cam operation.

For simple–harmonic motion,

$$s = \frac{h}{2} \left(1 - \cos \frac{\pi \theta}{\beta} \right)$$

$$V_c = \frac{V}{\omega} = \frac{\pi h}{2\beta} \sin \frac{\pi \theta}{\beta} .$$

During the lift period, $\beta = 120° = \dfrac{2}{3} \pi$ rad

$$V_{c\max} = \frac{\pi h}{2\beta} = \frac{1.5}{2 \left(\dfrac{2}{3} \pi \right)} = 1.125 \text{ cm.}$$

From Eq. (10-55),

$$e = V_{cmax} = 1.125 \text{ cm.}$$

From Eq. (10-57),

$$r_o = r_b + r_f = \frac{V_{cmax}}{\sin \alpha_c}$$

$$r_o = r_b + 1.0 = \frac{1.125}{\sin 30°}$$

$$r_b = 1.25 \text{ cm.}$$

During the fall period, $\beta = 150°$ or $\dfrac{5}{6} \pi$ rad

$$V_{cmin} = \frac{\pi h}{2\beta} = \frac{1.5}{2\left(\dfrac{5}{6}\pi\right)} = -0.90 \text{ cm.}$$

From Eq. (10-56),

$$e = V_{cmin} = -0.90 \text{ cm}$$

$$\tan \alpha_c = \frac{dV_c}{ds} \; .$$

From Eq. (10-54),

$$\frac{\pi}{\beta} \cot \frac{\pi\theta}{\beta} = \tan \alpha_c$$

$$\cot \frac{\pi\theta}{\beta} = \frac{\beta}{\pi} \tan \alpha_c = \frac{\dfrac{2}{3}\pi}{\pi} \tan 30°.$$

Therefore,

$$\frac{\pi\theta}{\beta} = 69.94° .$$

Substituting the displacement equation and the converted velocity equation of simple–harmonic motion gives

$$S_m = \frac{1.5}{2} (1 - \cos 69.94°) = 0.481 \text{ cm}$$

$$V_{cm} = \frac{1.5\pi}{2 \times \frac{2}{3}\pi} \sin 69.94° = 1.06 \text{ cm.}$$

Then, from Eq. (10-58) we obtain

$$r_o = r_b + 1.0 = \left[\left(\frac{1.06 + 0.90}{\tan 30°} - 0.481 \right)^2 + (-0.90)^2 \right]^{1/2}$$

or

$$r_b = 2.05 \text{ cm.}$$

Since $(r_b)_{\text{lift}} < (r_b)_{\text{fall}}$, $e = 1.125$ cm and $r_b = 1.25$ cm should be the final design choice.

Radial Cam with Swinging Roller Follower

Derivation by the Method of Pole. In Fig. 10-18 a disc cam rotates clockwise about the camshaft O imparting motion to an oscillating roller follower of length ℓ that is pivoted at point Q. The distance O and Q is c. The fixed angle ϕ_0 defines the lowest position of the follower. The pressure angle α is the angle between the common normal NN to the curve at the point of roller contact and BD, the normal to the centerline of the follower arm.

In the position shown, NN cuts the line of centers OQ at the pole I. Since OI and QI are in the same direction, both the cam and the follower will rotate in the same direction. Based on the geometry of Fig. 10-18, the velocity of the follower at point B is

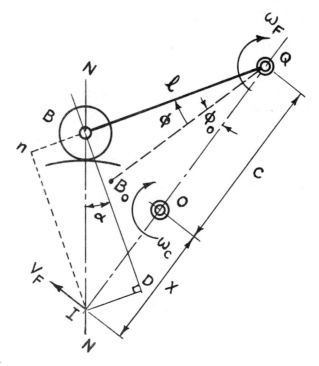

Fig. 10-18.

$$V_F = x\omega_c = (c + x)\,\omega_F \,,$$

where x is the distance OI. ω_F and ω_c represent the angular velocities of the follower and the cam, respectively. From this equation we obtain

$$x = \frac{c\omega_F}{\omega_c - \omega_F} \,. \tag{10-59}$$

Then

$$c + x = c\left(1 + \frac{\omega_F}{\omega_c - \omega_F}\right) = \frac{c\omega_c}{\omega_c - \omega_F}$$

or

$$c + x = \frac{c}{1 - \dfrac{\omega_F}{\omega_c}} \,.$$

Since the angular displacement of the follower is $\phi = f(\theta)$,

$$\frac{d\phi}{d\theta} = \frac{\dfrac{d\phi}{dt}}{\dfrac{d\theta}{dt}} = \frac{\omega_F}{\omega_c} ,$$

from which it follows that

$$c + x = \frac{c}{1 - \dfrac{d\phi}{d\theta}} . \qquad (10\text{-}60)$$

From Fig. 10-18,

$$\tan \alpha = \frac{\overline{ID}}{\overline{BD}} = \frac{\overline{nB}}{\overline{nI}} = \frac{(c + x) \cos (\phi + \phi_o) - \ell}{(c + x) \sin (\phi + \phi_o)}$$

or

$$\tan \alpha = \cot (\phi + \phi_o) - \frac{\ell}{(c + x) \sin (\phi + \phi_o)} .$$

Using Eq. (10-60) yields

$$\tan \alpha = \cot (\phi + \phi_o) - \frac{\ell \left(1 - \dfrac{d\phi}{d\theta}\right)}{c \sin (\phi + \phi_o)} . \qquad (10\text{-}61)$$

Clearly, the radius of the base circle r_o is OB_o. The relation between ϕ_o and r_o is

$$r_o = \sqrt{\ell^2 + c^2 - 2\ell c \cos \phi_o} .$$

In Eq. (10-61) $\dfrac{d\phi}{d\theta}$ is negative if ω_c is counterclockwise. If $\tan \alpha$ is negative, it signifies that the common normal NN lies on the other side of the perpendicular to the follower arm.

Alternative Derivation by Kloomok and Muffley (125). In Fig. 10-19, let

- θ = the angular rotation of the cam measured from a space fixed reference.
- ϕ = the angular rotation of the cam measured from a line joining the cam and the follower roller center.
- c = the distance from the cam center to the follower arm pivot.
- ℓ = the length of the follower arm.
- R = the radius measured from the cam center to the follower roller center.
- λ = the angle between NN and OB'.

Angles ψ, δ, and ϵ are defined as labeled in Fig. 10-19.

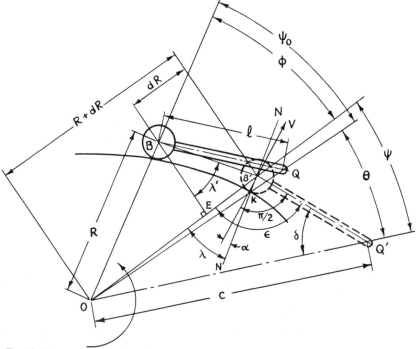

Fig. 10-19.

Let us use kinematic inversion by imagining that the cam is held fixed and the follower arm pivot Q is to rotate clockwise through angle θ to point Q'. Subsequently, the follower roller center B will move to B'. As the follower swings up, the ray from the cam center to the follower roller center will shift slightly.

Hence $\phi \neq 0$.

From Fig. 10-19,

$$\lambda' = \tan^{-1} \frac{B'E}{BE} \ .$$

As $d\phi$ decreases approaching zero as a limit, λ' approaches λ . Thus

$$\lambda = \tan^{-1} \frac{1}{R} \frac{dR}{d\phi} \ . \tag{10-62}$$

From the geometry we also have

$$\alpha = \pm \frac{\pi}{2} \mp \epsilon + \lambda \tag{10-63}$$

$$\phi = \pm \psi_o \mp \psi + \theta \ . \tag{10-64}$$

In Eq. (10-63) and (10-64) the upper sign corresponds to the case of rotating "away" from the follower pivot as in Fig. 10-20a, and the lower sign corresponds to the case of rotating "toward" the pivot as in Fig. 10-20b.

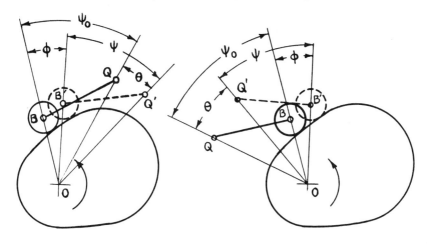

(a)

(b)

Fig. 10-20.

From triangle $OB'Q'$ we can find the expressions for R, ϵ, and ψ

$$R = (\ell^2 + c^2 - 2\ell c \cos \delta)^{1/2} \tag{10-65}$$

$$\epsilon = \sin^{-1}\left(\frac{c}{R}\sin\delta\right) \tag{10-66}$$

$$\psi = \cos^{-1}\left(\frac{c^2 + R^2 - \ell^2}{2Rc}\right). \tag{10-67}$$

Differentiating Eq. (10-65) with respect to θ and taking reciprocals give

$$\frac{d\theta}{dR} = \frac{R}{\ell c \sin\delta \dfrac{d\delta}{d\theta}}. \tag{10-68}$$

Differentiating Eq. (10-67) with respect to R gives

$$\frac{d\psi}{dR} = \frac{c^2 - R^2 - \ell^2}{2R^2 c \sin\psi}. \tag{10-69}$$

Differentiating Eq. (10-64) with respect to R gives

$$\frac{d\phi}{dR} = \frac{d\theta}{dR} + \frac{d\psi}{dR}, \tag{10-70}$$

where the two right side terms are defined in Eqs. (10-68) and (10-69).

Substituting into Eq. (10-63) using Eqs. (10-62), (10-66), and the reciprocal expression of (10-70), we finally obtain

$$\alpha = \pm\frac{\pi}{2} + \sin^{-1}\left(\frac{c}{R}\sin\delta\right) + \tan^{-1} \tag{10-71}$$

$$\left(\frac{1}{\dfrac{R^2}{\ell c \sin\delta \dfrac{d\delta}{d\theta}} - \dfrac{c^2 - R^2 - \ell^2}{2Rc \sin\psi}}\right).$$

In using Eq. (10-71), care must be exercised to distinguish between rotation "away" from the follower pivot (the upper sign) and rotation "toward" the pivot (the lower sign). Eq. (10-71) can be evaluated for a given motion of the follower arm by substituting the appropriate expression for δ and $\dfrac{d\delta}{d\theta}$. For example, if the motion of the follower arm is to be harmonic,

$$\delta = \delta_o + \frac{\tau}{2} \left(1 - \cos \frac{\pi\theta}{\beta} \right),$$

where δ_o is the initial value of δ, and τ is the total angular rotation of the follower arm.

Also note that Eq. (10-71) is more complicated than Eq. (10-60), which was derived by using the method of pole. Other methods for deriving the pressure angle are also available, for example, a method using differential geometry given by Baxter (45).

Design Charts for Maximum Pressure Angle — Radial Cam with Swinging Roller Follower. Again, finding the maximum pressure angle of a radial cam with an oscillating roller follower is an optimization problem of a function with a single independent variable. We may use differential calculus to do this. However, differentiation of either Eq. (10-60) or Eq. (10-71) to compute a maximum yields an unwieldy transcendental equation. Rather than attempting to calculate maxima in this way, we evaluate the equations through computer programming for a given set of parameters, $\ell, c, \tau,$ and β, for which the ratio of $\dfrac{\theta}{\beta}$ is varied from 0 to 1. The individual maxima so determined have been plotted versus $\dfrac{\beta}{\tau}$, with $\dfrac{c}{R_o}$ as a varying parameter. This is shown in the representative chart, Fig. 10-21. For a more extensive collection of these charts the reader should refer to the paper by Kloomok and Muffley (125). A FORTRAN program CAMPA is given in Appendix B for generation of these charts. In these charts, all linear dimensions have been converted to dimensionless form so that they can be applied to mechanisms of any size. The effect of rotation "toward" or "from" the follower arm pivot has been accommodated by plotting two complete sets of curves on each chart.

Example 10-5

To illustrate the use of the design charts, assume that a cam with an oscillating roller follower moves with cycloidal motion for rise between two dwells. Let R_o = 4.0 cm, ℓ = 6.0 cm, c = 6.75 cm, τ = 10°, β = 60°, and let the rotation of the cam be away from the pivot. Then

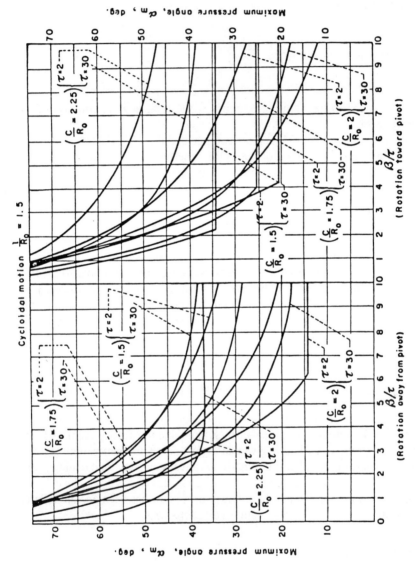

Fig. 10-21. Nomogram for determining maximum pressure angle for cam with swinging roller follower (Kloomok and Muffley).

$$\frac{\ell}{R_o} = 1.5$$

$$\frac{c}{R_o} = 1.69$$

$$\frac{\beta}{\tau} = 6 .$$

It is necessary to interpolate for both $\frac{c}{R_o}$ and τ; however, this interpolation is not critical since an approximate value of the pressure angle is usually sufficient. Chart values from Fig. 10-21 are

$\frac{c}{R_o}$	τ	α_m
1.50	2	41.5°
1.75	2	29.5°
1.50	30	43.0°
1.75	30	33.5°

Interpolation of α_m for $\frac{c}{R_o} = 1.69$ ($\tau = 2$) is

$$\alpha_m = 41.5° - \left[\frac{1.69 - 1.50}{1.75 - 1.50} (41.5 - 29.5) \right] = 32.4° .$$

Interpolation of α_m for $\frac{c}{R_o} = 1.69$ ($\tau = 30$) is

$$\alpha_m = 43.0° - \left[\frac{1.69 - 1.50}{1.75 - 1.50} (43.0 - 33.5) \right] = 35.8° .$$

Finally, interpolation of α_m for $\frac{c}{R_o} = 1.67$ and $\tau = 10$ is

$$\alpha_m = 32.4° + \left[\frac{10 - 2}{30 - 2} (35.8 - 32.4) \right] = 33.4° .$$

The design charts give only the information on α_m. The location of the maximum is not given, nor is it needed for most applications.

It is understood that the motion involves a "rise." For a "fall" motion, the value of α_m can be determined by the same techniques as used for the "rise," provided that the direction of cam rotation is reversed, as illustrated in Fig. 10-22, before using the charts.

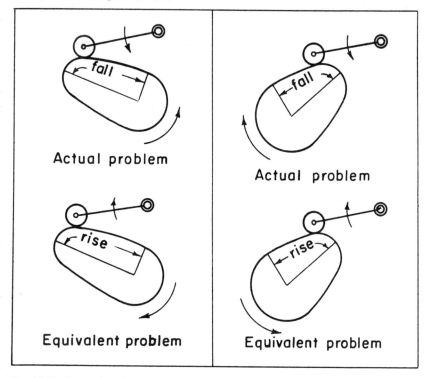

Fig. 10-22. Conversion of "fall" portion of cam to an equivalent "rise" to permit use of the nomogram.

10-7. NUMERICAL SCHEME FOR CALCULATING THE PRESSURE ANGLE WHEN THE CAM PROFILE IS IN TABULAR FORM

Thus far we have assumed that the cam profile can be expressed by a mathematical function, either of the trigonometric or of the polynomial type. Under these circumstances we can analytically calculate the pressure angle based on the derived equations. However, if the cam profile is described graphically or expressed in tabular form, what can we do? In the past, this design was often based on measurements from graphical layouts. When the cam–and–follower system is designed for high–speed applications and for mass production, graphical measurement of the pressure angle is not adequate. With the availability of numerical differentiation techniques and digital computers, we can overcome this difficulty.

Numerical differentiation is the process of calculating the derivatives of a function by means of a set of given values of that function. The problem is solved by representing the function with an interpolation formula and then differentiating this formula as many times as desired.

If the function is given by a table of values for equidistant values of the independent variable, it may be represented by an interpolation formula employing differences. One of the interpolation formulas that gives a high degree of accuracy for the derivative at or near the middle of the tabulated data is Stirling's interpolation formula. In the following material, we will write down Stirling's formula without derivation, and show how it can be differentiated to give the first approximate derivative. One should refer to a standard textbook (99) of numerical analysis for the derivation of Stirling's interpolation formula.

When data are tabulated for uniformly spaced abscissa with spacing h, it is convenient to express the formulations for interpolation and related processes in terms of a difference table. In connection with the difference table (Table 10-1), Stirling's interpolation formula may be written as

$$y = y_i + U \frac{\delta y_{i-1} + \delta y_i}{2} + \frac{U^2}{2} \delta^2 y_{i-1}$$

$$+ \frac{U(U^2 - 1)}{3!} \frac{\delta^3 y_{i-2} - \delta^3 y_{i-1}}{2} + \frac{U^2(U^2 - 1)}{4!} \delta^4 y_{i-2}$$

$$+ \frac{U(U^2 - 1)(U^2 - 2^2)}{5!} \frac{\delta^5 y_{i-3} + \delta^5 y_{i-2}}{2}$$

$$+ \frac{U^2(U^2 - 1)(U^2 - 2^2)}{6!} \delta^6 y_{i-3} + \dots , \tag{10-72}$$

where $U = \dfrac{x - x_i}{h}$.

Differentiating Eq. (10-72) with respect to x gives

Table 10-1. Difference Table

y	δy	$\delta^2 y$	$\delta^3 y$	$\delta^4 y$	$\delta^5 y$	$\delta^6 y$	$\delta^7 y$	$\delta^8 y$
y_{i-4}								
	δy_{i-4}							
y_{i-3}		$\delta^2 y_{i-4}$						
	δy_{i-3}		$\delta^3 y_{i-4}$					
y_{i-2}		$\delta^2 y_{i-3}$		$\delta^4 y_{i-4}$				
	δy_{i-2}		$\delta^3 y_{i-3}$		$\delta^5 y_{i-4}$			
y_{i-1}		$\delta^2 y_{i-2}$		$\delta^4 y_{i-3}$		$\delta^6 y_{i-4}$		
	δy_{i-1}		$\delta^3 y_{i-2}$		$\delta^5 y_{i-3}$		$\delta^7 y_{i-4}$	
y_i		$\delta^2 y_{i-1}$		$\delta^4 y_{i-2}$		$\delta^6 y_{i-3}$		$\delta^8 y_{i-4}$
	δy_i		$\delta^3 y_{i-1}$		$\delta^5 y_{i-2}$		$\delta^7 y_{i-3}$	
y_{i+1}		$\delta^2 y_i$		$\delta^4 y_{i-1}$		$\delta^6 y_{i-2}$		$\delta^8 y_{i-3}$
	δy_{i+1}		$\delta^3 y_i$		$\delta^5 y_{i-1}$		$\delta^7 y_{i-2}$	
y_{i+2}		$\delta^2 y_{i+1}$		$\delta^4 y_i$		$\delta^6 y_{i-1}$		
	δy_{i+2}		$\delta^3 y_{i+1}$		$\delta^5 y_i$			
y_{i+3}		$\delta^2 y_{i+2}$		$\delta^4 y_{i+1}$				
	δy_{i+3}		$\delta^3 y_{i+2}$					
y_{i+4}		$\delta^2 y_{i+3}$						
	δy_{i+4}							
y_{i+5}								

$$\frac{dy}{dx} = \frac{dy}{dU}\frac{dU}{dx} = \frac{1}{h}\frac{dy}{dU}$$

$$= \frac{1}{h}\left[\frac{\delta y_{i-1} + \delta y_i}{2} + U\delta^2 y_{i-1} + \frac{3U^2 - 1}{3!}\frac{\delta^3 y_{i-2} + \delta^3 y_{i-1}}{2}\right.$$

$$+ \frac{4U^3 - 2U}{4!}\delta^4 y_{i-2} + \frac{5U^4 - 15U^2 + 4}{5!}$$

$$\left.\frac{\delta^5 y_{i-3} + \delta^5 y_{i-2}}{2} + \frac{6U^5 - 20U^3 + 8U}{6!}\delta^6 y_{i-3} + \cdots\right].$$

$$(10\text{-}73)$$

For the point $x = x_i$, we have $U = 0$. Hence, upon substitution of this value of U into Eq. (10-73), we obtain

$$\left(\frac{dy}{dx}\right)_{x_i} = \frac{1}{h}\left[\frac{\delta y_{i-1} + \delta y_i}{2} - \frac{1}{6}\frac{\delta^3 y_{i-2} + \delta^3 y_{i-1}}{2}\right.\qquad(10\text{-}74)$$

$$\left.+ \frac{1}{30}\frac{\delta^5 y_{i-3} + \delta^5 y_{i-2}}{2} + \cdots\right].$$

Eq. (10-74) is the approximate formula for finding the derivative that is needed for calculating the cam pressure angle. We will illustrate this in the following example.

Example 10-6

A disc cam, which operates at a uniform speed, imparts motion to a follower. The follower is a reciprocating roller with an offset. During 12° of cam rotation, the follower moves outward 1 cm from rest with cycloidal motion. If the cam prime circle radius is 5 cm and the amount of offset is 1 cm, determine the pressure angle.

For the purpose of demonstrating the accuracy of the numerical method, the kinematic characteristics of cycloidal motion are computed by using the finite difference formula, and the results are then compared with the results obtained from the exact solution. The exact motion, of course, calls for knowing the cycloidal equations, which give the displacement and the velocity of the follower in terms of the cam angular rotation θ. These are

$$s(\theta) = h \left(\frac{\theta}{\beta} - \frac{1}{2\pi} \sin \frac{2\pi\theta}{\beta} \right)$$

$$s'(\theta) = \frac{h}{\beta} \left(1 - \cos \frac{2\pi\theta}{\beta} \right),$$

where h is the follower's stroke, and β is the total angular rotation of the cam. The exact equation for calculating the pressure angle α is Eq. (10-44)

$$\alpha = \tan^{-1} \left(\frac{s' - e}{s + \sqrt{r_o^2 - e^2}} \right),$$

in which $r_o = 5$ cm and $e = 1$ are known quantities.

Based on the initial displacement data, a difference table (Table 10-2) is first constructed. Table 10-3 exhibits the results of the computations. Values of both exact solutions and approximate solutions are given for values of θ, which increase from 0° to 12° by increments of 1° column (3) contains the results of the approximate values of s' (θ) that were computed from Eq. (10-74) using three-term approximation. For instance, when $\theta = 5°$,

$$s' = \frac{ds}{d\theta} = \frac{1}{h} \left[\frac{\delta s_{i-1} + \delta s_i}{2} - \frac{1}{6} \frac{\delta^3 s_{i-2} + \delta^3 s_{i-1}}{2} \right.$$

$$\left. + \frac{1}{30} \frac{\delta^5 s_{i-3} + \delta^5 s_{i-2}}{2} + \ldots \right]$$

$$= \frac{1}{1} \left\{ \frac{1}{2} (0.141588 + 0.162910) \right.$$

$$- \frac{1}{12} [(-0.015610) + (-0.021321)]$$

$$\left. + \frac{1}{60} (0.004186 + 0.005710) \right\}$$

$$= 0.155491 .$$

Table 10-2. Difference Table for Example 10-6

		δ	δ^2	δ^3	δ^4	δ^5	δ^6	δ^7	δ^8
0	0.000000								
		0.003755							
1	0.003755		0.021324						
		0.025079		0.015608					
2	0.028834		0.036932		−0.009895				
		0.062011		0.005713		−0.001531			
3	0.090845		0.042645		−0.011426		0.003060		
		0.104656		−0.005713		0.001529		−0.000403	
4	0.195501		0.036932		−0.009897		0.002657		−0.000730
		0.141588		−0.015610		0.004186		−0.001133	
5	0.337089		0.021322		−0.005711		0.001524		−0.000387
		0.162910		−0.021321		0.005710		−0.001520	
6	0.499999		0.000001		−0.000001		0.000004		−0.000015
		0.162911		−0.021322		0.005714		−0.001535	
7	0.662910		−0.021323		0.005713		−0.001531		0.000413
		0.141588		−0.015609		0.004183		−0.001122	
8	0.804498		−0.036932		0.009896		−0.002653		0.000715
		0.104656		0.005713		0.001530		−0.000407	
9	0.909154		−0.042645		0.011426		−0.003060		
		0.062011		0.005713		−0.001530			
10	0.971165		−0.036932		0.009896				
		0.025079		0.015609					
11	0.996244		−0.021323						
		0.003756							
12	1.000000								

In comparison with the exact value s' $(\theta = 5°) = 0.155502$, listed in column (2), this gives an error of only 0.007%. This high degree of accuracy is more than that required for pressure angle calculations. Knowing the derivative s', the corresponding pressure angle α can be readily calculated. Columns (4) and (5) in Table 10-3 show the exact values and the approximate values of the pressure angle, respectively.

Table 10-3. Numerical Results of Computation for Example 10–6

(1)		(2)	(3)	(4)	(5)
θ (°)	s	s' Exact	s' Approximate	Pressure Angle α (°)	
				Exact	Approximate
0	0.000000	0.000000	0.000000	11.537	11.537
1	0.003755	0.011164	0.013117	11.403	11.381
2	0.028834	0.041666	0.041748	11.005	11.004
3	0.090845	0.083333	0.083333	10.409	10.409
4	0.195501	0.125000	0.124990	9.745	9.745
5	0.337089	0.155502	0.155491	9.162	9.162
6	0.500000	0.166666	0.166646	8.774	8.774
7	0.662910	0.155502	0.155488	8.633	8.633
8	0.804498	0.125000	0.124990	8.722	8.722
9	0.909154	0.083333	0.083333	8.968	8.968
10	0.971165	0.041666	0.041748	9.272	9.271
11	0.996244	0.011164	0.013117	9.521	9.503
12	1.000000	0.000000	0.000000	9.621	9.621

In view of the explicit nature and the high degree of accuracy of the method, once implemented by a computer program the method may be regarded as an efficient alternative method for calculating the cam pressure angle, regardless of whether the displacement profile is described in functional form or in tabular form. For a further description of the method, one should refer to the paper by Chen (44). A FORTRAN program, named PARAD using this numerical method, is included in Appendix B.

11
Cam Radius of Curvature

11-1. INTRODUCTION

As discussed in Chapter 10, the pressure angle and the cam size are directly related, and the cam size should be as small as possible. As the cam size is reduced, both the pressure angle and the "radius of curvature," which is another important cam geometric parameter, tend to approach their limiting values so that, in most cases, they both are the critical design parameters. The minimum radius of curvature must be larger than a prescribed minimum to obtain the required motion of the follower and to ensure that the compressive contact stresses at the cam–follower interface are not excessive.

11-2. RADIUS OF CURVATURE OF A CURVE

The radius of curvature of a curve is a measure of the rapidity with which the curve changes direction. Suppose that a curve is given by the equation $y = f(x)$ and that f has a continuous second derivative. As shown in Fig. 11-1, at a particular point $P_0(x_0, y_0)$ the tangent to the curve makes an angle ϕ with the positive x direction. From the definition of a derivative, we know that $\phi = f'(x_0)$ or that at a point $P(x, y)$

$$\phi(x) = \tan^{-1} [f'(x)] .$$

The way ϕ changes as we move along a curve is a measure of the sharpness of the curve. Therefore, the curvature k is the rate of change of the angle ϕ with respect to the arc length s. That is

$$k = \frac{d\phi}{ds} .$$

The radius of curvature ρ of an arc at a point is defined as the reciprocal of the absolute value of the curvature at that point; that is

$$\rho = \frac{1}{|k|} .$$

The circle of curvature of an arc at a point P is that circle passing through P that has a radius equal to ρ, and whose center C lies on the concave side of the curve along the normal through P.

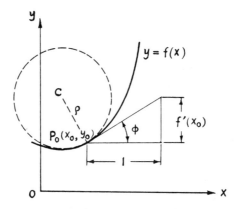

Fig. 11-1.

From calculus we know that if the curve is given in the Cartesian coordinate form $y = f(x)$, the radius of curvature is

$$\rho = \frac{\{ 1 + [f'(x)]^2 \}^{3/2}}{f''(x)} . \qquad (11\text{-}1)$$

If a curve is given in polar coordinate form $r = f(\theta)$, the radius of curvature is given by the formula

$$\rho = \frac{\{ f^2(\theta) + [f'(\theta)]^2 \}^{3/2}}{[f(\theta)]^2 + 2[f'(\theta)]^2 - f(\theta)f''(\theta)} . \qquad (11\text{-}2)$$

It can be shown that the magnitude of the curvature k or the radius of curvature ρ of a curve is an intrinsic property of the curve and does not depend on the coordinate system.

It is clear that each arc has two possible orientations, depending upon whether we go along it in one direction or in the opposite direction. However, once we choose an orientation, the direction of positive arc length is decided and, along with it, the sign of the curvature.

As shown in Fig. 11-2, if ϕ is increasing so that the curve is "turning to the left" as the parameter increases, then k is positive; k is negative if ϕ is decreasing. This is equivalent to saying that the concave side of the curve is on the left if $k > 0$ and is on the right if $k < 0$.

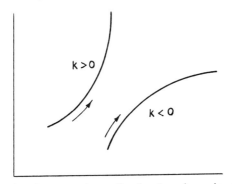

Fig. 11-2. Sign convention of curvature (arrow direction shows increasing parameter).

11-3. UNDERCUTTING PHENOMENON

When the follower or cam cutter cannot follow the desired cam path, a condition known as "undercutting" will result.

Undercutting of Cam with Roller Follower

Fig. 11-3 illustrates the undercutting conditions of a cam with a roller follower. Point (a) in Fig. 11-3 shows a proper operating condition without undercutting. The radius of curvature of the convex path of the follower is ρ, and the cam will at that point have a pitch curve radius of curvature of $r_o = \rho - r_f$.

With the convex curve at point (b) of Fig. 11-3, we have the conditions $\rho = r_f$ and $r_0 = 0$. Therefore, the actual cam will have a sharp corner. Theoretically, the stresses at this sharp corner are infinite in magnitude, and the cam surface wears rapidly. This situation should thus be avoided. At point (c) in Fig. 11-3 it is shown again with a convex curve for the case where $\rho < r_f$. This case is not possible because undercutting will result, and the actual motion of the roller follower will deviate from the intended one. An auxiliary enlarged view may be used to explain this situation. Originally, we intend to constrain a roller follower having a radius $r_f = AA_1$ along a motion profile ABCD, which contains a segment BC with a radius $\rho = BJ$ less than r_f. The roller, moving from A to B, passes through point C_1, which is needed later to constrain the follower to point C. Also, the roller, moving from C to D, passes through point B_1, which is needed earlier to constrain it to point B. The best the cam can do in this situation is to constrain the center of the roller to a path AI_1I_2D, which contains a segment I_1I_2 with I as the center and r_f as the radius. The result is an unintended undercutting from I_1 to I_2.

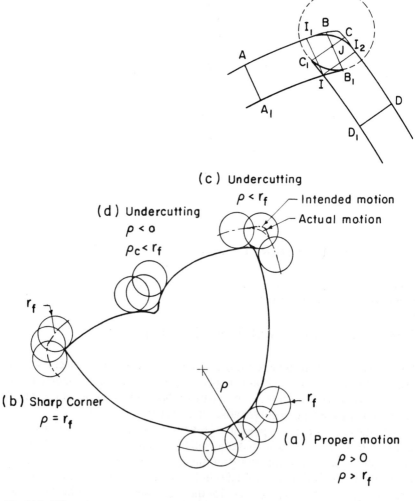

Fig. 11-3. Effect of curvature on cam and roller follower.

Undercutting is not likely to occur on the concave portion of the cam curve, but care should be exercised in ensuring that the radius of curvature of the actual cam curve is not equal to or less than the radius of the roller. This condition would occur if there is a concavity or cusp on the displacement curve, such as the one shown at point (d) in Fig. 10-3.

With these concepts in mind we can make the following observations and suggestions:

- Examination of Eq. (11-1) shows that radius of curvature ρ and the acceleration factor $f''(x)$ are inversely proportional to each other, and that any reasonably large increase in the acceleration factor $f''(x)$ with little increase in the slope $f'(x)$ will result in a decrease in the radius of curvature. This may explain why the minimum radius of curvature usually occurs in the vicinity of the region where the negative acceleration is a maximum.
- The radius of curvature decreases with decreases in the prime circle radius of the roller follower. The radius of curvature must be greater than the follower roller radius. Use a roller size that is as small as possible.
- To minimize wear, increase the radius of curvature as far as practicable. This is the easiest procedure to alleviate the condition of undercutting or sharp corners, but it generally has a practical limitation. As a rule of thumb, ρ equal to three times r_f is generally recommended for proper cam operation.
- The curvature effect is not as critical in internal cams as in external cams. In an internal cam the contact stresses due to a given force are smaller than in an external convex cam. Therefore, employ an internal cam if it is adequate.
- Other cam dimensional parameters (such as the amount of offset in cams with reciprocating followers and the pivot location, and the follower length in cams with swinging followers) will also affect the radius of curvature. But their relationships are complicated, and their effects are not critical.

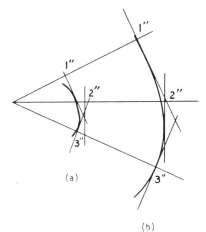

(a)

(b)

Fig. 11-4. Undercutting with flat–faced follower.

Undercutting of Cam with Flat–Faced Follower

In Fig. 11-4 (a) shows the face of a flat–faced follower in its relative positions $1''$, $2''$, and $3''$, and the cam drawn tangent to these lines. The cam profile, drawn tangent to the flat–faced follower, cannot reach tangency to the face at position $2''$. We may say that the follower positions $1''$ and $3''$ eliminate or undercut position $2''$. The cam thus developed is incapable of driving the follower according to the originally intended movement. To remedy this, we increase the cam size until the undercutting phenomenon disappears. This is depicted in Fig. 11-4 (b).

11-4. MINIMUM RADIUS OF CURVATURE OF CONCAVE CAM — RECIPROCATING ROLLER FOLLOWER

In Fig. 11-5 we observe that the radial distance to any point of the pitch curve is

$$r(\theta) = r_0 + s(\theta) , \tag{11-3}$$

where r_0 is the radius of the prime circle, and s is the follower motion, which is a function of cam angle θ.

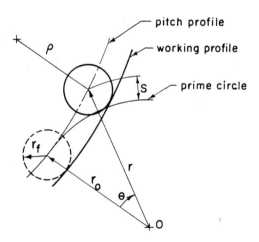

Fig. 11-5. Typical concave cam.

Substituting Eq. (11-3) into Eq. (11-2) gives the radius of curvature of the pitch profile

$$\rho = \frac{\left[(r_0 + s)^2 + \left(\dfrac{ds}{d\theta} \right)^2 \right]^{3/2}}{(r_0 + s)^2 + 2\left(\dfrac{ds}{d\theta} \right)^2 - (r_0 + s)\dfrac{d^2 s}{d\theta^2}} \qquad (11\text{-}4)$$

By inspection of Eq. (11-4) we can see that ρ is usually a minimum at the same point on the profile as where s is maximum, that is, where $\dfrac{ds}{d\theta} = 0$. In this case, the minimum radius of curvature of the pitch profile is

$$\rho_{\min} = \frac{r^2}{r - \left(\dfrac{d^2 s}{d\theta^2} \right)_{\text{at } \theta = 0}} , \qquad (11\text{-}5)$$

or, in terms of an independent variable t,

$$\rho_{\min} = \frac{r^2}{r - \dfrac{1}{\omega^2}\left(\dfrac{d^2 s}{dt^2} \right)_{\text{at } t = 0}} . \qquad (11\text{-}6)$$

Example 11-1

A radial roller follower is actuated by a lobe cam rotating at a uniform angular velocity ω. It is required that the stroke of the follower be $\pm b$ about the mean position with simple harmonic motion for one–third a revolution of the cam. Three motion cycles of the follower thus occur for one complete revolution of the cam. If the radius of the roller is $2.4b$, determine the minimum size of the cam.

The displacement of the follower can be expressed as

$$r = r_o + b \cos 3\omega t.$$

Fig. 11-6 shows the curve of follower displacement versus cam rotation. For an arbitrary value of $r_o > b$, we see that the curve has its minimum radius of curva-

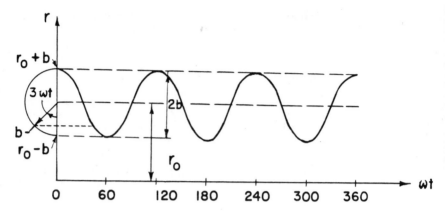

Fig. 11-6.

ture at the point where r is a maximum and equal to $(r_o + b)$, the corresponding value of ωt being $0°$, $120°$, and $240°$.

Substituting into Eq. (11-6) gives

$$\rho_{min} = \frac{r^2}{r + \dfrac{1}{\omega^2}(9b\omega^2)} .$$

To avoid undercutting we must have $\rho_{min} > r_f$.

For the prescribed value of the roller radius $r_f = 2.4b$ the minimum size of the cam can be obtained by setting $\rho_{min} = 2.4b$ in the above equation. Thus

$$(2.4b)r + (9b)(2.4b) - r^2 = 0$$

or

$$r^2 - 2.4br - 21.6b^2 = 0 .$$

Solving for the two roots of the quadratic equation in r we obtain

$$r = 6.0b \quad \text{positive root}$$

$$r = -3.6b \quad \text{negative root} .$$

The positive root solution corresponds to the case of an external cam (the roller runs on the outside of the cam profile), while the negative root solution

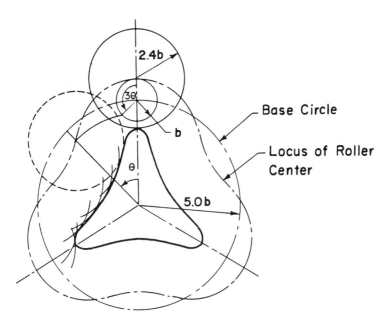

Fig. 11-7. External lobe cam for example problem 11–1.

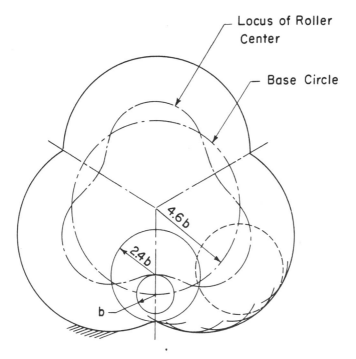

Fig. 11-8. Internal lobe cam for example problem 11–1.

corresponds to an internal cam. Figs. 11-7 and 11-8 show the layouts of these two cases.

The maximum values of r_o for the two cases are therefore

$$r_o = 6.0b - b = 5.0b$$

and

$$r_o = -3.6b - b = -4.6b.$$

11-5. ANALYTICAL DETERMINATION OF RADIUS OF CURVATURE

As we can see from the discussion up to this point, the condition of cam undercutting is attributable to the radius of curvature of the cam, the follower acceleration, and the cam size. In the case of (a) concave cams with reciprocating followers and (b) reciprocating cams with flat–faced followers, the determination of the maximum radius of curvature is a simple matter. However, general derivations of the radius of curvature for reciprocating followers with offset and for swinging followers are mathematically involved. Textbooks on kinematics do not even mention them.

We also know that the easiest procedure to avoid undercutting and sharp corners is to employ a larger cam, but we do not want to have a cam with need-less bulk either. In the past, this design step was often based on measurements from graphical layouts or by a hit–or–miss type of approach, depending heavily on guesswork, intuition, and experience. When designing cams for modern automatic machines, especially for mass production, graphical measurement of the radius of curvature is inadequate. It is often desirable to know accurately the radius of curvature so that we can find the corresponding magnitudes of the contact stresses between the cam and the follower. With the availability of digital computers, once the equations are established and computer programs are implemented, computations of the radius of curvature become merely a simple routine, regardless of the complexity of the mathematics involved in the derivation.

In this section we will analytically derive the radius of curvature for the case of offset reciprocating followers and swinging followers by different methods. Different methods of derivation give different expressions for the radius of curvature, but the final answers are the same.

Derivation of Radius of Curvature by the Method of Pole

Offset Reciprocating Roller Follower. As shown in Fig. 11-9, a cam has a prime circle radius r_o and an offset e. Counterclockwise rotation of the cam about cam center 0 through an angle θ causes the follower to travel a distance s along a straight line. Angle B_0BI is the pressure angle α. The common normal line NN cuts the line of centers OQ at the pole I. If we let $OI = x$, then from section 10-6 we know that

$$V_f = \frac{ds}{dt} = \frac{ds}{d\theta}\frac{d\theta}{dt} = \omega_c \frac{ds}{d\theta} , \qquad (10\text{-}43)$$

and that the acceleration of the follower is

$$A_f = \frac{dV_f}{dt} = \frac{d}{d\theta}\left(\omega_c \frac{ds}{d\theta}\right)\frac{d\theta}{dt} = \omega_c^2 \frac{d^2s}{d\theta^2} . \qquad (11\text{-}7)$$

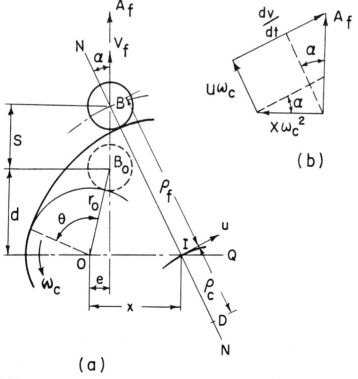

(a)

(b)

Fig. 11-9.

Using the method of pole, we consider the cam and the follower as two rotating bodies in contact. In Fig. 11-9a point B is the center of curvature of the follower roller, and point D is assumed to be the center of curvature of the cam. Note that B, D, and I are all on the common normal line NN. Let ρ_f and ρ_c represent the radii of curvature of the roller and cam, respectively. The pole velocity for pure rolling contact is found (244) to be

$$U = \frac{\rho_f \omega_c}{1 + \dfrac{\rho_f}{\rho_c}} \tag{11-8}$$

where U is directed as shown in Fig. 11-9a.

Based on the acceleration polygon shown in Fig. 11-9b, we have

$$\frac{U\omega_c + x\omega_c^2 \sin \alpha}{\cos \alpha} = A_f \tag{11-9}$$

or

$$A_f \cos \alpha = U\omega_c + x\omega_c^2 \sin \alpha = \frac{\rho_f \omega_c^2}{1 + \dfrac{\rho_f}{\rho_c}} + x\omega_c^2 \sin \alpha \, ,$$

from which

$$\frac{A_f}{\omega_c^2} \cos \alpha = \frac{\rho_f \rho_c}{\rho_f + \rho_c} + x \sin \alpha \, . \tag{11-10}$$

From the geometry of Fig. 11-9(a) we can also write

$$\rho_f \cos \alpha = s + \sqrt{r_o^2 - e^2} \, . \tag{11-11}$$

Designating the radius of curvature of the cam pitch curve by $\rho = \rho_f + \rho_c$ and using Eqs. (10-43), (11-7), (11-11) and some algebra, we obtain

$$\frac{1}{\rho} = \Gamma[\, 1 + \Gamma(s' \sin \alpha - s'' \cos \alpha)\,] \, , \tag{11-12}$$

where $\Gamma = \dfrac{\cos \alpha}{s + \sqrt{r_o^2 - e^2}}$

$$s' = \frac{ds}{d\theta}$$

$$s'' = \frac{d^2s}{d\theta^2} \ .$$

In using Eq. (11-12), the following sign conventions are important:

$$s' \text{ is } \begin{pmatrix} \text{positive} \\ \text{negative} \end{pmatrix} \text{ when the cam rotates } \begin{pmatrix} \text{counterclockwise} \\ \text{clockwise} \end{pmatrix}.$$

$$\sin \alpha \begin{pmatrix} \text{positive} \\ \text{negative} \end{pmatrix} \text{ if } \tan \alpha \text{ in Eq. (10-44) is } \begin{pmatrix} \text{positive} \\ \text{negative} \end{pmatrix}.$$

Positive ρ refers to a convex pitch profile; negative ρ refers to concave pitch profile. The radius of curvature of the working profile is $\rho - r_f$ for a convex profile and $\rho + r_f$ for a concave one.

As a special case, when the follower is radial, $e = O$, and $d = r_o$. Using Eq. (10-45), the pressure angle may be eliminated from Eq. (11-12) to give

$$\rho = \frac{\left[(r_o + s)^2 + \left(\frac{ds}{d\theta} \right)^2 \right]^{3/2}}{(r_o + s)^2 + 2 \left(\frac{ds}{d\theta} \right)^2 - (r_o + s) \frac{d^2s}{d\theta^2}} \ ,$$

which is the standard expression of radius of curvature in the polar coordinate system, Eq. (11-4). We could have written this directly. It may serve as a double check here.

Swinging Roller Follower. In Fig. 11-10(a) a cam rotates clockwise about cam center O, transmitting motion to a swinging roller follower of length ℓ pivoted at point Q. The center–to–center distance OQ is c. Angle ϕ_o defines the initial position of the follower. Angle DBI is the pressure angle α. The common normal NN cuts the line of centers OQ at the pole I. Consequently, both cam and followers will rotate in the same direction. Designating OI by x from section 10-6, we have

$$x = \frac{c\omega_f}{\omega_c - \omega_f} \ , \tag{10-59}$$

and

$$c + x = \frac{c}{1 - \dfrac{d\phi}{d\theta}} . \tag{10-60}$$

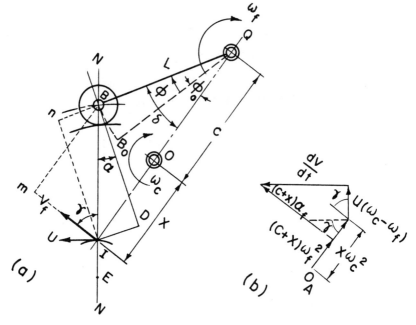

Fig. 11-10.

Consider the cam and the follower as two bodies in direct contact. In Fig. 11-10 (a) point B is the center of curvature of the follower roller, and point E is assumed to be the center of curvature of the cam. Note again that these three points (B, E, and I) are on the common normal NN. Regard $\rho_f = BI$ and $\rho_c = EI$ as the radii of curvature of the follower roller and the cam, respectively, and note that both are directed quantities.

The pole velocity for pure rolling contact in this case is

$$U = \frac{\rho_f (\dot{\omega}_c - \omega_f)}{1 + \dfrac{\rho_f}{\rho_c}} , \tag{11-13}$$

where U is directed downward and perpendicular to NN, as shown in Fig. 11-10 (a). Because $\omega_c > \omega_f$, $(\omega_c - \omega_f)$ is clockwise.

From the acceleration polygon shown in Fig. 11-10 (b), projection of the acceleration vectors along the common normal results in the relationship

$$(c + x)\dot{\omega}_f \cos \gamma = U(\omega_c - \omega_f) + [\, x\omega_c^2 - (c + x)\omega_f^2 \,] \sin \gamma . \qquad (11\text{-}14)$$

In the first term of the right–hand side of Eq. (11-14), we know from Eq. (10-59) that

$$\omega_c - \omega_f = \omega_c - \frac{x}{c + x}\,\omega_c = \frac{c}{c + x}\,\omega_c .$$

This, together with Eq. (11-13), gives

$$U(\omega_c - \omega_f) = \frac{\rho_f}{1 + \dfrac{\rho_f}{\rho_c}}\,(\omega_c - \omega_f)^2 \qquad (11\text{-}15)$$

$$= \frac{\rho_f \rho_c}{\rho_f + \rho_c}\left(\frac{c}{c + x}\right)^2 \omega_c^2$$

$$= \rho_f - \frac{\rho_f^2}{\rho_f + \rho_c}\left(\frac{c}{c + x}\right)^2 \omega_c^2 .$$

Again using Eq. (10-59), the second term of the right–hand side of Eq. (11-14) becomes

$$x\omega_c^2 - (c + x)\,\omega_f^2 = x\omega_c^2 - x\omega_c\left(\frac{x\omega_c}{c + x}\right) \qquad (11\text{-}16)$$

$$= \left(\frac{cx}{c + x}\right)\omega_c^2 .$$

Designating the radius of curvature of the cam pitch curve by $\rho = (\rho_f + \rho_c)$ and dividing Eq. (11-14) by ω_c^2 after substituting Eqs. (11-15) and (11-16) into Eq. (11-14), we obtain

$$\frac{1}{\rho} = \frac{\rho_f \left(\dfrac{c}{c+x}\right)^2 + \dfrac{cx}{c+x} \sin\gamma - (c+x)\dfrac{d^2\phi}{d\theta^2}\cos\gamma}{\rho_f^{\,2}\left(\dfrac{c}{c+x}\right)^2} ,$$

(11-17)

in which we have used the relationship $\dfrac{\dot\omega_f}{\omega_c^{\,2}} = \dfrac{d^2\phi}{d\theta^2}$.

Designating the angle $(\phi_o + \phi)$ by δ, with the aid of the triangle QIn in Fig. 11-10 (a) we can write

$$BI = \rho_f = \frac{(c+x)\sin\alpha}{\cos\alpha}$$

(11-18)

and also

$$\rho_f = \frac{(c+x)\cos\delta - L}{\sin\alpha} .$$

(11-19)

Equating these two expressions gives

$$L = (c+x)\,[\,\cos\delta - \sin\delta\tan\alpha\,] .$$

(11-20)

Referring to the triangle BIm in Fig. 11-10 (a) and using Eq. (11-18) yield

$$\cos\gamma = \frac{L\sin\delta}{\rho_f} = \frac{L\sin\delta\cos\alpha}{(c+x)\sin\delta} = \frac{L\cos\alpha}{c+x} .$$

(11-21)

Since $\gamma = \delta + \alpha$,

$$\sin\gamma = \sin\delta\cos\alpha + \cos\delta\sin\alpha .$$

(11-22)

Substituting Eqs. (11-18), (11-20), (11-21), and (11-22) into Eq. (11-17) leads to

$$\frac{1}{\rho} = \frac{\cos\alpha}{c\sin\delta} + \frac{Lx}{c(c+x)^2}\frac{\sin\alpha\cos^2\alpha}{\sin^2\delta} - \frac{L\dfrac{d^2\phi}{d\theta^2}\cos^3\alpha}{c^2\sin^2\delta} .$$

Finally, using Eqs. (10-59) and (10-60) in the above expression, we obtain

$$\frac{1}{\rho} = \lambda \{ 1 + \lambda [(1 - \phi') \phi' \sin \alpha - \phi'' \cos \alpha] \} , \qquad (11\text{-}23)$$

where

$$\lambda = \frac{\cos \alpha}{c \sin \alpha} \quad \text{with } \delta = \phi_o + \phi$$

$$\phi' = \frac{d\phi}{d\theta}$$

$$\phi'' = \frac{d^2\phi}{d\theta^2} .$$

In using Eq. (11-23), the following sign convention should be observed:

ϕ' is $\begin{pmatrix} \text{negative} \\ \text{positive} \end{pmatrix}$ when the cam and the follower are in the $\begin{pmatrix} \text{same} \\ \text{opposite} \end{pmatrix}$

direction of rotation during the outward motion stroke.

$\sin \alpha$ is $\begin{pmatrix} \text{positive} \\ \text{negative} \end{pmatrix}$ when $\tan \alpha$ in Equation (10-61) is $\begin{pmatrix} \text{positive} \\ \text{negative} \end{pmatrix}$.

When ρ is positive, the pitch curve is convex and conversely.

Reciprocating Flat-Faced Follower. In Fig. 11-11 C is the center of curvature of the cam at the point of contact P with the flat–faced follower. Point I is the pole and is located at the intersection between the common normal NN and the line of center OQ. Note that in this case the pressure angle is zero.

The radius of curvature ρ of point P of the cam profile is expressed by

$$\rho = s + r_b + (\overline{IC}) , \qquad (11\text{-}24)$$

where s is the displacement of the follower from its initial position, and r_b is the base circle radius of the cam. Using the concept of pole, if we let $x = OI$, then

$$V_f = \omega_c x$$

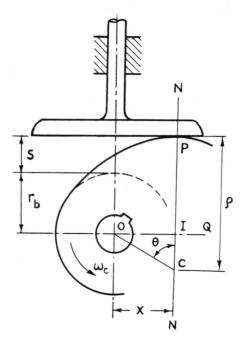

Fig. 11-11.

or

$$x = \frac{V_f}{\omega_c} = \frac{ds}{d\theta} \quad .$$

From Fig. 11-11 we can also write

$$x = (\overline{OC}) \sin \theta \ .$$

The acceleration of the follower is

$$A_f = \frac{d}{dt}(x\omega_c) = \frac{d}{dt}[\,(\overline{OC})\omega_c \sin \theta\,] = (\overline{OC})\omega_c^2 \cos \theta = (\overline{IC})\omega_c^2$$

or $$\overline{IC} = \frac{A_f}{\omega_c^2} \quad .$$

Substituting this into Eq. (11-24) gives the rather simple expression of the radius of curvature of the cam profile

$$\rho = s + r_b + \frac{A_f}{\omega_c^2} \,, \qquad (11\text{-}25)$$

where A_f is positive if it is directed away from the cam.

Swinging Flat–Faced Follower. The case of the swinging flat–faced follower shown in Fig. 11-12 is similar to that shown in Fig. 11-10 for a swinging roller follower. The only difference between the two is that in the flat–faced follower case the pressure angle is zero, and length of swinging arm L is not a constant. Without further elaboration, the steps of the derivation can be outlined as follows.

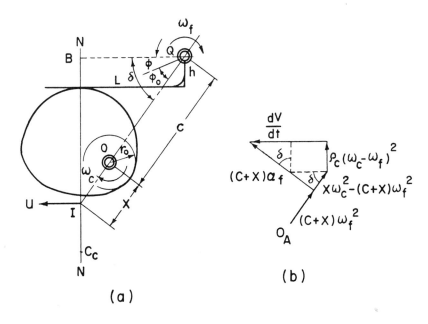

Fig. 11-12.

Locating the pole I as usual and setting $x = OI$, we may write

$$\frac{x}{c + x} = \frac{\omega_f}{\omega_c} = \frac{d\phi}{d\theta} \qquad (11\text{-}26)$$

$$\frac{c}{c + x} = 1 - \frac{d\phi}{d\theta}$$

or

$$c + x = \frac{c}{1 - \dfrac{d\phi}{d\theta}} \tag{10-60}$$

$$\frac{d^2\phi}{d\theta^2} = \frac{\dot{\omega}_f}{\omega_c^2} \ . \tag{11-27}$$

From the acceleration polygon shown in Fig. 11-12(b)

$$(c + x)\dot{\omega}_f = [\, x\omega_c^2 - (c + x)\omega_f^2 \,] \tan \delta + \frac{\rho_c(\omega_c - \omega_f)^2}{\cos \delta} \ . \tag{11-28}$$

Making use of Eqs. (11-26) and (10-60),

$$(c + x)\dot{\omega}_f = \frac{c}{1 - \dfrac{d\phi}{d\theta}} \dot{\omega}_f \tag{11-29}$$

$$x\omega_c^2 - (c + x)\omega_f^2 = x\omega_c^2 - \frac{(c + x)x^2}{(c + x)^2}\omega_c^2$$

$$= \frac{xc}{c + x}\omega_c^2$$

$$= c\frac{d\phi}{d\theta}\omega_c^2 \tag{11-30}$$

$$\rho_c(\omega_c - \omega_f)^2 = \rho_c\left(1 - \frac{d\phi}{d\theta}\right)^2\omega_c^2 \ . \tag{11-31}$$

Substituting Eqs. (11-29), (11-30), and (11-31) into Eq. (11-28) gives

$$\frac{c\dot{\omega}_f}{1 - \dfrac{d\phi}{d\theta}} \cos \delta = c\frac{d\phi}{d\theta}\omega_c^2 \sin \delta + \rho_c\left(1 - \frac{d\phi}{d\theta}\right)^2\omega_c^2.$$

Using Eq. (11-27), the explicit expression of ρ_c becomes

$$\rho_c = \frac{c}{1 - \left(\dfrac{d\phi}{d\theta}\right)^3} \frac{d^2\phi}{d\theta^2} \cos \delta - \frac{c}{1 - \left(\dfrac{d\phi}{d\theta}\right)^2} \frac{d\phi}{d\theta} \sin \delta \,. \qquad (11\text{-}32)$$

From Fig. 11-12(a),

$$\rho = \rho_c + (c + x) \sin \delta \qquad (11\text{-}33)$$

$$L = (c + x) \cos \delta \,. \qquad (11\text{-}34)$$

Therefore,

$$L = \frac{c}{1 - \phi'} \cos \delta \,, \qquad (11\text{-}35)$$

and $\quad \rho = \dfrac{c}{(1 - \phi')^2} \left[\phi'' \dfrac{\cos \delta}{1 - \phi'} + (1 - 2\phi') \sin \delta \right] - h \,, \qquad (11\text{-}36)$

where $\delta \quad = \phi + \phi_o$

$$\phi' \quad = \frac{d\phi}{d\theta}$$

$$\phi'' \quad = \frac{d^2\phi}{d\theta^2} \quad .$$

In Eqs. (11-35) and (11-36) ϕ is positive when ω_c and ω_f are in the same direction during the rise; otherwise, it is negative. The radius of curvature at all points on the cam can be increased by increasing r_o and c. The relation between r_o, ϕ_o, and c is given by

$$\sin \phi_o = \frac{r_o + h}{c} \,.$$

Derivation of Radius of Curvature by Complex Variable Method

The complex variable method devised by Raven (188) requires the use of "independent position equations" to describe the position of a point on a mechanism as a function of the geometry of the system and of the desired motion, and the successive differentiation of the independent position equations to obtain the kinematic information from which the desired unknown parameters may be derived. When the method is applied to the analysis of cams, the unknown parameters are the pressure angle and the radius of curvature. We will show the application of this method for the following two cases only.

Reciprocating Roller Follower. In Fig. 11-13 the follower roller center B is offset an amount h from the cam center O. Point C is the center of curvature of the pitch curve, and ρ is the radius of curvature of the pitch curve. The length R is the distance from the cam center O to the point C. The pressure angle is denoted by α.

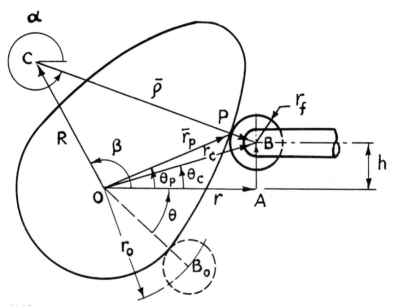

Fig. 11-13.

Given the displacement function

$$r = r_o + f(\theta) ,$$

where r_o is the minimum value of r, the two independent position equations for the trace point B are

$$\bar{r}_c = \overline{OC} + \overline{CB} = Re^{i\beta} + \rho e^{i\alpha} \qquad (11\text{-}37)$$

$$\bar{r}_c = \overline{OA} + \overline{AB} = r + ih, \qquad (11\text{-}38)$$

where i is the complex number. Equating the right–hand sides of Eqs. (11-37) and (11-38), using the trigonometric identity $e^{i\theta} = \cos \theta + i \sin \theta$, and separating the real and the imaginary components, one finds that

$$r = R \cos \beta + \rho \cos \alpha \qquad (11\text{-}39)$$

$$h = R \sin \beta + \rho \sin \alpha . \qquad (11\text{-}40)$$

Substituting $r = r_o + f(\theta)$ into Eq. (11-39) and differentiating Eqs. (11-39) and (11-40) with respect to θ give

$$f'(\theta) = - R \sin \beta \frac{d\beta}{d\theta} - \rho \sin \alpha \frac{d\alpha}{d\theta} \qquad (11\text{-}41)$$

$$O = R \cos \beta \frac{d\beta}{d\theta} + \rho \cos \alpha \frac{d\alpha}{d\theta} . \qquad (11\text{-}42)$$

For an infinitesimal rotation of the cam, ρ may be considered to remain constant. Thus point C and distance R may be regarded as fixed to the cam for an incremental rotation $d\theta$. Therefore, the magnitude of $d\beta$ is equal to $d\theta$, and since β decreases as θ increases, it follows that

$$\frac{d\beta}{d\theta} = - 1 .$$

Substituting this into the foregoing equations leads to

$$f'(\theta) = R \sin \beta - \rho \sin \alpha \frac{d\alpha}{d\theta} \qquad (11\text{-}43)$$

$$0 = R \cos \beta + \rho \cos \alpha \frac{d\alpha}{d\theta} . \qquad (11\text{-}44)$$

Eliminating $\frac{d\alpha}{d\theta}$ from this pair of equations, we obtain

$$f'(\theta) = R \sin \beta - R \tan \alpha \cos \beta . \qquad (11\text{-}45)$$

Substituting Eqs. (11-39) and (11-40) into Eq. (11-45) and solving for the pressure angle α yield

$$\tan \alpha = \frac{h - f'(\theta)}{r} .$$
(11-46)

The position of point P on the cam working profile is

$$\bar{r}_p = r_p e^{i\theta_p} = r + ih - r_f e^{i\alpha} .$$

To measure point P from the reference station of the cam, it is necessary to rotate vector $\bar{r}_p$ through angle θ. Thus the general equation for a point on the working profile with respect to the reference position of the cam is

$$r_p e^{i(\theta + \theta_p)} = (r + ih - r_f e^{i\alpha}) e^{i\theta}$$

$$= [(Re)^2 + (\vartheta m)^2]^{1/2} e^{i\left[\theta + \tan^{-1} \frac{(\vartheta m)}{(Re)} \right]} ,$$
(11-47)

where $Re = r - r_f \cos \alpha$

$\vartheta m = h - r_f \sin \alpha .$

To determine the radius of curvature ρ, first differentiate Eq. (11-46) with respect to θ. Thus

$$r \sec^2 \alpha \frac{d\alpha}{d\theta} + \tan \alpha f'(\theta) = - f''(\theta) .$$

The term $\dfrac{d\alpha}{d\theta}$ may be eliminated from this expression by substitution from Eq. (11-44). Then, with the aid of Eqs. (11-39) and (11-46), one can obtain the following expression for ρ :

(11-48)

$$\rho = \frac{\{ [h - f'(\theta)]^2 + r^2 \}^{3/2}}{r^2 + [h - f'(\theta)] \{ 2[h - f'(\theta)] - h \} - r[f''(\theta)]} .$$

Swinging Roller Follower. In Fig. 11-14, O is the cam center, and Q is the swinging follower pivot. The radius of curvature of the pitch profile is designated by ρ, while its direction is governed by β. The dimensions a, b, ℓ, and r_f are all given. The angular displacement of the swinging arm is ϕ, which is given by the relation

$$\phi = \phi_o + f(\theta) \, ,$$

where ϕ_o is the value of ϕ when the reference line OK on the cam has rotated through angle θ to coincide with the x–axis. $f(\theta)$ is the desired motion function.

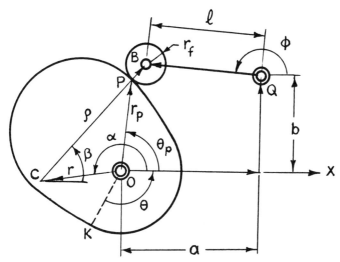

Fig. 11-14.

Referring to Fig. 11-14, the position equations for the roller center B are

$$\bar{r}_B = re^{i\alpha} + \rho e^{i\beta} \tag{11-49}$$

$$\bar{r}_B = a + ib + \ell e^{i\phi} \, . \tag{11-50}$$

Equating the right–hand sides of Eqs. (11-49) and (11-50), and separating the real and imaginary components, one finds that

$$r \cos \alpha + \rho \cos \beta = a + \ell \cos \phi \tag{11-51}$$

$$r \sin \alpha + \rho \sin \beta = b + \ell \sin \phi \tag{11-52}$$

Differentiating Eqs. (11-51) and (11-52) with respect to θ, and noting as before that

$$\frac{d\alpha}{d\theta} = -1$$

$$\frac{d\phi}{d\theta} = f'(\theta) \, ,$$

one finds that

$$r \sin \alpha - \rho \sin \beta \, \frac{d\beta}{d\theta} = - \ell f'(\theta) \sin \phi \tag{11-53}$$

$$- r \cos \alpha + \rho \cos \beta \, \frac{d\beta}{d\theta} = \ell f'(\theta) \cos \phi . \tag{11-54}$$

Eliminating $\dfrac{d\beta}{d\theta}$ from these two equations, and removing α–terms by means of Eqs. (11-51) and (11-52), one obtains

$$\tan \beta = \frac{\Gamma}{\Lambda} , \tag{11-55}$$

where $\Gamma = a + \ell [1 + f'(\theta)] \cos \phi$

$\Lambda = b + \ell [1 + f'(\theta)] \sin \phi$.

From Fig. 11-14 the position equation of point P on the cam working profile is

$$r_p e^{i(\theta + \theta_p)} = [a + ib + \ell e^{i\phi} - r_f e^{i\beta}] e^{i\theta}$$

$$= [(Re)^2 + (\vartheta m)^2]^{1/2} e^{i\left(\theta + \tan^{-1} \frac{\vartheta m}{Re} \right)} , \tag{11-56}$$

where $Re = a + \ell \cos \phi - r_f \cos \beta$

$\vartheta m = b + \ell \sin \phi - r_f \sin \beta$.

The radius of curvature ρ is obtained by differentiating Eq. (11-55) with respect to θ and eliminating unknown terms. Thus

$$\rho = \tag{11-57}$$

$$\frac{(\Gamma^2 + \Lambda^2)^{3/2}}{(\Gamma^2 + \Lambda^2) [1 + f'(\theta)] - (a\Gamma + b\Lambda)f'(\theta) + (a \sin \phi - b \cos \phi)\ell f''(\theta)}$$

Derivation of Radius of Curvature by Approximate Methods

A number of approximate methods for finding the cam radius of curvature are available. We will present the one developed by Krasnikov (138) for disc cams with both reciprocating roller followers and swinging roller followers. The

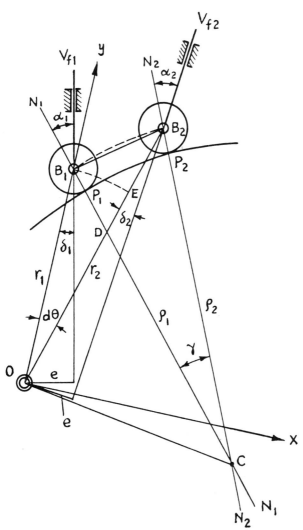

Fig. 11-15.

degree of accuracy of the method depends upon the incremental step size of the cam angular displacement. Limiting the step size to less than 2° provides sufficient accuracy.

Offset Reciprocating Roller Follower. In Fig. 11-15 consider two consecutive positions of the follower, where $d\theta$ is the incremental step of the cam rotation. The common normals $N_1 N_1$ and $N_2 N_2$, drawn from the roller centers B_1 and B_2 and passing through the points of contact between the cam and follower roller P_1 and P_2, intersect with the directions of the follower velocity vectors V_{f1} and V_{f2} to form the pressure angles α_1 and α_2, respectively. The two common normals intersect at point C, which is the center of curvature of the pitch profile segment B_1B_2, which is also the working profile segment P_1P_2. Then the radial distances CB_1 and CB_2 are, respectively, the pitch radii of curvature ρ_1 and ρ_2. This is approximately true if B_1 and B_2 are so close to each other that the pitch profile segment B_1B_2 may be treated as a circular arc, thus giving $\rho_1=\rho_2=\rho$. Let

$\quad r_1, r_2$ = the radius vectors of the pitch profile
$\quad \delta_1, \delta_2$ = the angle of offset
$\quad e$ = the amount of offset.

From the triangles OB_1C and OB_2C in Fig. 11-15, application of the law of cosines gives

$$\overline{OC}^2 = r_1^2 + \rho_1^2 - 2r_1\rho_1 \cos(\alpha_1 + \delta_1) \tag{11-58}$$

$$\overline{OC}^2 = r_2^2 + \rho_2^2 - 2r_2\rho_2 \cos(\alpha_2 + \delta_2) \tag{11-59}$$

Realizing that $d\theta$ is small, $\rho_1 = \rho_2 = \rho$, and solving for ρ using Eqs. (11-58) and (11-59), one can obtain

$$\rho \cong \frac{r_1^2 - r_2^2}{2\,[\,r_1 \cos(\alpha_1 + \delta_1) - r_2 \cos(\alpha_2 + \delta_2)\,]} \tag{11-60}$$

In Eq. (10-60) the pressure angles α_1 and α_2 can be calculated from Eq. (10-44), and the offset angles δ_1 and δ_2 are known because e, r_1 and r_2 are prescribed quantities. The angles δ_1 and δ_2 will have the sign corresponding to the location of the offset of the follower and the direction of rotation of the cam.

Swinging Roller Follower. A disc cam with cam center O imparting motion to a swinging roller follower pivoted at Q is shown in Fig. 11-16 for two adjacent follower positions. As in the reciprocating follower case, we construct the common normals N_1N_1 and N_2N_2 and define the pressure angles α_1 and α_2, respectively. Note that for this case we have a variable offset e_1 and e_2. Next, using the two common normals, we locate the center of curvature C and define the radii of curvature ρ_1 and ρ_2. Referring to the triangles OB_1C and OB_2C, the following relationships can readily be written:

$$(\overline{OC})^2 = r_1^2 + \rho_1^2 - 2r_1\rho_1 \cos(\delta_1 - \alpha_1) \tag{11-61}$$

$$(\overline{OC})^2 = r_2^2 + \rho_2^2 - 2r_2\rho_2 \cos(\delta_2 - \alpha_2) \tag{11-62}$$

Taking into account that $\rho_1 = \rho_2 = \rho$ when angle γ becomes small, and solving for ρ from Eqs. (11-61) and (11-62) give

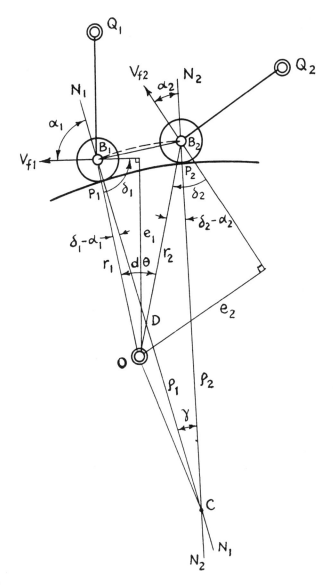

Fig. 11-16.

$$\rho = \frac{r_2^2 - r_1^2}{2 \left[r_2 \cos (\delta_2 - \alpha_2) - r_1 \cos (\delta_1 - \alpha_1) \right]} .$$ (11-63)

In Eq. (11-63), the pressure angles α_1 and α_2 can be computed from Eq. (10-61). Since r_1 and r_2 are known, the offsets e_1 and e_2 or equivalently the offset angles δ_1 and δ_2 can be readily precalculated.

There are other methods of derivation for determining the exact radius of curvature. Baxter (15) uses a differential geometry approach, which produces the same set of formulas for the radius of curvature as the method of poles produces. Derivations by Kloomok and Muffley (128) which are not shown here because of their complexity, are purely based on the geometry of mechanism and on the kinematic inversion. Although there is a difference in the degree of mathematical complexity of the exact formulas derived between the method of poles and the method used by Kloomok and Muffley, they give the same numerical answer from the same given data. The difference can be attributed chiefly to taste. For an interesting argument regarding the choice of formulas, the reader is referred to the discussion by Baxter (16).

11-6. DETERMINATION OF MINIMUM RADIUS CURVATURE OF CONVEX CAM

In the previous section we derived the formulas for the cam radius of curvature ρ. After this is accomplished, the resulting expression can be differentiated with respect to cam angle θ to determine the minimum value of ρ. If this is equated to the least allowable value, we obtain an expression for the smallest possible size of the cam. The whole process, in most cases, leads to transcendental or higher order algebraic equations, the analytical solution of which is difficult to obtain without the aid of digital computer programming. However, in a few restricted cases, e.g., a disc cam with a reciprocating flat–faced follower, the general trends can be developed analytically or geometrically without the use of programmed computers.

Analytical Method for Determining Minimum Radius of Curvature for Reciprocating Flat–Faced Follower

Simple–Harmonic Motion. The kinematic equations for simple–harmonic motion are

$$s = \frac{L}{2}\left(1 - \cos\frac{\pi\theta}{\beta}\right)$$

$$V_f = \frac{\pi L \omega_c}{2\beta}\sin\frac{\pi\theta}{\beta}$$

$$a_f = \frac{\pi^2 L \omega_c^2}{2\beta^2}\cos\frac{\pi\theta}{\beta}.$$

Substituting these into Eq. (11-25) gives

$$\rho = r_b + s + \frac{a_f}{\omega_c^2} \qquad (11\text{-}64)$$

$$= r_b + \frac{L}{2} + \frac{L}{2} \left(\frac{\pi^2}{\beta^2} - 1 \right) \cos \frac{\pi\theta}{\beta} \; .$$

Differentiating Eq. (11-64) with respect to θ and setting the result equal to zero, one obtains

$$\frac{\pi L}{2\beta} \left(\frac{\pi^2}{\beta^2} - 1 \right) \sin \frac{\pi\theta_m}{\beta} = 0 \; ,$$

where θ_m is the value of θ for which ρ is minimum. This can also be written

$$\sin \frac{\pi\theta_m}{\beta} = 0 \; , \qquad (11\text{-}65)$$

which has solution at $\theta_m = 0, \beta, 2\beta, 3\beta$, etc.

The minimum solution occurs when $\theta_m = 0$, and the corresponding value of the minimum radius of curvature is

$$\rho_{\min} = r_b + \frac{L\pi^2}{2\beta^2} \; .$$

Or, in nondimensional form

$$\frac{\rho_{\min}}{r_b} = 1 + \frac{L}{r_b} \frac{\pi^2}{2\beta^2} \; . \qquad (11\text{-}66)$$

Cycloidal Motion. The kinematic equations for cycloidal motion are

$$s = \frac{L}{\pi} \left(\frac{\pi\theta}{\beta} - \frac{1}{2} \sin \frac{2\pi\theta}{\beta} \right)$$

$$V_f = \frac{L\omega_c}{\beta} \left(1 - \cos \frac{2\pi\theta}{\beta} \right)$$

$$a_f = \frac{2\pi L \omega_c^2}{\beta^2} \sin \frac{2\pi\theta}{\beta} .$$

Substituting these into Eq. (11-25) gives

$$\rho = r_b + \frac{L\theta}{\beta} + \frac{L}{2\pi} \left[\left(\frac{2\pi}{\beta} \right)^2 - 1 \right] \sin \frac{2\pi\theta}{\beta} . \tag{11-67}$$

Differentiating Eq. (11-67) with respect to θ and setting the result equal to zero yield

$$\frac{L}{\beta} + \frac{L}{\beta} \left[\left(\frac{2\pi}{\beta} \right)^2 - 1 \right] \cos \frac{2\pi\theta_m}{\beta} = 0$$

$$\cos \frac{2\pi\theta_m}{\beta} = \frac{1}{1 - \left(\frac{2\pi}{\beta} \right)^2} \tag{11-68}$$

$$\theta_m = \frac{\beta}{2\pi} \cos^{-1} \left[\frac{1}{1 - \left(\frac{2\pi}{\beta} \right)^2} \right] .$$

For a cosine function

$$-1 \le \cos \frac{2\pi\theta_m}{\beta} \le 1$$

or

$$\left| \frac{1}{1 - \left(\frac{2\pi}{\beta} \right)^2} \right| \le 1 ,$$

from which one obtains

$$\beta \leqq \sqrt{2}\ \pi \qquad\qquad (11\text{-}69)$$

$$1 - \left(\frac{2\pi}{\beta}\right)^2 \leq -1 . \qquad\qquad (11\text{-}70)$$

These expressions are independent of all but one of the parameters, β, of the cam profile.

Eq. (11-68) therefore states that

$$\cos \frac{2\pi\theta_m}{\beta} \leq 0 .$$

Thus

$$\frac{\pi}{2} \leq \frac{2\pi\theta_m}{\beta} \leq \frac{3\pi}{2}$$

or

$$\frac{\beta}{4} \leq \theta_m \leq \frac{3}{4}\beta . \qquad\qquad (11\text{-}71)$$

For minimization, $\dfrac{d^2\rho}{d\theta^2}$ must be positive. Thus

$$-\frac{2\pi L}{\beta^2}\left[\left(\frac{2\pi}{\beta}\right)^2 - 1\right]\sin\frac{2\pi\theta_m}{\beta} > 0 .$$

We know from Eq. (11-70) that

$$1 - \left(\frac{2\pi}{\beta}\right)^2 \leq -1 .$$

Therefore,

$$\pi \leq \frac{2\pi\theta_m}{\beta} \leq 2\pi$$

or

$$\frac{\beta}{2} \le \theta_m \le \beta . \tag{11-72}$$

To satisfy both Eqs. (11-71) and (11-72), the following single condition must prevail:

$$\frac{\beta}{2} \le \theta_m \le \frac{3}{4} \beta . \tag{11-73}$$

Substituting Eq. (11-68) into Eq. (11-67) and designating $\dfrac{2\pi\theta_m}{\beta}$ by ϕ give the minimum value of ρ,

$$\rho_{min} = r_b + \frac{L\theta_m}{\beta} + \frac{L}{2\pi} \left[\left(\frac{2\pi}{\beta} \right)^2 - 1 \right] \frac{1}{\left(1 - \dfrac{2\pi}{\beta} \right)^2} \tan\phi$$

$$\rho_{min} = r_b + \frac{L\theta_m}{\beta} - \frac{L}{2\pi} \tan\phi$$

$$\rho_{min} = r_b - \frac{L}{2\pi} \left(\tan\phi + \frac{2\pi\theta_m}{\beta} \right)$$

$$\rho_{min} = r_b - \frac{L}{2\pi} (\tan\phi - \phi)$$

$$\rho_{min} = r_b - \frac{L}{2\pi} \, \text{inv}\,\phi , \tag{11-74}$$

where $\phi = \dfrac{2\pi\theta_m}{\beta}$.

If $\rho_{min} = r_b$, then Eq. (11-74) gives $\phi = 4.4934$ radians and $\beta = 152.1°$. The following two cases occur:

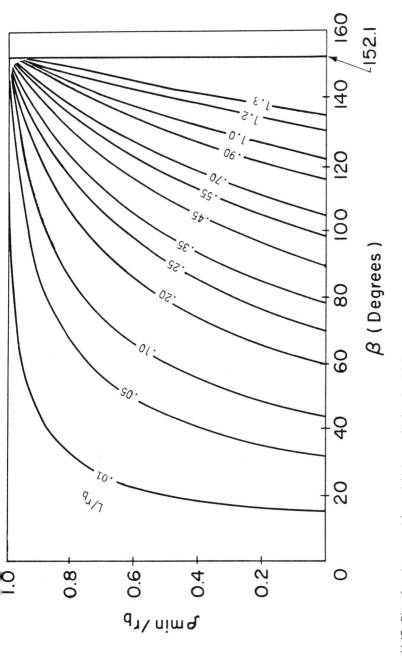

Fig. 11-17. Plot of ρ_{min}/r_o versus β for cycloidal cam with flat-faced follower.

263

Case 1. When $\beta < 152.1°$, inv ϕ is positive, and $\rho_{min} > r_b$; then ρ_{min} can be computed from Eq. (11-74).

Case 2. When $\beta > 152.1°$ inv ϕ is negative, and $\rho_{min} > r_b$, then the minimum radius of curvature is the radius of the base circle and occurs on the base circle.

Fig. 11-17 shows a plot of $\dfrac{\rho_{min}}{r_b}$ versus β for a cycloidal cam with a flat–faced follower.

Graphical Method for Determining the Minimum Radius of Curvature for Reciprocating Flat–Faced Follower

Recall from Eq. (11-25) that

$$\rho = s + r_b + \frac{A_f}{\omega_c^{2}} .$$

Thus

$$\rho_{min} = \left(s + r_b + \frac{A_f}{\omega_c^{2}} \right)_{min} . \tag{11-75}$$

If we preset the right–hand side of Eq. (11-75) equal to ρ_c, a critical value of the radius of curvature based on the criteria of no undercutting and an acceptable limit of contact stresses, we can write

$$(r_b)_{min} = \rho_c - (s + A_c)_{min} , \tag{11-76}$$

where the converted acceleration $A_c = \dfrac{A_f}{\omega_c^{2}}$.

To find the minimum of $s + A_c$, we differentiate $(s + A_c)$ with respect to s and set the result equal to zero,

$$\frac{d(s + A_c)}{ds} = 0 ,$$

which gives $\dfrac{dA_c}{ds} = -1$. $\tag{11-77}$

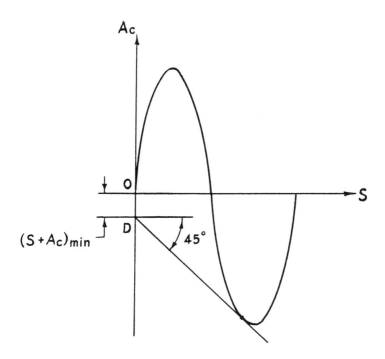

Fig. 11-18.

From Eq. (11-77) it can be seen that if the converted acceleration A_c is plotted against the follower displacement s with the same scale as shown in Fig. 11-18, a line at $-45°$ to the positive s-axis and tangent to the A_c versus s curve will exactly represent $\dfrac{dA_c}{ds} = -1$. Therefore, the intersection D of this extended tangent line with the A_c-axis is measured at a distance from O equal to

$$OD = (s + A_c)_{min} .$$

This forms the basis of the graphical method. Since only a portion of the A_c versus s curve is required to be actually drawn in the vicinity of the point of tangency between the tangent line and the curve, the solution can be obtained rather quickly. The following example is used to illustrate the method.

Example 11-2

A disc cam is to move a flat–faced follower according to the following motion:

Cam rotation		Follower motion
$0 \sim \dfrac{\pi}{4}$	$(0° \sim 45°)$	1–cm rise, constant acceleration
$\dfrac{\pi}{4} \sim \dfrac{3}{4}\pi$	$(45° \sim 135°)$	4–cm rise, constant velocity
$\dfrac{3}{4}\pi \sim \pi$	$(135° \sim 180°)$	1–cm rise, constant deceleration
$\pi \sim \dfrac{5}{4}\pi$	$(180° \sim 225°)$	dwell
$\dfrac{5}{4}\pi \sim 2\pi$	$(225° \sim 360°)$	6–cm fall, cycloidal motion

The total stroke is 6 cm. Suppose that the minimum radius of curvature specified is 5 cm, based on the limit of contact stresses, determined by the graphical method of the minimum base circle size.

The equations for $s(\theta)$, $V_f(\theta)$, and $A_f(\theta)$, which are determined from the motion specifications, are shown in Table 11-1.

Fig. 11-19 shows a closed curve for the complete plot of A_c versus s. A tangent making an angle of $-45°$ with the positive s-axis is drawn to the curve. The extended tangent cuts the A_c-axis at point -1.32. Therefore,

$$(s + A_c)_{min} = -1.32$$

or

$$(r_b)_{min} = 1.32 + \rho_c = 1.32 + 5.0 = 6.32 \text{ cm.}$$

Note that there is no need to plot a complete curve of A_c versus s. Only a solid lined portion of the curve in the vicinity of point C in Fig. 11-19 is required to obtain the graphical solution.

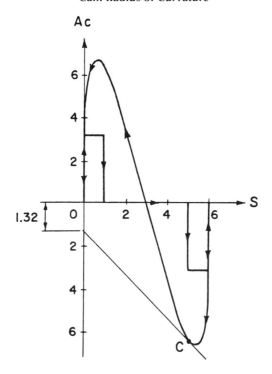

Fig. 11-19.

11-7. NOMOGRAM FOR MINIMUM RADIUS OF CURVATURE

The derivations related to the flat–faced follower shown in the previous section are exact. In the cases of both the reciprocating and the swinging followers, any attempt to derive a closed form solution for the minimum value of the radius of curvature leads to an unmanageable transcendental equation. As a result of this difficulty, the minimum radius of curvature is more readily obtained by computing the radius of curvature ρ from Eq. (11-4) at points throughout the active cam angle β and scanning the maximum values of ρ for a given type of motion program. Then the design nomograms are constructed by plotting the dimensionless ratio $\dfrac{\rho_{min}}{r_o}$ versus angle β with $\dfrac{r_o}{L}$ as a variational parameter. Figs. 11-20 and 11-21 show, respectively, the sample nomograms for the simple–harmonic motion and for the cycloidal motion for cams with reciprocating roller followers. Unfortunately, the original nomograms for cams with reciprocating roller followers published by Kloomok and Muffley in References (126) and (128) in 1955 were incorrect. The corrections have been recently made by Ganter and Uicker (86). Figs. 11-20 and 11-21 show the corrected version. A computer program named RAD1 in FORTRAN language for generating these nomograms is given in Appendix B.

Table 11-1 Expressions Representing Motion of Cam Follower for Example 11-2

θ (°)	$s(\theta)$	$v_f(\theta)$	$a_f(\theta)$
0-45	$\dfrac{16\theta^2}{\pi^2}$	$\dfrac{32\theta}{\pi^2}$	$\dfrac{32}{\pi^2}$
45-135	$1 + \dfrac{8}{\pi}\left(\theta - \dfrac{\pi}{4}\right)$	8	0
135-180	$6 - \dfrac{16}{\pi^2}(\pi - \theta)^2$	$\dfrac{32(\pi - \theta)}{\pi^2}$	$-\dfrac{32}{\pi^2}$
180-225	6	0	0
225-360	$6 - \left[\dfrac{8}{\pi}\left(\theta - \dfrac{5}{4}\pi\right) - \dfrac{3}{\pi}\sin\dfrac{8}{3}\left(\theta - \dfrac{5}{4}\pi\right)\right]$	$-\dfrac{8}{\pi} + \dfrac{8}{\pi}\cos\dfrac{8}{3}\left(\theta - \dfrac{5}{4}\pi\right)$	$-\dfrac{64}{3\pi}\sin\left(\theta - \dfrac{5}{4}\pi\right)$

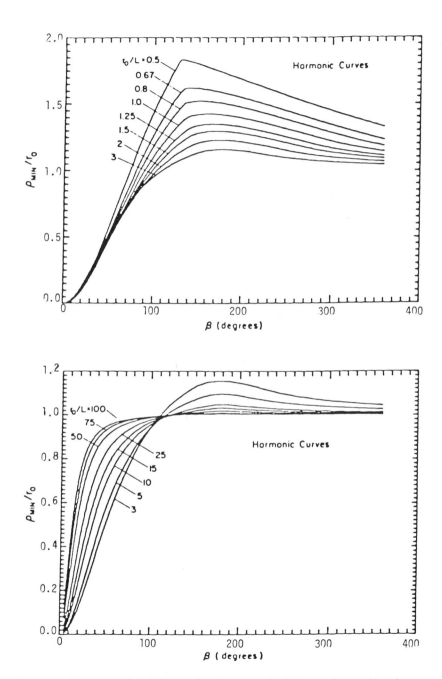

Fig. 11-20. Nomogoram for minimum radius of curvature for full harmonic cam with reciprocating roller follower.

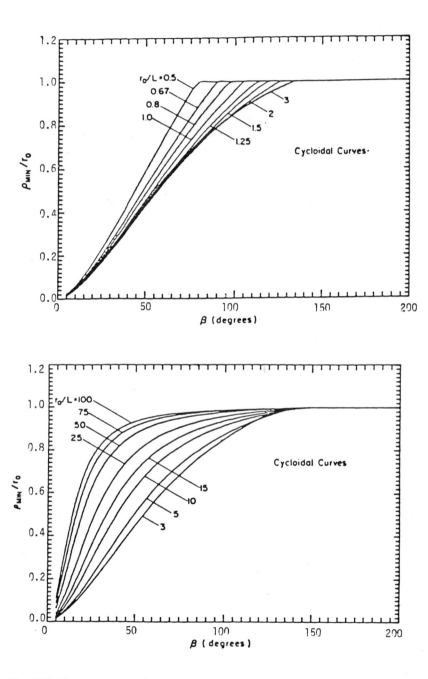

Fig. 11-21. Nomogram for minimum radius of curvature for full cycloidal cam with reciprocating roller follower.

Example 11-3

A reciprocating roller follower moves with a stroke $L = 1.5$ cm with cycloidal motion while the cam rotates $\beta = 50°$. The follower dwells for 40° and then returns with cycloidal motion in 70°. If the prime circle radius is $r_o = 4.5$ cm and the roller radius is $r_f = 0.75$ cm check the cam for undercutting.

$$\frac{r_o}{L} = \frac{4.5}{1.5} = 3.0 .$$

The outward motion will govern because of its smaller range of motion β. Therefore, from Fig. 11-21 for $\dfrac{r_o}{L} = 3.0$ and $\beta = 50°$,

$$\frac{\rho_{min}}{r_o} = 0.44 ,$$

and

$$\rho_{min} = 0.44 \times 4.5 = 1.98 \text{ cm.}$$

The cam will not be undercut because $\rho_{min} > r_f$.

A different design chart prepared by Koumans (136), shown in Fig. 10-14, can also be used for determining the minimum radius of curvature of cams.

In a similar manner, design nomograms for cams with swinging roller followers can be plotted using $\dfrac{\rho_{min}}{r_o}$ as the ordinate and $\dfrac{\beta}{\tau}$ as the abscissa. The angular motion stroke of the follower τ and the dimensionless ratios $\dfrac{c}{r_o}$ and $\dfrac{\ell}{r_o}$ may be used as varying parameters. Fig. 11-22 shows sample plots of this kind for cycloidal motion with the ratio $\dfrac{\ell}{r_o}$ equal to 1.0 and 1.5. Note that the effect of roller rotation "away from pivot" or "toward pivot" has been accommodated by plotting two complete sets of charts. A FORTRAN program called RAD2 for generating nomograms for determining the radius of curvature for swinging followers is also given in Appendix B.

In using the nomogram of Fig. 11-22, an interpolation is sometimes required to obtain $\dfrac{\rho_{min}}{r_o}$. This is illustrated as follows.

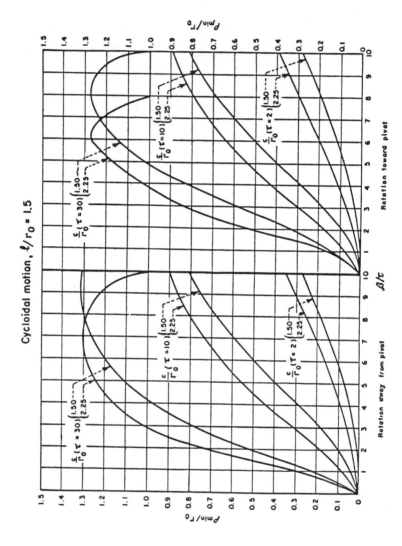

Fig. 11-22. Nomogram for minimum radius of curvature for cycloidal cam with swinging roller follower ($L/r_o = 1.5$).

Example 11-4

A disc cam imparts motion to a swinging roller follower by cycloidal motion with $\tau = 10°$ and $\beta = 60°$. If $\ell = 6.0$ cm, $c = 6.75$ cm, $r_o = 4.0$ cm, $r_f = 1.0$ cm, and the follower roller is away from pivot, check the cam for undercutting.

$$\frac{\ell}{r_o} = \frac{6.0}{4.0} = 1.5$$

$$\frac{c}{r_o} = \frac{6.75}{4.0} = 1.69$$

$$\frac{\beta}{\tau} = \frac{60}{10} = 6 \; .$$

From Fig. 11-22 we can tabulate the data and perform the interpolation as follows:

$\dfrac{\ell}{r_o}$	$\dfrac{c}{r_o}$	$\dfrac{\rho_{min}}{r_o}$
1.5	1.5	0.50
1.5	2.25	0.65

The interpolation of $\dfrac{\rho_{min}}{r_o}$ for $\dfrac{c}{r_o}$ ($\tau = 10$ deg.) is

$$\frac{\rho_{min}}{r_o} = 0.50 + \left(\frac{1.69 - 1.5}{2.25 - 1.5} \right)(0.65 - 0.5) = 0.54 \; ,$$

which gives

$$\rho_{min} = 0.54 \times 4.0 = 2.16 \text{ cm.}$$

Since $\rho_{min} > r_f$, there is no undercutting.

11-8. NUMERICAL SCHEME FOR CALCULATING RADIUS OF CURVATURE WHEN THE CAM PROFILE IS IN TABULAR FORM

All equations derived in this chapter for calculating the cam radius of curvature thus far require the cam displacement profile to be described in functional form. Difficulty occurs if the displacement profile is expressed in tabular form. In this situation, a numerical differentiation scheme such as the one introduced in Chapter 10 may be extended for use, although there are other numerical differentiation methods available.

Let us again recall Stirling's interpolation formula, Eq. (10-72). Using the same notation as before and differentiating this formula with respect to x gives Eq. (10-73), which will not be reproduced here. If we differentiate Eq. (10-73) with respect to x another time, we obtain

(11-78)

$$
\frac{d^2y}{dx^2} = \frac{1}{h^2} \left[\delta^2 y_{i-1} + U \frac{\delta^3 y_{i-2} + \delta^3 y_{i-1}}{2} + \frac{12U^2 - 2}{4!} \delta^4 y_{i-2} \right.
$$

$$
+ \frac{20U^3 - 30U}{5!} \frac{\delta^5 y_{i-3} + \delta^5 y_{i-2}}{2}
$$

$$
\left. + \frac{30U^4 - 60U^2 + 8}{6!} \delta^6 y_{i-3} + \ldots \right].
$$

For the point $x = x_i$, we have $U = O$. Substituting this value of U into Eq. (11-78), we obtain

$$
\left(\frac{d^2y}{dx^2} \right)_{x_i} = \frac{1}{h^2} \left[\delta^2 y_{i-1} - \frac{1}{12} \delta^4 y_{i-2} + \frac{1}{90} \delta^6 y_{i-3} + \ldots \right]. \quad (11-79)
$$

Eq. (11-79) can also be derived in other ways. A method of employing the difference operator for deriving the same is given by Chen (44).

Both the first derivative, Eq. (10-74), and the second derivative, Eq. (11-79), will be needed in the process of computing the cam radius of curvature.

Example 11-5

A disc cam, which operates at a uniform speed, translates motion to a flat-faced follower. Through 12° of cam rotation the follower travels a unit

Table 11-2 Numerical Results of Computation for Example 11-5

	(1)	(2)	(3)	(4)	(5)	(6)	(7)
		Half Face Width of Follower				Radius of Curvature	
θ	s	s' Exact	s' Approx	s'' Exact	s'' Approx	ρ Exact	ρ Approx
0	0.000000	0.000000	0.000000	0.000000	0.000000	0.000000	0.000000
1	0.003755	0.011164	0.013117	0.021816	0.021324	0.025571	0.025079
2	0.028834	0.041666	0.041748	0.037787	0.037756	0.066621	0.066590
3	0.090845	0.083333	0.083333	0.043633	0.043631	0.13478	0.13476
4	0.195501	0.125000	0.124990	0.037787	0.037786	0.233288	0.233287
5	0.337089	0.155502	0.155491	0.021816	0.021815	0.358905	0.358902
6	0.499999	0.166666	0.166646	0.000000	0.000000	0.499999	0.499999
7	0.662910	0.155502	0.155488	−0.021816	−0.021816	0.641094	0.641094
8	0.804498	0.125000	0.124990	−0.037787	−0.037786	0.766711	0.766703
9	0.909154	0.083333	0.083333	−0.043633	−0.043631	0.865521	0.865523
10	0.971165	0.041666	0.041748	−0.037787	−0.037756	0.933378	0.933409
11	0.996244	0.011164	0.013117	−0.021816	−0.021323	0.974428	0.974921
12	1.000000	0.000000	0.000000	0.000000	0.000000	1.000000	1.000000

distance outward from rest with cycloidal motion. If the cam base circle radius is r_b, determine the radius of curvature of the cam as well as the bottom surface dimension of the flat–faced follower.

The equation for the radius of curvature ρ for a reciprocating flat–faced follower is governed by Eq. (11-25), which may be written as

$$\rho = r_b + s(\theta) + s''(\theta) .$$

One–half of the bottom surface dimension of the flat–faced follower is exactly equal to $s'(\theta)$.

Since the type of motion and the data given in this example are the same as in example 10-6, we can refer to the same difference table, Table 10-2.

Table 11-2 exhibits the results of the computations. Values of both the exact solutions and the approximate solutions are given for values of θ that increase from 0° to 12° by increments of 1°. The exact solution calls for knowing the equations of cycloidal motion, and the approximate solutions are based on the use of Eq. (10-74) and Eq. (11-79) for calculating the first two derivatives. In Table 11-2 Column (3) contains the results of the approximate values of $s'(\theta)$, which were computed from Eq. (10-74) using three–term approximation. For example, when $\theta = 5°$ $s'(\theta) = 0.155491$. This was illustrated in Table 10-3 for example 10-6. Column (5) in Table 11-2 contains the results of the values $s''(\theta)$ that were computed from Eq. (11-79), again using three–term expansion. For instance, when $\theta = 5°$,

$$s'' = \frac{d^2s}{d\theta^2} = \frac{1}{h^2}\left[\delta^2 s_{i-1} - \frac{1}{12}\delta^4 s_{i-2} + \frac{1}{90}\delta^4 s_{i-3} + \dots \right]$$

$$= \frac{1}{1}\left[0.021322 - \frac{1}{12}(-0.005711) + \frac{1}{90}(0.001524) - \dots \right]$$

$$= 0.021815 .$$

In comparison with the corresponding exact value $s''(5) = 0.021816$, this gives an error of 0.0046%.

When using Table 11-2, one must note that the values displayed in columns (6) and (7) should be added to the specified radius of the base circle r_b to produce the correct answers b or the radii of curvature.

The FORTRAN program PARAD listed in Appendix B may be used for automatic computation of the radius of curvature when the cam profile is described in tabular form.

12
Contact Stresses And Wear

12-1. INTRODUCTION

When two elastic bodies having curved surfaces, such as a cam and a follower, transmit loads from one member to another, an area of contact is developed, accompanied by compressive "contact" stresses. Contact stresses are functions of applied forces, body geometries, material properties, and surface treatment. A large magnitude of cyclic contact stresses will cause excessive wear. As a result, physical deterioration occurs on either or both of the engaged surfaces.

Although wear is a commonplace phenomenon, it is by no means an uncomplicated one; on the contrary, the mechanisms and theory of wear are very complex. Despite the voluminous published data in the literature reporting individual wear experiments, as yet, no quantitative empirical relations connecting the amount of wear with such operating parameters as load, speed, and the material constants have been developed. In fact, the search for such a single relation is somewhat meaningless because of the several quite distinct phenomena that are lumped together under the single word wear. Observations show that the performance of cam follower systems tested in the laboratory under controlled conditions deviates from their performance in the field. In this chapter, we will briefly outline various types of wear with greater emphasis on surface fatigue caused by rolling contact. This will provide the designer with an intuitive understanding that will guide his design decisions toward greater reliability of the finished product.

12-2. HERTZ THEORY OF ELASTIC CONTACT

The state of stress and strain between two elastic bodies in contact was established in the classic work by Hertz (240). Consider two elastic bodies, say two crowned rollers of different sizes, brought together so that they are touching at a point O, as sketched in Fig. 12-1. A plane tangent to each body at the touching point forms the tangent plane. If the bodies are now pressed together so that the collinear force is normal to the tangent plane, deformation takes place, and one may expect that a small contact area will replace the contact point O of the unloaded state. The first step is to find the size and the shape of this contact area and the distribution of normal pressure applied to it. Having done so, we can calculate the stresses and strains that the interfacial pressure induces in the contacting members. In the case of cams and followers, the strain computation is not of importance.

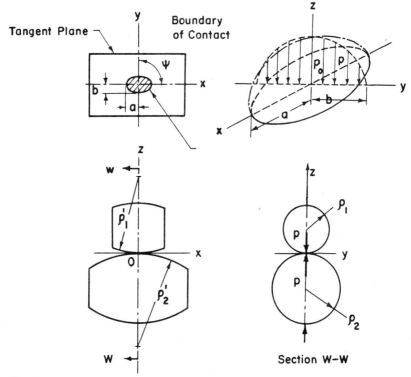

Fig. 12-1. Elastic contact of crowned rollers, showing pressure distribution and contacting boundary.

Hertz starts by assuming that
- The contacting bodies are isotropic and elastic in accordance with Hooke's law.

- In the vicinity of the contact interface, the contact area is small compared to the various radii of curvature of the undeformed bodies.
- Only normal pressures that arise during contact are considered. Relative displacements in the plane of x and y, and any shearing tractions that might arise therefrom are neglected.

Based on these assumptions, Hertz shows the following results by an application of potential theory:

1. The pressure distribution between the two contacting bodies forms a semiellipsoid, and the surface of contact traced on the tangent plane will have an elliptical boundary (Fig. 12.1).
2. The intensity of pressure p over the surface of contact is represented by the ordinates of the semiellipsoid

$$p = p_o \left[1 - \frac{x^2}{a^2} - \frac{y^2}{b^2} \right]^{1/2}, \tag{12-1}$$

where a and b denote the semiaxes of the elliptical boundary. The maximum pressure p_0 situated at the center of the surface of contact above point O is

$$p_o = \frac{3p}{2\pi ab}. \tag{12-2}$$

The semiaxes a and b of the ellipse of contact are

$$a = m \left[\frac{3}{4} \frac{P\Delta}{A + B} \right]^{1/3} \tag{12-3}$$

$$b = n \left[\frac{3}{4} \frac{P\Delta}{A + B} \right]^{1/3}, \tag{12-4}$$

where the values of m and n are given in Table 12-1.

In Eqs. (12-3) and (12-4) Δ is a factor determined by the relationship between Poisson's ratios μ_1, μ_2 and the moduli of elasticity E_1 and E_2 of the materials, where the subscripts 1 and 2 refer to the first and the second contacting bodies, respectively.

$$\Delta = \frac{1 - \mu_1^2}{E_1} + \frac{1 - \mu_2^2}{E_2}. \tag{12-5}$$

Table 12-1. Constants for Contact Ellipse

θ	m	n	θ	m	n
35°	2.397	0.530	65°	1.378	0.759
40°	2.136	0.567	70°	1.284	0.802
45°	1.926	0.604	75°	1.202	0.846
50°	1.754	0.641	80°	1.128	0.893
55°	1.611	0.678	85°	1.061	0.944
60°	1.486	0.717	90°	1.000	1.000

Note: $\cos\theta = \dfrac{B-A}{B+A}$

A and B are factors determined by various radii of curvature of the contacting bodies. If we designate ρ_1, ρ_2 as the minimum radii of curvature, ρ_1', ρ_2' as the maximum radii of curvature at the point of contact, and ψ as the angle between the planes containing the curvatures $\dfrac{1}{\rho}$ and $\dfrac{1}{\rho'}$, then

$$A + B = \frac{1}{2}\left(\frac{1}{\rho_1} + \frac{1}{\rho_1'} + \frac{1}{\rho_2} + \frac{1}{\rho_2'}\right) \tag{12-6}$$

$$B - A = \frac{1}{2}\left[\left(\frac{1}{\rho_1} - \frac{1}{\rho_1'}\right)^2 + \left(\frac{1}{\rho_2} - \frac{1}{\rho_2'}\right)^2\right. \tag{12-7}$$

$$\left. + 2\left(\frac{1}{\rho_1} - \frac{1}{\rho_1'}\right)\left(\frac{1}{\rho_2} - \frac{1}{\rho_2'}\right)\cos 2\psi\right]^{1/2}.$$

Therefore, the dimensions a and b of the ellipse depend on the shape, the applied force, and the material properties of the two contacting bodies.

Next, let us consider two cylinders of infinite length (finite length in practice) in contact. Theoretically, if the bodies were perfectly rigid, they would have straight–line contact. Actually, the bodies under load deflect to give area contact.

For two long elastic cylinders having radii ρ_1 and ρ_2 aligned so that their axes are parallel (Fig. 12-2), the "elliptical boundary" of contact degenerates into parallel lines. The contact area thus becomes a "rectangle" of infinite length (in practice, the length of the cylinder) and of width $2b$ given by

$$2b = \left(\frac{16P\rho}{\pi E}\right)^{1/2}, \tag{12-8}$$

where P is the normal force per unit length of the cylinder $\rho = \dfrac{\rho_1\rho_2}{(\rho_1 + \rho_2)}$.
In this limiting case of the Hertz contact problem, note that the contact zone's dimension varies as the $\dfrac{1}{2}$ power of the load, rather than the $\dfrac{1}{3}$ power as in the previous case. The normal pressure distribution is

$$p = p_o \left(1 - \frac{y^2}{b^2}\right)^{1/2},\tag{12-9}$$

where $p_o = \dfrac{2P}{\pi b}$.

From the geometry of circles (Fig. 12-2) the depressed depths h_1 and h_2 are

$$h_1 = \rho_1 - \sqrt{\rho_1^2 - b^2}\tag{12-10}$$

$$h_2 = \rho_2 - \sqrt{\rho_2^2 - b^2}\,.$$

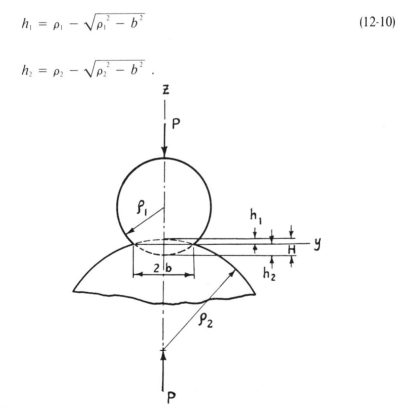

Fig. 12-2. Elastic contact of cylinders.

When a cylindrical roller is used on a disc cam, misalignment will exist so that the axes of the cam and the roller follower are no longer parallel to each other. This will increase wear. Misalignment can also take place in such a manner that the axis of the roller is parallel to the cam surface, but no longer parallel to the camshaft; this will cause the roller to roll on the cam at a certain point, but slide on it at all other points where contact occurs. Another factor that can cause sliding is the existence of a varying circumferential speed of the cam. Since misalignment almost always exits, a roller follower with a slightly spherical surface (achieved by means of a ground crown) is commonly recommended.

Contact Stresses

By using the Newtonian potential function, the equations for the entire stress field of two elastic bodies in contact can be obtained. The solution process involves the use of elliptic integrals and is a little complicated. We will not display the solution here. One can refer to Reference (242) for the details.

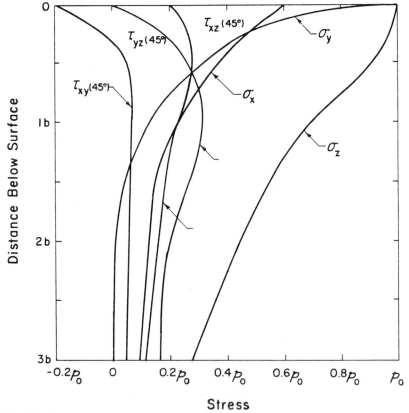

Fig. 12-3. Variation of Hertzian stresses with depth below surface.

The results of the stress distribution in the case of two cylinders, i.e., a disc cam with a roller follower, are plotted in Fig. 12-3. This is a plot of the three normal stresses (σ_x, σ_y, σ_z) in the direction of the applied load and the corresponding three shear stresses. The highest shear stress is τ_{yz} (45°), which has a maximum value of approximately $0.3p_0$ at a depth of $0.786b$. These stresses result from contact loading alone. While it is true that all principal stress components are compressive and have their largest values at the contact surface, the combination of these components results in a relatively small value of induced shear. However, the yielding of steel depends on shearing stress, and it is necessary to determine the point within the body at which the principal stresses combine to produce maximum shear. Thus, in the case of a disc cam with a roller follower made of steel, the maximum stress occurs below the cam surface. This explains why the cam surface commonly fails as a result of contact stress caused by pitting at the surface of contact. Failure results when the origin of such pits is located at the approximate depth of the point of maximum shearing stress.

When sliding is present, a combined rolling and sliding action makes the problem more complicated. This situation frequently changes the location of the failure origin.

Formulas of Maximum Compressive Contact Stress

For convenience of design computations, the contact stress equations are summarized in Table 12-2. As an example, two cylinders of dissimilar metal in contact and in perfect alignment produce a maximum compressive stress of

$$\sigma_{max} = 0.564 \left[\frac{P'\left(\dfrac{\rho_1 + \rho_2}{\rho_1 \rho_2}\right)}{\dfrac{1 - \mu_1^2}{E_1} + \dfrac{1 - \mu_2^2}{E_2}} \right]^{1/2} , \tag{12-11}$$

where the notations used are

P' = the normal load per unit width of the contacting members.

ρ_1, ρ_2 = the radii of curvature of the cam and the follower, respectively.

E_1, E_2 = the moduli of elasticity of the cam and the follower, respectively.

μ_1, μ_2 = Poisson's ratio for the cam and the follower, respectively.

Note that when the cam and the follower are made of identical materials, Eq. (12-11) degenerates to become

$$\sigma_{max} = 0.418 \left[P'E \left(\frac{\rho_1 + \rho_2}{\rho_1 \rho_2} \right) \right]^{1/2}. \tag{12-12}$$

This is also listed in the second column of Table 12-2 for ease of reference. The subsequent columns in the Table give the values of maximum shear stress τ_{max}, the depth from the surface of contact at which τ_{max} is located, and the dimensions of the semi–axes of the ellipse, a and b. Poisson's ratio for steel, $\mu = 0.3$, is used for tabulation. Study (245) shows that variations of Poisson's ratio in the usual range of common engineering materials do not have a strong influence on the important features of the stress pattern.

The radius of curvature of any cam may be determined by the methods described in Chapter 11. It is obvious that the radius of curvature is positive when the profile is convex and negative when the profile is concave. The radius of curvature of a flat–faced follower tends toward infinity.

Example 12-1.

Consider a disc cam with a tangent–type profile having a nose radius of 0.65 cm. The load between the cam and roller follower varies; at a constant angular velocity of 1,200 rpm, a maximum force of 600 N acts on the flank. The force on the cam nose is 650 N, the pressure angle at the flank point is 20°, and the roller follower is 2.0 cm in diameter. The cam thickness is 2.0 cm. Both the cam and the follower are made of steel. Determine the maximum contact stress for the nose and for the flank at this operational speed.

The force distribution gives the normal load on the cam flank per unit of thickness

$$P' = \frac{600}{2 \times \cos 20°} = 319.3 \text{ N}.$$

Since the cam and the follower are made of steel ($\mu = 0.3$), Eq. (12-12) gives the maximum contact stress at the flank,

$$\sigma_{max} = 0.418 \left[P'E \left(\frac{1}{\rho_1} + \frac{1}{\rho_2} \right) \right]^{1/2}$$

Table 12-2. Summary of Contact Stress Formulas

No.	GEOMETRY	DISSIMILAR METALS $p_0 = \sigma_z = \sigma_{max}$	SIMILAR METALS: $E_1 = E_2 = E,\ \mu_1 = \mu_2 = 0.3$			
			$p_0 = \sigma_z = \sigma_{max}$	τ_{max}	Depth at τ_{max}	$a = b^*$ (No 1,2,3) b (No 4,5,6)
1.	Sphere and Flat Plate	$0.578\left[\dfrac{P}{\rho^2\left(\dfrac{1-\mu_1^2}{E_1}+\dfrac{1-\mu_2^2}{E_2}\right)}\right]^{1/3}$	$0.388\left[\dfrac{PE^2}{\rho^2}\right]^{1/3}$	$.33 p_0$	$.25a$	$1.11\left[\dfrac{PR}{E}\right]^{1/3}$
2.	Two Spheres	$0.578\left[\dfrac{\dfrac{P\cdot\rho_1\rho_2}{\rho_1+\rho_2}}{\left(\dfrac{1-\mu_1^2}{E_1}+\dfrac{1-\mu_2^2}{E_2}\right)}\right]^{1/3}$	$0.388\left[PE^2\dfrac{\rho_1+\rho_2}{\rho_1\rho_2}\right]^{1/3}$	$.33 p_0$	$.25a$	$1.11\left[\dfrac{P}{E}\left(\dfrac{\rho_1\rho_2}{\rho_1+\rho_2}\right)\right]^{1/3}$
3.	Sphere and Spherical Socket	$0.578\left[\dfrac{\dfrac{P(\rho_1-\rho_2)}{\rho_1\rho_2}}{\left(\dfrac{1-\mu_1^2}{E_1}+\dfrac{1-\mu_2^2}{E_2}\right)}\right]^{1/3}$	$0.388\left[PE^2\dfrac{\rho_1-\rho_2}{\rho_1\rho_2}\right]^{1/3}$	$.33 p_0$	$.25a$	$1.11\left[\dfrac{P}{E}\left(\dfrac{\rho_1\rho_2}{\rho_1-\rho_2}\right)\right]^{1/3}$
4.	Cylinder and Flat Plate	$0.564\left[\dfrac{P'}{\rho\left(\dfrac{1-\mu_1^2}{E_1}+\dfrac{1-\mu_2^2}{E_2}\right)}\right]^{1/2}$	$0.418\left[\dfrac{P'E}{\rho}\right]^{1/2}$	$.30 p_0$	$.79b$	$3.04\left[\dfrac{P'\rho}{E}\right]^{1/2}$
5.	Two Cylinders	$0.564\left[\dfrac{P'\left(\dfrac{\rho_1+\rho_2}{\rho_1\rho_2}\right)}{\dfrac{1-\mu_1^2}{E_1}+\dfrac{1-\mu_2^2}{E_2}}\right]^{1/2}$	$0.418\left[P'E\left(\dfrac{\rho_1+\rho_2}{\rho_1\rho_2}\right)\right]^{1/2}$	$.30 p_0$	$.79b$	$3.04\left[\dfrac{P'}{E}\left(\dfrac{\rho_1\rho_2}{\rho_1+\rho_2}\right)\right]^{1/2}$
6.	Cylinder and Cylindrical Groove	$0.564\left[\dfrac{P'\left(\dfrac{\rho_1-\rho_2}{\rho_1\rho_2}\right)}{\dfrac{1-\mu_1^2}{E_1}+\dfrac{1-\mu_2^2}{E_2}}\right]^{1/2}$	$0.418\left[P'E\left(\dfrac{\rho_1-\rho_2}{\rho_1\rho_2}\right)\right]^{1/2}$	$.30 p_0$	$.79b$	$3.04\left[\dfrac{P'}{E}\left(\dfrac{\rho_1\rho_2}{\rho_1-\rho_2}\right)\right]^{1/2}$

P = Total load
$P' = P/a$ = Load per unit width

285

$$= 0.418 \left[319.3 \times 20.68 \times 10^6 \times \left(\frac{1}{1} + \frac{1}{\infty} \right) \right]^{1/2}$$

$$= 34,000 \ N/cm^2 .$$

The maximum contact stress occuring at the nose is

$$\sigma_{max} = 0.418 \left[319.3 \times 20.68 \times 10^6 \times \left(\frac{1}{1} + \frac{1}{0.65} \right) \right]^{1/2}$$

$$= 54,000 \ N/cm^2 .$$

We see that the nose is subjected to a larger stress than is the flank.

12-3. WEAR PHENOMENA

The effects of wear are the result of a complex set of factors that is a part of the specific condition of service. The properties of the material itself, the mating material, and the operational conditions of the design combine to cause different types of wear.

In simple terms, wear may be defined as the unwanted removal of solid material from rubbing surfaces. While this definition sounds quite simple, it does in fact lump together many quite diverse phenomena such as abrasion, corrosion, pitting, etc. In any particular instance of wear one may have any of these conditions present either singly or in combination. In the latter case, the situation may be even more complicated because of interaction between the several conditions. Several types of wear include adhesive wear, abrasive wear, corrosive wear, and surface fatigue, each of which can be described by its own characteristics. Although all forms of wear may occur at one time, surface fatigue is the dominant cause of failure in cam and follower systems. In the following we shall describe the working and the control of each of these different categories of wear, with an emphasis on surface fatigue.

Adhesive or Galling Wear

This is a reference to an attraction between the surface atoms of two contacting materials, leading to a transfer of material from one surface to the other and eventually to the formation of loose fragments.

Theoretically, metal surfaces are represented as being smooth and flat. However, microscopic examination of surfaces reveals small peaks (asperities) and

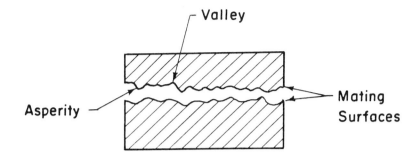

Fig. 12-4. Cross–sectional view of mating surfaces.

valleys, as shown in Fig. 12-4. The best machining or superfinishing practice still leaves surface roughness on the order of a good fraction of a micron at the very least, and waviness that is a fraction of a wave length of light in size. When two surfaces are placed one upon the other, only the asperities touch, and, as a result, surface contact is established in extremely small areas. High local pressure combined with the relative sliding motion along crystallographic planes causes roughening of the interface of contact. A slip plane with a slip direction lying in that plane forms a slip system. It is generally the case that several slip systems are operating during plastic deformation and, as a result, the roughening will take place in several different directions. When a pair of firmly interlocked high spots is forced apart, breakage will occur at some distance from the original interface, where the section is weakest.

Most of the energy released during the process of breaking the high spots is finally transformed into heat, which causes a sudden temperature flash. When the heat of the temperature flash is conducted through the interface, momentary diffusion occurs rapidly. If the diffusion process is rapid enough to cause welding of the sheared–off peak to the opposite high spot, a piece of transferred metal is formed. If the conditions are such that no appreciable diffusion occurs, the adhesive force (if strong enough) can still keep the metal particles on the opposite high spot. The small piece of metal sheared from the high spot will leave as a "loose particle" when both diffusion and adhesion are weak.

The amount of adhesive transfer and wear can be profoundly affected by the coefficient of surface friction and the ambient conditions. The coefficient of friction is a measure of the shearing force required to separate the contact, once it has been formed, for a given applied normal force. There are many factors affecting friction. Some of these are listed below.

Material combinations — Tests show that identical or similar materials have greater transfer than very dissimilar ones. For instance, it is well–known that one never runs steel against steel. Table 12-3 displays some interesting metal combinations.

Surface cleanliness — Sliding surfaces become coated with an amorphous substance, the so-called Beilby layer. Without this layer, metallic surfaces cannot slide, but weld solidly together when brought into contact. In the absence of plastic flow, the oxide layers remain intact and prevent cohesion of the metals.

Lubrication — Since the thickness of the oil film deposited on a sliding surface is much less than the height of the asperities of most commercially prepared surfaces, welding cannot be prevented, but it can be reduced considerably. It is mainly the static or inherent viscosity of the lubricant that can keep the metals apart. A thin lubricant (10 SSU at 38°C) is suggested for roller followers. A high–viscosity oil, grease, or chemical compound is employed for the flat–faced follower sliding surfaces.

Surface hardness and surface finish — Generally, friction is less with harder metals. Good surface finish with a lapping and a polishing action is essential with hardened materials.

Temperature — In general, high temperature increases and accelerates adhesive wear. This is to be expected because the formation of the weld is, on an atomic scale, the formation of an interatomic bond or, in other words, a surface chemical reaction. The rate of chemical reactions increases greatly with increased temperature.

Table 12-3. Some Proven Combinations of Dissimilar Materials

Hardened steel	and cast iron
	or soft bronze
	or phosphor bronze
	or nylon
Cast iron	and phosphor bronze
	or soft steel
Soft brass	and soft steel

Abrasive Wear

There is probably no metal–to–metal wear problem that is not aggravated by non–metallic abrasives, because abrasive grit is found everywhere in the form of ordinary dust. With this type of wear the removal of solid material from a surface is accomplished not by its sticking to the other surface and being pulled out, but rather by its being plowed or gouged out by a much harder surface or body. Hardness is always a major factor in combating attack by non–metallic abrasives.

Corrosive Wear

The occurrence of corrosive wear requires the presence of corrosion and rubbing. The most common environments, such as air at room temperature, contain humidity and other industrial vapors. Oxides or hydroxides of the metals in question are formed by exposure to such environments. As these compounds are loosely adherent to the metal base, rubbing serves to remove them. A combination of high unit loading and vibratory motion may result in fretting corrosion. The effect of fretting corrosion is to increase the susceptibility to fatigue failure of dynamically loaded machine–elements. An adequate lubricant generally exerts a marked effect on the corrosive wear that may take place. Its effect may be of two general types. It may protect the surface from the corroding environment, thus reducing or minimizing the corrosive wear that would otherwise result. The lubricant itself may react chemically with the surface, thus altering the type of compound and amount of wear that would otherwise occur.

Surface Fatigue

A cam and follower pair under rolling contact conditions suffers from surface fatigue failures as a result of the repetition of a contact load. This is characterized by load pitting and spalling of the surfaces, and occurs rather suddenly without any prior visible warning after a relatively long life or many cycles of revolution. However, when it does occur, the particle removed and the resulting pit are relatively large — many times larger than the typical wear particle produced by other types of wear condition — and the useful life of the rolling mechanism is terminated shortly after the pitting or the spalling begins. This pitting is the result of fatigue of the surfaces in question in exactly the same manner as other mechanical members fatigue under cyclic stresses. Pitting can be either incipient or destructive.

Incipient pitting starts as a superficial microcrack of irregular shape, less than 1.5 mm deep. It will not progress beyond the initial stage if induced surface compressive stresses exist. These compressive stresses increase slowly with the development of a plastic flow that may occur during rolling contact, sliding contact, or both. Eventually, the induced stresses become large enough to offset the tensile stress acting in a direction parallel to the surface; then pitting stops.

Destructive pitting may originate from either subsurface or surface fatigue. The phenomenon is progressive and occurs when the corrective action associated with incipient pitting is insufficient to halt the pit formation. Destructive pitting can lead to the disintegration of the surface.

The destructive nature of pitting involves a multitude of factors, such as high–contact stresses, sliding action accompanying rolling action, etc. Pits constitute stress raisers that can hasten fatigue failure. The size and the number of pits increase until smoothness of operation is impaired. Fracturing occurs either at the surface, or in the transition region between the case and the core of a case–hardened surface where the stress gradient is large enough to overcome the strength of the core in the region near the case.

Spalling is generally considered a special form of destructive pitting. One type of spalling occurs when large pits are formed by the joining of smaller, adjacent pits. Other forms are characterized by a flaking of the metal surface layer. In this case, the new, fractured surface is essentially parallel to the original surface. Flaking is usually associated with a severe stress gradient near the surface. The net result of one or more such flaked regions is to leave a badly pitted surface on the roller or the cam.

Macroscopic and microscopic obervations of fracture surfaces indicate that the macroscopic modes of pitting and spalling failure are different from one other, but that the microscopic modes of failure are similar.

The failure surfaces have been analyzed by means of light microscopy and transmission electron microscopy using replicas. Recently, the scanning electron microscope, which is suitable for the location of specific area of interest and which has a great depth of focus, has been used to advantage in the field of surface failure analysis. Various fracture surfaces have been analyzed using the scanning electron microscope, but the systematic observation and the analysis of surface failure due to rolling fatigue is far from complete.

When two rolling surfaces are in contact under load, Hertzian stress analysis shows that the maximum shear stress occurs not immediately at the surface of the two bodies, but at a small but finite distance beneath the surface as shown by the solid–line curve in Fig. 12-5. Hence, when a fatigue crack does develop, it is located in the general vicinity of this distance below the surface. In cases of combined rolling and sliding there is, superimposed on the shear stress pattern for pure rolling, an additional tangential stress distribution due to the sliding. The result is that the maximum value of the total stress is increased over that for pure rolling alone, but its location is raised nearer to the surface (see Fig. 12-5). As a result, the tendency toward pitting failure is increased somewhat, but when formed the pits are shallower. At the limit, with principally sliding motion with only a minor component of rolling, the point of maximum stress may be so near the surface that the wear particles resulting from surface fatigue become indistinguishable from those produced by the other sliding types of wear. With respect to reducing surface fatigue to lengthen the useful life of parts in rolling contact, the following observations may serve as guidelines:

1. Any design or operating changes that reduce contact stresses (and, in some instances, changes that reduce sliding velocity) help prevent pitting.
2. The resistance to pitting can be considerably increased by increasing surface hardness and by surface polishing. It is common practice to make the follower roller of softer or first–destroyed material for easy replacement.

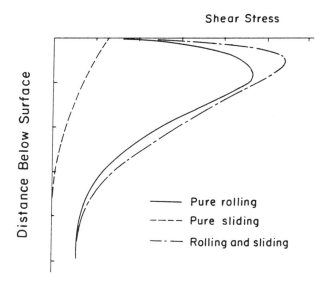

Fig. 12-5. Comparison of shear stress at various depths below surface in rolling, sliding, and combined rolling /sliding contact.

3. Lubrication is helpful, but its effect is primarily indirect in two respects. Its first function is to wash away grit that would otherwise score or damage the rolling surfaces, and its second function is to prevent corrosion that, even though it be very minute, will sufficiently roughen the smooth rolling surfaces and form minute pits, from which a fatigue crack can start owing to the local stress concentration.

12-4. CAM MATERIALS AND SURFACE TREATMENTS

It has been an established practice to harden materials to resist wear. Although the surface hardness of a material is not always the sole criterion for wear resistance, it is not possible to abandon hardness as an important factor. We shall outline in the following the commonly used cam materials and their surface treatments, starting with those materials with the least hardness.

Soft Metals — Acceptable materials in this range are aluminum, brass, bronze, cold rolled steel, etc. The selection of these materials is usually dictated by the requirements of the mechanism. These requirements can be many and varied, but the two that first come to mind are compatibility of materials and the weight factor. Soft cams require the same degree of accuracy as hardened cams. Profiles are milled, and good surface finish is still required.

Cast Iron or Meehanite — Cams of this type have largely been replaced on high–speed, high–load applications by hardened materials. However, there are specific applications where cams made of this material are still used and are an excellent choice. Meehanite–GA has good shock resistance and good vibratory damping, and through these two qualities it has a tendency to reduce noise in the mechanism.

Toughened Materials Only — These are normally materials in the SAE 6145 class, hardened up to approximately 30 to 35 Rockwell C. This process normally does not require grinding because it is usually used where conventional milling accuracies are sufficient and contact stresses are not excessive.

Surface Hardness Only Such as that Achieved by Flame Hardening or Induction Hardening — Either a SAE 6145 or a 6150 material is good for use. SAE 1045 is not. It is not as stable as the 6100 series and therefore has a tendency toward more distortion in the heat treatment cycle. The 6100 series steels are used when surface hardness only is required because profile accuracy requirements and follower loads do not call for any core hardness.

Flame Hardening Plus Core Hardening — This is nothing more than a refinement of the preceding method whereby the material is brought up to a core hardness of approximately 30 Rockwell C, machine finished, and flame hardened.

Carburized and Hardened — In a great majority of cases, this is by far the best method of achieving a good, accurate cam at a reasonable cost. The best material in this category is SAE 8620 steel. With 8620 steel, an inherent core hardness of approximately 35 Rockwell C is achieved. It is an oil quench material that in itself gives less heat treating distortion than a water quench and has much less danger of cracking. Carburizing and hardening overcome every disadvantage of flame hardening. Better heat treatment control, more uniform hardness, and much better metallurgy of the cam surface results. However, cams made of this material and hardened by this method definitely should be ground.

Through Hardened Materials Such as Tool Steels — These are the best for high follower loads and for high production machines where initial material and cost are small factors. They definitely require grinding in all cases. Here again, a water quench steel is not satisfactory. It is always better to use either an oil quench tool steel or an air–hardened tool steel. The best, naturally, is air hardening because of the higher hardness that can be achieved. The cost of air hardened tool steels is higher than that of oil quenched steels.

12-5. EXPERIMENTAL DATA OF SURFACE WEAR TESTS

Without information on the surface–endurance limits of mating materials, the design of direct–contact machine members for wear is essentially a matter of judgment and experience based on the past performance records of similar designs. Recognizing this, Buckingham was the first to design and to build a surface-wear testing machine. Since 1932, surface wear tests have been conducted by Talbourdet (212) of United Shoe Machinery Corporation. Considerable data have been gathered and made available to design engineers. They determine "load–stress K factors" for various materials and surface hardness combinations, and for various cycles of operation. With this information, the limitation on load capacity can be determined for a desired wear–life expectancy.

Fig. 12-6 shows the schematic of the roll–testing machine. The test rolls are mounted on gear–driven arbors, one of which is supported in a fixed frame, the other in a pivoted frame. The load is applied through a calibrated spring connecting the two frames. The rolls and their supporting bearing are adequately lubricated.

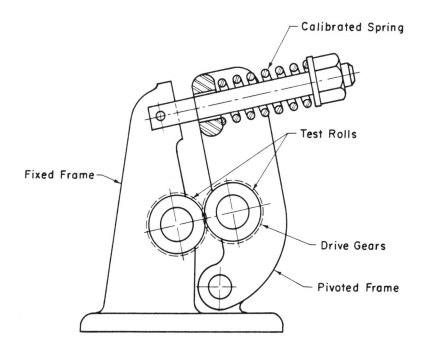

Fig. 12-6. Schematic of testing machine developed by United Shoe Machinery, Corp.

The Load–Stress K Factor

Recall that the Hertzian stress for two cyclinders of dissimilar metal in contact is given by Eq. (12-11). For a Poisson's ratio $\mu = 0.03$ (a common assumption for metal), Eq. (12-11) can be reduced to the form

$$P = \frac{K}{\left(\dfrac{1}{\rho_1} + \dfrac{1}{\rho_2} \right)} , \qquad (12\text{-}13)$$

where $K = \dfrac{\sigma_{max}}{0.35} \left(\dfrac{1}{E_1} + \dfrac{1}{E_2} \right).$ \qquad (12-14)

Quantity K is called the load–stress factor for cylinders in contact. Table 12-4 lists this K value for 100 million repetitions of stress for materials combinations subjected to rolling only and rolling combined with 9% sliding action. The values for rolling only are applicable to cam–follower applications where sliding is not anticipated. The values listed under 9% sliding are applicable to spur and helical gears, or to cams where a small amount of sliding is anticipated.

Percentage Sliding

Percent sliding is the ratio of relative sliding velocity to the surface velocity of either test roll. As such, it is dimensionless and independent of the speed of operation. The percentage sliding on each specimen of a combination will be different, and can vary from zero for rolling contact to infinity for pure sliding. Because of the nature of this parameter, the experimental load–stress factors listed in Table 12-4 for similar percent-sliding conditions can be used even though test-roll and gear or cam speeds differ.

Load–Life Curve

Values of K for various combinations of materials have been determined experimentally as a function of the number of stress cycles required to produce surface failure in the test specimens. Fig. 12-7 shows a typical load–life curve of test data obtained from 5.84–cm diameter gray cast iron rolls loaded in rolling contact.

   In plotting K versus life, a least-square curve fitting line is drawn through the normal scatter of significant points obtained from tests. The equation for the K–factor as a function of life is derived from the slope of these fitting lines

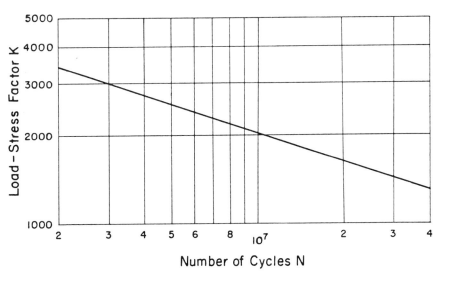

Fig. 12-7. A typical K–N curve for gray cast iron roll having a hardness 130 to 180 Brinell.

$$\log_{10} K = \frac{B - \log_{10} N}{A}, \tag{12-15}$$

where constant A and B are given in Table 12-4, and N is the number of stress cycles for which a K value is required.

The load–life curve represents probable values. Exact load–life factors, therefore, may be greater or less than those listed. In addition, tests are generally conducted under optimum conditions, which are not normally encountered in the field. Engineering judgment must still be applied in allowing for mounting errors, lubrication deficiencies, thermal effects, and other operating or geometric variables not accounted for in the laboratory tests. Therefore, it is logical that factors of safety should be considered when determining the safe wear load capacity of cams.

Example 12-2

Determine the maximum allowable contact force between the cam and the follower of Example 12-1 to avoid pronounced wear before 100 million stress cycles. The cam is made of 4150 heat treated steel, with 270 ∼ 300 BHN, and a phosphate–coated surface. The follower roller is made of roll–hardened tool steel with 60 ∼ 62 RC.

From Table 12-4, we find that the K–factor for the combination of materials is $K = 9000$. From Eq. (12-13) the total allowable normal contact load for a cam having a thickness of 2 cm is

Table 12-4. Experimental load/stress factors for gear and cam materials

Material Running Against Tool-Steel Roll Hardened to 60-62 Rc

Material	K_1	Rolling Only Hertz Stress (MPa)	A	B	K_1	Rolling & 9% Sliding Hertz Stress (MPa)	A	B
1020 steel carburized, 0.045 in. in depth, 50-60 Rc	87.6	1770	7.39	66.70	72.1	1610	13.20	111.73
1020 steel, 130-150 Bhn	—	—	—	—	11.8	650	4.78	41.80
1117 steel, 130-150 Bhn	10.6	610	4.21	37.57	8.0	530	3.63	33.05
X1340 steel, induction-hardened, 0.045" min depth, 45-58 Rc	69.0	1570	6.56	59.42	56.6	1420	8.51	73.98
Blue tempered spring-steel stampings, 40-50 Rc	17.0	780	4.00	36.92	—	—	—	—
1144CD steel, 260-290 Bhn (stressproof)	—	—	—	—	16.9	770	11.01	87.58
4140/4150 steel, 350-370 Bhn (etd 180)	—	—	—	—	78.1	1670	17.76	148.17
4150 steel, heat-treated, 270-300 Bhn, phosphate-coated	83.0	1720	11.40	98.28	59.8	1450	15.47	128.30
4150 steel, heat-treated, 270-300 Bhn, flash chromium-plated	41.8	1220	11.18	93.20	—	—	—	—
4150 steel, heat-treated, 270-300 Bhn	62.3	1490	8.80	76.59	43.4	1240	11.56	96.29
4150 ceramic cast steel, heat-treated, 270-300 Bhn	—	—	—	—	19.7	830	17.86	138.28
4340 steel, induction-hardened 0.045" min depth, 50-58 Rc	89.7	1790	14.15	120.54	62.1	1490	14.02	117.26
4340 steel, heat-treated, 270-300 Bhn	—	—	—	—	38.1	1170	18.05	144.84

Table 12-4. Cont'd.

Material	K_1	Rolling Only Hertz Stress (MPa)	A	B	K_1	Rolling & 9% Sliding Hertz Stress (MPa)	A	B
6150 steel, 300-320 Bhn	8.1	540	3.10	29.41	—	—	—	—
6150 steel, 270-300 Bhn	—	—	—	—	12.6	670	8.30	66.92
18% Ni maraging tool, air-hardened, 48-50 Rc	—	—	—	—	29.8	1010	3.90	37.15
Gray-iron, Class 20, 160-190 Bhn, phosphate-coated	6.5	370	3.90	34.57	—	—	—	—
Gray-iron, Class 20, 140-160 Bhn	5.4	340	3.83	33.79	5.1	320	4.09	35.42
Gray-iron, Class 30, 200-220 Bhn	7.7	430	4.24	37.20	—	—	—	—
Gray-iron, Class 30, heat-treated (austempered), 255-300 Bhn, phosphate-coated	20.0	700	5.52	48.30	17.4	650	6.01	51.51
Gray-iron, Class 30, oil-quenched, 270-415 Bhn	12.7	560	5.45	46.71	—	—	—	—
Gray-iron, Class 35, 225-255 Bhn	13.8	590	11.62	90.95	13.1	580	8.39	67.72
Gray-iron, Class 45, 220-240 Bhn	—	—	—	—	7.3	450	3.77	33.88
Nodular-iron, Grade 80-60-03, 207-241 Bhn	14.5	660	10.09	80.26	13.5	640	5.56	47.65
Nodular-iron, Grade 100-70-03, heat-treated, 240-260 Bhn	—	—	—	—	24.6	840	13.04	104.38
High-strength yellow brass, drawn, 157-162 Bhn	8.7	460	3.69	33.61	—	—	—	—
Nickel bronze, 80-90 Bhn	9.6	500	6.01	49.96	—	—	—	—
SAE 65 phosphor-bronze sand casting, 65-80 Bhn	5.0	360	2.84	27.03	2.4	250	2.39	23.25
SAE 660 continuous-cast bronze, 70-80 Bhn	—	—	—	—	2.2	230	1.94	20.32
Aluminum bronze	17.4	680	5.87	50.50	—	—	—	—
Zinc die casting, 70 Bhn	1.7	190	3.07	27.13	1.5	180	3.11	27.23

Table 12-4. Cont'd.

Material	Rolling Only				Rolling & 9% Sliding			
	K_1	Hertz Stress (MPa)	A	B	K_1	Hertz Stress (MPa)	A	B
Random-fiber cotton-base phenolic	6.9	—	6.03	49.26	6.3	—	5.95	48.44
Graphitized laminated phenolic	6.2	—	6.58	52.69	—	—	—	—
Nema Grade L laiminated phenolic	6.1	—	9.39	71.68	5.7	—	5.53	45.36
Linen-base laminated phenolic	5.7	—	8.54	65.68	4.6	—	6.46	51.05
Acetal resin	4.3	—	—	—	4.0	—	—	—
Polyurethane rubber	1.7	—	—	—	—	—	—	—
Polycarbonate resin	0.4	—	—	—	—	—	—	—
High-molecular-weight polyethylene	—	—	—	—	2.5	—	8.03	59.43
MC 901 nylon	—	—	—	—	6.2	76	17.04	123.74
Material Running Against Same								
AISI 1117 Hot rolled steel, 100-110 Bhn	—	—	—	—	11.0	630	5.23	44.83
1020 steel, 130-170 Bhn, and same but phosphate-coated	20.1	840	7.84	65.25	10.2	600	6.38	52.72
1144 CD steel, 260-290 Bhn, (stress-proof)	—	—	—	—	15.9	750	4.10	37.53
4150 steel, heat-treated, 270-300 Bhn, and same but phosphate-coated	46.9	1290	10.46	88.24	16.0	760	9.58	77.01
SAE 4150 Leaded steel, 270-300 Bhn	—	—	—	—	17.8	800	6.55	55.49
4150 leaded steel, phosphate-coated, heated-treated, 270-300 Bhn	—	—	—	—	21.0	860	6.63	56.55

Table 12-4. Cont'd.

Material	K_1	Rolling Only Hertz Stress (MPa)	A	B	K_1	Rolling & 9% Sliding Hertz Stress (MPa)	A	B
4340 steel, heat-treated, 320-340 Bhn, and same	70.9	1590	18.13	150.33	35.8	1130	26.19	205.84
but phosphate-coated	6.6	310	3.05	28.81	6.3	300	3.55	32.15
Gray-iron, Class 20, 130-180 Bhn								
Gray-iron, Class 30, heat-treated (austempered), 270-290 Bhn	26.3	700	7.25	61.80	24.2	670	7.87	66.11
Nodular-iron, Grade 80-60-03, 207-241 Bhn	24.5	810	4.69	42.65	12.1	570	4.18	37.61
Mechanite, 190-240 Bhn	11.1	550	4.76	41.54	10.1	530	4.94	42.60
Copper infiltrated iron powdered metal 15-25 Cu, 0-1C, BAL. Fe), 7.1-7.4 g/cm³	—	—	—	—	9.9	510	2.65	26.54
High strength alloy powdered metal (4600 alloy, 2 Cu, 1C), 6.4-6.7 g/cm³	—	—	—	—	13.9	520	8.13	66.08
Prefiltron 22 powdered metal (22 Cu, BAL. Fe), 7.2-7.3 g/cm³	—	—	—	—	4.7	340	3.62	32.15
Same as above three except contact surfaces ground	—	—	—	—	6.6	410	3.50	31.87
Special iron-ni alloy powdered metal (5 Ni, 2 Cu, BAL. IRON), 6.8-7.0 g/cm³	—	—	—	—	8.2	430	7.29	58.40
Medium density allow powdered metal (5 Cu, 1C, BAL. Fe), 6.4-6.6 g/cm³	—	—	—	—	4.8	300	2.17	22.50
6061-T6 aluminum, hard anodic coat	2.4	—	10.27	73.57	1.8	—	5.02	39.39
HK31XA-T6 Magnesium, HAE coat	1.2	—	6.46	47.33	1.9	—	11.07	77.51

$$F = \frac{2K}{\dfrac{1}{\rho_1} + \dfrac{1}{\rho_2}} = \frac{2 \times 9000}{\dfrac{1}{1} + \dfrac{1}{0.65}}$$

$$= 7090 \ N \ .$$

These calculations can be readily repeated for other materials combinations listed in Table 12-4.

12-6. ROLLER FOLLOWER

There are two types of cam followers: the roller and the flat–faced. The roller follower is used because of its low friction and low rolling wear. It is primarily used where high relative velocities exist between the cam surface and its contacting body. Although the roller shape may be cylindrical, conical, or hyperboloidal, the cylindrical roller follower is the most commonly used because of its simplicity, ease of manufacturing, and commercial availability.

Pure rolling action is desired, although a certain tolerable amount of sliding always exists. When the percent sliding is increased, the coefficient of friction follows an upward progression. In addition, the point of maximum shear stress approaches the surface. This is evident from the observation and the measurement of progressively shallower fatigue pits in the wear tests as percentage sliding is increased. Excessive sliding may be caused by misalignment, backlash, jamming in the bearing race, fluctuations in the cam peripheral speed, etc.

Plain Rollers

Rollers using a plain journal bearing have been employed in some applications, but they have drawbacks due to the excessive wear that occurs on the limited area of contact between the bearing stud and the cam roll. Careful consideration should be given to designs in which journal–bearing cam rolls are used. Nylon is a particularly effective roller material for moderate loadings.

Fig. 12-8 shows the forces acting on a follower roll. Let P be the applied load; R and r represent the radii of the cam roll and the cam roll stud, respectively; and μ and μ_1 represent the coefficients of friction between the cam and the roll and between the cam roll and the cam roll stud, respectively. The friction moment tending to rotate the cam roll is PR, and the friction moment resisting the rotation of the cam roll is $Pr\mu_1$. To avoid skidding, it is necessary to have $PR\mu > Pr\mu_1$ or $R\mu > r\mu_1$.

Obviously, the load–carrying capacity of the cam roll bearing must be greater than the maximum load imposed on the cam and the roll surfaces.

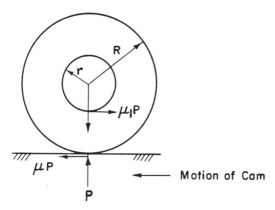

Fig. 12-8. Forces acting on follower roll.

As a rule of thumb, when the radius of the cam roll is approximately equal to one-third of the radius of curvature of the cam, the bearing capacity will be equal to approximately one-third of the catalog rating for quiet-running radial loads.

Anti–Friction Rollers

If possible, cam rolls should be straddle–mounted and supported by an antifriction bearing of ball, roller, or needle construction to maintain rolling contact. Some of these are available commercially. The commercial follower employs a needle bearing, which has an advantage over ball bearings because the large number of small–diameter, closely spaced rollers appreciably reduce the bending stress in the outer bearing race.

Two types of needle–bearing cam roll mountings are available, the stud type and the yoke type. Both types have an extra–heavy outer race to provide the strength and the shock absorbing properties required in applications where the outer race is not constrained in a housing, but rather is mounted on a raceway zone–hardened stud. Thrust surfaces are incorporated into the bearing design so that the outer race is non separable from the inner member. These thrust surfaces are primarily for axial location and cannot support appreciable thrust loads.

The stud–type cam roll is shown in Fig. 12-9. It has an integral threaded stud that serves as the inner race and as the bearing shaft. Grooves in the stud provide passageways for a lubricant. This design permits heavier stud cross sections than would be possible if a separate inner race and shaft assembly were used. Where cam followers are mounted as cantilevers, the increased rigidity of the integral stud is of advantage. The stud type also offers considerable convenience in mounting design. The yoke–type, or clevis–type, cam roll, as shown in Fig. 12-10, is used where it is possible to support the cam follower on both sides.

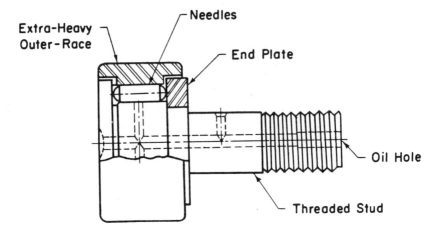

Fig. 12-9. Stud–type cam follower.

It cannot be used for the groove or the face cam, where the stud must be mounted on one side only. A pair of hardened steel endplates confines the rollers and the outer race. This yoke mounting is preferable to the cantilever stud type for use in avoiding bending and misalignment in heavily loaded systems. Accurate alignment is especially important for highly loaded systems because it distributes the load and the wear over the width of the cam and assures optimum performance from the bearing. Cam follower bearings are worn more rapidly by misalignment than by overloading with swinging follower systems; the designer may have a choice in the position of the follower assembly or in the direction of rotation of the cam. Whenever possible, the cam

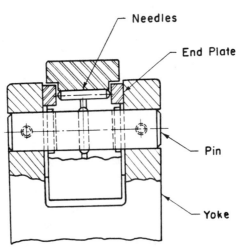

Fig. 12-10. Yoke–type cam follower.

should rotate away from the follower pivot. This reduces wobbling in the roller and results in better alignment of the bearing.

Seals should be specified when the unit is operated in a contaminating environment. The seal is made of specially treated nylon lips. Interference fits (in the outer–race undercut) and a lip–wiping fit (on the outer edge of the endplate or integral flange) hold the seal in place.

Selection of Needle Bearing Size

The selection of commercial needle–bearing cam followers is based primarily on load capacity, sometimes known as "Basic Dynamic Capacity." Generally, the catalog value of load rating is based on a rotational speed of 33.3 rpm, a B–10 life of 500 hours, and a track hardness of RC–40. When application characteristics vary from these norms, one has to account for the differences. The designer has to determine the effective load that the follower must carry. If no shock loading is expected, then this load is a constant. If shock loads are expected, the actual steady–state load must be multiplied by a shock factor. When the actual load varies with time, the root–mean load is used. This load capacity should be corrected by two factors:

1. the life factor, which accounts for the difference between the required life and the rated life.
2. the speed factor, which accounts for the difference between the required speed and the rated speed.

Details on determining these values are generally available in standard textbooks on machine design and also in manufacturers' catalogs, which provide tables and charts to streamline the selection process. We shall not elaborate on these here.

Lubrication

The cam–roll bearing must be lubricated to maintain rolling action. For rolling contact conditions, intermittent lubrication of the cam surface with a thin lubricant (10 SSU at 38°C) will prevent corrosion and dispose of particles of metal that may be sheared off the cam surface. The most widely accepted metal characteristic reducing the tendency to gall is self–lubrication. Self–lubricating followers have MoS_2–filled nylon rings at the ends of the needles. The rings reduce internal friction and temperatures, increasing grease life and allowable speed. When studs are likely to deflect or to be misaligned, the rings can boost bearing life by a factor of ten. Generally, self–lube followers cut relubrication frequency to about one–third that of the non–self–lube follower. For preloaded cam systems and for high–speed designs in which the rate of sliding may be high, lubrication of the cam surface may also be necessary to prevent sparking and surface welding and to dissipate the heat generated in operation. In some instances, surface welding and sparking can be eliminated by contaminating the cam surface with a phosphate coating (Parco–Lubrite). In others, where combinations of high loads and high sliding velocity are present, it may be necessary to use extreme–pressure lubricants containing chlorine or sulphur additives. However, the use of grease, semifluid grease, or other high–viscosity oils, which may be employed for lubricating the flat–faced follower, is not recommended for roller followers.

13
Force Analysis

13-1. INTRODUCTION

There are forces associated with the motions of all machine parts. In a design process, the magnitude, the direction, and the line of action of all forces and torques must be identified and evaluated so that the dimensions of the machine parts can be chosen to provide sufficient strength and rigidity, given the appropriate choice of materials. Generally speaking, the forces acting on a cam–and–follower system include the static and applied load, the inertia force, the frictional resistances, the vibratory forces, and the spring loads. In addition, the transfer of energy in a machine system must be known so that the power required for driving the machine can be calculated.

13-2. APPLIED LOAD OR WORKING LOAD

Working loads represent the useful work done by a mechanism. They may be gradually applied, suddenly applied, or applied through an impact. The static forces, when gradually applied, are the principal forces in a slowly moving cam. The static-force analysis of a cam with different types of followers has been presented in sections 10-5 through 10-7, when we dealt with the pressure-angle and its limitations. The application of working loads may augment or reduce the other forces in the system. For example, if applied during the forward cam stroke, they add to the inertia forces during the acceleration period. During the deceleration period, they have a tendency to retard the impact and vibratory forces by absorbing some of the energy stored in the follower mechanism.

Impact forces are caused by separation due to backlash or to clearance between the two mechanical parts in match. An inadequate preload of the constrained spring may cause separation with impact between the cam and the follower during operation. If the cam follower is engaged in a grooved cam, there is a chance that the combined forces will change the direction of force action (as during the deceleration period) to produce an impact when the cam follower moves from one side of the groove to the other.

13-3. INERTIA FORCES

Inertia forces are caused by the necessity of moving masses lineally or rotationally. A cam follower may have a lineal or angular movement, and it may produce a simple motion of a single mass or move different masses with strokes–lineal or angular–different from the stroke of the cam follower itself.

The inertia force is a product of the mass and the acceleration (the moment of inertia and the angular acceleration for a rotational system) of the follower system. The inertia force, passing through the center of gravity of the rigid body, has a direction opposite to that of the acceleration. By using D'Alembert's principle, we can make a free–body diagram of all of the forces involved and analyze the dynamic condition as an equivalent static problem.

13-4. FRICTION FORCES

Friction is inevitable between contacting parts in relative motion. The magnitude of the frictional effects is not always negligible. In frictional analysis we must consider both the static and the kinetic values of friction. The static coefficient of friction indicates the force required to commence sliding; the kinetic coefficient indicates the force required to maintain sliding. Tables of friction coefficients found in standard compilations generally show the static coefficients being about 40% greater than the kinetic.

The best and the most accurate way to include frictional resistances in a design is to measure them from the actual machine or prototype. Handbooks list these resistances for some combinations of materials, but the conditions under which the values are obtained are usually not given, and when they are, they seldom fit the specific conditions at hand. The applied load, the surface roughness, and the apparent area of contact have little influence on the coefficient of friction, but the following factors are important.

• Surface Cleanliness — Metal surfaces are usually contaminated. It is difficult to estimate the degree of contamination of a particular surface because many contaminants do not cover the surface completely. Ignorance of the degree of cleanliness is the main reason for the poor "predictability" of friction values.

• Velocity — The effect of velocity on friction is usually small. Typically, for every change in sliding velocity by a factor of 10, friction changes by about 10%.

• Temperature — The effects of temperature can be quite marked. In general, changes in the coefficient of friction are on the order of 0.1 per 38°C and tend to be of the same magnitude up to approximately 100°C. Superimposed on these may be "transition temperatures," at which the friction coefficients change by the large amount of 0.2 to 0.5 over a temperature range that may be as narrow as 10°C.

Fig. 13-1 shows a general-purpose friction chart. From this chart one can pick out realistic friction coefficients for a wide range of materials and lubrication conditions. Three groups of materials are plotted: nonmetal on nonmetal, dissimilar metals, and similar metals. The extent of the shading shows the probable range of values. There is roughly a 90 percent probability of getting a point within the shaded region. Note that the friction coefficient is plotted on a logarithmic scale. The lubrication conditions are plotted along the abscissa, ranging from no lubricant to cases where there are boundary conditions with a good lubricant.

As it is often difficult to ensure good lubrication between a cam and its follower, and between the follower and its guides, it is important to make generous allowances for the effects of friction in the design of cams.

13-5. VIBRATORY FORCES

Variations or sudden changes in elastic deformations create vibrations. These vibrations in turn produce stresses and forces that are superimposed on the inertia force in the follower system. The magnitude of these vibratory stresses and forces are influenced by the acceleration characteristics, the rigidity, and the damping of the follower mechanism. The vibration analysis of a cam-driven mechanism can be complicated. This topic will be separately treated in Chapters 15 and 16.

13-6. SPRING FORCE

The primary functions of the spring force in a cam-follower system are to counteract the inertia of the follower and to maintain contact between the follower and the cam throughout the motion cycle.

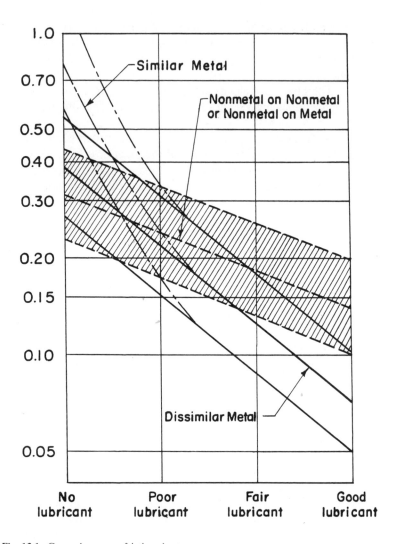

Fig. 13-1. General-purpose friction chart.

 The spring force is directly proportional to the follower body displacement. The load of the spring must be adequate but not overly large. If the load is too small, the follower will jump off the cam surface. Conversely, the use of a high spring force to prevent follower jump may be a poor solution, since the increased normal forces on the cam often result in undesirable dynamic forces and excessive wear. In this situation, rotating the cam will also require more power than desirable.

 Fig. 13-2 shows a cam–and–follower mechanism with its displacement and acceleration curves. The critical design point is where the inertia reaction of

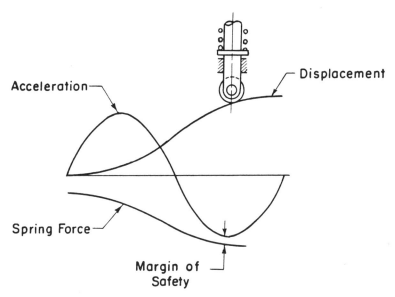

Acceleration

Displacement

Spring Force

Margin of
Safety

Fig. 13-2 Critical design point for spring.

the follower is a maximum and tends to eliminate contact between the follower and the cam. This point occurs in the vicinity of the maximum negative acceleration. Jump will occur when the negative inertia force of the system exceeds the available spring force. If a purely static evaluation is made, the spring loading curve represented here might be chosen for a specified speed of operation. When an additional reserve is found necessary to overcome the force caused by vibratory effects, a large spring rate increase might be considered.

Furthermore, if the follower train responds to a dynamic excitation, the spring will also respond to the same, since it has its own natural frequency. Surging, or coil flutter, is the common manifestation of this phenomenon. The surging of the spring is the result of forced vibration waves advancing and reflecting throughout the length of the spring. Thus, a complicated series of vibrations may be continually reinforcing and only partially canceling each other during the spring action. The vibrations of cam–and–follower systems will be treated separately in Chapter 16. All of the considerations in this chapter are on the basis of a static spring force.

Example 13-1

Fig. 13-3 shows the schematic of a spring–loaded, cam–driven hole punch. For simplicity of illustration and ease of calculation, let us assume that an unsymmetric parabolic motion curve with a dwell is used to allow the insertion and the removal of the work–piece between punches. To keep the spring size and the surface stresses small, the magnitude of positive acceleration is set equal to twice that of the deceleration during the working period. Also assume that the shearing load during punching starts at 200 Newtons and linearly decreases to zero as the work–piece is penetrated. Let the total distance traveled by the punch be 4 cm, consisting of 3 cm in approach, $\frac{1}{2}$ cm in penetrating the material thickness, and $\frac{1}{2}$ cm in overshoot. Other data are as follows:

Cam speed: 60 rpm, uniform.
Follower outward stroke: 4 cm in 45° of cam rotation.
Follower return stroke: 4 cm in 45° of cam rotation.
Weight of punch (including all attachments): 50 N.

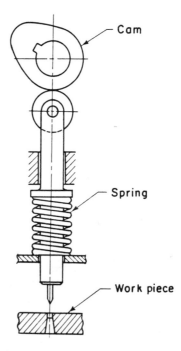

Fig. 13-3. Cam–driven hole puncher.

Design the helical spring with a margin of safety of at least 35 N in excess of the forces tending to eliminate the constraining of the follower on the cam. This margin will compensate for friction, error, etc.

We first note that the period of motion is 1 sec. The time of the outward motion stroke during the punching operation is $1 \times \frac{45}{360}$ or $\frac{1}{8}$ sec, which is also the time of the return stroke. The remaining $\dfrac{3}{4}$ sec is the dwell period.

Denoting the angular displacement of the cam by θ, the follower's displacement by y, and its acceleration by a, and using the subscripts 1 and 2 to indicate the periods of acceleration and deceleration, respectively, we can write

$$\theta_1 + \theta_2 = 45°$$

$$\frac{\theta_2}{\theta_1} = \frac{2}{1}\ .$$

Therefore,

$$\theta_1 = 15° \qquad \theta_2 = 30°$$

The corresponding time periods are

$$t_1 = \frac{15}{45}\left(\frac{1}{8}\right) = \frac{1}{24}\ \text{sec},$$

and

$$t_2 = \frac{30}{45}\left(\frac{1}{8}\right) = \frac{1}{12}\ \text{sec}.$$

Furthermore, from the relationship

$$y_1 + y_2 = 4\ ,$$

that is

$$\frac{1}{2}\,a_1 t_1^{\,2} + \frac{1}{2}\,a_2 t_2^{\,2} = 4$$

or

$$\frac{1}{2}\,a_1\left(\frac{1}{24}\right)^2 + \frac{1}{2}\,a_2\left(\frac{1}{12}\right)^2 = 4$$

and

$$a_1 = -2a_2,$$

we obtain

$$a_1 = 1536 \text{ cm/sec}^2$$

$$a_2 = -768 \text{ cm/sec}^2.$$

Hence,

$$y_1 = \frac{1}{2}(1536)\left(\frac{1}{24}\right)^2 = 1.333 \text{ cm.}$$

$$y_2 = \frac{1}{2}(768)\left(\frac{1}{12}\right)^2 = 2.667 \text{ cm.}$$

Then the follower displacement is

$$y = 768t^2 \qquad\qquad\qquad 0 \le t \le \frac{1}{24}$$

$$y = 4 - 6(1 - 8t)^2 \qquad\qquad \frac{1}{24} \le t \le \frac{5}{24}$$

$$y = 768(0.25 - t)^2 \qquad\qquad \frac{5}{24} \le t \le \frac{1}{4}$$

$$y = 0 \qquad\qquad\qquad\qquad \frac{1}{4} \le t \le 1,$$

and the acceleration is

$$\ddot{y} = 1536 \qquad\qquad\qquad 0 \le t \le \frac{1}{24}$$

$$\ddot{y} = -768 \qquad\qquad\qquad \frac{1}{24} \le t \le \frac{5}{24}$$

$$\ddot{y} = 1536 \qquad \qquad \frac{5}{24} \le t \le \frac{1}{4}$$

$$\ddot{y} = 0 \qquad \qquad \frac{1}{4} \le t \le 1.$$

The inertia load is

$$F = \frac{W}{g}\,\ddot{y} = \frac{50}{980.7}\,\ddot{y},$$

which gives

$$F = 78.31 \qquad \qquad 0 \le t \le \frac{1}{24}$$

$$F = -39.16 \qquad \qquad \frac{1}{24} \le t \le \frac{5}{24}$$

$$F = 39.16 \qquad \qquad \frac{5}{24} \le t \le \frac{1}{4}$$

$$F = 0 \qquad \qquad 0 \le t \le 1.$$

To this we add the force required to penetrate the material, which we have assumed starts at 200 N and diminishes linearly with y as the material is penetrated. This force will therefore be

$$P = 200 - 400(y - 3) \qquad \qquad 3.0 \le y \le 3.5.$$

Therefore,

$$P = 0\,, \qquad \qquad 0 \le t \le 0.074$$

$$\begin{aligned} P &= 200 - 400\,[4 - 6(1 - 8t)^2 - 3] \\ &= 2400(1 - 8t)^2 - 200, \qquad 0.074 \le t \le 0.089 \end{aligned}$$

$$P = 0 \qquad \qquad 0.089 \le t \le 1,$$

where the time regions can be calculated as follows:

From $y = 4 - 6(1 - 8t)^2$

$$t = \frac{1}{8} - \frac{1}{8}\sqrt{\frac{4 - y}{6}}$$

when $y = 3$ cm, $t = 0.074$ sec

when $y = 3.5$ cm, $t = 0.089$ sec.

Accordingly,

$$\theta = 2\pi(0.074) = 0.465 \text{ rad} = 26.64°$$

$$\theta = 2\pi(0.089) = 0.559 \text{ rad} = 32.04°$$

We also must subtract the weight of the punch. The total load without the spring is therefore

$$Q_1 = 28.31 \qquad\qquad\qquad\qquad 0 \leq t \leq \frac{1}{24}$$

$$Q_1 = -89.16 \qquad\qquad\qquad\qquad \frac{1}{24} \leq t \leq 0.074$$

$$Q_1 = 2400(1 - 8t)^2 - 250 \qquad\qquad 0.074 \leq t \leq 0.089$$

$$Q_1 = -89.16 \qquad\qquad\qquad\qquad 0.089 \leq t \leq \frac{5}{24}$$

$$Q_1 = -10.84 \qquad\qquad\qquad\qquad \frac{5}{24} \leq t \leq \frac{1}{4}$$

$$Q_1 = -50 \qquad\qquad\qquad\qquad\qquad \frac{1}{4} \leq t \leq 1.$$

Fig. 13-4(f) shows the superimposed loads without including the spring effect. We see a fluctuating load varying from 110.8 N to −89.2 N. It is necessary to

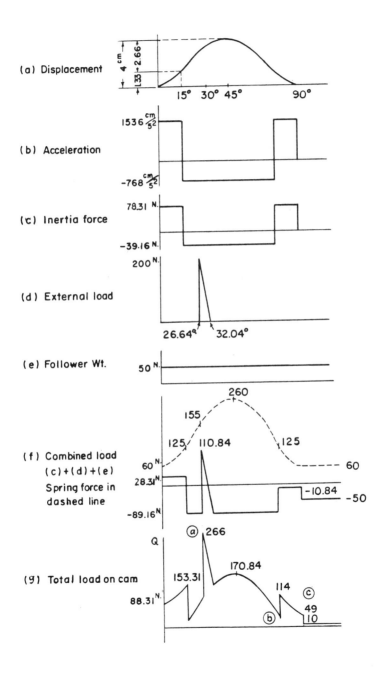

Fig. 13-4. Force diagram of cam follower for example 13-1.

provide a spring force to make the overall load on the cam always positive. Let us try a spring with an initial load of 60 N and a spring rate of 50 N/cm. The spring force is then given by

$$S = 60 + 50y \, ,$$

thus giving

$$S = 60 + 38400 t^2 \qquad\qquad 0 \le t \le \frac{1}{24}$$

$$S = 260 - 300(1 - 8t)^2 \qquad\qquad \frac{1}{24} \le t \le \frac{5}{24}$$

$$S = 60 + 38400(0.25 - t)^2 \qquad\qquad \frac{5}{24} \le t \le \frac{1}{4}$$

$$S = 60 \qquad\qquad \frac{1}{4} \le t \le 1 \, .$$

Finally, the overall load on the cam surface is

$$Q = 88.31 + 38400 t^2 \qquad\qquad 0 \le t \le \frac{1}{24}$$

$$Q = 170.84 - 300(1 - 8t)^2 \qquad\qquad \frac{1}{24} \le t \le 0.074$$

$$Q = 2100(1 - 8t)^2 + 10 \qquad\qquad 0.074 \le t \le 0.089$$

$$Q = 170.84 - 300(1 - 8t)^2 \qquad\qquad 0.089 \le t \le \frac{5}{24}$$

$$Q = 49.16 + 38400(0.25 - t)^2 \qquad\qquad \frac{5}{24} \le t \le \frac{1}{4}$$

$$Q = 10 \qquad\qquad \frac{1}{4} \le t \le 1 \, .$$

The overall load on the cam surface is shown in Fig. 13-4(g). When this is programmed into a computer with plotting capabilities, the values of Q will be plotted automatically. If this is done by hand, it is not necessary to draw a diagram at precisely every point in the motion cycle; only the peak magnitude and the magnitude at critical points are of concern. Point a, where the sum of all the forces is the highest, determines the maximum surface contact stresses between the follower and the cam. At point b the spring force exceeds the net load by a margin of 35.84 Newtons. The spring will itself have both weight and inertia that will affect the value of Q. However, in this case these are negligible. In a case where the spring weight and the inertia are significant the calculation is repeated, including the spring weight in the equivalent weight of the follower, and the spring is redesigned. The equivalent weight of the follower is commonly set equal to the actual weight of the follower linkage plus one–third of the spring weight.

It should be noted that the foregoing problem is meant to serve primarily as a guide for analysis. Flexibility present in the process can be used to improve the design. In the first place, we could change the acceleration curve as well as the ratio of acceleration to deceleration. We could also change the spring preload and the spring index. Cams with long strokes require a careful selection of springs to prevent unnecessary stresses.

Although the example deals with a cam with a reciprocating follower, the procedure of analysis computations applies to cams with swinging followers as well. The only difference for the latter is that the load Q is expressed as a torque.

13-7. MINIMUM PRESET OF FOLLOWER SPRING TO PREVENT CAM–FOLLOWER SEPARATION

The minimum spring preset necessary to maintain cam–follower contact depends upon the type of cam profile being used, the ratio of the forcing frequency to the natural frequency of the spring, and the frictional resistance in the follower. We will outline the method for determining this minimum value here for a typical case of the simple–harmonic motion profile.

The cam–follower system is modeled* to consist of a discrete follower mass m, a linear spring with stiffness k, and a viscous system damping with damping coefficient c. Applying Newton's second law of motion to the follower and accounting for all of the forces contributed by these elements result in the equation

---

* The modeling of cam–and–follower systems is described in Chapter 14.

$$m \frac{d^2 y}{dt^2} + c \frac{dy}{dt} + k(y + \delta) = F(t) , \qquad (13\text{-}1)$$

where y is the follower displacement from its lowest position on the cam surface. δ is the initial preset of the spring. If the follower is operating in the gravitational field, its weight can be included as an additional amount of preset expressed in the form $\frac{w}{k}$, and δ in Eq. (13-1) would in this case be replaced by $\delta + \frac{w}{k}$, where w is the weight of the follower.

For a harmonic cam

$$y = \frac{h}{2} (1 - \cos \omega t)$$

$$\frac{d^2 y}{dt^2} = \frac{h}{2} \omega^2 \cos \omega t ,$$

where h is the maximum amplitude of the cam lift, and ω is the cam angular velocity. Substituting these into Eq. (13-1) gives

$$F(t) = \frac{h}{2} (m\omega^2 - k) \cos \omega t + \frac{h}{2} c\omega \sin \omega t + k \left(\delta + \frac{h}{2} \right) .$$

Introducing nondimensional parameters

$$F_n = \frac{2F(t)}{hk}$$

$$\beta = \frac{\omega}{\omega_n}$$

$$\zeta = \frac{c}{m\omega_n}$$

and $\Delta = \dfrac{2\delta}{h}$,

this equation may be rewritten as

$$F_n(t) = (\beta^2 - 1) \cos \omega t + \zeta \beta \sin \omega t + \Delta + 1 \ . \tag{13-2}$$

Defining the phase angle ϕ by

$$\tan \phi = \frac{\beta^2 - 1}{\zeta \beta} \ ,$$

Eq. (13-2) is further simplified to the form

$$F_n(t) = \sqrt{(\beta^2 - 1)^2 + \zeta^2 \beta^2} \ \sin (\omega t + \theta) + \Delta + 1 \ . \tag{13-3}$$

The expression for the minimum contact force is found by setting the derivative of Eq. (13-3) equal to zero.

$$\frac{dF_n}{dt} = 0 = \omega \sqrt{(\beta^2 - 1)^2 + \zeta^2 \beta^2} \ \cos (\omega t + \phi) \ ,$$

from which

$$\cos (\omega t + \phi) = 0 \ ,$$

giving

$$(\omega t + \phi) = \frac{n \pi}{2} \ , \qquad n = 1, 3, 5, \ldots \tag{13-4}$$

Substituting Eq. (13-4) into Eq. (13-3) gives the expression for the minimum contact force

$$(F_n)_{\min} = \Delta + 1 - [(\beta^2 - 1)^2 - \zeta^2 \beta^2]^{1/2} \ . \tag{13-5}$$

Separation of the follower from the cam is imminent when the contact force goes to zero. Based on this concept, if we set Eq. (13-5) equal to zero and solve for Δ, we obtain

$$\Delta = [(\beta^2 - 1)^2 + \zeta^2 \beta^2]^{1/2} - 1 \ . \tag{13-6}$$

Eq. (13-6), which was derived by Hart and Zorowski (96), gives the preset in terms of the system frequency, the damping, and the cam frequency at which

separation is imminent. This equation compares favorably with an earlier derivation by Baumgarten (13) in which damping was not included. In Eq. (13-6)
for values of Δ greater than that defined by this equation the follower will
remain in contact with the cam throughout the entire cycle of operation. If the
value of Δ is less than that given by the equation, the contact force will become
negative, indicating that separation has occurred. In addition, Eq. (13-6) shows
that $\zeta = \sqrt{2}$ is a critical value of damping above which the onset of separation is predicted at $\beta = 0$ for $\Delta = 0$. In other words, for $\zeta \geq \sqrt{2}$ and
$\Delta = 0$ there is no value of β for which separation will not occur or at least
be imminent.

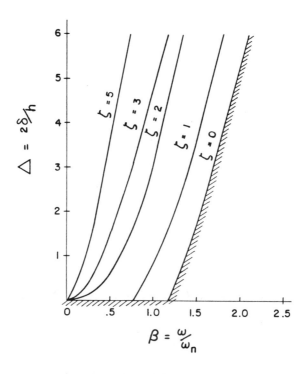

Fig. 13-5. Variation of precompression parameter with frequency ratio for harmonic cam.

Fig. 13-5 shows a plot of Δ versus β with ζ as a varying parameter. This permits easy determination of whether or not separation will occur in a specific
system if the system parameters are known. For a given value of ζ, any combi-
antion of values of Δ and β that lie to the right of that specific ζ curve defines a
situation in which separation will occur.

13-8. EXPERIMENTAL DETERMINATION OF FOLLOWER JUMP

Rao and Raghavacharyulu (187) have devised a simple but fairly accurate experimental method to measure and to investigate the jump phenomenon in a cam follower. Specifically, the minimum speed at which jump initiates, the cam–angle at which jump started, and the time period of cam–follower separation can be measured experimentally.

The experimental setup shown in Fig. 13-6 consists of a cam–follower system mounted on a rigid frame. The cam is driven by a 1 hp, 1475 rpm d.c. shunt motor through a gear–box assembly. By varying the field and the armature currents, it is possible to drive the cam through the gear box at speeds ranging from 30 rpm to 4,000 rpm with good control at all speeds. The roller follower actuated by the cam reciprocates vertically in the stationary guides.

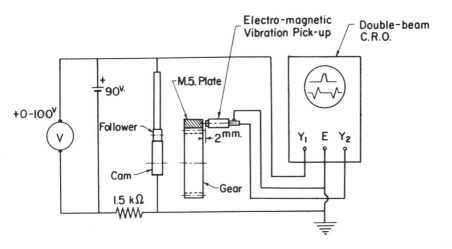

Fig. 13-6. Schematic of experimental set–up for measuring cam follower jump.

When there is no contact separation of the cam from the follower, the beam on the dual channel cathode–ray–oscillograph (CRO) screen remains stationary. The jump phenomenon is observed on the scope with the beam breaking when separation occurs between the cam and the follower.

To predict the cam–angle at which jump occurs, a reference point on the cam is transferred to an indirect but more convenient one on the surface of one of the gears of the gear–box. A small mild steel piece is fixed to the circumference of the gear, which now indicates the 0° position of the cam. An electromagnetic vibration pick–up is used as shown in the Figure, which is connected to the second beam of the dual–channel oscillograph, thus providing the reference position. The position of the jump signal in beam 1 with

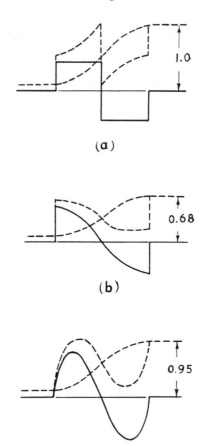

Fig. 13-7. Effect of cam profile on spring forces.

respect to the left reference kink signal in beam 2 gives the angle at which jump initiates. The time period of cam–follower separation can also be measured from the first beam.

Experiments have been conducted on a variety of cam profiles consisting of RDRD motion with different rates of compression springs being used. The results show that the simple harmonic and the parabolic cams have better jump characteristics than the cycloidal and the polynomial cams.

13-9. EFFECT OF CAM PROFILE ON SPRING FORCES AND CONTACT FORCES

The main function of the spring is to maintain contact between the follower and the cam during the motion stroke, especially during the deceleration period. To minimize the rate of wear and to reduce unnecessary side thrust on the follower, the size of the spring should be as small as possible. The space occupied by a spring is practically proportional to the maximum spring load, if the initial load is small. The curves in Fig. 13-7 indicate the relative maximum spring loads necessary to maintain contact between the follower and the cam during deceleration. Three cam curves — the parabolic cam, the harmonic cam, and the cycloidal cam — were compared on the basis of the same operational conditions. These curves had 1″ lift in 120° of cam rotation. The base circle radius was 7.1 cm. The moving parts were assumed to weigh 4.4 N, and the spring had an initial load of 8.9 N, at zero lift and allowed a 5% margin above the highest deceleration force elsewhere. For further information, the reader is referred to the article by Jennings (111).

In Fig. 13-7 we see that the simple–harmonic motion curve is excellent as it requires a spring to sustain a maximum load only 68% as often as the parabolic cam. The variation of contact force is also shown in Fig. 13-7. Sudden changes in the follower contact force result in sudden changes in elastic deformation at the contact region. It is apparent that undesirable vibratory motions will be mitigated if the contact force varies as smoothly as possible. Among the three curves compared, the cycloidal cam gives the smoothest variation of contact force.

Equations of spring preset for other types of cam profiles can be derived in a similar manner. The method also applies analogously to cams with swinging followers. In such cases we deal with rotational inertia and summed external torques instead of forces.

13-10. TORQUE

The torque created by a cam is often overlooked. However, torque may be important, especially for those cam mechanisms carrying heavy loads. From the torque information we can determine the cam–shaft loads and the power needed to drive the follower system, and thus the driving motor size. In finding the torque, the effect of friction may be negligible for cams with roller follower, but it may be significant for cams with flat–faced followers.

Reciprocating Roller Follower

Fig. 13-8 shows a radial cam with a roller follower. Let

T = the torque
F = the force on the cam surface
r = the radial distance to the trace point
s = the follower displacement measured from the prime circle
α = the pressure angle

Neglecting friction, the torque at any cam angle θ is

$$T = Fr \tan \alpha, \tag{13-7}$$

which is the same as Eq. (10-27).

But we know

$$\tan \alpha = \frac{\dot{s}}{r\omega} \, ,$$

where the dot represents differentiation with respect to time. Substitution yields the torque

$$T = \frac{F\dot{s}}{\omega} \, . \tag{13-8}$$

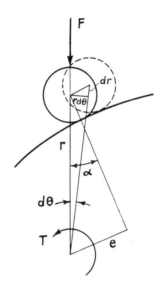

Fig. 13-8.

Thus we see that the torque is proportional to the follower velocity and to the total load. The torque is continuously changing because both the follower velocity and the total load are variables. The total load consists of the static load, the friction, the inertia load, and the spring forces. In high speed applications, the inertia load predominates. Table 13-1 shows a comparison of the torques created by the inertia loads for three different types of motion — the cycloidal motion, the modified sine motion, and the modified trapezoidal motion. In the Table the location of positive and negative maximum torques is expressed in terms of $\dfrac{\theta}{\beta}$, where θ is the cam angle at any time, and β is the total cam rotation.

Table 13-1. Comparison of Torque Created by Inertia Loads

	Comparative Values of Maximum Torques	Location of Positive (Negative) Max Torques
Cycloidal motion	1.0	0.333 (0.667)
Modified sine motion	0.76	0.287 (0.713)
Modified trapezoidal motion	1.27	0.393 (0.607)

It is obvious that the modified sine motion is more advantageous when inertia loads are predominant. This is because the modified sine curve has the lowest maximum value of torque, and its switch from a maximum positive torque to a maximum negative torque is the most gradual.

Reciprocating Flat–Faced Follower

A cam with a reciprocating flat–faced follower is shown in Fig. 13-9(a). Let

T = the torque.
P = the total normal load on the cam.
r_b = the base circle radius.
s = the follower displacement measured from the base circle.
ω = the cam angular velocity.
V_s = the sliding component of velocity.
μ = the coefficient of friction between the follower and the cam.

By the principle of virtual work

$$T\omega = P\dot{s} + \mu P V_s$$

or

$$T = P\,\frac{\dot{s}}{\omega} + \mu P\,\frac{V_s}{\omega}\,, \tag{13-9}$$

where the dot represents differentiation with respect to time. From the similarity of the velocity diagram, Fig. 13-9(b), and triangle OBA of Fig. 13-9(a), it is apparent that

$$V_s = \omega \, \overline{BA}$$

or

$$V_s = \omega(s + r_b).\tag{13-10}$$

Substituting Eq. (13-10) into Eq. (13-9) gives

$$T = P\left[\frac{\dot{s}}{\omega} + \mu(s + r_b)\right].\tag{13-11}$$

Eq. (13-11) shows that the torque is a variable function of the displacement of the follower and the converted velocity $\dfrac{\dot{s}}{\omega}$ (or the slope of the cam surface). The torque is also dependent on the coefficient of friction and on the base circle radius of the cam.

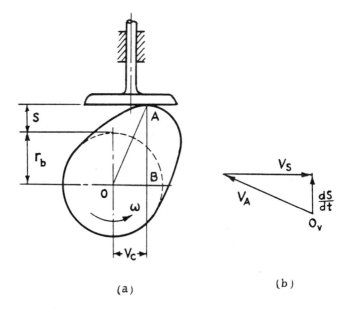

(a)   (b)

Fig. 13-9. Counterbalance mechanism for station wagon tailgate.

In Eq. (13-11) the total load P is a variable: it is the resultant of the weight and the loading of the follower, and the resistance, the inertia, and the spring forces. If the relationship between P and the displacement of the follower is known, the cam driving torque at each instant, its maximum and minimum values, and the average torque can easily be found.

Cam with Prescribed Torque Variations

In many slow–speed cam–activated mechanisms, we can design the cam profile to coordinate the desired input (force) and output (torque) relationships for a finite range of operation. We will use a radial cam with a roller follower to illustrate this.

From Fig. 13-8 we see that

$$\tan \alpha = \frac{dr}{rd\theta} .$$

Substituting this into Eq. (13-7) gives

$$T = \frac{Fdr}{d\theta} . \tag{13-12}$$

Suppose a design requires that the output torque T be proportional to the angle of rotation θ while the input force F be proportional to the follower displacement. Then

$$T = T_i + C_1\theta \tag{13-13}$$

$$F = F_i + C_2(r - r_i) , \tag{13-14}$$

where T_i, F_i, and r_i are initial values of torque, force, and radial distance, respectively. C_1 and C_2 are constants of proportionality.

Substituting Eqs. (13-13) and (13-14) into Eq. (13-12) and integrating, we obtain

$$T_i\theta + \frac{C_1\theta^2}{2} = F_ir + \frac{C_2}{2}(r - r_i)^2 + C_3 ,$$

where the integration constant C_3 can be evaluated by the condition $r = r_i$ when $\theta = 0$. Thus

$$C_3 = -F_ir_i .$$

With this, the final equation can be written as

(13-15)

$$r^2 + \frac{2}{C_2}(F_i - C_2 r_i)r + r_i^2 - \frac{2F_i r_i}{C_2} - \frac{C_1}{C_2}\theta^2 - \frac{2T_i\theta}{C_2} = 0 .$$

Eq. (13-15) is a quadratic equation in r when angle θ and other values are specified.

Next, suppose a constant torque is required in the output, disregarding the change in the spring force as the follower moves. Then C_1 is equal to zero in Eq. (13-13). Subsequently Eq. (13-15) becomes

$$r^2 + \frac{2}{C_2}(F_i - C_2 r_i)r + r_i^2 - \frac{2F_i r_i}{C_2} - \frac{2T_i\theta}{C_2} = 0 . \qquad (13-16)$$

In this way, we can find the cam profile with a prescribed torque pattern. The following example given by Garrett (87) is used for illustration.

Example 13-2.

Fig. 13-10 shows a cam that might be used to raise the upper section of a station wagon tailgate. The output torque required to balance the gate varies sinusoidally with respect to θ according to

$$T = C_1 \sin\left(\theta + \frac{\pi}{6}\right).$$

This is shown in Fig. 13-11. The input torque is supplied by the spring–loaded follower. The spring force decreases as the gate rises, but the torque supplied by the spring increases to a maximum, then gradually drops off to balance the gate. The spring force may be described by

$$F = F_i - C_2(r_i - r) .$$

In this case, the change in r is negative, and

$$Td\theta = -Fdr .$$

When the torque equation and the spring–force equation are substituted into this equation and when the results are integrated and evaluated with the boundary condition $r = r_i$ when $\theta = 0$, we obtain the following quadratic equation in r:

$$r^2 - \frac{2}{C_2}(C_2 r_i - F_i)r - \frac{2F_i r_i}{C_2} + \frac{C_2 r_i^2}{C_2} + \sqrt{3}\ \frac{C_1}{C_2} \tag{13-17}$$

$$(1 - \cos\theta) + \frac{C_1}{C_2}\sin\theta = 0 ,$$

where C_2, F_i, and r_i are given data. The constant C_1 can be determined as follows.

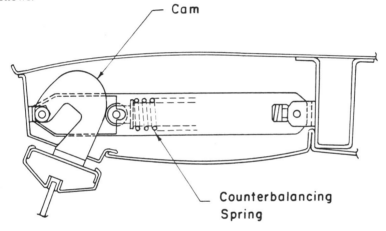

Fig. 13-10. Station wagon tailgate.

With reference to Fig. 13-11, the maximum torque caused by the weight of the tailgate is 1412 N–cm. This torque varies according to

$$T_G = C_3 \sin\left(\theta + \frac{\pi}{12}\right).$$

When $\theta = \dfrac{\pi}{2}$, $T = T_G$, and

$$C_1 = C_3 \ \frac{\sin\left(\dfrac{\pi}{2} + \dfrac{\pi}{12}\right)}{\sin\left(\dfrac{\pi}{2} + \dfrac{\pi}{6}\right)} .$$

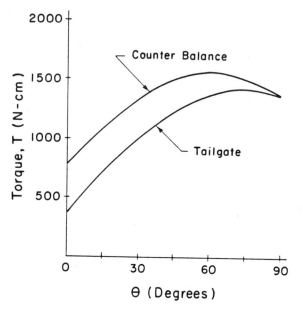

Fig. 13-11. Torque versus angle of rotation for example 13–2.

Since $C_3 = (T_G)_{max} = 1412$ N-cm, $C_1 = 1570$ N-cm .

Assume that $C_2 = 565$ N-cm, $r_i = 7.62$ cm, and $F_i = 890$ N are given. Eq. (13-17) then gives

$$r = 6.044 + [1534 - 2720(1 - \cos \theta) - 1570 \sin \theta]^{1/2} .$$

This is the required pitch profile of the cam as a function of θ.

14
Cam System Dynamics — Modeling

14·1 RATIONALE OF STUDY IN CAM SYSTEM DYNAMICS

If a machine is running relatively slowly, the response of the follower mass will largely accord with the kinematic values calculated on the basis of the static cam command. As the operational speed of machines increases so must consideration of the interactive dynamics of the system.

The difference in action between the cam and the follower is basically due to elasticity in the follower linkages; elastic members are prone to deflection. Machine elements operating at high speeds are subject to high accelerations and large inertia loads. Under these conditions, the follower train acts as a stiff spring. If this spring is compressed by the large inertia forces during the initial acceleration phase, it can subsequently release sufficient energy to overcome the spring force during periods of low or negative inertia forces. This will momentarily cause uncontrollable motion. Thus the follower will vibrate, and the vibration normally remains after the cam rise is completed. This vibratory response of the follower induces wear and may cause malfunctioning of and damage to the machine. Design evaluation of a high–speed cam–actuated system requires an assessment of the response of the follower to the input motion excitation. For every cam motion input a gradually programmed and carefully monitored prototype test can always be carried out to verify the adequacy of the dynamic characteristics of a particular system. Mathematical assessment through modeling and computer simulation is normally used for the study of cam system dynamics. This is especially useful when design parameter trade-offs or compromises must be made and to conduct "worst case" studies of the performance of a system safely and economically. Through the use of this method we can avoid the burden of expensive experimental setups and the time-consuming process of hardware modifications.

14-2 A BRIEF ACCOUNT OF EARLY DEVELOPMENT

In the early twenties, machines were generally run at low speeds, and cam design relied heavily on empirical knowledge and geometric constructions. At that time, cam contours were generally composed of circular arc segments and tangents tailored by trial and error. Little attention was paid to the understanding of the mechanics involved, and when it was, it remained restricted to kinematic considerations, specifically to the value of maximum nominal acceleration with the intent of keeping inertial loading low. Since only nominal accelerations were considered and the vibratory type of acceleration was not taken into account, simple analytical functions, such as the parabolic curves and the sine curves, soon became popular. At increased machine speeds, however, the dynamic properties of these cam curves proved to be rather poor. Designers did not realize that cam curves with a low value of nominal acceleration, such as the parabolic, generate sudden acceleration changes and are prone to vibration.

As engine speeds in the early 1930's increased, mechanical failure of some automotive and aircraft poppet valve units raised questions that could not be explained by conventional analysis. It became increasingly accepted that abrupt changes in the acceleration values of high-speed cams were to be avoided. Thus, not only the maximum value of the acceleration curve was important, but also its derivatives with respect to time, "jerk," and "quirk." The design of such a "jerk-free" and/or "quirk-free" cam provided quite a puzzle. Furthermore, because of the permissible machining tolerances, the practical significance of smoothing out theoretical ripples by demanding higher continuous derivatives was open to discussion. The significance of the flexibility of the follower linkage in cam mechanism dynamics was pointed out by Olmstead (177) and Hrones (104). Hrones first simulated the dynamics of the cam-follower system using a simple spring-mass model on a differential analyzer.

The first experimental verification of poppet valve dynamics was conducted by Mitchell (161) in 1950. He recorded the vibration characteristics of the follower for three basic motions — parabolic, simple harmonic, and cycloidal.

Turkish (217) introduced techniques for measuring the valve gear frequency of vibration and actual acceleration records by monitoring the cam velocity through a magnetic velocity transducer mounted on the engine unit. He also employed an electronic acceleration analyzer in the measurement of the true acceleration of a cam. Thoren, Engemann, and Stoddart (215) measured the valve jump behavior with high–speed motion picture photography. Barkan (11) used a resistance–type strain gage mounted on the upper rocker arm of the valve gear unit to obtain dynamic strain records.

As better laboratory equipment became available, investigations into the true behavior of the valve train of internal combustion engines confirmed that the valve motion at high speeds could deviate considerably from the theoretical values calculated on the basis of static follower lift.

Awareness of valve train vibration led to a number of investigations in the early fifties and later in an attempt to produce various modifications of cam profiles. The modified parabolic, the modified cycloidal (232), the trapezoidal, the modified trapezoidal (172) and the modified sinusoidal curves (202) are examples of these investigations. The use of attenuated harmonic series was also suggested (9) as a means for establishing cam profile specifications. As was shown in Chapter 6, in the category of harmonic series cam curves the accuracy in calculating cam profiles is primarily dependent upon the number of terms in the Fourier series representing the profile. The necessity of truncation in the actual use of such a series and the uncertainty of its mathematical convergence make it difficult to decide how many terms should be included in the computation to guarantee the intended accuracy at the end points of the motion range.

The "polydyne" method (an acronym derived from the words polynominal and dynamics) of Stoddart (209) aroused a great deal of interest. This method, which requires the simultaneous solution of a set of equations to satisfy the imposed kinematic boundary conditions, resulted in the generation of algebraic polynominals for cams. When calculating the cam profile at a given engine speed, the deflection of the valve linkage due to spring and dynamic forces is taken into account. The poly part of the polydyne has been discussed in Chapter 3. This approach is, however, not without shortcomings. While it does produce very smooth valve lift curves, they are of a fixed shape and lack the flexibility of local motion control. The acceleration curves obtained by the polydyne method often have the location of the crossover point (where the acceleration changes sign) erratically shaped toward one end of the motion stroke. As one can see from Chapter 3, the evolution of an acceptable cam profile for automotive application may involve a tedious process of alteration of the polynominal powers.

The key factor that has contributed to the widening interest in and discussion of cam dynamics is the advent of computer technology capable of dealing with complex mathematical problems and of simplifying the solution of the equations describing the system.

Modeling is one of the major tasks in the study of cam dynamics. Modeling involves distribution of system parameters, cam motion excitation, and environmental influences. Decisions pertinent to the modeling task may enhance or constrain the results of the mathematical analyses.

The models proposed in the past for the study of cam dynamics relied mainly on the simplified linear models. Recent studies, however, have extended the analysis and the simulation of complex multi–degree–of–freedom linear and nonlinear models. In this chapter, we will treat the subject of modeling in considerable details.

14-3 DYNAMIC MODELING

In the most general sense, a model is a conceptualization of a real system. It has no inherent meaning other than in its correspondence to the real system that, for the convenience of the investigator, it represents. If the quantitative behavior of the model accurately represents the behavior of the real system, the investigator then has a concise method of describing that system. If the model can be used as the object of experimentation, standing in place of the real system, new insights into the behavior of the real system may be gained; but such insights must be checked against the behavior of the system itself.

If the model cannot be made to reproduce the behavior of the real system by the manipulation of model parameters within ranges of reasonable values, the investigator should reject that model as being an inappropriate representation of a real system. The accuracy with which the simplified system reproduces the dynamic characteristics of the original system depends, to some extent, upon experience and judgment.

Discretization and Degrees of Freedom

Every physical component is a continuum, the motion of which can be described by an infinite number of coordinates distributed along the component. It is necessary to replace the actual system by a finite number of lumped parameters. In general, a greater number of lumped parameters will result in a more accurate model, but will also require more work, since there will be more loads and more deflections to calculate for more positions. At each concentrated mass, the system may be given up to six degrees of freedom (three translational components and three rotational components). If all six degrees of freedom associated with each mass are treated as generalized displacements, the computational effort becomes very large. Simplification can be introduced depending upon the particular situation and the intended design objective and requirements. Some of the degrees of freedom that are not important may be deleted.

The actual cam–and–follower system may consist of one or more rods, levers, and springs, all of which have mass and elasticities distributed throughout the system in accordance with their physical dimensions. A typical example is the automotive overhead valve gear system shown in Fig. 14-1(a). A simplification can usually be made by lumping discrete masses at certain points of the follower linkage. The mass points are separated by corresponding elasticities of the linkage. The actual system of Fig. 14-1(a) is properly divided into several regions, and the masses included within each of these regions are lumped into concentrated masses interconnected by weightless springs of appropriate stiffness, as shown in Fig. 14-1(b) (damping may be included too). Note that the coil spring itself may be further discretized as a string of small masses and springs, if the representation of spring surge is accounted for in the modeling process.

In the dynamic modeling of a cam–and–follower system it has been a fairly common practice to reduce it further to a simple spring–mass system by lumping the effective mass of the follower at one point, with its linkage elasticity approximated by a single spring supporting the effective mass. The values of the effective mass and the spring stiffness can be calculated based on the principle of kinetically equivalent systems described in standard textbooks.

While experimental evidence indicates that the one–degree–of–freedom model is satisfactory for the study of automotive valve gears, the dynamic studies of cam–actuated systems in automatic machines on other occasions can be expressed realistically only by means of two or more independent displacement coordinates.

In general, more elaborate models will result in a more accurate system, but will require more complex mathematical solutions and modal analysis. While a one–degree–of–freedom model may sometimes be considered oversimplified, a highly refined model may not be sufficiently economical. For a particular machine, one has to weigh both validity and economy to insure compatibility between the evolved design and its intended application in modeling.

Kinetically Equivalent Systems

In many problems concerning the dynamics of a rigid body it is convenient to construct an equivalent model using two lumped masses appropriately sized and appropriately located. One example is the connecting rod of a reciprocating engine or a compressor. The piston end of the connecting rod translates, while the crank end rotates.

So that the two–mass system is dynamically equivalent to the rigid body, it must react to a given system of forces in exactly the same manner as the rigid

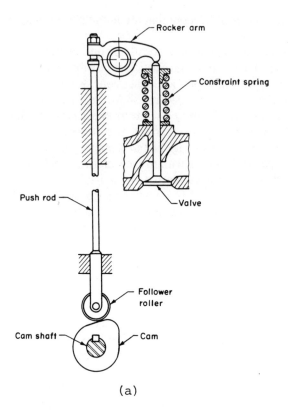

(a)

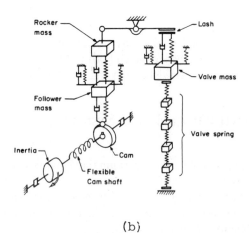

(b)

14-1. (a) Automotive overhead valve gear system. (b) Lumped spring–mass system model.

body reacts. Obviously the conditions that must be satisfied by the two–mass system are:
• The total mass must be equal to that of the rigid body.
• The c.g. must coincide with that of the rigid body.
• The total moment of inertia about an axis through the c.g. must be equal to that of the rigid body.

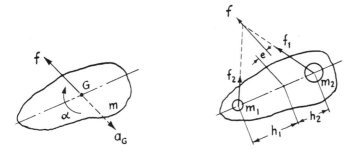

Fig. 14-2. Kinetically equivalent system.

For the rigid body shown in Fig. 14-2, let m be the mass and I_G the moment of inertia about an axis through G. Also, let m_1 and m_2 be two masses that form kinetically equivalent systems, and let h_1 and h_2 be the distances of m_1 and m_2, respectively, from G. Then the three conditions stated above lead to the following equations:

$$m_1 + m_2 = m \qquad (14\text{-}1)$$

$$m_1 h_1 = m_2 h_2 \qquad (14\text{-}2)$$

$$m_1 h_1^2 + m_2 h_2^2 = mk^2 . \qquad (14\text{-}3)$$

Substituting for $m_2 h_2$ in Eq. (14-3) from Eq. (14-2), we get .

$$m_1 h_1^2 + m_1 h_1 h_2 = mk^2 = I_G ,$$

where k is the radius of gyration of the body with respect to point G.

Thus

$$m_1 = \frac{mk^2}{h_1(h_1 + h_2)} . \qquad (14\text{-}4)$$

But from (14-1) and (14-2),

$$m_1 = \frac{mh_2}{h_1 + h_2} \, .$$
(14-5)

Equating (14-4) and (14-5) gives

$$k^2 = h_1 h_2 \, .$$
(14-6)

From Eq. (14-6) it is clear that either h_1 or h_2, but not both, may be chosen arbitrarily. If h_1 is fixed, then the distance h_2 will follow from the above equation. The location of m_2 is called the center of percussion.

Mode Coupling

The rotational or torsional modes of vibration are usually not as obvious as the translational modes. They may be coupled together with the translational mode. For coupled modes in translation and rotation, it is often possible to determine whether the system is coupled or uncoupled for motion in a certain direction. All we need to do is to make a simple test if the part is available. The test is carried out by applying a steady load to the body of the system at its center of gravity in a specific direction. If the body moves in the direction of the applied load without rotation, then the translational mode is not coupled with the rotational mode for motion along the direction of the applied load. Frequently, some degrees of freedom may be uncoupled from others.

Conversely, torsional modes sometimes may be coupled with bending modes and produce resonant frequencies that are much lower than expected. If this low–frequency torsional mode is not foreseen, it can lead to unexpectedly large displacements and stresses that will ultimately shorten the fatigue life of the member.

Modeling of Constituent Parameters

The problem of converting a complex mechanical system into a simpler one can be described in terms of the constituent system parameters: masses, springs, and dampers. What parts of the system should be designated as masses and what parts should be designated as springs? There is no simple answer to this question, since it depends upon the geometry and the arrangement of the parts of each system component and of assembly. We will discuss each separately.

Equivalent Masses or Moments of Inertia. Mass enters the consideration of dynamic systems through Newton's second law. Thus

$$F = m\ddot{x}$$
(14-7)

for a translational system, and

$$T = J\ddot{\theta} \tag{14-8}$$

for a torsional system.

Large, heavy components may be condensed into single points located at the center of mass of the body. Here we assume that the body is rigid. Hence, all points move together, permitting condensation into a single point. The mass m is given by Eq. (14-7). The moment of inertia is given by Eq. (14-8).

$$m = \int \rho \, dV$$

$$J = \int r^2 dm = mk^2 ,$$

where ρ is the mass density, V is the volume of the rigid body, and r is the distance from the polar axis to mass dm.

The kinetic energy KE associated with a mass m translating at velocity $\dot{x}$ is given by

$$KE = \frac{1}{2} m\dot{x}^2 . \tag{14-9}$$

In an analogous manner, the kinetic energy of a rotating body whose moment of inertia is J is given by

$$KE = \frac{1}{2} J\dot{\theta}^2 . \tag{14-10}$$

The equivalent mass may not be the total mass of the members. Certain approximations and equivalences must be determined based on the energy principle. A number of common configurations, masses, and moments of inertia are summarized in Table 14-1.

Group of Masses. To satisfy equivalency, the kinetic energy KE of the system containing two masses connected by a rigid link, as shown in Fig. 14-3(a), must be equal to the kinetic energy $(KE)_{eq}$ of the single equivalent mass shown in Fig. 14-3(b).

Table 14-1. Equivalent Masses and Moments of Inertia

Cantilever beam	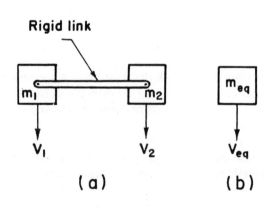	$M_{eq} \cong \dfrac{M}{4}$
Simply supported beam		$M_{eq} = \dfrac{M}{2}$
Coiled spring		$M_{eq} = \dfrac{M}{3}$
Bellow		$M_{eq} = \dfrac{M}{3}$
Shaft in torsion		$J_{eq} = \dfrac{J}{3}$

Rigid link

(a)   (b)

Fig. 14-3.

$$KE = \frac{1}{2} m_1 v_1^2 + \frac{1}{2} m_2 v_2^2$$

$$(KE)_{eq} = \frac{1}{2} m_{eq} v_{eq}^2 .$$

Equating these two and solving for the equivalent mass give

$$m_{eq} = \frac{m_1 v_1^2 + m_2 v_2^2}{v_{eq}^2} . \tag{14-11}$$

Similarly, for two rotating bodies with moments of inertia J_1 and J_2, we can write

$$J_{eq} = \frac{J_1 \dot{\theta}_1^2 + J_2 \dot{\theta}_2^2}{\dot{\theta}_{eq}^2} . \tag{14-12}$$

Depending upon the configuration and the distribution of the masses and the velocities, the following cases will follow the same principle.

Translational Mechanical Transformers. Assume that the two masses are fastened to a lever, a rocker arm, or a bell crank that pivots at one end. Let the arm length ℓ_i represent the distance of mass m_i from the pivot (see Fig. 14-4). We may conveniently locate the equivalent at any point, say, at the site of mass m_1. Thus all velocities can be obtained in terms of v_1. Then, for small angles of rotation,

$$v_{eq} = v_1$$

$$v_2 = \frac{\ell_2}{\ell_1} v_1 .$$

Applying Eq. (14-11) gives

$$m_{eq} = m_1 + m_2 \left(\frac{\ell_2}{\ell_1} \right)^2 . \tag{14-13}$$

Rotational Mechanical Transformers. In an analogous manner, when the load is coupled to the drive unit by gears, it may be reduced to a single equivalent load at the drive shaft if each inertia term is multiplied by the gear angular

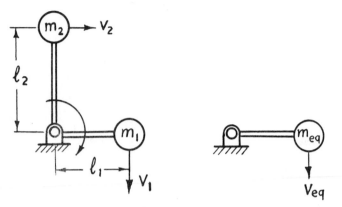

Fig. 14-4. Translational mechanical transformer.

speed ratio squared. If the load must be turned faster than the drive shaft, the load inertia is increased by the gear speed ratio squared, and vice versa.

Consider a system consisting of two pairs of spur gears, and let the angular speed of the gears be n_1, n_2, n_3, and n_4 as denoted in Fig. 14-5. Then the moment of inertia of the first pair of gears with reference to the driving shaft is

$$J_1 + J_2 \left(\frac{n_2}{n_1} \right)^2 .$$

The moment of inertia of the second pair of gears with reference to the driving shaft is

$$J_3 + J_4 \left(\frac{n_4}{n_3} \right)^2 .$$

Therefore, the equivalent moment of inertia of the two–stage gear reduction system with reference to the input shaft is

$$J_{\text{gear}} = J_1 + J_2 \left(\frac{n_2}{n_1} \right)^2 + \left(\frac{n_2}{n_1} \right)^2 \left[J_3 + J_4 \left(\frac{n_4}{n_3} \right)^2 \right] . \qquad (14\text{-}14)$$

In a typical mechanical power drive, the pivot of the motor does not connect directly to the load. It transmits through a set of gears. Suppose there exists a number of gear pairs for speed reduction between the motor and the terminal load, as shown in Fig. 14-5. Then the moment of inertia J of the entire drive system with reference to the motor shaft is

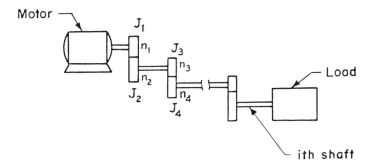

Fig. 14-5. Gear system.

$$J = J_{motor} + J_{gear} + \frac{1}{r^2} J_{load} , \tag{14-15}$$

where r is the overall speed reduction ratio of the gear train.

Coupled Rotating and Translating Masses. Consider two direct-contact members, one of which rotates about an axis while the other translates. A typical example is the pinion–rack pair (Fig. 14-6). The object is to combine the two, either as a single equivalent translating mass or as a single equivalent rotating inertia.

For the former case, the kinetic energy is given by

$$KE = \frac{1}{2} m_{eq} v_{eq}^2 = \frac{1}{2} mv^2 + \frac{1}{2} J\dot{\theta}^2 .$$

Since $v_{eq} = v$ and $\dot{\theta} = \dfrac{v}{R}$,

then

$$\frac{1}{2} m_{eq} v^2 = \frac{1}{2} mv^2 + \frac{1}{2} J\left(\frac{v}{R}\right)^2$$

or

$$m_{eq} = m + \frac{J}{R^2} . \tag{14-16}$$

For the latter case,

$$KE = \frac{1}{2} J_{eq} \dot{\theta}_{eq}^{2} = \frac{1}{2} mv^{2} + \frac{1}{2} J\dot{\theta}^{2} .$$

Since $\dot{\theta}_{eq} = \dot{\theta}$ and $v = R\dot{\theta}$,

then

$$\frac{1}{2} J_{eq}\dot{\theta}^{2} = \frac{1}{2} J\dot{\theta}^{2} + \frac{1}{2} m(R\dot{\theta})^{2}$$

or

$$J_{eq} = J + mR^{2} . \tag{14-17}$$

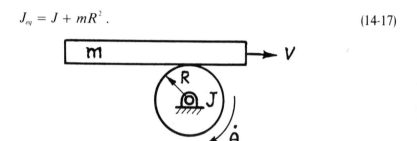

Fig. 14-6. Coupled rotating and translating masses.

Example 14-1

Fig. 14-7 is an example of a cam mechanism. The total reduced weight of the follower system consists of the effective weight contributed from the push rod, the pivoted arm, and the side element.

The kinetic energy of the push rod is

$$(KE)_{p} = \frac{1}{2} \frac{W_{p}}{g} v_{p}^{2} ,$$

and the kinetic energy of the side element is

$$(KE)_{t} = \frac{1}{2} \frac{W_{t}}{g} v_{t}^{2} ,$$

where W_{p} and v_{p} are the weight and velocity of the push rod, respectively, and W_{t} and v_{t} are the weight and the velocity of the side element.
Equating these two expressions, we obtain

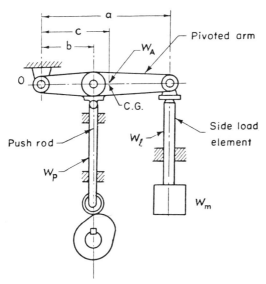

Fig. 14-7. Cam mechanism.

$$W_\ell = W_p \left(\frac{b}{a} \right)^2 ,$$

where a and b represent the distances of the side element and the push rod, respectively, measured from the pivot 0.

The reduced weight of the pivoted arm is derived from the moment of inertia. The moment of inertia about the pivoted center is

$$I_o = I_G + \frac{W_A}{g} c^2 ,$$

where I_G is the moment of inertia of the arm about $c.g.$ of the arm, W_A is the weight of the arm, and c is the distance between $c.g.$ and the pivot. But I_o may be written as if the equivalent weight W of the arm were concentrated at a distance a from the pivot

$$I_o = \frac{W_\ell}{g} a^2$$

or

$$W_\ell = \frac{I_o g}{a^2} .$$

Therefore, the equivalent weight of the entire system with reference to the side element is

$$W = W_m + \left(\frac{b}{a}\right)^2 W_p + (I_G g + W_A c^2)/a^2 \,,$$

where W_m is the actual load attached to the side element.

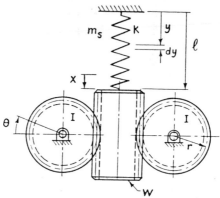

Fig. 14-8. Spring–constrained pinion–rack system.

Maximum Energy Principle for Conservative Systems. For a conservative system, the maximum kinetic energy is equal to the maximum potential energy. This simple relation may be used to an advantage for establishing the equivalent mass or the equivalent moment of inertia of a system.

Consider the pinion–and–rack system shown in Fig. 14-8. Assume that the spring mass is not negligible. It has a length ℓ and a mass density ρ. Since the motion of the system can be described by

$$x = x_o \sin \omega t$$

$$\theta = \theta_o \sin \omega t \,,$$

where x_o and θ_o are the amplitudes of sinusoidal motion with circular frequency ω, we can write the maximum kinetic energy

$$(KE)_{max} = I(\theta_o \omega)^2 + \frac{1}{2}\frac{W}{g}(r\theta_o \omega)^2 + \frac{1}{2}\rho \int_o^\ell \left(\frac{y x_o \omega}{\ell}\right)^2 dy$$

$$= \omega^2 \left(I + \frac{1}{2} \frac{W}{g} r^2 + \frac{m_s}{6} r^2 \right) \theta_o^2 \, ,$$

where m_s is the total mass of the spring. The maximum potential energy is

$$(PE)_{max} = \frac{1}{2} k(x_o)^2 = \frac{1}{2} k(r\theta_o)^2 \, .$$

Equating $(KE)_{max}$ and $(PE)_{max}$, we obtain the frequency of vibration

$$\omega = r \sqrt{\frac{k}{2I + \dfrac{Wr^2}{g} + \dfrac{m_s}{3} r^2}}$$

Therefore, the equivalent moment of inertia of the system is

$$I_{eq} = 2I + \frac{Wr^2}{g} + \frac{m_s}{3} r^2 \, . \tag{14-18}$$

Other Adjustments. Sometimes, adjustments and corrections should be made for the mass of shafting, slender rods, springs, and linkages. The following are suggestions for handling the equivalent mass or the moment of inertia associated with these members.

Shafting. In dealing with torsion, we find that the mass of a shaft can be neglected if the product of the length of the shaft in meters, multiplied by the frequency in vibrations per second, does not exceed a value of 305.

If the mass of the shaft is not negligible but is small compared with that of the rotor mounted on it (Fig. 14-9(a)), the moment of inertia of the shaft is dynamically equivalent to one–third that of the end rotor.

The situation is a little complicated when two rotors with masses M_A and M_B are connected by a shaft (Fig. 14-9(b)). One must first make an estimate of the possible position of the node of vibration. Then, one must add to it one–third of the moment of inertia of the length of the shaft between the node and the mass M_A to J_A, and also add one–third of the moment of inertia of the length of the shaft between the node and the mass M_B to J_B.

Slender Rods. The total mass of long slender rods that act as springs is not used directly. Textbooks on vibration show that a cantilever beam should have

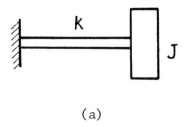

(a)

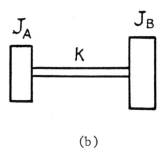

(b)

Fig. 14-9.

23 percent of its distributed mass concentrated at the end; similarly, a simply supported beam should have one–half of its mass concentrated at the midspan.

Helical Springs. Theory and experimentation have shown that the effective mass of a helical spring varies from $\dfrac{4}{\pi^2}$ to one–third of the mass of the spring as the mass varies from zero to infinity. For average masses roughly one–third of the actual mass is effective. This is due to flexibilities that prevent all of the mass from being accelerated at the same rate. Thus, the acceleration wave does not affect the other two–thirds of the mass.

Linkages. Unlike other mechanical components, mechanical linkages are characterized by large ranges of motion. The kinematic and dynamic characteristics of a linkage vary with time.

Consider a slider–crank mechanism (Fig. 14-10). Assume that the driving crank is counterbalanced so that the center of gravity of the driving crank coincides with the center of the crank shaft. The kinetic energy of the mechanism is

$$KE = \frac{1}{2}\left(I_2\omega_2^{\,2} + m_3v_3^{\,2} + I_3\omega_3^{\,2} + m_4v_B^{\,2}\right).$$

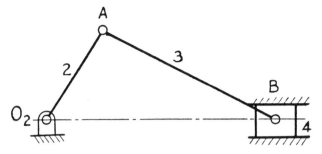

Fig. 14-10. Slider–crank 4–bar linkage.

To determine the equivalent mass with reference to the piston, we rewrite the kinetic energy expression in the form

$$KE = \frac{1}{2} M_{eq} v_B^2 = \frac{1}{2} v_B^2 \left[m_4 + m_3 \left(\frac{v_3}{v_B} \right)^2 \right.$$

$$\left. + I_3 \left(\frac{\omega_3}{v_B} \right)^2 + I_2 \left(\frac{\omega_2}{v_B} \right)^2 \right].$$

Therefore, the equivalent mass of the linkage is the expression inside the bracket.

Similarly, the equivalent moment of inertia with reference to the input crank can be found to be

$$I_{eq} = I_2 + m_3 \left(\frac{v_3}{\omega_2} \right)^2 + I_3 \left(\frac{\omega_3}{\omega_2} \right)^2 + m_4 \left(\frac{v_4}{\omega_2} \right)^2. \tag{14-19}$$

One must remember that the obtained M_{eq} and I_{eq} are both functions of the instantaneous velocities of the linkage, which vary as the configuration of the linkage changes with time, and are highly dependent upon the geometry of constraint of the given mechanism.

Although we have used a slider–crank mechanism for illustration, the same technique can be applied to other link mechanisms as well.

Experimental Methods for Determining Moments of Inertia. It is generally difficult to compute the mass moment of inertia when one or more of the following conditions exist: the body shape is irregular, the material density is unknown, or the parts must be disassembled before precise dimensions can be found.

There are several experimental methods available for finding the mass moment of inertia if the part is obtainable. These are the torsional pendulum method, the compound pendulum method, the bifilar or the trifilar pendulum method, the inclined surface experiment, the rolling oscillation technique, and the stereologic method. The first five methods listed here are generally described in standard textbooks on the dynamics of machinery. The last method (150) is a novel concept that requires an overlay of a polar moment of inertia grid on the irregular plane section of which the moment of inertia is to be determined.

Equivalent Spring Stiffness. Every mechanical member acts as a spring of different stiffness. If the machine part or model is already in existence, the most convenient way to determine the spring stiffness is by actual tests. This is done by loading the component or the assembly and accurately measuring the deflection. The values of the loads and the deflections when plotted form a hysteresis loop, which can be approximated by a straight line. The spring rate equals the slope of the approximate straight line.

The stiffness of a spring is defined as the ratio of the force exerted to the deflection produced by that force. Therefore, if an equation is available that gives the relation between the force and the deflection, then we can use the equation to compute the spring stiffness.

Beams, for example, act as a most common type of structural spring, since they experience deflection when acted upon by a force. Beams have a wide variety of edge conditions varying from free to fixed end, and a variety of deflection modes including tension, bending, shear, and torsion. Table 14-2 contains some equivalent spring stiffnesses of standard elements.

Group of Springs. Springs may be combined in parallel, in series, or in a combination of parallel and series. Parallel springs are such that the displacement for each spring is the same, and the total spring force equals the sum of the individual spring forces.

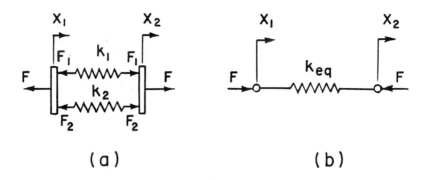

(a)   (b)

Fig. 14-11. Springs in parallel.

As shown in Fig. 14-11,

$$F = F_1 + F_2 ,$$

with $F_1 = k_1(x_1 - x_2)$

$$F_2 = k_2(x_1 - x_2) ,$$

and for the equivalent spring

$$F = k_{eq}(x_1 - x_2) .$$

Equating the right–hand side of the two cases gives

$$k_{eq} = k_1 + k_2 . \tag{14-20}$$

For the series springs, the force in each spring is the same, and the total displacement is the sum of the individual spring displacements. Thus referring to Fig. 14-12, we can write

$$F_1 = F_2 = F$$

$$x_1 - x_2 = \frac{F_1}{k_1} = \frac{F}{k_1}$$

$$x_2 - x_3 = \frac{F_2}{k_2} = \frac{F}{k_2} ,$$

and for the equivalent spring

$$x_1 - x_3 = \frac{F}{k_{eq}} .$$

Combining these gives

$$\frac{1}{k_{eq}} = \frac{1}{k_1} + \frac{1}{k_2}$$

or

$$k_{eq} = \frac{k_1 k_2}{k_1 + k_2} . \tag{14-21}$$

Table 14-2. Equivalent Spring Stiffnesses

Direct load	Straight rod		$\dfrac{EA}{L}$
	Coil spring (n active coils)		$\dfrac{Gd^4}{8nD^3}$
	Conical spring (n active coils)		$\dfrac{Gd^4}{n(d_1+d_2)^3}$
Bending	Cantilever beam		$\dfrac{Eb}{4}\left(\dfrac{h}{L}\right)^3$
	Simple beam		$4Eb\left(\dfrac{h}{L}\right)^3$
	Clamp-clamp beam		$16Eb\left(\dfrac{h}{L}\right)^3$
	Leave spring (i = leaves)		$\dfrac{Eibh^3}{4L^3}$

Table 14-2. Cont'd.

Shear	Round cantilever bar		$\dfrac{GA}{t(1+0.44r^2)}$ $r=\dfrac{\ell}{d}$
	Rectangular cantilever		$\dfrac{GA}{t(1+0.33\gamma^2)}$ $\gamma=\dfrac{t}{h}$
Torsion	Solid shaft		$\dfrac{\pi G d^4}{32L}$
	Hollow shaft		$\dfrac{G\pi(d_o^4-d_i^4)}{32L}$
	Rectangular bar		$\dfrac{Gbh(b^2+h^2)}{12L}$
	Solid taperred shaft		$\dfrac{0.295d_1^4 G}{L\left[\dfrac{d_1}{d_2}+\left(\dfrac{d_1}{d_2}\right)^2+\left(\dfrac{d_1}{d_2}\right)^3\right]}$
	Shaft with keyway		$\dfrac{\pi G d^4}{32L}$
	Splined shaft		$\dfrac{\pi G d^4}{32L}$

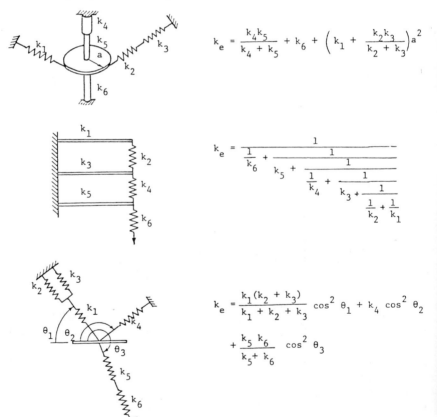

Fig. 14-12. Springs in series.

When the spring system is a combination of springs in parallel and in series, it is only necessary to combine the equivalent springs of the parallel groups into a series combination with other springs. Fig. 14-13 shows some typical examples of finding the equivalent spring stiffness. Note that the force output and the system stiffness are a function of angles θ in addition to the spring stiffness when the spring axes are not parallel.

$$k_e = \frac{k_4 k_5}{k_4 + k_5} + k_6 + \left(k_1 + \frac{k_2 k_3}{k_2 + k_3} \right) a^2$$

$$k_e = \cfrac{1}{\cfrac{1}{k_6} + \cfrac{1}{k_5 + \cfrac{1}{\cfrac{1}{k_4} + \cfrac{1}{k_3 + \cfrac{1}{\cfrac{1}{k_2} + \cfrac{1}{k_1}}}}}}$$

$$k_e = \frac{k_1(k_2 + k_3)}{k_1 + k_2 + k_3} \cos^2 \theta_1 + k_4 \cos^2 \theta_2$$

$$+ \frac{k_5 k_6}{k_5 + k_6} \cos^2 \theta_3$$

Fig. 14-13. Equivalent spring stiffnesses.

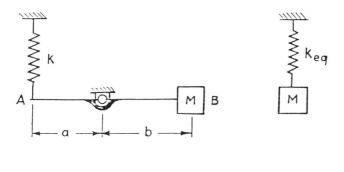

(a)   (b)

Fig. 14-14.

Mechanical Transformers. The spring in the system shown in Fig. 14-14(a) can be replaced by an equivalent spring with stiffness k_{eq} acting at point B, where the mass is attached. If we equate the potential energy of the spring at point A to that of an equivalent spring at point B, we obtain

$$\frac{1}{2} \, kx_A^2 = \frac{1}{2} \, k_{eq}x_B^2 \, ,$$

where x_A and x_B are the spring deflections at stations A and B, respectively.

Since the deflections at A and B are directly proportional to the lever arm distances relative to the pivot

$$x_B = \frac{b}{a} \, x_A \, ,$$

we obtain the equivalent spring stiffness with reference to the mass as

$$k_{eq} = \left(\frac{a}{b}\right)^2 k \, . \tag{14-22}$$

In an analogous manner, for a pair of gears the equivalent torsional spring stiffness of the driven shaft B with reference to the driving shaft A can be written as

$$k_{eq} = k_B \left(\frac{n_B}{n_A}\right)^2 \, , \tag{14-23}$$

where n_A and n_B are the angular speeds of gears A and B, respectively.

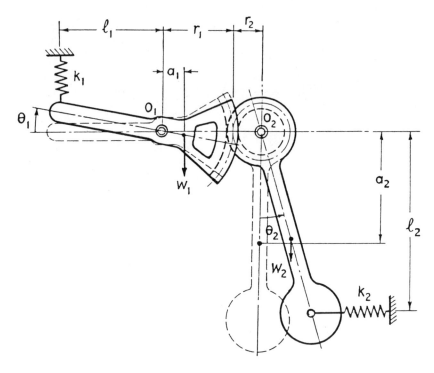

Fig. 14-15.

Energy Principle for Conservative Systems. Consider the system of Fig. 14-15, where a pinion and a sector gear are engaged together to produce an angular displacement ratio

$$n = \frac{r_1}{r_2} = \frac{\theta_2}{\theta_1} \, ,$$

where r_1 and r_2 are the pitch radii of the sector gear and the pinion, and θ_1 and θ_2 are the angular displacement of the same.

Based on the equilibrium position of the figure shown in dashed lines, the kinetic energy and the potential energy of the system are

$$KE = \frac{1}{2} I_1 \dot{\theta_1}^2 + \frac{1}{2} I_2 (n\dot{\theta_1})^2$$

$$PE = \frac{1}{2} k_1 (\ell_1 \theta_1)^2 + \frac{1}{2} k_2 (n\ell_1 \theta_1)^2 + W_2 a_2 (1 - \cos \theta_2) \, .$$

For a conservative system, we have

$$\frac{d}{dt}(KE + PE) = 0, \tag{14-24}$$

which leads to the equation of motion

$$(I_1 + n^2 I_2)\ddot{\theta}_1 + [k_1 \ell_1^2 + n^2(k_2 \ell_1^2 + W_2 a_2)]\theta_1 = 0.$$

Therefore, the equivalent spring stiffness and the moment of inertia in terms of the motion of W_1 are seen to be

$$k_{eq} = k_1 \ell_1^2 + n^2(k_2 \ell_2^2 + W_2 a_2), \tag{14-25}$$

and

$$I_{eq} = I_1 + n^2 I_2,$$

I_1 and I_2 being the moments of inertia of W_1 and W_2 about their pivoted points O_1 and O_2, respectively.

Other Adjustments.

Effect of Adjoining Junction. A stepped shaft is somewhat more flexible than it appears, since an abrupt change in the shaft diameter creates a junction effect in which some of the material in the larger diameter portion adjoining the step is inactive. The extent of this effect depends upon the diameter ratio and the fillet radius at the junction. The actual formulas for shafts with keyways and splines can be derived mathematically from the theory of elasticity, but the results are extremely complicated. The formulas quoted here in Table 14-2 for shafts with keyways and splines are empirical in origin, but are generally considered to be very nearly correct.

Effect of Boundary Conditions. The amount of error involved in a poor estimate of the boundary conditions will often be much greater than the error involved in the use of concentrated loads in place of uniform loads. For example, just changing the ends of a uniform beam from a fixed condition to a simply supported condition will reduce the resonance frequency by approximately 55 percent. However, if a uniformly distributed load is replaced by a concentrated load at the center of a simply supported beam, the resonant frequency of the beam will only be reduced by roughly 30 percent.

Equivalent Length. The torsional spring stiffness of the shafts of a noncircular cross section is usually expressed in terms of a solid round shaft having an equivalent length L_e and an equivalent diameter D_e. Table 14-3 contains expressions for calculating the equivalent lengths of some common non–circular cross sections.

It is interesting to note that the torsional rigidity of any solid symmetrical section is nearly the same as that of an elliptical section having the same area and the same polar moment of inertia as the actual section. A long thin rectangular torsion member is not as stiff as a member having a square section of the same cross–sectional area.

Table 14-3. Equivalent Lengths of Non–circular Cross–sectional Shafts Based on Equal Torsional Rigidity

Cross-section	Equivalent Length of Circular Cross-sectional Shaft of Diameter D_e L_e
	$\dfrac{D_e^4}{D^4} L$
	$\dfrac{D_e^4}{D^4 - d^4} L$
	$0.5 \dfrac{(a^2 + b^2)}{a^3 b^3} D_e^4 L$
	$3.23 \dfrac{(b^3 + h^3)}{b^3 h^3} D_e^4 L$
	$0.7 \dfrac{D_e^4}{b^4} L$

L = Length of the actual non-circular cross-sectional shaft

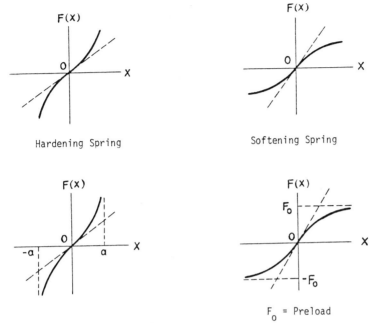

Fig. 14-16. Power-law nonlinear springs.

Nonlinear Springs. It has been common practice to assume linearity for an actually nonlinear system. The reasons for neglecting nonlinearities are twofold: (a) a nonlinear system is inherently more complicated and more difficult to analyze than a linear one, and (b) many systems are quasi-linear over the operational range, and performance predictions based upon a linear model are sufficiently accurate to satisfy design objectives. Most nonlinearity arising in components is unavoidable. Occasionally, nonlinearity may also be introduced intentionally into a design to accomplish a specific objective. As the nonlinear properties of a system become more pronounced and their effects become significant, a linear approximation is no longer adequate.

Fig. 14-16 shows the force and the deflection relationship of nonlinear springs, which can be represented by a continuous curve. A hardening spring characteristic is a frequently observed nonlinearity, the restoring force exerted by a spring under deformation increasing more rapidly with strain than Hooke's Law predicts. A hardening spring may be described by a power series

$$F(x) = kx + \sum \alpha_n x^n, \qquad (n = 3, 5, \ldots, \text{odd}), \qquad (14\text{-}26)$$

where $F(x)$ is a single–valued function of displacement x, and k and the α's are constants. It may also be described by a tangent function

Table 14-4. Nonlinear Spring Characteristics

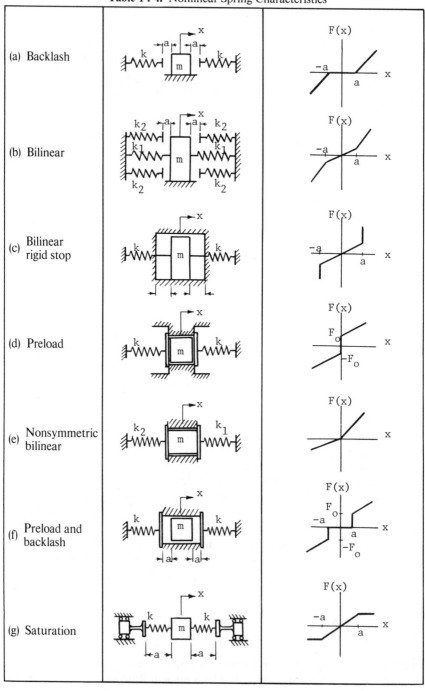

$$F(x) = \frac{2ka}{\pi} \tan \frac{\pi}{2a} x \qquad (-a < x < a), \qquad (14\text{-}27)$$

with a being a constant.

A "softening" spring characteristic is observed less often than a hardening one because resilient elements that soften appreciably are not capable of supporting heavy loads. Most resilient elements that soften may be thought of as buckling in some way. A softening spring may be described by a power series of the form

$$F(x) = kx - \sum \alpha_n x^n, \qquad (n = 3, 5, \ldots, \text{odd}), \qquad (14\text{-}28)$$

or by a hyperbolic tangent function

$$F(x) = F_o \tan h \left(\frac{kx}{F_o} \right). \qquad (14\text{-}29)$$

Table 14-4 illustrates some piecewise–linear spring combination. In this Table case (a) shows a spring–mass system in which the springs do not contact the mass for displacement within the band $x < \pm a$. This nonlinearity is commonly referred to as backlash. In mechanical systems, backlash is frequently encountered in the analysis of gears, cams, and linkages. Backlash in grooved cams will be described in the section immediately following this one. Mechanical errors may result from tolerances in machine parts, play in the joints, and misalignment in assembly. The existence of backlash may also be caused by load deformations as well as by a temperature gradient due to the thermal effect.

Case (b) shows a symmetrical bilinear type of nonlinear spring. One set of springs is in contact with the mass for any displacement x, while another set of springs makes contact only for $x > \pm a$. As the second set of springs becomes stiffer, the case of a spring–mass system with stiff elastic stops is obtained. The limiting case would be an infinite spring rate for a rigid wall, case (c). An unsymmetric bilinear spring and the corresponding force–deflection curve are given in case (e). One application of a bilinear spring is in the suspension of an automobile.

Case (d) shows a preload nonlinearity. The springs have an initial compression. The mass cannot move until a force is applied to it, equal to the initial compressive force F_o of the springs. A combination of preload and backlash is also possible. This is represented in case (f).

Case (g) shows a saturation type of nonlinearity. Saturation is frequently the mechanism by which the spring force stops to increase when the deflection exceeds a certain limit.

Backlash in Cams. If a grooved cam is used, then there is normally no follower spring and backlash between the cam–groove walls, and the roller will be traversed when the direction of the load on the roller reverses. Such traversal may take place at the beginning of the motion, when the accelerating force begins to increase, and also wear the point where accelerations change sign. Van der Hoek (221) and Koster (133) have considered the problem of backlash traversal based on the following model. (Koster incorporated into the model the fluid film squeeze effect. Film squeeze is a nonlinear damping phenomenon to be discussed in the next section after damping).

With reference to Fig. 14-17, the force transmitted by film squeeze for a grooved cam with a pressure angle of less than $\dfrac{\pi}{4}$ radian may be approximated by

$$F = \frac{d}{dt} \left(\epsilon_c - \epsilon_r \right) \eta_s \left(c' + c'' \right), \qquad (14\text{-}30)$$

where $\eta_s = 12\pi\eta b \left(\dfrac{R_e}{2} \right)^{3/2}$

$$c' = \left| \frac{1}{\epsilon_r - \epsilon_c} \right|^{3/2} \qquad (\epsilon_r > \epsilon_c)$$

$$c'' = \left| \frac{1}{\epsilon_c + \epsilon - \epsilon_r} \right|^{3/2} \qquad (\epsilon_c + \epsilon > \epsilon_r).$$

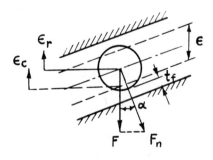 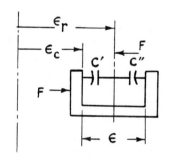

Fig. 14-17. Backlash traversal of grooved cam.

As is shown in Fig. 14-17, if $\dot{\epsilon}_c > \dot{\epsilon}_r$, $c'' = 0$, and if $\dot{\epsilon}_c < \dot{\epsilon}_r$, $c' = 0$. In the above equations, the displacements ϵ_r, ϵ_c, and ϵ are defined as labeled in Fig. 14-17. Symbols R_e, η, b, and t_f are the same as those defined in conjunction with Eq. (14-31).

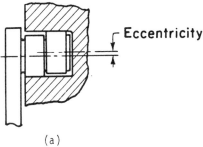

(a)

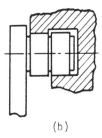

(b)

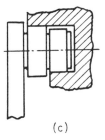

(c)

Fig. 14-18. (a) Eccentrically located roller, (b) Undercut groove, (c) Stepped groove.

The elimination of backlash is essential to the reduction of unwanted sliding action, vibration, and wear. One way to accomplish this is to use two rollers in contact on either side of one groove. Fig. 14-18 shows three different roller and groove arrangements. Fig. 14-18(a) shows two eccentric rollers in a single groove. These rollers have equal diameters; they are free to rotate, and they ride on opposite groove surfaces. In Fig. 14-18(b), we see concentric rollers of the same diameter but in a relieved groove. The undercut is difficult to produce accurately. The third type, shown in Fig. 14-18(c), has two concentric rollers of different diameters in a stepped groove. Another way of avoiding backlash in rib cams is to arrange rollers on both sides of the rib, as shown in Fig. 1-10. A most effective positive–drive action can also be obtained by the application of conjugate or complementary cams (Fig. 1-7 and 1-8).

Damping. Any mechanical components having relative translation or rotation with either perfect or partial lubrication will have damping loss given the fact that there are slips and boundary shear effects at mating surfaces.

Although complex descriptions of damping mechanisms are possible, if the range of relative motion between parts is small, the phenomenology can be modeled by a simple description, that of viscous damping. The magnitude of the resistive force of viscous damping is the product of the velocity and a (constant) viscous damping coefficient.

Damping characteristics must be examined carefully for each element having relative motion. For example, a slider pair dissipates a substantial amount of energy through friction along the contacting surfaces. Other factors that affect damping include load and lubrication in bearings, tolerances in machine members, bolted assemblies with different interface pressures and dif- ferent surface finishes, and temperature changes that produce dimensional changes.

In cam–actuated mechanisms, when a film of viscous fluid lubricant is forced out from between a pair of approaching and contacting surfaces of the cam and the follower, pressures are developed that resist the tendency of the surfaces to come together. Under such conditions, the fluid layer is described as having "squeeze–film" properties. Many problems involving hydrodynamic squeeze–films arise in the general treatment of journal bearing theory, and the effect is significant in the lubrication of rolling contact elements.

Table 14-5 shows some typical damping properties of mechanical dampers.

Squeeze-Film Effect. We will here consider the squeeze–film effect of a lubri- cant between the surfaces of a disc cam and its follower roller just prior to con- tact. Based on the theorem of two–dimensional viscous flow, and with the assumptions of constant viscosity of the lubricant and constant pressure throughout the film thickness, the magnitude of squeeze force can be derived (133) as

$$F = 12\pi\eta v b \left(\frac{R_e}{2t_f}\right)^{3/2} , \qquad (14\text{-}31)$$

where R_e is the effective radius, which may be expressed in terms of roller radius R_1 and cam radius R_2 as

Table 14-5. Typical Mechanical Dampers

Translating Surface		$D_{eq} = \dfrac{\mu A}{h}$
Rotating Disk		$D_{eq} = \dfrac{\pi \mu d^4}{16h}$
Translating Cylinder		$D_{eq} = \dfrac{\mu A}{h}$
Rotating Cylinder		$D_{eq} = \dfrac{\pi \mu d^3 L}{4h}$
Dashpot		$D_{eq} = \dfrac{6\pi\mu L}{h^3}\left[\left(a - \dfrac{h}{2}\right)^2 - r^2\right]$ $\left[\dfrac{a^2 - r^2}{a - \dfrac{h}{2}} - h\right]$

A = Wetted surface area
μ = Coefficient of absolute viscosity

$$R_e = \frac{R_1 R_2}{R_1 + R_2} \; .$$

t_f is the film thickness, η is the viscosity of the fluid, b is the thickness of the cam or of the roller, and v is the approach velocity of the cam and the roller toward each other.

Energy Dissipated by a Damper. The energy dissipated by a viscous damper is given by the integral

$$\int D d\dot{x} \; ,$$

where $D = c\dot{x}$ is the force exerted by the damper, c is the coefficient of viscous damping, and $\dot{x}$ is the velocity.

Upon integrating we have the energy dissipated by a viscous damper equal to $\frac{1}{2} c\dot{x}^2$. Similarly, in a torsional system the energy dissipated is equal to $\frac{1}{2} c_t \dot{\theta}^2$, where c_t is the coefficient of torsional viscous damping, and θ is the angular velocity. The dissipated energy is usually accounted for by the formation of heat.

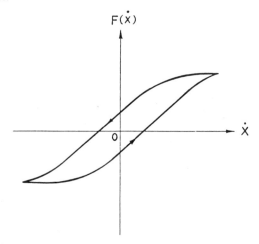

Fig. 14-19. Hysteresis loop.

When most materials are stressed, the stress–strain diagram forms a hysteresis loop instead of being just a back–and–forth path. The area inside the loop is directly proportional to the energy that is lost in the cyclic process.

Hysteresis is said to possess the "memory" property; it is multi-valued. The hysteresis loop can take many forms. Fig. 14-19 shows a typical one.

Experimental Determination of Damping. Only test data and testing experience can really provide adequate information on damping. For the purpose of performing a vibration analysis, testing experience should be used to estimate the approximate transmissibility of each mechanical element that is treated as a single-degree-of-freedom system. The transmissibility may be expressed in terms of the frequency ratio $r = \dfrac{\omega}{\omega_n}$ as

$$TR = \sqrt{\frac{1 + (2r\zeta)^2}{(1 - r^2)^2 + (2r\zeta)^2}} \qquad (14\text{-}32)$$

where ζ is the damping factor that is equal to $\dfrac{c}{2m\omega_n}$, with c representing the viscous damping coefficient, m representing mass, and ω_n representing the natural frequency of the system.

For a lightly damped system at resonance

$$TR \cong \frac{1}{2\zeta}$$

or $\qquad TR \cong \dfrac{\sqrt{km}}{c}$.

Hence, $\quad c = \dfrac{\sqrt{km}}{TR}$. $\qquad (14\text{-}33)$

Therefore, an increasing damping ratio tends to reduce the transmissibility at resonance.

In setting up the test, a rigid vibration fixture should be used to support the member that is to be tested to prevent fixture resonances from influencing the part resonances.

Nonlinear Dampings. A general form of the velocity dependent resistance force, $D(x)$, may be expressed in the form

$$D(\dot{x}) = c\dot{x} \, |\, \dot{x}\,|^{\,n-1}, \qquad\qquad (14\text{-}34)$$

where c is the damping coefficient, and n is an integer index. For $n = 0$, one obtains the resistance law for Coulomb friction; for $n = 1$, viscous damping; for $n = 2$, quadratic damping, etc. The actual damping element consists of viscous, quadratic, Coulomb, and stiction combined, the characteristics of which are shown in Fig. 14-20.

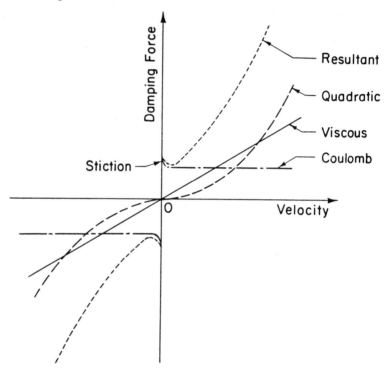

Fig. 14-20. Combined nonlinear damping characteristic.

It is possible to replace the actual nonlinear damping by an approximate and an equivalent viscous damping c_{eq} if the damping is reasonably small and if the input force is sinusoidal. The equivalence is based on equal dissipative work done by the damping forces. Vibration theory shows that for a quarter cycle of vibration the equivalence of dissipative work can be expressed as

$$\int_0^{\frac{\pi}{2\omega}} c_n \dot{x}^n dx = c_{eq} \int_0^{\frac{\pi}{2\omega}} \dot{x}\, dx,$$

from which we obtain

$$c_{eq} = c_n X^{n-1} \omega^{n-1} \gamma_n, \tag{14-35}$$

where $\gamma_n = \dfrac{4}{\pi}$ for $n = 0$ (Coulomb damping); $\gamma_n = 1$ for $n = 1$ (viscous damping); and $\gamma_n = \dfrac{8}{3\pi}$ for $n = 2$ (quadratic damping). X represents the amplitude of vibration.

To determine the generalized dissipative force, we define a "power function" P such that the generalized dissipative forces are given by

$$D(\dot{x}_n) = \frac{\partial P}{\partial \dot{x}_n}. \tag{14-36}$$

Table 14-6 summarizes some useful forms of the power function for a system containing lumped masses. Note that the power function for the case of viscous damping is the well-known Rayleigh dissipation function. If a system is acted upon by a combination of forces, the total P may be added together.

Table 14-6. Summary of Typical Forms of Power Function

Type of Damping	Power Function
Coulomb damping	$P = \displaystyle\sum_{i=1}^{p} c_i \dot{x}_i$
Viscous damping	$P = \dfrac{1}{2} \displaystyle\sum_{i=1}^{p} c_i \dot{x}_i^{2}$
Damping described by power series $D(\dot{x}) = c_i \dot{x}_i^{n}$	$P = \dfrac{1}{n+1} \displaystyle\sum_{i=1}^{p} c_i \dot{x}_i^{n+1}$
Surface contact $dD = c\dot{x}^n \, dA$	$P = \dfrac{1}{n+1} \displaystyle\int c\dot{x}^{n+1} \, dA$

14-4. MODELING OF AN AUTOMOTIVE VALVE–GEAR SYSTEM — A PRACTICAL EXAMPLE

Automotive valve–gear systems can be arranged in a number of configurations. Some typical arrangements were given in Chapter 1 (Figs. 1-2a, b, c, d). For the purpose of showing the principles and the procedures involved in

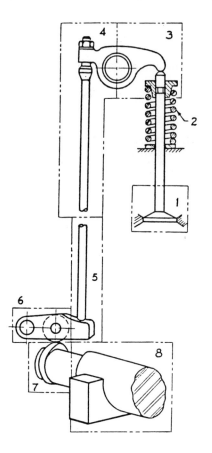

Fig. 14-21. Automotive overhead valve–gear system (model A).

dynamic modeling we will use a classical overhead valve–gear system (Fig. 1-2a or 14-1a) for illustration. This model was employed by Barkan (11)* in a study of the dynamic response of an automot24 depict the evolution of the reduced system. Starting with Fig. 14-21, the actual system is divided into several sections. The exhaust valve, the spring, the spring cap, and the pushrod undergo simple reciprocating motion, while the upper rocker arm and the lower rocker lever undergo oscillating motion. In addition, because of the flexibility in the camshaft and the camshaft bearings, the camshaft and its journals can be considered to undergo a reciprocating motion.

The reciprocating parts may be directly weighed, if the prototype is available, or their weight may be carefully calculated based on design drawings if

_____

*The model used by Barkan contains a lower–rocker lever.

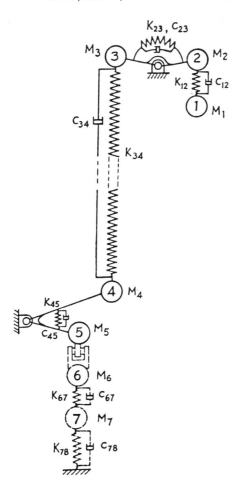

Fig. 14-22. Lumped spring–mass–damper system model of automotive overhead valve-gear system (model B).

the actual parts are not available. The two oscillating members, the lower rocker lever and the upper rocker arm, are reduced as follows:

Lower Rocker Lever. The mass of lever M is given as equal to 0.3442 kg. We wish to replace it by a reduced concentrated mass system. Masses M_a, M_b, and M_c are to be located at the center lines of the pivot, the cam, and the pushrod, respectively (Fig. 14-25). Since M_a is exactly at the pivot, it will not contribute to the kinetic energy of the equivalent system and need not be evaluated. Masses M_b and M_c will be contributed to the reduced masses M_4 and M_5, respectively, of the intermediate system shown in Fig. 14-22. Also known are the distances $h_b = r_{OG} = 0.0368 \ m$, $h_c = 0.0691 \ m$, and $R_{GS} = 0.0442 \ m$, as

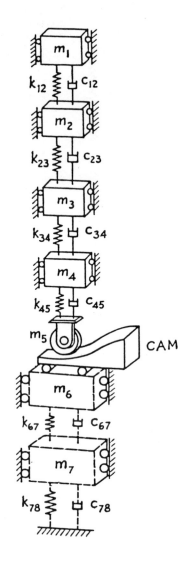

Fig. 14-23. Reduced system model (model C).

labeled in Fig. 14-25. The moment of inertia of the lever can be determined experimentally by swinging it on a knife edge S as a simple pendulum. The period of this pendulum is $\tau = 0.465$ sec. Therefore, the moment of inertia with respect to point S can be calculated

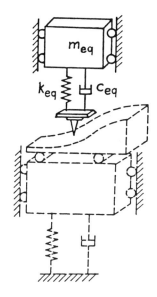

Fig. 14-24. Reduced system model (model D).

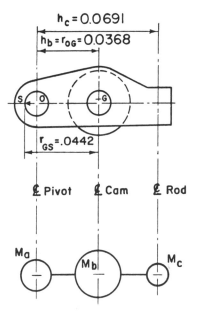

O – Pivot
G – Mass Center
S – Knife-edge Support

Fig. 14-25. Kinetically equivalent system of lower rocker lever.

$$I_s = Mgr_{GS} \frac{\tau^2}{(2\pi)^2}$$

$$= 0.344 \, (9.807) \, (0.0442) \left(\frac{0.465}{2\pi} \right)^2$$

$$= 0.000816 \text{ N-m}^2.$$

Then the moment of inertia about *c.g.* is

$$I_G = I_s - Mr_{GS}^2$$

$$= 0.000816 - 0.344 \, (0.0442)^2$$

$$= 0.000145 \text{ N-m}^2,$$

and the moment of inertia about the pivoted axis is

$$I = I_G + Mr_{OG}^2$$

$$= 0.000145 + 0.344 \, (0.0368)^2$$

$$= 0.000612 \text{ N-m}^2.$$

Kinetic equivalency requires

$$M = M_a + M_b + M_c$$

$$Mr_{OG} = M_b h_b + M_c h_c$$

$$I = M_b h_b^2 + M_c h_c^2.$$

Solving for M_c and M_b, we obtain

$$M_c = \frac{I - Mr_{OG} h_b}{h_c (h_c - h_b)} = \frac{0.000612 - 0.344 \, (0.0368)^2}{0.0691 \, (0.0691 - 0.0368)}$$

$$= 0.0652 \text{ kg}.$$

$$M_b = \frac{Mr_{OG} - M_c h_c}{h_b} = \frac{0.344 \, (0.0368) - 0.0652 \, (0.0691)}{0.0368}$$

$$= 0.223 \text{ kg}.$$

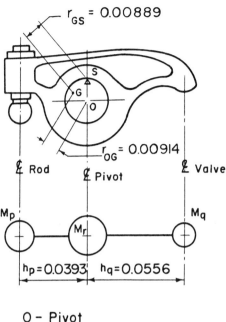

$r_{GS} = 0.00889$

S
G
O

$r_{OG} = 0.00914$

℄ Rod   ℄ Valve
℄ Pivot

M_p M_q

M_r

$h_p = 0.0393$ $h_q = 0.0556$

O – Pivot
G – Mass Center
S – Knife-edge Support

Fig. 14-26. Kinetically equivalent system of upper rocker arm.

Upper Rocker Arm. Based on Fig. 14-26, the upper rocker arm can be replaced by a kinetically equivalent system containing three masses: M_p at the pushrod line, M_r at the pivot, and M_q at the valve axis. We follow the same procedure of computation as outlined for the lower rocker lever. The given or measurable data are:

Mass of the rocker arm $M = 0.253$ kg

Distance from G to S $r_{GS} = 0.00889$ m

Distance from O to G $r_{OG} = 0.00914$ m

Distance between M_p and M_r $h_p = 0.0393$ m

Distance between M_q and M_r $h_q = 0.0556$ m

Period of pendulum oscillation $\tau = 0.667$ sec .

The moments of inertia about various points are

about the knife-edge support,

$$I_s = Mgr_{GS} \frac{\tau^2}{(2\pi)^2} = (0.253)(9.807)(0.00889) \left(\frac{0.667}{2\pi}\right)^2$$

$$= 0.000249 \text{ N-m}^2 \text{ ;}$$

about the mass center,

$$I_G = I_s - Mr_{GS}^2 = 0.000249 - 0.253(0.00889)^2$$

$$= 0.000228 \text{ N-m}^2 \text{ ; and}$$

about the pivot of rotation,

$$I = I_G + Mr_{OG}^2 = 0.000228 + 0.253(0.00914)^2$$

$$= 0.000249 \text{ N-m}^2.$$

Kinetic equivalency requires

$$M = M_p + M_q + M_r$$

$$M(h_p - r_{OG}) = M_r h_p + M_q(h_p + h_q)$$

$$I = M_p h_p^2 + M_q h_q^2 .$$

M_r, coinciding with the pivot, will not contribute to the kinetic energy and need not be evaluated.

Solving for M_p and M_q gives

$$M_p = \frac{I + Mr_{OG}h_q}{h_p(h_p + h_q)} = \frac{0.000249 + 0.253(0.00914)(0.0556)}{0.0393(0.0393 + 0.0556)}$$

$$= 0.0702 \text{ kg}$$

$$M_q = \frac{M_p h_p - Mr_{OG}}{h_q} = \frac{0.0702(0.0393) - (0.253)(0.00914)}{0.0556}$$

$$= 0.00801 \text{ kg .}$$

Table 14-7. Summary of Mass Distributions and Spring Stiffnesses in the Example of Valve Gear System (Reduction from Model A to Model B)

Region	Mass Distributions (Kg.)	Spring Stiffnesses ($\times 10^8 \text{N/m}$)
1	M_1 = valve head + 1/2 valve stem = 0.187 + 0.047 = 0.234	K_{12} = valve stem = 3.389
2	M_2 = 1/2 valve stem + spring cap + 1/3 valve spring + upper rocker arm = 0.0467 + 0.0689 + 0.0426 + 0.00801 = 0.166	K_{23} = upper rocker arm = 0.8078
3	M_3 = upper rocker arm + 1/2 pushrod = 0.101 + 0.0689 = 0.170	K_{34} = push rod = 1.553
4	M_4 = 1/2 push-rod + lower rocker lever (push-rod section) = 0.0689 + 0.0652 = 0.134	K_{45} = lower rocker lever = 2.672
5	M_5 = lower rocker lever (cam section) = 0.223	K_{56} = cam and roller interface = ∞
6	M_6 = 2/3 camshaft between journals = 0.998	K_{67} = camshaft in bending = 4.971
7	M_7 = 1/3 camshaft between journals + camshaft journals = 0.499 + 3.354 + 18.550 = 22.403	K_{78} = oil film compressibility on camshaft bearings = 7.976

M_p and M_q are components of M_3 and M_2 of Fig. 14-22. This completes the resolution of the two oscillating parts into assemblies of point masses.

The masses included within each of these sections and the appropriate stiffnesses of the interconnected springs in model B of Fig. 14-22 are summarized in Table 14-7. Reciprocating parts are weighted and combined with the equivalent oscillating parts just calculated. Note that one–third of the valve spring should be used in M_2, and about two–thirds of the mass of the center section of the camshaft should be used in mass M_6, the remainder of the camshaft mass being placed in M_7. The spring stiffnesses are experimentally determined by loading the component or the assembly and accurately measuring the deflections.

The reduction from model B (Fig. 14-22) to model C (Fig. 14-23) takes place with reference to the valve axis. Based on the principle of kinetic energy, the reduced mass m in model C is related to the mass m in model B by

$$m = \frac{M}{(lever\ ratio)^2} \ .$$

On the basis of potential energy equivalence, the component stiffnesses of the two modeled systems are related by

$$k = \frac{K}{(lever\ ratio)^2} \ .$$

The details of these reductions have been discussed in the section dealing with mechanical transformers as reflected in Equations (14-13) and (14-22).

The lever ratios for the given valve–gear system are

Valve to pushrod lever ratio $r = 1.41$

Valve to cam lever ratio $R = 2.63$.

Table 14-8 summarizes the transition from model B to model C and the related computations.

Finally, the transition from the multi–degree–of–freedom model C to the single–degree–of–freedom model D (refer to Fig. 14-24, disregarding the dashed lines) requires (a) the equivalence of mass, and (b) the equivalence of the fundamental natural frequency of vibration between the two models. The magnitude of mass m_{eq} of system D is equal to the sum of the five masses of system C. Thus

$$m_{eq} = \sum_{i=1}^{5} m_i$$

$$= 0.234 + 0.166 + 0.0855 + 0.0675$$

$$= 0.585\ kg \ .$$

The fundamental natural frequency of the single mass system can be estimated by

$$\omega_n = \sqrt{\frac{k_{eq}}{m_{eq}}} \ ,$$

where the equivalent spring stiffness k_{eq} can be computed from Eq. (14-21).

Table 14-8. Reduction from Model B to Model C of the Example of Valve Gear System Based on Kinetically Equivalent Principle

Region	Masses (Kg.)	Spring Stiffnesses ($\times 10^8 N/m$)
1	$m_1 = M_1 = 0.234$	$k_{12} = K_{12} = 3.389$
2	$m_2 = M_2 = 0.116$	$k_{23} = K_{23} = 0.8078$
3	$m_3 = \dfrac{M_3}{r^2} = 0.0855$	$k_{34} = \dfrac{K_{34}'}{r^2} = 0.7811$
4	$m_4 = \dfrac{M_4}{r^2} = 0.0675$	$k_{45} = \dfrac{K_{45}}{r^2} = 1.344$
5	$m_5 = \dfrac{M_5}{R^2} = 0.0322$	$k_{56} = \dfrac{K_{56}}{R^2} = \infty$
6	$m_6 = \dfrac{M_6}{R^2} = 0.144$	$k_{67} = \dfrac{K_{67}}{R^2} = 0.7186$
7	$m_7 = \dfrac{M_7}{R^2} = 3.239$	$k_{78} = \dfrac{K_{78}}{R^2} = 1.153$

Valve-to-pushrod lever ratio $r = 1.41$
Valve-to-cam lever ratio $R = 2.63$

Thus

$$\frac{1}{k_{eq}} = \sum_{i=1}^{6} \frac{1}{k_i}$$

$$= 10^{-8} \times \left(\frac{1}{3.389} + \frac{1}{0.8078} + \frac{1}{0.7811} + \frac{1}{1.344} \right.$$

$$\left. + \frac{1}{0.7186} + \frac{1}{1.153} \right)$$

$$= 5.825 \times 10^{-8}$$

$$k_{eq} = 0.1717 \times 10^8 \; N/m .$$

Therefore,

$$\omega_n = \sqrt{\frac{0.1717 \times 10^8}{0.585}} = 5{,}418 \text{ rad/sec.}$$

The actual fundamental frequency of system C will be somewhat lower than 5,418 rad/sec because we have not taken masses m_6 and m_7 into account. A more accurate estimate of the value of ω_n can be obtained by many other methods, for instance, the Holzer method. We shall not elaborate on Holzer's method here, but will rather recommend that the readers refer to a standard vibration book for it. Also note that we do not consider damping effect here.

For further detailed discussions on modeling of the valve gear system one should refer to the papers by Barkan (11), Johnson (117), and Stoddart (209).

We have outlined the general principles of dynamic modeling and described the various constituent parameters by which a dynamic system may be represented. What remains is to write the system equations on the basis of the model formed. This aspect of the modeling process will be treated in Chapter 15.

15
Formulation and Solution of Cam–And–Follower Systems

This chapter deals with the development of mathematical models in the form of one or more differential equations describing the cam–and–follower system with different degrees of sophistication in modeling. Also presented are several techniques for solving the formulated differential equations.

15-1. LINEAR MODEL OF A SINGLE DEGREE OF FREEDOM

The simplest model of a cam–follower system, as shown in Fig. 15-1, is obtained by assuming that the equivalent mass of the follower is lumped in one point. The elasticity of the follower corresponds to a linear spring with stiffness k supporting the mass. Here we assume that the cam support is rigid and that the damping is of a viscous nature with the coefficient of damping c. If x is the displacement of the follower with respect to the equilibrium position of the system and $y(t)$ is the time–dependent displacement of the cam, then in the absence of backlash, the equation of motion of the system with reference to the absolute coordinate of the follower mass is

$$m\ddot{x} + c\dot{x} + kx = c\dot{y}(t) + ky(t) , \qquad (15\text{-}1)$$

where the dots represent differentiation with respect to time. Sometimes, it is

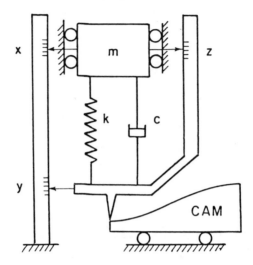

Fig. 15-1. Linear model of cam–follower system of single degree of freedom.

more convenient to refer to the relative coordinate $z = x - y$, since the stresses
in the follower system, the contact stress at the cam surface, and the deviation
between the input and the output motion are all directly proportional to z. The
equation of motion of the system with reference to the relative motion of the
follower mass is

$$m\ddot{z} + c\dot{z} + kz = -m\ddot{y}(t) . \tag{15-2}$$

Eq. (15-2) may be written in the form

$$\ddot{z} + 2\zeta\omega_n\dot{z} + \omega_n^2 z = -\ddot{y}(t) , \tag{15-3}$$

where $\omega_n = \sqrt{\dfrac{k}{m}}$

$\zeta = \dfrac{c}{2m\omega_n}$

are the undamped system's characteristic frequency (natural frequency) and
damping factor, respectively.

Without a loss of generality, the initial conditions of the system may be
expressed as $z(0) = z_o$ and $\dot{z}(0) = \dot{z}_o$. Eq. (15-3) is in the real time domain. If we
conduct time scaling process by letting $\tau = \omega_n t$, then

$$\dot{z} = \frac{dz}{dt} = \omega_n \frac{dz}{d\tau}$$

$$\ddot{z} = \frac{d^2 z}{dt^2} = \omega_n^2 \frac{d^2 z}{d\tau^2} \ .$$

Substituting these into Eq. (15-3), we may transform the equation of motion into a fictitious time of τ domain

$$z'' + 2\zeta z' + z = y''(\tau) \ , \tag{15-4}$$

with initial conditions $z(0) = z_o$ and $z'(0) = z_o'$, where the primes represent differentiation with respect to τ.

We have formulated the modeled cam–and–follower system of a single degree of freedom in the form of a second–ordered differential equation. This form may be further reduced by two first–order vector–matrix differential equations using the state variable approach (144). The state variable method greatly simplifies the mathematical representation of systems and is particularly suited for solutions in the time domain. We will also see that the state variable method is general enough to treat systems of multiple degrees of freedom.

Normalizing Eq. (15-3) by setting

$$z = X_1 \ ,$$

we obtain

$$\dot{X}_1 = X_2$$

$$\dot{X}_2 = -\omega_n^2 X_1 - 2\zeta\omega_n X_2 + \ddot{y}(t) \ ,$$

where X_1 and X_2, which represent the system's relative displacement and relative velocity, respectively, are the chosen state variables. The vector–matrix equation can be casted in the form

$$\begin{bmatrix} \dot{X}_1 \\ \dot{X}_2 \end{bmatrix} = \begin{bmatrix} 0 & 1 \\ -\omega_n^2 & -2\zeta\omega_n \end{bmatrix} \begin{bmatrix} X_1 \\ X_2 \end{bmatrix} + \begin{bmatrix} 1 & 0 \\ 0 & 1 \end{bmatrix} \begin{bmatrix} 0 \\ \ddot{y}(t) \end{bmatrix} \ . \tag{15-5}$$

The associated initial conditions are $X_1(0) = X_{10}$, and $X_2(0) = X_{20}$.

15-2. LINEAR MODEL OF MULTIPLE DEGREES OF FREEDOM

Fig. 15-2 shows a lumped model of a multi–degree–of–freedom cam–and–follower system. We have assumed that the vibrations of the follower masses take place with respect to the equilibrium positions of the system and that the cam and its follower remain in continuous contact.

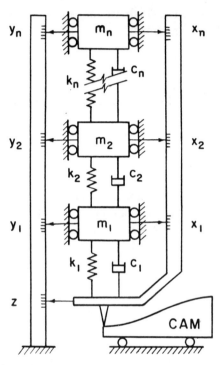

Fig. 15-2. Linear model of cam–follower system of multiple degrees of freedom.

Let x_1, x_2, ..., x_n represent the absolute displacements of the masses and $y(t)$ represent the motion excitation. The differential equations of motion of the system may be written as

(15-6)

$$m_1 \ddot{x}_1 + c_1(\dot{x}_1 - \dot{y}) + k_1(x_1 - y) - c_2(\dot{x}_2 - \dot{x}_1) - k_2(x_2 - x_1) = 0$$

$$m_2 \ddot{x}_2 + c_2(\dot{x}_2 - \dot{x}_1) + k_2(x_2 - x_1) - c_3(\dot{x}_3 - \dot{x}_2)$$

$$- k_3(x_3 - x_2) = 0$$

− − − − − −

$$m_i \ddot{x}_i + c_i(\dot{x}_i - \dot{x}_{i-1}) + k_i(x_i - x_{i-1}) - c_{i+1}(\dot{x}_{i+1} - \dot{x}_i)$$
$$- k_{i+1}(x_{i+1} - x_i) = 0$$

$$- - - - - -$$

$$m_{n-1}\ddot{x}_{n-1} + c_{n-1}(\dot{x}_{n-1} - \dot{x}_{n-2}) + k_{n-1}(x_{n-1} - x_{n-2}) - c_n(\dot{x}_n - \dot{x}_{n-1})$$
$$- k_n(x_n - x_{n-1}) = 0$$

$$m_n \ddot{x}_n + c_n(\dot{x}_n - \dot{x}_{n-1}) + k_n(x_n - x_{n-1}) = 0 \,,$$

in which the dot denotes differentiation with respect to time t; m_i is the ith mass; c_i is the ith viscous damping coefficient; and k_i is the ith spring stiffness. Eq. (15-6) can also be written in terms of the relative displacement

$$z_1 = x_1 - y$$

$$z_2 = x_2 - x_1$$

$$z_3 = x_3 - x_2$$

$$\cdots \cdots$$

$$z_i = x_i - x_{i-1}$$

or

$$x_i = \sum_{j=1}^{i} z_j + y, \qquad (i = 1, 2, \dots, n) . \tag{15-7}$$

Substituting Eq. (15-7) into (15-6) gives

$$m_1 \ddot{z}_1 + c_1 \dot{z}_1 + k_1 z_1 - c_2 \dot{z}_2 - k_2 z_2 = -m_1 \ddot{y} \tag{15-8}$$

$$m_2(\ddot{z}_1 + \ddot{z}_2) + c_2 \dot{z}_2 + k_2 z_2 - c_3 \dot{z}_3 - k_3 z_3 = -m_2 \ddot{y}$$

$$- - - - - -$$

$$m_{n-1}\left(\sum_{j=1}^{n-1} \ddot{z}_j\right) + c_{n-1}\dot{z}_{n-1} + k_{n-1}z_{n-1} - c_n \dot{z}_n - k_n z_n = -m_{n-1}\ddot{y}$$

$$m_n\left(\sum_{j=1}^{n} \ddot{z}_j\right) + c_n \dot{z}_n + k_n z_n = -m_n \ddot{y} .$$

Therefore, Eq. (15-8) can be expressed in vector–matrix form as

$$\underline{m}\ddot{\underline{z}} + \underline{c}\dot{\underline{z}} + \underline{k}\underline{z} = - \underline{M}\ddot{\underline{y}}, \tag{15-9}$$

where

$$\underline{m} = \begin{bmatrix} m_1 & & & & & \\ m_2 & m_2 & & & \text{zero} & \\ m_3 & m_3 & m_3 & & & \\ \cdots \cdots & & & & & \\ m_{n-1} & m_{n-1} & \cdots \cdots & & m_{n-1} & \\ m_n & m_n & \cdots \cdots & & m_n & m_n \end{bmatrix},$$

$$\underline{c} = \begin{bmatrix} c_1 & -c_2 & & & \text{zero} & \\ & c_2 & -c_3 & & & \\ & & c_3 & -c_4 & & \\ & & & \cdot & \cdot & \\ & & & & \cdot & \cdot \\ & \text{zero} & & & c_{n-1} & -c_n \\ & & & & & c_n \end{bmatrix},$$

$$\underline{k} = \begin{bmatrix} k_1 & -k_2 & & & & \text{zero} \\ & k_2 & -k_3 & & & \\ & & k_3 & -k_4 & & \\ & & & \ddots & \ddots & \\ & & & & k_{n-1} & -k_n \\ \text{zero} & & & & & k_n \end{bmatrix},$$

and

$$\underline{M} = \begin{bmatrix} m_1 & & & \\ & m_2 & & \\ & & \vdots & \\ & & m_{n-1} & \\ & & & m_n \end{bmatrix},$$

or

$$\ddot{\underline{z}} = -\underline{m}^{-1}\underline{c}\dot{\underline{z}} - \underline{m}^{-1}\underline{k}\underline{z} - \underline{m}^{-1}\underline{M}\ddot{y}. \tag{15-10}$$

Introducing state variables

$$X(t) = \left\{ -\frac{\underline{z}}{\underline{p}} - \right\}$$

in which

$$\dot{\underline{z}} = \underline{p},$$

we can recast Eq. (15-10) in the form

$$\dot{\underline{X}}(t) = \underline{A}\underline{X} + \underline{B}\underline{u}, \tag{15-11}$$

where

$$\underline{A} = \left[\begin{array}{c|c} 0 & I \\ \hline -m^{-1}k & -m^{-1}c \end{array} \right]$$

$$\underline{B} = \underline{I}$$

$$\underline{u} = \left[\begin{array}{c} 0 \\ \hline -\underline{m}^{-1}\underline{M}\ddot{y} \end{array} \right].$$

The initial condition is $X(0) = X_o$.

15-3. SYSTEM MODELS CONTAINING NONLINEAR PASSIVE PARAMETERS

Nonlinearities in cam–and–follower systems can be caused by the passive parameters in the modeled system. These include nonlinear damping of various kinds, such as Coulomb friction, quadratic damping, stiction, and combinations of these; backlash or play in components; and other types of nonlinear mechanisms described earlier in Chapter 14.

Single–Degree–of–Freedom Systems

Fig. 15-3 shows a single–degree–of–freedom system model containing a nonlinear damping element. The damping mechanism is a combination of viscous, quadratic, and Coulomb friction types. Let c, α, and β represent the coefficients of viscous, quadratic, and Coulomb damping, respectively. Other symbols are as defined previously. The equation of motion with reference to the equilibrium position is

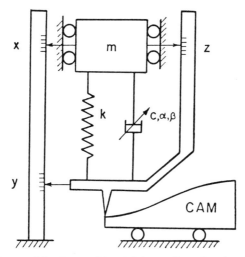

Fig. 15-3. Single–degree–of–freedom model containing nonlinear damping element.

$$m\ddot{x} + c(\dot{x} - \dot{y}) + k(x - y) + \alpha \,|\, \dot{x} - \dot{y} \,|\, (\dot{x} - \dot{y})$$

$$+ \,\beta \,\frac{(\dot{x} - \dot{y})}{|\dot{x} - \dot{y}|} = 0 \,.$$

In terms of the relative coordinate $z = x - y$, this becomes

$$m\ddot{z} + c\dot{z} + kz = -m\ddot{y} - \alpha \,|\, \dot{z} \,|\, \dot{z} - \beta \,\frac{\dot{z}}{|\dot{z}|} \,. \qquad (15\text{-}12)$$

Eq. (15-12) can be rewritten as

$$\ddot{z} + 2\zeta\omega_n\dot{z} + \omega_n^2 z = -\omega_n^2 \delta \,, \qquad (15\text{-}13)$$

where

$$\delta = \frac{\ddot{y}}{\omega_n^2} + \frac{\alpha}{m\omega_n^2} \,|\, \dot{z} \,|\, \dot{z} + \frac{\beta}{m\omega_n^2} \,\frac{\dot{z}}{|\dot{z}|} \,.$$

ω_n is the natural frequency, and ζ is the viscous damping factor of the system.

If the backlash in the system is taken into account, we can formulate the equations of motion based on a single–degree–of–freedom model as shown in Fig. 15-4, where x_o represents the backlash. In this situation, we must realize

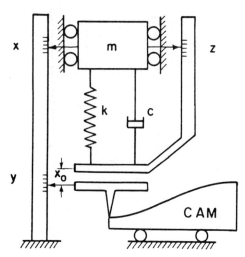

Fig. 15-4. Single–degree–of–freedom model with backlash.

that

when $y - x > x_o$, contact exists;

when $y - x < x_o$, there is no contact.

Based on Fig. 15-4, we can write the equations of motion

$$m\ddot{x} + kx = 0 \qquad\qquad \text{if } y - x < x_o \qquad (15\text{-}14)$$

$$m\ddot{x} + c\dot{x} + kx = ky + c\dot{y} \qquad \text{if } y - x > x_o .$$

Multiple–Degrees–of–Freedom Systems

Fig. 15-5 shows a nonlinear model of n–degrees of freedom, in which x_1, $x_2, \ldots , x_n$ are the absolute displacements of the follower masses, and $y(t)$ represents the input motion. Using the relative coordinates $z_1 = x_1 - y$, $z_2 = x_2 - x_1 , \ldots , z_n = x_n - x_{n-1}$, the equations of motion of the system may be written in general form as

$$m_i\ddot{z_i} + G_i(\dot{z}_1, \dot{z}_2, \ldots, \dot{z}_n) + H_i(z_1, z_2, \ldots, z_n) = f_i(t) \qquad (15\text{-}15)$$

$$i = 1, 2, \ldots, n$$

$$f_i(t) = -m_i\ddot{y}(t) + F_1(t) \qquad \text{for } i = 1$$

$$f_i(t) = F_i(t) \qquad\qquad \text{for } i \neq 1 ,$$

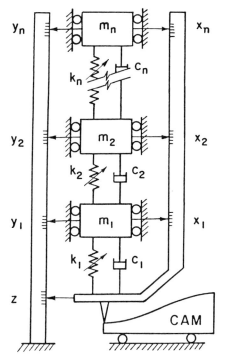

Fig. 15-5. Non-linear model of cam–follower system of multiple degrees of freedom.

where $G_i(\dot{z}_1, \dot{z}_2, \ldots, \dot{z}_n)$ represents the ith nonlinear damping force, and $H_i(z_1, z_2, \ldots, z_n)$ represents the ith nonlinear spring force. $F_i(t)$ is the ith external forcing term, if any exists. The G and H may be any form or complicated nonlinear function.

Eq. (15-15) may be rewritten in the form

$$\ddot{z}_i + 2\zeta_i\omega_{ni}\dot{z}_i + \omega_{ni}^2 z = -\omega_{ni}^2\Gamma \qquad i = 1, 2, \ldots, n, \qquad (15\text{-}16)$$

where

$$\Gamma_i = \frac{1}{\omega_{ni}^2}\left(G_i + H_i - 2\zeta_i\omega_{ni}\dot{z}_i - \omega_{ni}^2 z_i - \frac{f_i}{k_i}\right),$$

for $i = 1, 2, \ldots, n$, where k_i is the linear spring stiffness associated with the ith nonlinear spring, ω_{ni} is the ith natural frequency, and ζ_i is the ith viscous damping factor of the system.

Note that in Eq. (15-16), if the system is linear, all δ's do not contain nonlinear terms. If the system is undamped, all damping factors are dropped. These situations may be considered to be special cases.

Example 15-1

For the purpose of illustration, let us consider a two–degree–of–freedom non-linear system as shown in Fig. 15-6. The nonlinearity here is mainly due to the cubic power law springs. Based on the free–body diagrams, through the application of Newton's second law we obtain

$$m_1\ddot{x}_1 = c_2\dot{z}_2 + k_2 z_2 + \beta_2 z_2^3 - c_1\dot{z}_1 - k_1 z_1 - \beta_1 z_1^3 \qquad (15\text{-}17)$$

$$m_2\ddot{x}_2 = -c_2\dot{z}_2 - k_2 z_2 - \beta_2 z_2^3 \,,$$

where $z_1 = x_1 - y$ and $z_2 = x_2 - x_1$ are the relative coordinates.

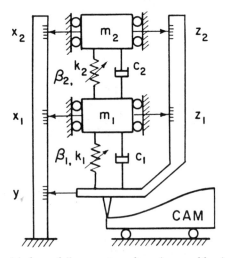

Fig. 15-6 Nonlinear model of cam–follower system of two degrees of freedom.

Eq. (15-17) can be rearranged as

$$\qquad\qquad\qquad\qquad\qquad\qquad\qquad\qquad\qquad\qquad\qquad (15\text{-}18)$$

$$m_1\ddot{z}_1 + c_1\dot{z}_1 + k_1 z_1 = c_2\dot{z}_2 + k_2 z_2 + \beta_2 z_2^3 - \beta_1 z_1^3 - m_1\ddot{y}$$

$$m_2\ddot{z}_2 + c_2\dot{z}_2 + k_2 z_2 = -\beta_2 z_2^3 - m_2(\ddot{z}_1 + \ddot{y}) \,.$$

Substituting the first expression for $\ddot{z}_1$ into the second in Eq. (15-18) leads to the following

$$\ddot{z}_1 + 2\zeta_1\omega_{1n}\dot{z}_1 + \omega_{1n}^2 z_1 = -\omega_{1n}^2 \delta_1 \qquad (15\text{-}19)$$

$$\ddot{z}_2 + 2\zeta_2\omega_{2n}\dot{z}_2 + \omega_{2n}^2 z_2 = -\omega_{2n}^2 \delta_2 \,,$$

where

$$\delta_1 = \frac{\ddot{y}}{\omega_{1n}^2} - \frac{c_2}{k_1}\dot{z}_2 - \frac{k_2}{k_1}z_2 + \frac{\beta_1}{k_1}z_1^3 - \frac{\beta_2}{k_1}z_2^3$$

$$\delta_2 = -\frac{c_1}{m_1\omega_{2n}^2}\dot{z}_1 + \frac{c_2}{m_1\omega_{2n}^2}\dot{z}_2 - \frac{\omega_{1n}^2}{\omega_{2n}^2}z_1 + \frac{m_2}{m_1}z_2$$

$$- \frac{1}{m_1\omega_{2n}^2}z_1^3 + \frac{\beta_2}{k_2}\left(1 + \frac{m_2}{m_1}\right)z_2^3 .$$

Note that the formulation of Eq. (15-19) follows the general pattern of Eq. (15-16).

15-4. COUPLED SYSTEMS OF CAM–FOLLOWERS AND DRIVE SHAFTS

In the usual analysis of cam–operated systems the cam drive shaft is assumed to be infinitely rigid. In systems where high loads and high speeds are encountered and where a relatively long flexible shaft is used, the dynamic effect of cam shaft elasticity has to be considered. The following three models will be treated.

Model 1   Single Degree–of–Freedom Translation Model

The first model, shown in Fig. 15-7, is obtained by assuming that the equivalent mass m of the follower is lumped in one point and constrained to move in the vertical direction only. The elasticity of the follower corresponds to a linear spring, with stiffness k supporting the mass. Damping in the follower is represented by the viscous damping coefficient c. The flexible camshaft is represented by the torsional stiffness k_θ and by the transverse (bending) stiffnesses k_x and k_y in the x and y directions, respectively. The input angular velocity is considered to be constant. Backlash is neglected, and it is assumed that the return spring exerts sufficient force to keep the roller in contact with the cam. This model has been described by Koster (134) and utilized by Ardayfio (4) for studying the effects of flexibility in the drive shaft on the vibratory response of the cam–follower.

The motion of the center of the follower roller is a function of the cam rotation θ and the elastic deflections of the camshaft in the y– and x–directions. Because of the relatively slight shaft deflection y in comparison with the instan-

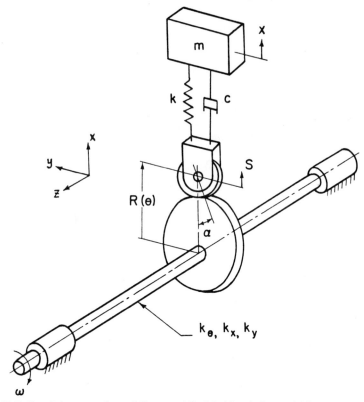

Fig. 15-7. Coupled system of cam–follower and flexible drive shaft – model 1.

taneous cam pitch radius $R(\theta)$, the slope of the cam, $\tan \alpha$, is assumed to remain independent of y. The slope may be defined as

$$\tan \alpha = \frac{1}{R(\theta)} \frac{ds}{d\theta} .$$

Thus the nominal follower velocity is

$$\dot{s} = \omega R(\theta) \tan \alpha , \tag{15-20}$$

where ω is the constant input angular velocity of the shaft. Integrating Eq. (15-20) gives the nominal displacement at the roller

$$s = \omega \int_0^t R(\theta) \tan \alpha \, dt . \tag{15-21}$$

The equivalent stiffness k_{eq} of the system is derived in Reference (134) as

$$\frac{1}{k_{eq}} = \frac{1}{k_c} + \frac{1}{k_t} \tan^2 \alpha \,, \tag{15-22}$$

where the equivalent vertical spring stiffness is

$$k_c = \frac{kk_x}{k + k_x} \,,$$

and the equivalent tangential spring stiffness is

$$k_t = \frac{k_y k_\theta}{k_y + k_\theta} \,.$$

It is apparent that k_{eq} thus obtained is time–dependent.

The original model with four degrees of freedom may be approximated by a model with a single degree of freedom with variable stiffness. The equation of motion of the system may be written as

$$m\ddot{x} + c(\dot{s} - \dot{x}) + k_{eq}(s - x) = 0 \,,$$

where the dots represent differentiation with respect to time.

Using Eq. (15-22) gives

$$m\ddot{x} + c(\dot{s} - \dot{x}) + \frac{k_c}{1 + \dfrac{k_c}{k_t}\left(\dfrac{1}{\omega R}\dot{s}\right)^2}(s - x) = 0 \,. \tag{15-23}$$

The effect of the flexibility of the shaft is greatest for the position of the cam corresponding to $\alpha = \alpha_{max}$. For many cam profiles this occurs at the midstation of the cam lift. As a first approximation, $R(\theta)$ can be replaced by the mean pitch radius of the cam R_m, i.e.,

$$R(\theta) = R_m \,. \tag{15-24}$$

Eq. (15-23) can now be rewritten as

$$m\ddot{x} + c(\dot{s} - \dot{x}) + \cfrac{k_c}{1 + \cfrac{k_c}{k_t}\left(\cfrac{1}{\omega R_m}\dot{s}\right)^2}(s - x) = 0 \,. \qquad (15\text{-}25)$$

Next, the following non-dimensional parameters are introduced:

$$\tau = \frac{t}{T_1}$$

$$\Gamma = \frac{s}{h} \qquad\qquad \dot{\Gamma} = \frac{\dot{s}\,T_1}{h}$$

$$X = \frac{x}{h} \qquad\qquad \dot{X} = \frac{\dot{x}\,T_1}{h} \qquad\qquad \ddot{X} = \frac{\ddot{x}\,T_1^2}{h} \,,$$

and

$$T = \frac{2\pi}{T_1}\,\sqrt{\frac{m}{k_c}}$$

$$\varsigma = \frac{cT}{4\pi}$$

$$F = \frac{k_c}{k_t}\left(\frac{h}{R_m\beta}\right)^2 \qquad \beta = \omega T_1 \,,$$

where h is the cam lift in a dwell–rise–dwell motion input, and T_1 is the period of such input. Substituting these into Eq. (15-25) yields

$$(1 + \dot{\Gamma}^2 F)\,\ddot{X} + 2\,\varsigma(1 + \dot{\Gamma}^2 F)\left(\frac{2\pi}{T}\right)\dot{X} + \left(\frac{2\pi}{T}\right)^2 X \qquad (15\text{-}26)$$

$$= 2\varsigma(1 + \dot{\Gamma}^2 F)\left(\frac{2\pi}{T}\right)\dot{\Gamma} + \left(\frac{2\pi}{T}\right)^2\Gamma \,.$$

This is a second–order linear differential equation with variable coefficients.

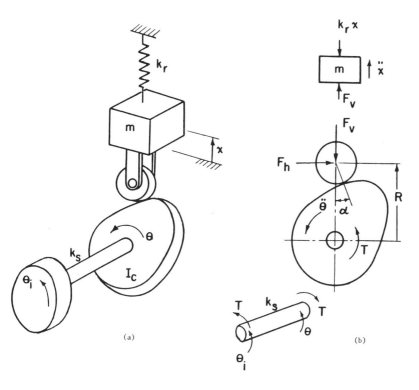

Fig. 15-8 (a). Coupled system of cam–follower and flexible drive shaft–model 2; (b). Free–body diagram of model 2.

Model 2   Single Degree-of-Freedom Torsional Model

In high–speed camera studies of cam–driven systems, Rothbart (195) observed a phenomenon that he termed "shaft wind–up." This phenomenon is most likely to arise under the conditions of a high inertia load, a large pressure angle, and a flexible drive shaft. Although the power input end of the shaft generally turns at a nearly uniform speed, the speed of the cam itself is reduced at the twists up to the instant of maximum torque. During this period, the follower is at first reluctant to move and later moves slower than intended. Beyond the instant of maximum torque, the energy stored in the shaft is released and drives the cam at an increasing speed, thus causing the follower mass to catch up with the forcing cam action and then to overshoot it.

As shown in Fig. 15-8(a), this system model includes the polar moment of inertia I_c of the cam about its axis of rotation, the mass m of the follower, and the stiffnesses of the massless drive shaft and follower return spring, k_s and k_r, respectively. The driving shaft rotates at a constant angular velocity ω, whereas the cam rotates at an angular velocity $\dfrac{d\theta}{dt}$, different from ω be-

cause of the drive shaft torsional deflections. The angular displacement of the cam is defined by θ, and the cam configuration is defined by an arbitrary geometric function $f(\theta)$. Based on the free–body diagram of this system shown in Fig. 15-8(b), we can write the following equations:

$$m\ddot{x} = F_v - k_r x \tag{15-27}$$

$$I_c\ddot{\theta} = T - F_h R \tag{15-28}$$

$$T = k_s(\theta_i - \theta) \tag{15-29}$$

$$\tan \alpha = \frac{F_h}{F_v} , \tag{15-30}$$

where F_v and F_h represent the vertical and the horizontal components of the contact forces, respectively. α is the pressure angle, and T is the cam shaft torque.

Eliminating F_v between (15-27) and (15-30), and substituting the result and (15-29) into (15-28) give

$$I_c\ddot{\theta} + m\ddot{x}R \tan \alpha + k_s\theta = k_s\theta_i - k_r x R \tan \alpha , \tag{15-31}$$

since

$$x = f(\theta) \tag{15-32}$$

$$\ddot{x} = f''(\theta) \dot{\theta}^2 + f'(\theta) \ddot{\theta} , \tag{15-33}$$

where the primes represent differentiations with respect to θ.

For a radial cam

$$R = R_o + f(\theta) , \tag{15-34}$$

with R_o being the base circle radius,

and

$$\tan \alpha = \frac{1}{R} \frac{dR}{d\theta} = \frac{f'(\theta)}{R_o + f(\theta)} . \tag{15-35}$$

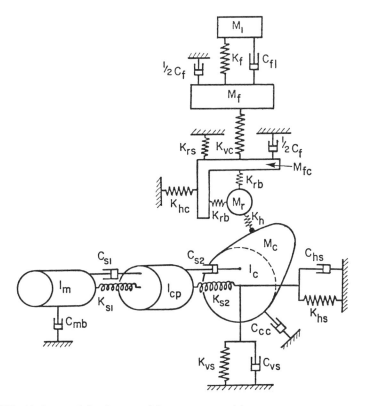

Fig. 15-9. 11–degree–of–freedom cam–follower system model.

Substituting Eqs. (15-32) through (15-35) into Eq. (15-31) yields

$$\{I_c + m\,[f'(\theta)]^2\}\,\ddot{\theta} + mf'(\theta)f''(\theta)\dot{\theta}^2 + k_s\theta \qquad (15\text{-}36)$$

$$= k_s\theta_i - k_r f(\theta)f'(\theta)\,.$$

Eq. (15-36), again, is a second–order time variant nonlinear differential equation.

Model 3   Multiple Degree–of–Freedom Model

As we can see from the above discussion, the first model has the merit of simplicity, so that merely three dimensionless characteristics (two if damping is ignored) are needed to describe the dynamic behavior of a cam mechanism driven by a relatively flexible shaft. The real question, however, is how accurately dynamic behavior can be described with the model, particularly because in the determination of the response the assumption of Eqs. (15-22) and (15-23)

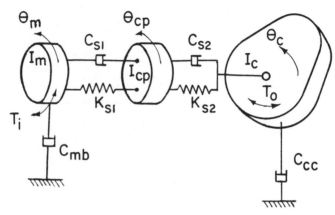

Fig. 15-10. 3–degree–of–freedom torsional system model.

have been made. In the more complicated dynamic models with multiple degrees of freedom, many limitations may be relaxed, and the random nature of the machining tolerances of both the cam profile and the follower together with all possible system flexibility errors can be taken into account by simulation. A simulation study based on an eleven–degrees–of–freedom model has been carried out by Kim and Newcombe (124).

Fig. 15-9 shows the third dynamic model, resolved into the driving or torsional system, Fig. 15-10, and the driven or translational system, Fig. 15-11. The latter is divided into two subsystems according to the vertical motion (y–axis) and the horizontal motion (x–axis) of the parts.

Using Newton's second law or applying the Lagrange equation, we can write the following sets of equations of motion.

For translational movement of the follower (Fig. 15-11) along the y–axis direction

$$M_i \ddot{y}_5 + c_{f1}(\dot{y}_5 - \dot{y}_4) + k_f(y_5 - y_4) = 0 \qquad (15\text{-}37)$$

$$M_f \ddot{y}_4 - c_{f1}(\dot{y}_5 - \dot{y}_4) + \frac{1}{2} c_f \dot{y}_4 + k_{vc}(y_4 - y_3) - k_f(y_5 - y_4) = 0$$

$$M_{fc} \ddot{y}_3 + \frac{1}{2} c_f \dot{y}_3 + k_{rb}(y_3 - y_2) - k_{vc}(y_4 - y_3) + F_p + k_{rs} y_3 = 0$$

$$M_r \ddot{y}_2 - k_{rb}(y_3 - y_2) - F_n \cos \alpha = 0$$

$$M_c \ddot{y}_1 + c_{vs} \dot{y}_1 + k_{vs} y_1 + F_n \cos \alpha = 0 \; ,$$

and along the x-axis direction

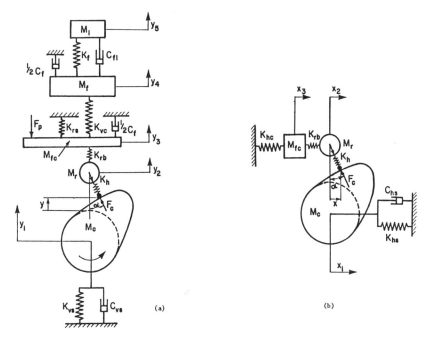

Fig. 15-11 (a). 8–degree–of–freedom translational system model, (b). 8–degree–of–freedom translational system model.

$$M_{fc}\ddot{x}_3 - k_{rb}(x_2 - x_3) + k_{hc}x_3 = 0 \tag{15-38}$$

$$M_r\ddot{x}_2 + k_{rb}(x_2 - x_3) + F_n \sin \alpha = 0$$

$$M_c\ddot{x}_1 + c_{hs}\dot{x}_1 + k_{hs}x_1 - F_n \sin \alpha = 0 \ .$$

For torsional movement of the drive shaft (Fig. 15-10)

$$I_m\ddot{\theta}_m + c_{s1}(\dot{\theta}_m - \dot{\theta}_{cp}) + c_{mb}\dot{\theta}_m + k_{s1}(\theta_m - \theta_{cp}) - T_i = 0 \tag{15-39}$$

$$I_{cp}\ddot{\theta}_{cp} - c_{s1}(\dot{\theta}_m - \dot{\theta}_{cp}) + c_{s2}(\dot{\theta}_{cp} - \dot{\theta}_c) - k_{s1}(\theta_m - \theta_{cp})$$
$$+ k_{s2}(\theta_{cp} - \theta_c) = 0$$

$$I_c\ddot{\theta}_c - c_{s2}(\dot{\theta}_{cp} - \dot{\theta}_c) + c_{cc}\dot{\theta}_c - k_{s2}(\theta_{cp} - \theta_c) + T_o = 0 \ .$$

In the expressions above

$$T_o = \frac{\dot{y}}{\dot{\theta}} F_c \cos \alpha \ ,$$

where

F_n = the contact force between the cam and the follower roller.
α = the pressure angle.

Other symbols are as labeled in Figs. 15-9, 15-10, and 15-11.

The damping forces $\dfrac{1}{2} c_f \dot{y}_4$ and $\dfrac{1}{2} c_f \dot{y}_3$ are to be replaced by the friction forces F_1 and F_2 caused by the contact force F_n, which will be found later. To be able to simulate the simultaneous differential Eqs. (15-37) through (15-39), the parameters such as the mass, the spring stiffness, and the damping coefficient must first be determined. These are analyzed as follows.

If we denote δ_{rs} as the length of the spring subjected to compression, F_p as the spring preload, and k_t as the total equivalent spring constant, then

$$\delta_{rs} = \frac{F_p}{k_t} = \frac{F_p}{k_{rs}} + \frac{F_p}{k_{rb}} + \frac{F_p \cos^2 \alpha}{k_n} + \frac{F_p}{k_{vs}}$$

and

$$\frac{1}{k_t} = \frac{k_{rb} k_h k_{vs} + k_{rs} k_h k_{vs} + k_{rs} k_{rb} k_{vs} \cos^2 \alpha + k_{rs} k_{rb} k_h}{k_{rs} k_{rb} k_h k_{vs}} ,$$

Then

$$F_p = \delta_{rs} k_t$$

$$= \frac{k_{rs} k_{rb} k_h k_{vs} \delta_{rs}}{k_{rb} k_h k_{vs} + k_{rs} k_h k_{vs} + k_{rs} k_{rb} k_{vs} \cos^2 \alpha + k_{rs} k_{rb} k_h} .$$

The normal contact force F_n is obtained according to the criterion of separation of contact between the cam and the roller,

$$y_2 \lessgtr y + y_1 + \frac{F_p}{k_h} .$$

For $y_2 < y + y_1 + \dfrac{F_p}{k_h}$, contact is maintained, thus

$$F_n = k_h (y + y_1 - y_2) \cos \alpha + F_p \cos \alpha ,$$

and for $y_2 \geq y + y_1 + \dfrac{F_p}{k_h}$, separation occurs, thus

$$F_n = 0 .$$

Therefore, we may regard $y_2 = y + y_1 + \dfrac{F_p}{k_h}$ as the threshold of contact separation.

To calculate the contact force, the spring stiffness k_h for contact between the cam and the roller should be defined. We recall that for two cylinders having thickness w (Fig. 12-2), the width of the rectangular contact area, $2b$, can be obtained from Eq. (12-11), the well–known Hertzian stress formula. Thus

$$b = \left[\frac{2P}{\pi w} \frac{\dfrac{1 - \mu_1^2}{E_1} + \dfrac{1 - \mu_1^2}{E_1}}{\left(\dfrac{1}{\rho_1} + \dfrac{1}{\rho_2} \right)} \right]^{1/2}$$

where

$\mu_1, \mu_2 =$ Poisson's ratio of materials for the roller and the cam, respectively.

$E_1, E_2 =$ the modulus of elasticity of materials for the roller and the cam, respectively.

$\rho_1, \rho_2 =$ the radius of the roller and the cam, respectively.

Note that ρ_2 varies according to the contact position and is given by Eq. (11-4), i.e.,

$$\rho_2 = \frac{\left[(r_o + s)^2 + \left(\dfrac{ds}{d\theta} \right)^2 \right]^{3/2}}{(r_o + s)^2 + 2 \left(\dfrac{ds}{d\theta} \right)^2 - (r_o + s) \dfrac{d^2s}{d\theta^2}} ,$$

where $R_o = R_b + r_1$, R_b is the base circle radius. Also, from Eq. (12-10), with reference to the geometry of Fig. 12-2, the depth of deformations h_1 and h_2 are

$$h_1 = \rho_1 - \sqrt{\rho_1^2 - b^2}$$

$$h_2 = \rho_2 - \sqrt{\rho_2^{\,2} - b^2} \quad .$$

Since $k_h = \dfrac{P}{H}$, and by assuming unity P, we finally get

$$k_h = \frac{1}{h_1 + h_2} \quad .$$

Referring to Fig. 10-6, the frictional forces between the follower stem and the follower guide can be calculated at

$$F_1 = \mu N_1$$

$$F_2 = \mu N_2 \, ,$$

where μ is the coefficient of friction between the follower and its guide. From static force equilibrium,

$$N_1 = \zeta F_n \sin \alpha$$

$$N_2 = (1 + \zeta) \, F_n \sin \alpha \, ,$$

in which F_n is the normal contact force, α is the pressure angle, and ζ is a dimension ratio as defined in Fig. 10-6.

The modeling of passive system parameters such as masses, moments of iner-tia, and spring stiffnesses is carried out in a standard way as described in Chap-ter 14. The choice for the value of the damping factor of 0.03 for structural damping and of 0.05 to 0.07 for well–lubricated machine components is consid-ered reasonable.

Because of the stochastic nature of the machining accuracy of the cam pro-file, an input representing the actual random characteristic of the cam profile must be added to the dynamic effects. This is described in the next section.

15-5. PROBABILISTIC MODEL OF CAM PROFILES

Referring to Figs. 15-12 and 15-13, we see that the desired location of the cutter can only be guaranteed within a tolerance band in both the x and the y directions. Thus, the resulting profile shape will have a random waviness. Sur-faces produced by milling, turning, grinding, and honing have an almost Gaus-sian, or normal, distribution. For the cam profile, a normally distributed random value with a given mean and a standard deviation is generated from a

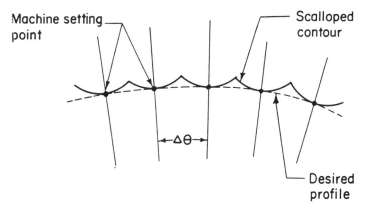

Fig. 15-12. Scalloped cam surface.

sequence of uniform random numbers. To obtain a smooth wavy shape, the random points that lie within a selected tolerance band are connected by a cubic spline curve (Fig. 15-14).

The probabilistic approach used by Kim and Newcombe (124) provides the stochastic information and the 3σ band, based on the two-dimensional tolerance of the cam profile and the roughness of the roller surface, assuming both obey the Gaussian distribution. The displacement of the follower at any cam angle is generated using a different 3σ. The randomly generated displacement points are then connected with a spline curve (Fig. 15-15), and the resulting continu-

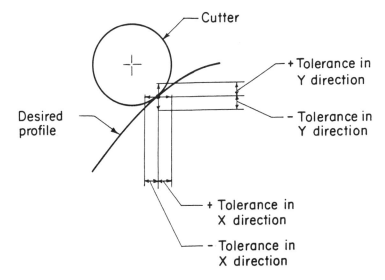

Fig. 15-13. Tolerance band for setting cutter.

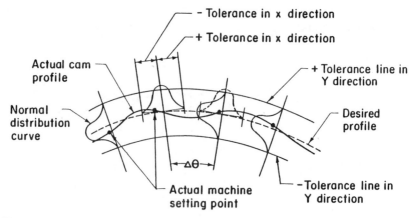

Fig. 15-14. Cam profile waviness produced by tolerance band in setting cutter.

ous spline function can be differentiated to obtain the theoretical velocity and the acceleration aspects. This velocity and acceleration information can then be used to calculate the pressure angle and the radius of curvature of the cam profile so that the dynamic simulation can be carried out.

15-6. METHODS OF SOLUTION AND SYSTEM RESPONSE

Up to this point we have emphasized the development of mathematical models in the form of one or more differential equations describing system performance. Now, we have to find solutions for these formulated equations. In this section, three methods of solution are presented: the Laplace transform

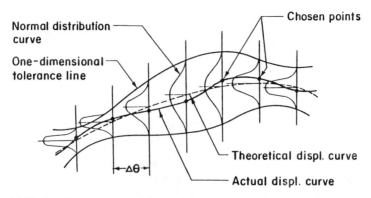

Fig. 15-15. Combined effects of cam and follower tolerance on follower displacement curve.

method, the state variable method, and a numerical method using finite differences.

Laplace Transform Method

The Laplace transform technique is an algebraic means of solving linear, time invariant differential equations. This technique transforms the differential equations into algebraic equations, including all initial conditions. Straightforward algebraic manipulation of these equations provides the transformed solution, including both the transient and the steady–state components. Many special characteristics of transform solutions may be applied to simplify the algebra. To complete the solution, the inverse transform must be found. In some cases the inverse–transform operation can be performed by direct reference to transform tables. We will demonstrate this method by solving Eq. (15-4)

$$z'' + 2\zeta z' + z = y''(\tau)$$

with the initial conditions $z(0) = z_o$, and $z'(0) = z_o'$.

Taking the Laplace transform gives

$$s^2 Z(s) + 2\zeta s Z(s) + Z(s) = \mathscr{L}[y''(\tau)] + z_o(s + 2\zeta) + z_o',$$

where $\mathscr{L}$ is the symbol of the Laplace transform, and s is the transform operator. It follows that

$$Z(s) = \frac{\mathscr{L}[y''(\tau)]}{s^2 + 2\zeta s + 1} + \frac{z_o(s + 2\zeta)}{s^2 + 2\zeta s + 1} + \frac{z_o'}{s^2 + 2\zeta s + 1}$$

Noting that $\eta^2 = 1 - \zeta^2$, we can write

$$Z(s) = \frac{\mathscr{L}[y''(\tau)]}{(s + \zeta)^2 + \eta^2} + \frac{z_o(s + 2\zeta)}{(s + \zeta)^2 + \eta^2} + \frac{z_o'}{(s + \zeta)^2 + \eta^2}$$

Taking the inverse transform, we obtain the solution z in the τ–domain as

$$(15\text{-}40)$$

$$z(\tau) = \mathscr{L}^{-1}\left[\frac{\mathscr{L}(y'')}{(s + \zeta)^2 + \eta^2}\right] + e^{-\zeta\tau}\left(\frac{z_o' + \zeta z_o}{\eta} \sin \eta\tau + z_o \cos \eta\tau\right)$$

$$= z_{ss}(\tau) + z_{tr}(\tau).$$

In Eq. (15-40) the first term $z_{ss}(\tau)$ represents the steady–state displacement response, and the second term $z_{tr}(\tau)$ represents the transient displacement response. The velocity and the acceleration responses may be obtained by differentiation. Depending upon the acceleration input function $y''(\tau)$, the Laplace transform $L\,(y'')$ and its subsequent inverse transform may be complicated.

Example 15-2

Use the Laplace transform method to find the system displacement response for a dwell–rise–dwell cycloidal motion cam. The acceleration function for cycloidal motion is a full–sine pulse. A full–sine pulse may be regarded as the superposition of two half–sine pulses, $y_1''(\tau)$ and $y_2''(\tau)$. Thus

$$y''\,(\tau) = y_1''\,(\tau) + y_2''\,(\tau)\,,$$

$$\text{with}\quad y_1''\,(\tau) = Y''\,\sin \omega\tau \qquad \left(0 < \tau < \frac{\pi}{\omega}\right) \tag{15-41}$$

$$y_1''\,(\tau) = 0 \qquad \left(\tau > \frac{\pi}{\omega}\right)\,,$$

$$\text{and}\quad y_2''\,(\tau) = -y_1''\left(t - \frac{\pi}{\omega}\right)\,, \tag{15-42}$$

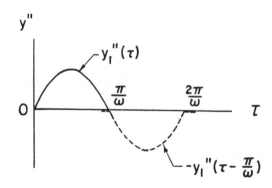

Fig. 15-16.

where $\dfrac{\pi}{\omega}$ is the duration of a half-sine pulse, as shown in Fig. 15-16. Thus $[z(\tau)]_{ss}$, the relative displacement response of $y''(\tau)$, is given by

$$[z(\tau)]_{ss} = [z_1(\tau)]_{ss} + [z_2(\tau)]_{ss} \tag{15-43}$$

$$= [z_1(\tau)]_{ss} + \left[-z_1 \left(\tau - \frac{\pi}{\omega} \right) \right]_{ss},$$

where $z_1(\tau)$ is the displacement response of the system due to the half-sine pulse excitation $y_1''(\tau)$, and $z_2(\tau)$ is the displacement response due to $y_2''(\tau)$. Therefore, we must first find $z_1(\tau)$.

To find $z_1(\tau)$ we take the Laplace transform of Eq. (15-41) and substitute it into Eq. (15-40) without regard for the initial value solution. This gives

$$[z_1(\tau)]_{ss} = \mathscr{L}^{-1} \left\{ Y'' \frac{\omega\left(1 + e^{-\frac{\pi}{\omega}s}\right)}{(s^2 + \omega^2)\,[(s + \zeta)^2 + \eta^2]} \right\} \tag{15-44}$$

or

$$\frac{[z_1(\tau)]_{ss}}{Y''} = \mathscr{L}^{-1} \left[\frac{\omega\left(1 + e^{-\frac{\pi}{\omega}s}\right)}{(s^2 + \omega^2)\,(s^2 + 2\zeta s + 1)} \right]. \tag{15-45}$$

$$= \frac{\omega}{\sqrt{(1 - \omega^2)^2 + 4\zeta^2\omega^2}} \left\{ \frac{1}{\omega} \sin(\omega\tau - \psi_1) + \frac{e^{-\zeta\tau}}{\eta} \right.$$

$$\sin(\eta\tau - \psi_2) + \frac{1}{\omega} \sin\left[\omega \left(\tau - \frac{\pi}{\omega} \right) - \psi_1 \right]$$

$$H\left(\tau - \frac{\pi}{\omega} \right) + \frac{e^{-\zeta\left(\tau - \frac{\pi}{\omega}\right)}}{\eta}$$

$$\sin\left[\eta \left(\tau - \frac{\pi}{\omega} \right) - \psi_2 \right] H\left(\tau - \frac{\pi}{\omega} \right) \right\},$$

where H represents the Heaviside unit function, and the phase angles are

$$\psi_1 = \arctan\left(\frac{2\zeta\omega}{1 - \omega^2}\right), \qquad 0 \le \psi_1 \le \pi$$

$$\psi_2 = \arctan\left(\frac{-2\zeta\eta}{\omega^2 + 2\zeta^2 - 1}\right), \qquad \pi \le \psi_2 \le 2\pi.$$

We must consider separate solutions for the two time intervals.

For the interval $0 < \tau < \dfrac{\pi}{\omega}$,

$$\frac{[z_1(\tau)]_{ss}}{Y''} = \frac{\omega}{\sqrt{(1 - \omega^2)^2 + 4\zeta^2\omega^2}} \tag{15-46}$$

$$\left[\frac{1}{\omega}\sin(\omega\tau - \psi_1) + \frac{e^{-\zeta\tau}}{\eta}\sin(\eta\tau - \psi_2)\right].$$

For the interval $\tau > \dfrac{\pi}{\omega}$,

$$\frac{[z_1(\tau)]_{ss}}{Y''} = \frac{\omega}{\sqrt{(1 - \omega^2)^2 + 4\zeta^2\omega^2}} \left\{\frac{1}{\omega}\sin(\omega\tau - \psi_1)\right.$$

$$+ \frac{e^{-\zeta\tau}}{\eta}\sin(\eta\tau - \psi_2) + \frac{1}{\omega}\sin\left[\omega\left(\tau - \frac{\pi}{\omega}\right) - \psi_1\right]$$

$$\left. + \frac{e^{-\zeta\left(\tau - \frac{\pi}{\omega}\right)}}{\eta}\sin\left[\left(\tau - \frac{\pi}{\omega}\right) - \psi_2\right]\right\}$$

$$= \frac{\omega}{\sqrt{(1 - \omega^2)^2 + 4\zeta^2\omega^2}} \; \frac{e^{-\zeta\tau}}{\eta} \left[\sin(\eta\tau - \psi_2) + e^{\frac{\zeta\pi}{\omega}} \right.$$

$$\left. \sin\left(\eta\tau - \psi_2 - \eta\frac{\pi}{\omega}\right) \right]. \qquad (15\text{-}47)$$

For the displacement response to the full–sine pulse within the interval $0 \le \tau \le \dfrac{2\pi}{\omega}$, Eq. (15-46) still holds valid. However, for the interval $t > \dfrac{2\pi}{\omega}$, we have to apply Eq. (15-43), which leads to

$$\frac{[z(\tau)]_{ss}}{Y''} = [z_1(\tau)]_{ss} + \left[-z_1\left(\tau - \frac{2\pi}{\omega}\right) \right]_{ss}$$

$$= \frac{\omega}{\sqrt{(1 - \omega^2)^2 + 4\zeta^2\omega^2}} \; \frac{e^{-\zeta\tau}}{\eta} \sin(\eta\tau - \psi_2) + e^{\frac{\zeta\pi}{\omega}}$$

$$\sin\left(\eta\tau - \psi_2 - \eta\frac{\pi}{\omega}\right) - \sin\left(\eta\tau - \frac{2\eta\pi}{\omega} - \psi_2\right) - e^{\frac{\zeta\pi}{\omega}}$$

$$\sin\left(\eta\tau - \frac{3\eta\pi}{\omega} - \psi_2\right). \qquad (15\text{-}48)$$

If there is no damping, $\zeta = 0$, $\eta = 1$, and Eq. (15-46) becomes

$$\frac{[z(\tau)]_{ss}}{Y''} = \frac{1}{1 - \omega^2}(\sin\omega\tau + \omega\sin\tau) \qquad \text{for } \tau < \frac{2\pi}{\omega}, \qquad (15\text{-}49)$$

and Eq. (15-48) becomes

$$\frac{[z(\tau)]_{ss}}{Y''} = \frac{\omega}{1 - \omega^2}\left[+ \sin\tau + \sin\left(\tau - \frac{\pi}{\omega}\right) - \sin\left(\tau - \frac{2\pi}{\omega}\right) \right.$$

$$\left. - \sin\left(\tau - \frac{3\pi}{\omega}\right) \right] \qquad \text{for } \tau > \frac{2\pi}{\omega}. \qquad (15\text{-}50)$$

State Variable Method

The state variable approach recasts differential equations of motion in a form amenable to direct matrix manipulation, thereby permitting a unified treatment of the solution of the system, whether it has a single degree of freedom or multiple degrees of freedom. With state variables the solution of linear differential equations can be easily derived, concisely stated, and directly coded for digital computation.

In the previous section, we used the vector–matrix notation and derived the differential equation for a general, multiple–degree–of–freedom system, Eq. (15-11).

$$\dot{\underline{X}} = \underline{A}\underline{X} + \underline{B}\underline{u} .$$

The solution of this equation, given $\underline{X}(0) = \underline{X}_o$, can be found by use of the matrix exponential. Premultiplying the above equation by $e^{-\underline{A}t}$, we obtain

$$e^{-\underline{A}t}\dot{\underline{X}} = e^{-\underline{A}t}\underline{A}\underline{X} + e^{-\underline{A}t}\underline{B}\underline{u} ,$$

or equivalently,

$$\frac{d}{dt}(e^{-\underline{A}t}\underline{X}) = e^{-\underline{A}t}\underline{B}\underline{u} .$$

Integrating between 0 and t gives

$$e^{-\underline{A}t}\underline{X} \Bigg]_0^t = \int_0^t e^{-\underline{A}\tau}\underline{B}u \, d\tau$$

$$e^{-\underline{A}t}\underline{X} - \underline{X}(0) = \int_0^t e^{-\underline{A}\tau}\underline{B}\underline{u}(\tau) d\tau .$$

Premultiplying $e^{\underline{A}t}$ gives

$$\underline{X}(t) = e^{\underline{A}t}\underline{X}(0) + e^{\underline{A}t}\int_0^t e^{-\underline{A}\tau}\underline{B}\underline{u}(\tau) \, d\tau , \tag{15-51}$$

where $e^{\underline{A}t}$ is known as the transition matrix defined by

$$e^{\underline{A}t} = \underline{I} + \underline{A}t + \underline{A}^2 \frac{t^2}{2!} + \ldots + \underline{A}^n \frac{t^n}{n!} + \ldots \tag{15-52}$$

When $t = nT$, where T is an increment of time and $n = 0, 1, 2\ldots$, from (15-51) we obtain

$$\underline{X}(nT) = e^{AnT}\underline{X}_0 + e^{AnT}\int_0^{nT} e^{-A\tau}\underline{Bu}(\tau)\, d\tau .\qquad (15\text{-}53)$$

Similarly, when $t = (n + 1)T$,

$$\underline{X}[(n + 1)T] = e^{A(n + 1)T}\underline{X}_0 + e^{A(n + 1)T}\int_0^{(n + 1)T} e^{-A\tau}\underline{Bu}(\tau)d\tau .\qquad (15\text{-}54)$$

Multiplying (15-53) by e^{AT} and subtracting it from Eq. (15-54), we obtain

$$\underline{X}[(n + 1)T] = e^{AT}\underline{X}(nT) + e^{A(n + 1)T}\int_{nT}^{(n + 1)T} e^{-A\tau}\underline{Bu}(\tau)d\tau .\qquad (15\text{-}55)$$

When the excitation function is arbitrary but continuous, the integral in (15-55) can be evaluated by applying Simpson's rule to give the following recursive formula

$$\qquad (15\text{-}56)$$

$$\underline{X}[(n + 1)T] = e^{AT}\left[\underline{X}(nT) + \frac{T}{6}\,\underline{Bu}(nT)\right] + \frac{2T}{3}\,e^{A\left(\frac{T}{2}\right)}$$

$$\underline{Bu}\left[\left(n + \frac{1}{2}\right)T\right] + \frac{T}{6}\,\underline{Bu}\,[(n + 1)T] + R ,$$

where R is the error term, which can be neglected when T is sufficiently small. The error analysis of this method has been provided by Liou (144). Eq. (15-56) gives the displacement and the velocity responses as a function of time for various follower masses in a multi–degree–of–freedom system. Knowing the displacement and the velocity responses, one can always substitute them back into the original differential equation to find the time response for acceleration. Cam– follower systems of a single degree of freedom are handled in exactly the same manner.

A FORTRAN program using the state–variable solution method for finding time response, program TRESP, is given in Appendix B.

Numerical Solution Method Using Finite Differences

Nonlinear systems are usually cumbersome to solve. In most cases they require numerical methods and computers for solution. The finite difference method introduced in this section represents one of the typical approximate solution methods involving iteration. This method can be used to solve both linear and nonlinear system equations. Without a loss of generality, let us consider the solution for a nonlinear system of multiple degrees of freedom governed by Eq. (15-16).

The general solution of Eq. (15-16) is made up of the complementary solution, which is governed by the initial state, and the particular solution, which may be expressed in terms of a convolution integral. That is

$$(15\text{-}57)$$

$$z_i(t) = \left[z_o e^{-\zeta \omega_n t} \left(\cos \omega_d t + \frac{\zeta}{\sqrt{1 - \zeta^2}} \sin \omega_d t \right) + \frac{\dot{z}_o}{\omega_d} e^{-\zeta \omega_n t} \right.$$

$$\left. \sin \omega_d t \right]_i - \left[\frac{1}{\omega_d} \int_0^t \Gamma(\tau) e^{-\zeta \omega_n (t - \tau)} \sin \omega_d (t - \tau) \, d\tau \right]_i \, ,$$

$$i = 1, 2, \ldots, n \, ,$$

where z_o and $\dot{z}_o$ are the initial displacement and velocity, respectively. ω_d is the damped natural frequency, which is equal to $\omega_n \sqrt{1 - \zeta^2}$.

The derivative of Eq. (15-57) is

$$\dot{z}_i(t) = z_o e^{-\zeta \omega_n t} \left[-\zeta \omega_n \left(\cos \omega_d t + \frac{\zeta}{\sqrt{1 - \zeta^2}} \sin \omega_d t \right) \right. \qquad (15\text{-}58)$$

$$\left. - \omega_d \sin \omega_d t + \frac{\omega_d \zeta}{\sqrt{1 - \zeta^2}} \cos \omega_d t \right]_i$$

$$+ \left[\frac{\dot{z}_o}{\omega_d} e^{-\zeta \omega_n t} (-\zeta \omega_n \sin \omega_d t + \omega_d \cos \omega_d t) \right]_i$$

$$+ \left[\frac{1}{\omega_d} \int_0^t \Gamma(\tau) e^{-\zeta \omega_n (t - \tau)} \left[\zeta \omega_n \sin \omega_d (t - \tau) \right. \right.$$

$$\left. \left. - \omega_d \cos (t - \tau) \right] d\tau \right]_i$$

$$i = 1, 2, \ldots, n \, .$$

Eqs. (15-57) and (15-58) cannot be conveniently evaluated for an arbitrary curve of $\Gamma(t)$, since the excitation function may be known only as a graphical function, in digital data form, or as a complicated analytic function. However, if $\Gamma(t)$ is divided into finite segments of time and represented in some approximate manner using an interpolating polynomial, a step–by–step approximate numerical integration can be carried out.

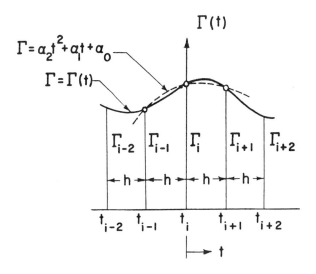

Fig. 15-17. Passing a parabola through three pivotal points.

Consider the situation defined in Fig. 15-17. Three consecutive pivotal points $i - 1$, i, and $i + 1$ are equally spaced by h on the t–axis. Designating the corresponding pivotal values Γ_{i-1}, Γ_i, and Γ_{i+1}, and passing a parabola through these three points, we obtain a central–difference interpolating polynomial of the type

$$\Gamma(t) = \frac{1}{2h^2}(\Gamma_{i-1} - 2\Gamma_i + \Gamma_{i+1})t^2 + \frac{1}{2h}(\Gamma_{i+1} - \Gamma_{i-1})t + \Gamma_i .$$

This can be rearranged and expressed in terms of difference notation as follows:

$$\Gamma(t) = \frac{1}{2h^2}[(\Gamma_{i-1} - \Gamma_i) - (\Gamma_i - \Gamma_{i+1})]t^2 \qquad (15\text{-}59)$$

$$+ \frac{1}{2h}[-(\Gamma_{i-1} - 2\Gamma_i + \Gamma_{i+1}) + (\Gamma_{i+1} - \Gamma_{i-1})]t + \Gamma_i$$

$$= \left(\frac{\Delta_{i-1}^2}{2h^2}t^2 - \frac{\Delta_{i-1}^2}{2h}t + \frac{\Delta_{i-1}}{h}t + 1 \right)\Gamma_i ,$$

or

$$\Gamma(t) = \left[1 + \Delta_{i-1}\left(\frac{t}{h}\right) + \frac{1}{2}\left(\frac{t}{h}\right)\left(\frac{t}{h} - 1\right)\Delta_{i-1}^2 \right]\Gamma_i . \qquad (15\text{-}60)$$

Eq. (15-60) is essentially a terminated Gauss' backward interpolating formula.

In a similar manner, it is an easy task to develop the second–order interpolation polynomials in terms of known function values forward of the point in question to give

$$\Gamma(t) = \frac{1}{2h^2}(\Gamma_i - 2\Gamma_{i+1} + \Gamma_{i+2})t^2 + \frac{1}{2h} \qquad (15\text{-}61)$$

$$(-3\Gamma_i + 4\Gamma_{i+1} - \Gamma_{i+2})t .$$

This can be rearranged to become

$$\Gamma(t) = \left[1 + \Delta_i\left(\frac{t}{h}\right) + \frac{1}{2}\left(\frac{t}{h}\right)\left(\frac{t}{h} - 1\right)\Delta_i^2 \right]\Gamma_i . \qquad (15\text{-}62)$$

which corresponds to a terminated Newton's forward–difference interpolating formula.

The more terms used, the higher the degree of accuracy resulting. However, sufficient accuracy can be obtained by using parabolic interpolation, as in Eqs. (15-61) and (15-62), making further complication unnecessary.

Eq. (15-61) is the expression used for all intermediate segments of the curve. Eq. (15-62) is derived to avoid the nonexistent term Δ_{i-1}^2 in which Γ_{i-1} falls outside the range of variables of interest. It should be used to represent the curve during the first increment in the march of points.

Next, we have to choose an appropriate quadrature formula for numerical integration. Note that the area under a parabola between $-h$ and h in Fig. 15-17 is

$$\int_{-h}^{h} \Gamma(t)\,dt = \frac{h}{3}\,(\Gamma_{i-1} + 4\Gamma_i + \Gamma_{i+1}), \tag{15-63}$$

which is the well–known Simpson's one–third rule, with its remainder term on the order of h^5.

For numerical integration involving end points, a one–sided formula is needed for integration between t_i and t_{i+1}. We choose the formula

$$\int_{t_{i+1}}^{t_i} \Gamma(t)\,dt = \frac{h}{12}\,(-\Gamma_{i-1} + 8\Gamma_i + 5\Gamma_{i+1}), \tag{15-64}$$

which is recognizable as Simpson's rule for partial area, with error on the order of h^4.

Having established the interpolation polynomials for the representation of functions and mechanical quadrature formulas for performing integration, we now have a numerical instrument for evaluating the convolution integral of Eq. (15-57). If the parabolic representation of the function given by Eq. (15-60) is substituted for the function Γ in Eq. (15-57), and the integration is performed and evaluated, there results, for oscillatory response, the following set of recurrence formulas:

$$z_{i+1} = (z_i)_{comp} - \frac{\overline{\Gamma_i}}{k}\,(A - \zeta\lambda_1 B)$$

$$- \frac{\Delta_{i-1}\overline{\Gamma_i}}{k}\left(1 - \frac{2\zeta}{\omega_n t}A - \frac{\lambda_2}{\omega_d t}B\right) \tag{15-65}$$

$$\tag{15-66}$$

$$\dot{z}_{i+1} = (z_i)_{comp} - \frac{\overline{\Gamma_i}}{k}\left(\frac{1}{\omega_d t}B\right) - \frac{\Delta_{i-1}\overline{\Gamma_i}}{k}\left(\frac{1}{\omega_n t}A - \frac{\zeta}{\omega_d t}B\right),$$

in which $(z_i)_{comp}$ and $(\dot{z}_i)_{comp}$ are complimentary solutions of z_i and $\dot{z}_i$, respectively.

$$A = 1 - e^{-\zeta \omega_n t} \cos \omega_d t$$

$$B = e^{-\zeta \omega_n t} \sin \omega_d t$$

$$\lambda_1 = \frac{1}{\sqrt{1 - \zeta^2}} ,$$

and

$$\lambda_2 = 1 - 2\zeta^2 .$$

In Eqs. (15-65) and (15-66), Γ_i is the average value of the function $\Gamma(t)$ during each increment. The parabolic average Eq. (15-64) is used in computing Γ_i. For equidistant h the trigonometric coefficients at $t = h$ are calculated just once for the entire solution process. After all substitution in Eqs. (15-65) and (15-66) are made, the resulting numerical integration equations of a system of n degrees of freedom may be cast in the following functional form using matrix notation

$$\{z_j\}_{i+1} = F_j (\tilde{\Gamma}_{i-1}, \tilde{\Gamma}_i, \tilde{\Gamma}_{i+1}, \tilde{z}_{i-1}, \tilde{z}_i, \tilde{z}_{i+1}, \tilde{\dot{z}}_i, h) \tag{15-67}$$

$$\{\dot{z}_j\}_{i+1} = G_j (\tilde{\Gamma}_{i-1}, \tilde{\Gamma}_i, \tilde{\Gamma}_{i+1}, \tilde{z}_{i-1}, \tilde{z}_i, \tilde{z}_{i+1}, \tilde{\dot{z}}_i, h) , \tag{15-68}$$

where the symbols $\dot{F}$ and G are functional expressions, and

$$\tilde{\Gamma} = (\Gamma_1, \Gamma_2, \ldots, \Gamma_n)$$

$$\tilde{z} = (z_1, z_2, \ldots, z_n)$$

$$\tilde{\dot{z}} = (\dot{z}_1, \dot{z}_2, \ldots, \dot{z}_n) .$$

The following systematic procedures are to be carried out:
1. The initial conditions $\tilde{z}_o$ and $\tilde{\dot{z}}_o$ are always known at the beginning.
2. Since everything on the right side of Eqs. (15-67) and (15-68) is known except $\tilde{z}_{i+1}$, this value may be set equal to $\tilde{z}_i$ in the initial step. Since the term $\tilde{z}_{i-1}$ does not exist at the beginning in the parabolic average formula of Eq. (15-64), a linear average should be used for the first increment.

3. The value $\tilde{z}_i$ is used for $\tilde{z}_{i+1}$ in the right side of Eq. (15-67) to compute a new value of $\tilde{z}_{i+1}$. This iteration process is repeated until the succeeding values of $\tilde{z}_{i+1}$ converge to a prescribed degree of accuracy.
4. The converged value of $\tilde{z}_{i+1}$ is then used in Eq. (15-68) to find the velocity $\dot{\tilde{z}}_{i+1}$.
5. This process is followed until all required response data have been obtained.

We can also apply this finite–difference approach to obtaining an approximate solution of a nonlinear time invariant differential equation, such as Eqs. (15-26) and (15-36), arising from a cam–follower system with an elastic drive shaft coupling. For instance, if we substitute into Eq. (15-26) the three–point central–difference formula for the approximation of the velocity and the acceleration at any instant,

$$\dot{X}_n = \frac{X_{n+1} - X_{n-1}}{2\Delta\tau} \tag{15-69}$$

$$\ddot{X}_n = \frac{X_{n+1} - X_{n-1} - 2X_n}{(\Delta\tau)^2} \ , \tag{15-70}$$

where $\Delta\tau$ is a small time interval, we obtain the following recursive relation:

$$X_{n+1} = \frac{1}{c_n} \left(\Gamma_n + 2f_n\dot{\Gamma}_n + a_n X_n + b_n X_{n-1} \right) ,$$

where

$$a_n = \frac{2d_n}{(\Delta\tau)^2} - 1$$

$$b_n = \frac{f_n}{\Delta\tau} - \frac{d_n}{(\Delta\tau)^2}$$

$$c_n = \frac{f_n}{\Delta\tau} - \frac{d_n}{(\Delta\tau)^2}$$

$$d_n = (1 + \Gamma_n^2 F) \left(\frac{\tau}{2\pi} \right)^2$$

$$f_n = (1 + \dot{\Gamma}_n^2 F) \left(\frac{\tau}{2\pi} \right) \zeta .$$

This iterative method, which is not too accurate, has been used by Ardayfio (4) for the solution of Eq. (15-26). Midha *et. al.* (159) have suggested a more accurate method of solution in which they have discretized the continuum of the system parameters and reduced the solution to that of linear second-order differential equations with constant coefficients. Other numerical methods of solution, such as the fourth-order Runge-Kutta method, the predictor-and-corrector methods, and so forth, are also frequently used for the solution of the differential equations. Further discussion of numerical solution methods, as well as their properties of convergence and error bounds, are beyond the scope of this work.

16
Dynamic Response of
Cam-and-Follower Systems

16-1. INTRODUCTION

A study of the response of an electrical network or system to the input of transients in the form of short-duration pulses is an established method of analysis of the network. By comparing the input and the output, conclusions may be drawn as to the respective merits of the various components. In an analogous manner, a cam-actuated mechanism system is an example of the application of transients to a mechanical system. In studying the dynamic response of such a system, we have the following considerations.

First, we want to know the characteristics of the driving motion produced by the cam. This driving motion is referred to as the "base excitation," although other external disturbing forces may also act on the follower at the same time.

Second, we want to know the composition of the resilient medium interposed between the excitation-producing base and the terminal component of the follower. Properties of primary concern are the distribution of mass and elastic flexibilities as well as damping throughout the follower system.

Third, we want to know the behavior of the follower caused by the transmitted excitation, which is known as the "response."

The three factors do not exist independently, but are closely related, and are governed by the formulated equation (or equations) of motion based on a system model.

In this chapter, after the basic concept and some definitions are established, the various factors that influence the transient response will be presented and discussed based on the following two models:
• the linear model with a single degree of freedom.
• the linear model with a flexible drive shaft.

Generally, models with many degrees of freedom give a more accurate representation of system response. Nevertheless, it has been proved (133) that the representation of a cam–follower mechanism by means of a simple–degree–of–freedom model having a natural frequency equal to the fundamental natural frequency of the actual system is satisfactory, since the fundamental natural frequency dominates the transient follower response. Throughout the chapter, the response of multiple–degree–of–freedom systems may be mentioned and presented on occasion, but we do not intend to go into the details of the complicated modal analysis involved. Furthermore, current knowledge on the difficult topic of nonlinear system response is rather meager and inconclusive, so we can only refer the reader to the pertinent but limited literature available for more advanced studies. We also assume that the reader has a working knowledge of the fundamental linear theory of mechanical vibration.

16-2. BASIC CONCEPTS AND DEFINITIONS

To determine the response of a typical dynamic system, one generally considers both steady–state response and transient response. For cam–and–follower systems, it is the transient response that is of concern. Steady–state vibration will not occur, because in practice the angular velocity of the camshaft is low in comparison with the natural frequency of the follower system. Rothbart (193) suggested the use of a steady–state response consideration if dwell periods were short in relation to cam rise time. This is a misconception. In general, the vibrations excited by the first acceleration period will last into the second acceleration period if the dwell period is short and if the system is not heavily loaded and efficiently damped. The vibrational amplitude of the first period may be reduced or reinforced by the second, depending upon the phase of the vibration as it reaches the second period. For simplicity of analysis and for ease in providing a common ground for the comparison of the merits of different cam curves on the basis of their responses, we assume that the vibration damps out during the dwell period and does not carry over to the next motion cycle. Two periods of interest to the designer are:
1. The response produced during the period of application of base excitation or during the stroke, which is called the primary response.
2. The response that continues after the removal of excitation, which is called the residual response.

For many relatively flexible cam–follower systems, a rapid exchange of energy takes place between the elastic regions and the masses during operation, manifesting itself in the form of an unwanted vibratory motion of the follower. The actual follower response often may be appreciably different from the motion that the cam surface would impart to a perfectly rigid follower system. Intuitively, we must agree that the follower response resulting from cyclic changes in base excitation increases as the magnitude of the excitation increases and as the speed of the machine increases. The disturbance in the follower is accentuated if the change in base acceleration is sudden, because then the effect of the action is as though it were suddenly applied — not an impact such as a right to the jaw, but more analogous to the results of placing one's hands on somebody and suddenly thrusting strongly forward (as contrasted to a gradual increase in the thrust). The action is also similar to that of an explosion, particularly to an underwater explosion at close range or a near–miss. We may term this kind of action a "mechanical shock," and its associated system response a "shock response." A shock is defined as the physical manifestation of the transfer of mechanical energy from one body to another during an extremely short interval of time.

The "shock response spectrum," or simply the "response spectrum," is one of the two most commonly used methods of analyzing mechanical shock. The other method is the Fourier spectrum. In either case, the time history of the transient is spectrally decomposed; that is, the amplitude versus the time picture of the transient is converted into an amplitude versus frequency picture, or spectrum. These spectral analysis methods are very useful for understanding and working with mechanical shock. The response spectrum representation has long been used by structural dynamicists and packaging designers. Neklutin (171) was the first to utilize this technique in the study of cam–driven systems. We will talk more about the response spectrum after having studied the time response.

Now, let us examine Fig. 16-1, where the vibratory response characteristics, with and without damping, of the three systems — parabolic, simple harmonic, and cycloidal — are displayed. The damping value used is 10 percent of the critical value. For each motion, the dashed line represents the excitation. In Fig. 16-1 the simple harmonic and the parabolic curves, with their infinite pulse characteristic, show large vibrations, the magnitudes of which are about twice as great as expected. The cycloidal curve, on the other hand, has small values of magnification. All vibrations occur at the natural frequency of the follower linkage. The vibrations take place during the stroke and the dwell periods, with their peak magnitudes influenced by the sudden application, reversal, or removal of the excitation. As the excitational frequency approaches a value that is a small odd integer multiple of the natural frequency of the system, the vibration becomes more drastic because of resonance. Experimental results by Mitchell (161) found, in the absence of damping, the actual response in acceler-

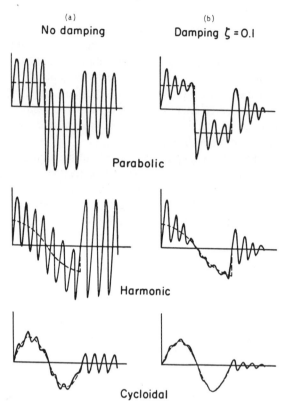

Fig. 16-1. Vibratory response characteristics of cam–follower system for parabolic, simple-harmonic and cycloidal input (a) no damping (b) with 10% damping.

ation to be in the ratios 1, 0.834, and 0.584 for parabolic, simple harmonic, and cycloidal curves, respectively. With damping, the differences in the responses are not as great.

16-3. TIME RESPONSE OF LINEAR SYSTEM OF SINGLE DEGREE OF FREEDOM

The solution of the equation of motion for a single–degree–of–freedom cam–follower system subjected to a motion excitation of the dwell–rise–dwell type has been treated in Chapter 15. A typical example of the primary responses in displacement, velocity, and acceleration of the follower of such a system subjected to simple–harmonic excitation is shown in Figure 16-2. The response curves in Fig. 16-2 portray a typical resilient system such as an auto-motive valve–gear and a textile machine, for which we have small values of n,

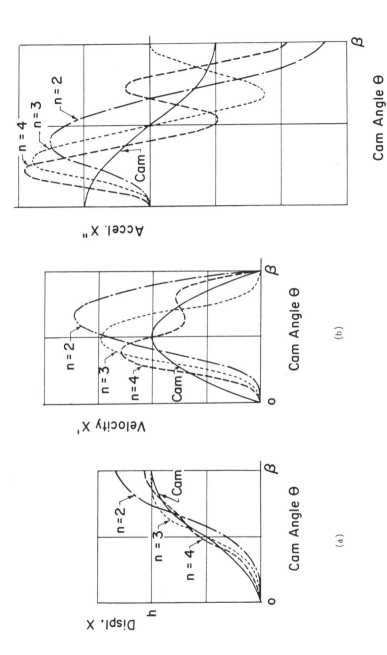

Fig. 16-2. Primary responses in (a) displacement, (b) velocity, and (c) acceleration of an undamped single-degree-of-freedom system.

425

where n is the ratio of the natural frequency to the excitational frequency. For more rigid systems ($n > 4$) the analysis and the curves will be similar, having higher frequencies and smaller amplitudes. In Fig. 16-2a it should be noted that the follower mass catches up with and overshoots the forcing cam displacement. Here, the dynamic compression of the highly flexible follower linkage results in a subsequent release of energy that causes the end of the follower to surge ahead of or fall behind the cam lift. When damping is present, the amplitudes produced by this action will be somewhat reduced.

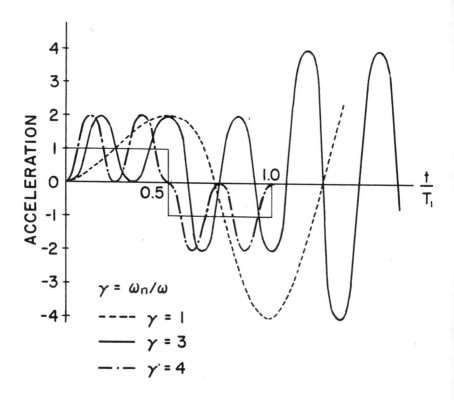

Fig. 16-3. Time response during and beyond the excitation period (parabolic input).

Although the follower response in displacement, which provides information on the positional accuracy of the follower, is of interest to cam designers, the follower response in acceleration is more important because in design the requirements concerning residual vibration have to be fulfilled over a finite range of cam operational speed. Even if these vibrations are not visible to an observer, the product handled by the machine may be disturbed by them. As a result, a lower efficiency and a greater wear of moving parts can result; the latter is usually manifested by noise.

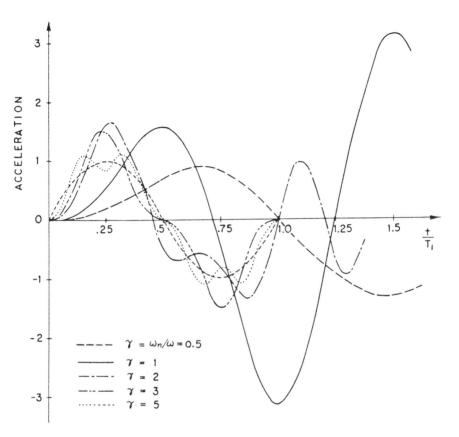

Fig. 16-4. Time response during and beyond the excitation period (cycloid input).

Examples of acceleration time responses that occur during and beyond the excitation period and that are caused by a parabolic cam input, a cycloidal cam input, and a modified trapezoidal cam input are shown in Figs. 16-3, 16-4, and 16-5, respectively, for a number of natural frequencies of an undamped single-freedom cam–follower system.

It is interesting to observe that in the case of parabolic acceleration, the magnitude of the residual vibrations can be up to four times greater than the background excitation when there are 3, 5, 7, etc. free vibrations during the stroke. But when the number of free vibrations during the stroke is even, such as 4, 6, 8, etc., no residual vibrations exist. In the case of cycloidal acceleration, residual vibrations vanish when this number is 2, 3, 4, 5, etc. Residual vibrations reached their maxima when there were 2½, 3½, 4½, 5½, etc. cycles of free vibrations during a stroke. The physical interpretation of this phenomenon is that when the mass comes to rest at a peak of oscillation (kinetic energy vanishes), the pulse ends, returning the spring to its original length (potential

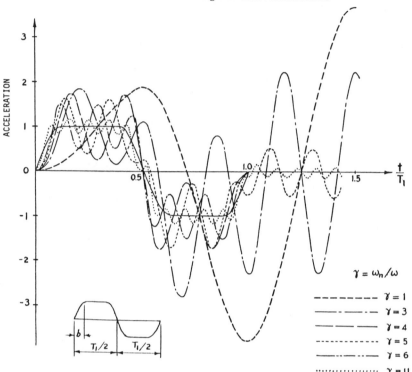

Fig. 16-5. Time response during and beyond the excitation period (modified trapezoidal input).

energy vanishes). No energy remains in the system at this moment; therefore, motion ceases. This phenomenon also occurs for other symmetric or anti–symmetric excitational pulses. For non–symmetric pulses, the magnitude of the residual vibrations is not to be zero at certain points, although it is nearly zero.

This phenomenon may be used to advantage in design considerations. Theoretically speaking, one may purposely tune and maintain the natural frequency of a system to produce zero residual vibration. Nevertheless, this is difficult to achieve in reality because the camshaft speed generally varies from time to time, and the designer cannot predict in advance a precise speed of the machine.

16-4. RESPONSE REPRESENTATION IN FREQUENCY DOMAIN — DYNAMIC RESPONSE SPECTRA

Dynamic Response Spectra

As mentioned earlier, one very useful way to express the dynamic response characteristic of a cam–follower system is to use that cam's excitational motion to compute dynamic response spectra (DRS). Such response spectrum analysis provides unique information to help designers quickly visualize the effects of mechanical shock upon a system. It also offers two popular and useful benefits:

1. It gives a designer a concise indication of the maximum dynamic loads various parts of his system will experience, which is helpful in predicting damage potential; and
2. It gives test engineers a very sensitive technique for helping insure repeatability of the transient response test.

A DRS is defined as a plot of individual peak–acceleration responses of a multitude of single–degree–of–freedom, mass–spring systems subject to a particular input transient. The ordinate is usually acceleration, or some normalized expression relating to acceleration, while the abscissa is in terms of the system natural frequency, or the ratio of pulse duration to the system natural period. Damping is a parameter, and its values should be stated. If it is not stated, it is assumed to be zero.

The graphic definition of a DRS is illustrated in Fig. 16-6. We start with a given input pulse and carry out a mathematical computation to obtain the response of a single–degree–of–freedom linear system subject to that input. We might, for example, first compute the follower acceleration as a function of time. We then take the maximum follower acceleration and plot it on a graph versus the fundamental period of the one–degree–of–freedom system. One such mathematical operation gives one point on the diagram. If we hold the damping of the system constant but vary the system's natural frequency or period by changing its spring stiffness, and carry out the calculation again and again, we get a number of such points, which altogether define a curve called a response spectrum. Then we must carry out the calculation again with other assumed values for the damping ratio, obtaining a set of curves, each applicable for a different damping ratio. This set of curves constitutes the DRS.

The maximum response that occurs during the application of the input transient is called the "primary spectrum." These acceleration magnitudes are unidirectional, occuring in either the positive or the negative direction, but never in both. The peak response after the termination of the input transient is called the "residual spectrum." Characteristically, the residual spectrum always represents positive and negative acceleration responses of magnitudes equal to or less than the primary values. Residual responses are usually associated with nondirectional fatigue stresses.

When we talk about response spectra, we have a choice of talking about displacement response spectra, velocity response spectra, or acceleration response spectra. By multiplying the maximum displacement by the fundamental circular frequency of the system ω_n, we get a quantity that has units of velocity and is referred to as spectral velocity or pseudo–velocity. Multiplying pseudo–velocity once again by ω_n, we get still another quantity that is called pseudo–acceleration, or spectral acceleration. Thus we can define the DRS according to the following relations:

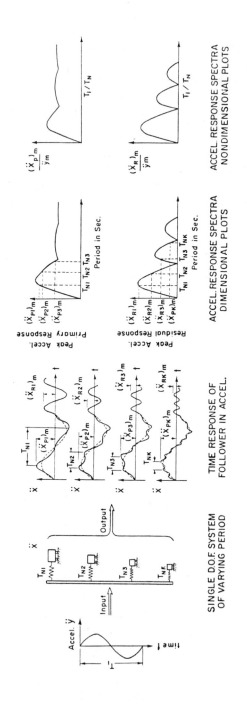

Fig. 16-6. Graphic definition of DRS.

$$S_D = X_{max}$$

$$S_V = \omega_n S_D \qquad\qquad (16\text{-}1)$$

$$S_A = \omega_n^2 S_D .$$

When working with an undamped system, s_V and s_A as defined above are exact. When damping is present, these are approximations because the response is not perfectly sinusoidal, and the values of ω_n and the damped natural frequency ω_d are not exactly the same. However, when damping is small, the approximations are generally good enough for practical applications.

The plot of a normalized DRS is of greater utility than the regular dimensional plot, because one normalized plot will suffice for all magnitudes of excitations of similar pulse shapes. The normalized displacement, velocity, and acceleration DRS are defined as

$$S_{ND} = \frac{X_{max}}{y_{max}}$$

$$S_{NV} = \frac{\omega_n X_{max}}{\dot{y}_{max}} \qquad\qquad (16\text{-}2)$$

$$S_{NA} = \frac{\omega_n^2 X_{max}}{\ddot{y}_{max}}$$

Figs. 16-7 and 16-8 show an example of a DRS plotted in perspective view. These are the response spectra for the modified trapezoidal cam for damping of 0%, 0.05%, 0.1%, 0.2%, and 0.3%. These figures show the characteristic shapes and nature of such spectra. The curves tend to peak at one or more values of natural periods of the system; that is to say, systems with certain natural periods are especially excited by this particular input transient because of matching between the frequency content of the input motion and the natural frequency of the system.

Response spectra such as this are quite useful in design, because from such spectra a designer can readily assess how systems of different periods respond to some specified input excitations. Programs SPEC1, SPEC2, and SPEC3 listed in Appendix B have been developed for generating the primary and residual response spectra.

Example 16-1

For illustration, consider a modeled cam-follower system with a single-degree-of-freedom used in a high-speed automatic machine. The follower is actuated by a dwell-rise-dwell cam with a modified trapezoidal pro-

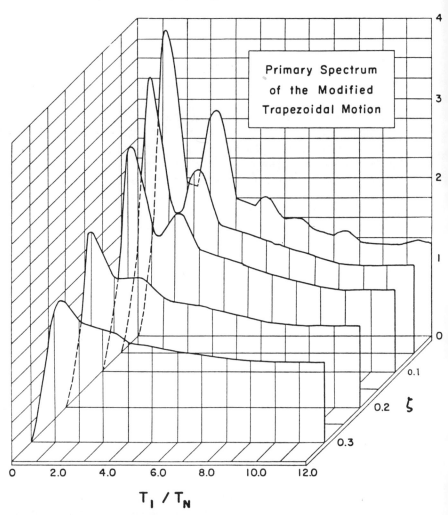

Fig. 16-7. Primary spectrum of modified trapezoidal cam.

file. The peak input acceleration is 500 m/sec^2, and the duration of the excitation is 0.015 sec. If the follower linkage of the system is such that it has a natural frequency of 100 Hz, what will be the peak acceleration response of the follower during the lift stroke and during the dwell period? Let us assume that damping factor is $\zeta = 0.05$.

With reference to Figs. 16-7 and 16-8, with $\zeta = 0.05$ and at time ratio $\dfrac{T_1}{T_N} = 0.015 \times 100 = 1.5$, the primary acceleration attenuation is 2.98, and the residual acceleration attenuation is 1.88. Therefore, the primary acceleration response will be 2.98 times the input or 1,445 m/sec^2, and the residual

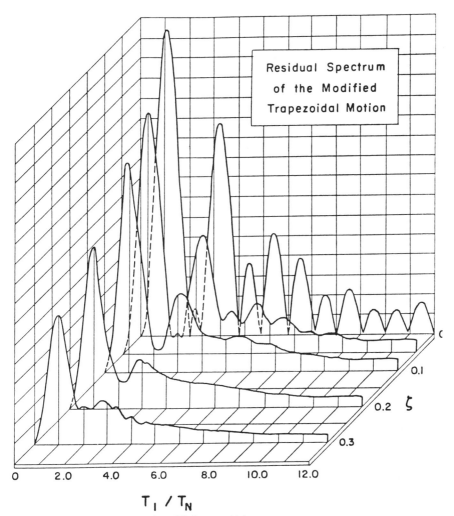

Fig. 16-8. Residual spectrum of modified trapezoidal cam.

acceleration response will be 1.88 times the input or 940 m/sec^2. If the effective mass of the follower weighs 40 Newtons, the corresponding inertial load of the follower is 5,892 Newtons due to primary vibration and 3,833 Newtons due to residual vibration.

The Damping Effect

The values of damping in machines vary in accordance with the constituent components in the follower assembly and are different in different parts of a

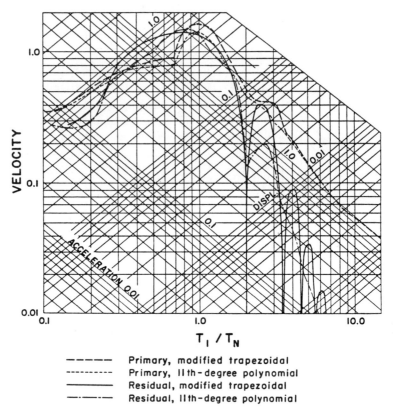

VELOCITY

T_1 / T_N

— — — — Primary, modified trapezoidal
- - - - - - - - - - Primary, 11th-degree polynomial
———————— Residual, modified trapezoidal
—·——·— Residual, 11th-degree polynomial

Fig. 16.9 Four-grid plot of primary and residual spectra for modified trapezoidal and 11th degree polynomial cams.

machine, depending largely upon the condition of surfaces having relative motion, as well as the condition of lubrication. Damping appears to be the most difficult parameter to pin down in analysis. Static tests should be conducted to establish damping factors for each case under consideration. In automotive valve gear systems, Barkan (11) suggested using a viscous damping factor of $\zeta = 0.05$ to 0.15. Roggenbuck (191) used $\zeta = \dfrac{3}{16}$ in a simulation study of an automotive valve linkage. According to Rothbart (193), ζ may vary between 0.1 to 0.25 in other cam–driven machines and systems. Damping has a more pronounced effect on the residual vibration response than on the primary response. The effect of damping is also to smooth out the wiggles and to reduce the sharpness of the peaks in the response. In the modified trapezoidal cam, for instance, the presence of moderate damping, say $\zeta = 0.1$, tends to reduce sharply the peak value for $\dfrac{T_1}{T_N}$ when $\dfrac{T_1}{T_N}$ is slightly larger than 2.0, and to annihilate almost all of the humps at which the peak values occur when $\dfrac{T_1}{T_N} > 4.0.$

Four-Grid Logarithmic Representation

Fig. 16-9 represents a four-grid or tripartite plot of the primary and the residual spectra for a modified trapezoidal cam, in which the normalized displacement, velocity, and acceleration characteristics of the response are plotted versus the $\dfrac{T_1}{T_N}$ value. One can therefore use this plot to represent simultaneously the corresponding three types of response spectra. The normalized displacement and the velocity response values, in terms of frequency, are given as $\dfrac{Z_{max}}{y_{max}}$ and $\dfrac{\omega_n Z_{max}}{\dot{y}_{max}}$, respectively. Here we plot the normalized amplitude versus $\dfrac{T_1}{T_N}$ with the superimposed normalized acceleration response values on an inclined line with negative slope and the normalized displacement response values on another inclined line with positive slope. Logarithmic scales are used for all coordinates.

Comparison of DRS by Means of Response Envelopes

In this section we attempt to provide a quantitative comparison of the dynamic characteristics of a class of cam profiles of the dwell-rise-dwell type. Based on a single-degree-of-freedom model, the author (45) analyzes and presents a comprehensive display in non-dimensional form of the dynamic characteristics of a number of important practical, classical, modified, and new cam profiles.

   To be able to make a direct comparison of the dynamic characteristics of different cam profiles, at the expense of accuracy, a simplified envelope for a portion of the residual vibration is used instead of the exact shapes of the residual vibration curves. This may be a little too conservative. However, it is believed that the inaccuracy caused by the use of an envelope will not affect the results of and the conclusions drawn from the comparison.

   Fig. 16-10 shows the s_{NA} of 12 different cams. In the figure the solid line curves represent the residual response, and the dashed line curves represent the primary response. Fig. 16-11 shows a comparison of the maximum primary vibrations of all of the important profiles considered, and Fig. 16-12 shows a comparison of the residual vibration envelopes of these profiles when the ratio $\dfrac{T_1}{T_N}$ increases. The construction of the envelope of a residual response

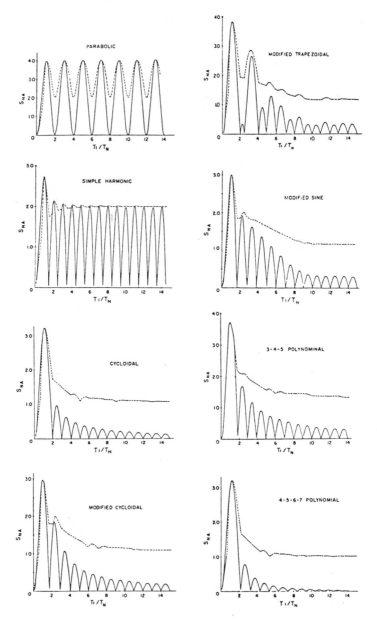

Fig. 16-10. Plot of S_{NA} versus T_1/T_N for 12 different cams solid–line curve — residual response dashed–line curve — primary response.

spectrum is shown in Fig. 16-13. The corresponding equations of acceleration for this class of cams, except those that have been presented earlier, are given at the end of this section.

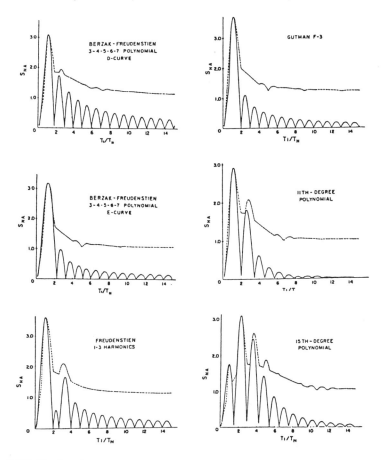

Fig. 16-10. Continued

A study of these figures and the summarized results in Table 16-1 yield the following observations:

1. Of the cam forms analyzed, the modified trapezoidal, the Gutman F-3, the Freudenstein 1-3 harmonic, the modified sine, the Berzak-Freudenstein 3-4-5-6-7 polynomial (D-curve), and the modified cycloidal are among those having low values of peak acceleration. The 11th-degree polynomial, the Berzak-Freudenstein 3-4-5-6-7 polynomial (D-curve), the 4-5-6-7 polynomial, and the Freudenstein 1-3 harmonic are among those having a low level of residual vibrations in the frequency range $\dfrac{T_1}{T_N} > 4$, with the 11th-degree polynomial function being the lowest.

2. Generally speaking, the speeds of cam-driven mechanisms often vary. Coincidence of one or more of the excitational frequencies (harmonics) with

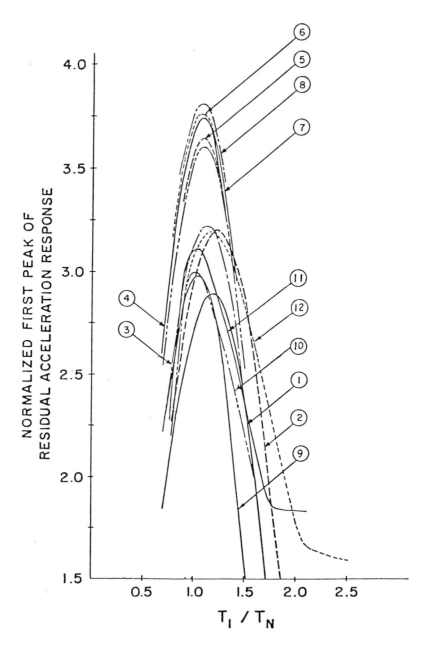

Fig. 16-11. Comparison of normalized peak acceleration magnitudes for primary vibration (1) 11th-degree polynomial; (2) the 4-5-6-7 polynomial; (3) the cycloidal; (4) Freudenstein's 1-3 harmonic; (5) Gutman F-3; (6) the 3-4-5 polynomial; (7) Freudenstein's 1-3-5 harmonic; (8) the modified trapezoidal; (9) the modified cycloidal; (10) the modified sine; (11) Berzak–Freudenstein 3-4-5-6-7 polynomial–D curve; (12) Berzak-Freudenstein 3-4-5-6-7 polynomial–E curve.

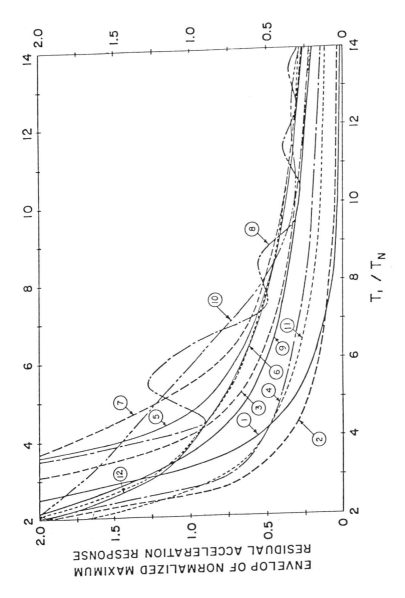

Fig. 16-12. Comparison of normalized peak acceleration magnitudes envelope for residual vibration (same numbering identifications as in Figure 16-11).

439

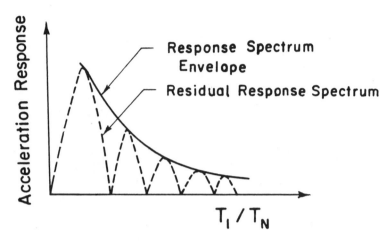

Fig. 16-13. Construction of an envelope to a residual response spectrum.

the natural frequencies of the follower system will likely occur. The level of vibratory response is proportional to the amplitude of the harmonic in coincidence. A cam acceleration curve with a limited number of or no high-frequency harmonics may avoid this coincidence if the frequency of the highest and the last harmonic is lower than the first dangerous frequency of the system. This probably explains why the cam curves containing relatively few harmonics such as the Gutman F–3, the Freudenstein 1–3 harmonic, and even the cycloidal (with peak acceleration of 6.28) do produce generally sound dynamic response.

3. It seems difficult and unreasonable to claim that a single cam form is optimal and dynamically superior for all applications. The response spectrum can be controlled only on the basis of an imposed condition or in certain frequency regions, and this control may be exercised at the expense of other factors or of increased response in other frequency regions. The designer needs to weigh the two most important but conflicting factors, the maximum magnitude of acceleration and the level of residual vibration, together with other factors such as displacement accuracy and velocity, in one or more parts of the entire system in making his final choice of a cam. Each design should be evaluated separately based upon its particular requirements.

Many of the kinematic equations of the class of cam profiles used for plotting Figs. 16-10 through 16-12 have been made available earlier. Those cam profiles that have not been presented are outlined in the following expressions, in which $\tau = \dfrac{\theta}{\beta}$:

Table 16-1. Summary of Kinematic and Dynamic Factors of Cam Profiles

Type of Profile	Kinematic			Dynamic			
	Max Velocity Factor	Max Accel. Factor	Max Jerk Factor	Max Primary	Stabilizing Level	Max Residual	Stabilizing Level
Parabolic	2.00	4.00	∞	4.0	4.0	4.0	4.0
Simple–harmonic	1.57	4.93	∞	2.75	2.0	2.75	2.0
Cycloidal	2.00	6.28	40	3.24	u	3.24	v
Modified cycloidal	1.76	5.89	67	2.98	u	2.98	v
Modified trapezoidal	2.00	4.89	61	3.83	u	3.82	v
Modified sine	1.76	5.53	23	3.00	u	3.00	v
3–4–5 polynomial	1.89	5.77	60	3.76	u	3.76	v
4–5–6–7 polynomial	2.19	7.52	52	3.23	u	3.20	v
Freudenstein 1–3	2.00	5.39	51	3.61	u	3.61	v
Gutman F–3	2.00	5.15	168	3.65	u	3.64	v
11th-degree polynomial	2.05	7.91	55	2.91	u	2.90	v
15th-degree polynomial	1.50	8.58	89	3.20	u	3.20	v
Berzak-Freudenstein 3–4–5–6–7 polyn, D–curve	1.80	5.60	73	3.11	u	3.11	v
Berzak-Freudenstein 3–4–5–6–7 polyn, E–curve	2.00	6.50	41	3.20	u	3.20	v

u — approaching to unit
v — vanishing

11-degree polynomial

$$S = 336\tau^5 - 1,890\tau^6 + 4,740\tau^7 - 6,615\tau^8$$
$$+ 5,320\tau^9 - 2,310\tau^{10} + 420\tau^{11}$$

$$V = 1,680\tau^4 - 11,340\tau^5 + 33,180\tau^6 - 52,920\tau^7$$
$$+ 47,880\tau^8 - 23,100\tau^9 + 4,620\tau^{10}$$

$$A = 6,720\tau^3 - 56,700\tau^4 + 199,080\tau^5 - 370,440\tau^6$$
$$+ 383,040\tau^7 - 207,900\tau^8 + 46,200\tau^9$$

$$J = 20,160\tau^2 - 226,800\tau^3 + 995,400\tau^4 - 2,222,640\tau^5$$
$$+ 2,681,280\tau^6 - 1,663,200\tau^7 + 415,800\tau^8.$$

The 11th-degree polynomial function has a maximum velocity of 2.05 $\dfrac{h}{\beta}$ and a maximum acceleration of 7.91 $\dfrac{h}{\beta^2}$.

Berzak and Freudenstein 3-4-5-6-7 polynomial (D-curve)

$$S = 12.1\tau^3 - 25.5\tau^4 + 24.9\tau^5 - 14.7\tau^6 + 4.2\tau^7$$

$$V = 36.3\tau^2 - 102.0\tau^3 + 124.5\tau^4 - 88.2\tau^5 + 29.4\tau^6$$

$$A = 72.6\tau - 306.0\tau^2 + 498.0\tau^3 - 441.0\tau^4 + 176.4\tau^5$$

$$J = 72.6 - 612\tau + 1,494\tau^2 - 1,764\tau^3 + 882\tau^4.$$

This polynomial function has a maximum velocity of 1.80 $\dfrac{h}{\beta}$ and a maximum acceleration of 5.60 $\dfrac{h}{\beta^2}$.

Berzak and Freudenstein 3-4-5-6-7 polynomial (E-curve)

$$S = 5.35\tau^3 + 8.20\tau^4 - 35.74\tau^5 + 32.46\tau^6 - 9.27\tau^7$$

$$V = 16.05\tau^2 + 32.80\tau^3 - 178.70\tau^4 + 194.76\tau^5 - 64.89\tau^6$$

$$A = 32.1\tau + 98.40\tau^2 - 714.8\tau^3 + 973.8\tau^4 - 389.34\tau^5$$

$$J = 32.1 + 196.8\tau - 2144.4\tau^2 + 3895.2\tau^3 - 1946.70\tau^4.$$

This function has a maximum velocity of $2.00 \dfrac{h}{\beta}$ and a maximum acceleration of $6.50 \dfrac{h}{\beta^2}$.

16-5. DYNAMIC RESPONSE OF LINEAR MULTIPLE DEGREE-OF-FREEDOM SYSTEMS

Although the differential equation of motion for systems of multi-degree-of-freedom or nonlinear systems can be readily written, the large number of parameters that may be involved in the problem makes it advisable to organize the study of these systems by first making a dimensional analysis and writing a functional relationship between the parameters. To make the dimensional analysis, all of the factors believed to be of significance are listed. These factors are then combined in dimensional groups. The number of groups required is equal to the difference between the number of factors and the number of fundamental dimensions involved in the factors. The dimensionless groups can be formed in many ways, subject only to the restrictions that they be independent and that each factor in the list be used in at least one group. Usually, the groups are chosen so as to have some physical significance or so they can be conveniently varied in experimental studies.

For example, the acceleration response of the follower masses of a linear two-degrees-of-freedom system subject to a given transient pulse may be expressed in terms of three groups of dimensionless parameters in the absence of damping,

$$\frac{\omega_n^2 (x_i)_{max}}{\ddot{y}_{max}} = f \left(\frac{m_1}{m_2} , \frac{\dfrac{k_1}{m_2}}{\dfrac{k_1}{m_1}} , \frac{T_1}{T_N} \right) \tag{16-3}$$

$i = 1$ and 2 ,

and that of an undamped linear three–degrees–of–freedom system may be expressed in terms of five groups of dimensionless parameters,

$$\frac{\omega_n^2 (x_i)_{max}}{\ddot{y}_{max}} = f \left(\frac{m_1}{m_2}, \frac{m_2}{m_3}, \frac{\dfrac{k_1}{m_2 + m_3}}{\dfrac{k_1}{m_1}}, \frac{\dfrac{k_2}{m_3}}{\dfrac{k_1}{m_1}}, \frac{T_1}{T_N} \right) \tag{16-4}$$

$i = 1$ and 2 and 3 ,

Eqs. (16-3) and (16-4) provide a guide for the systematic investigation of all of the parameters that enter the problem. The responses of a multi–degree–of–freedom linear system can be computed individually for each normal mode, and the total response can be obtained by superimposing the response of the individual mode. Since the vibration mode shapes of any multi–degree–of–freedom system have two orthogonality properties that make possible an important simplification in the general equations of motion [Equation (15-9)], any arbitrary displacement shape of the system can be expressed as a linear combination of natural modes. Modal analysis permits each mode to be represented by an equivalent single–degree–of–freedom system. We do not intend to present here the details of modal analysis. It is also possible to apply the response spectrum technique, developed earlier for simple systems, to give an assessment of the maximum response of the follower during the excitation. It must be recognized, however, that in general the modal response maxima do not occur simultaneously, and thus they cannot be superposed directly to obtain the total maximum. A direct superposition of the modal response maxima overestimates the true maximum response.

All of these modal analyses, together with the repeated, systematic change of the parameters in Eq. (16-3) or Eq. (16-4), would be a long and an expensive procedure to use in investigating all of the parametric groups and their relationships to the response.

Many automatic machines are complex structures with many degrees of freedom. However, under certain conditions they behave like simple systems. For conditions under which a complex structure does not behave like a simple system, many vital parts of the machine can be considered decoupled from the complete system and analyzed as simple systems. Therefore, it may be justifiable to consider such a part a simple system that is amenable to simpler mathematical analysis, if it can replace the complex system or part of the complex system and give insight into the probable behavior of the more complicated system.

16-6. DYNAMIC RESPONSE OF NONLINEAR SYSTEMS

Nonlinear systems are not easy to handle, since superposition does not apply. Generalization of results is difficult if not impossible, and each type of nonlinear element has its own peculiar characteristics. Although theoretical and practical consideration of nonlinear systems has been of interest to engineers and mathematicians for over a century, the literature on nonlinearity effects associated with cam system dynamics is rather limited. The knowledge in this area is far from being conclusive.

The cam-and-follower system containing a nonlinear power law spring of either the stiffening or the softening type has been studied by Chen (37). In a recent report by Chen and Polvanich (38), dynamic response spectra were presented for cam-driven systems containing a damping mechanism of combined viscous, quadratic, coulomb and stiction type. Chen (40) also investigated the dynamic response characteristics of a cam-actuated system with a pneumatic mechanism of the hysteretic type.

The design of nonlinear systems has usually been accomplished by a simulation of some sort, and this method still has great merit, despite its lack of rigor. Computer simulation of a cam-actuated soap machine containing coulomb damping has been conducted by Benedict and Tesar (18). Koster (134) has used computer simulations for the study of the dynamic behavior of cam mechanisms with drive shaft couplings, using models of progressing degrees of complexity up to and including a model with four degrees of freedom. In the latter model the mass of the cam is accounted for in all directions of deflection of the shaft, in addition to the direction of rotation, and nonlinear effects such as backlash, lubricant film squeeze, and dry friction are admissible. A digital computer simulation program called "DYNACAM," a continuous simulation language, has been developed by Koster for the simulation of such a complex model. The reader should refer to Koster's book for details.

16-7. DYNAMIC RESPONSE OF CAM-FOLLOWER SYSTEM WITH FLEXIBLE DRIVE SHAFTS

In Chapter 15 we formulated three models of cam mechanisms driven by a relatively flexible shaft. The first model, governed by Eq. (15-26), has the simplicity of needing merely three dimensionless characteristics to describe the dynamic response of the system. These three dimensionless parameters are

$$T = \frac{2\pi}{T_1} \sqrt{\frac{m}{k_c}}$$

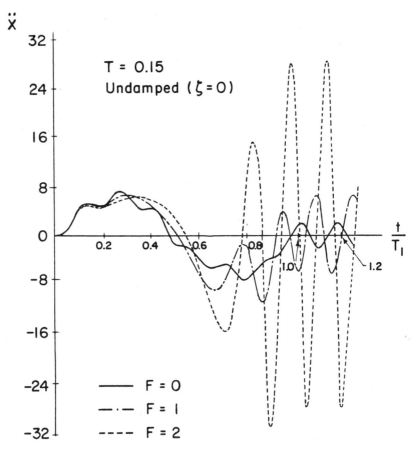

Figure 16-14. Acceleration response for cycloidal cam with $T = 0.15$, $\zeta = 0$, and different degrees of drive shaft flexibility.

$$\zeta = \frac{cT}{4\pi}$$

$$F = \frac{k_c}{k_t}\left(\frac{h}{R_m \omega T_1}\right)^2,$$

where all symbols are as defined previously.

Fig. 16-14 shows the acceleration response of a cycloidal cam with $T = 0.15$ when damping is not taken into account. Note that when $F = 0$ (corresponding to an infinitely rigid shaft), the curve resembles that of nominal acceleration shown in Fig. 16-4. With F increasing, the amplitudes of the residual vibration increase markedly; at $F = 1$ the residual amplitude is already largely equal to the maximum nominal acceleration of 6.28; at $F = 2$ the residual amplitude is nearly four and one-half times as great.

The reason for this phenomenon is that at big values of F, i.e., with a relatively flexible shaft, a large amount of energy is stored in windup and bending during the first half of the cam lift. During the second half, with the decreasing slope of the cam, the shaft relaxes and acts as a catapult. At the increased angular velocity of the cam, the deceleration of the follower may appreciably exceed the nominal value, so that heavy vibrations will persist after the end of the cam rise.

Fig. 16-15 shows a plot of the residual amplitude of acceleration versus T, with F as a varying parameter for the cycloidal cam. This figure, given by Koster, may serve as a design chart to aid the engineer in selecting a satisfactory combination of T and F.

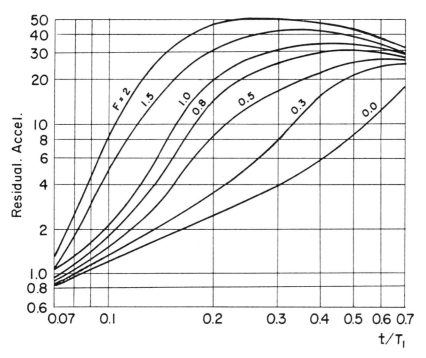

Fig. 16-15. Residual amplitude of acceleration versus T with F as varying parameter (cycloidal cam).

If the damping effect is considered, the dynamic response of a cam mechanism driven by a flexible shaft may be presented in a three-dimensional surface to portray the effect of the various design parameters on the response. This has been done by Ardayfio (4). Fig. 16-16 shows the residual acceleration response surface for the 3–4–5 polynomial cam for a flexible shaft $(F=1)$ and the various values of ζ and $\dfrac{t}{T_1}$. It is apparent that, for a fixed value of shaft flexibility, the residual vibration is minimized by decreasing the turning (T) and increasing the damping.

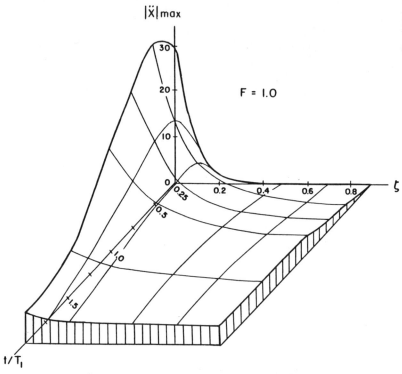

Fig. 16-16. Residual acceleration response surface for 3–4–5 polynomial cam $(F=1)$.

The second model of a cam mechanism driven by a relatively flexible shaft, as formulated in Eq. (15-36), is based on an equivalent single–degree–of–freedom model using cam shaft rotational angle θ as a dependent variable. Four dimensionless parameters are used to characterize the dynamic response of the system. These parameters, according to Szakallas and Savage (210), are the frequency ratio η, the reflected inertia ratio Q_m, the maximum drive windup ratio β_m, and the maximum radial force ratio γ_m, defined as follows

$$\eta = \frac{\omega\ell}{\omega_b} \frac{\theta_f}{2\pi\dot{\theta}_i} \sqrt{\frac{k_s}{I_c}}$$

$$Q_m = \frac{m(x'_{max})^2}{I_c}$$

$$\beta_m = \left(\frac{\theta_i - \theta}{\theta_f}\right)_{max}$$

$$\gamma_m = \frac{F_v}{F_n} = \frac{k_r x + m\ddot{x}}{mx_f\left(\frac{\dot{\theta}_i}{\theta_f}\right)^2},$$

where

θ_i = the angular position of the input power source.

$\dot{\theta}_i$ = the angular speed of the input power source.

β = the total duration of the rise.

h = the total rise.

x'_{max} = the maximum cam slope.

k_r = the follower spring rate.

ω_ℓ = the limit natural frequency.

ω_b = the base natural frequency.

Other symbols are as defined previously.

Figs. 16-17 and 16-18 show a plot of the maximum windup ratio β_m versus η with Q_m as a varying parameter for the harmonic cam curve and for the cycloidal cam curve, respectively. Q_m is a measure of the degree of severity of the drive shaft windup. For $Q_m = 0$, there is no windup in the drive train, since the drive train vibration is caused by the accelerating and the decelerating torques required to move the follower mass through its rise. Thus, the greater is Q_m, the greater is this forcing function. The jump line indicates the limiting condition at which the required follower force reverses direction. This means the separation of the follower from the cam surface — a condition for which the vibration model is invalid. Thus response data above this line is not plotted.

From these charts, one can see that increasing the value of the frequency ratio η and decreasing the value of the reflected inertia ratio Q_m imply stiffer systems, thus reducing the drive system windup effect. Furthermore, the harmonic rise produces lower drive shaft windup than the cycloidal one. This will be illustrated by the following example.

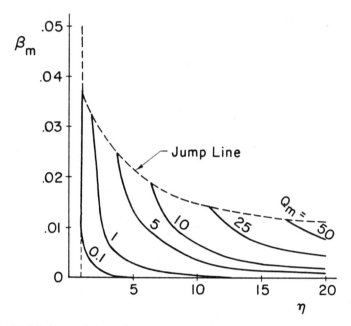

Fig. 16-17. Maximum windup ratio β_m versus η with Q_m as varying parameter (harmonic cam).

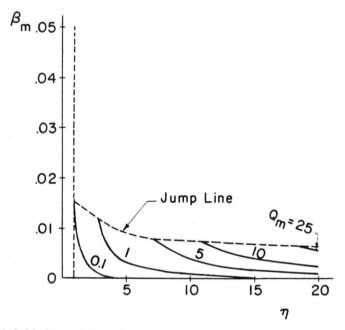

Fig. 16-18. Maximum windup ratio β_m versus η with Q_m as varying parameter (cycloidal cam).

Example 16-2

Consider a modeled cam–follower–drive shaft system with the following data:

Cam speed   350 rpm (36.65 rad/sec)
Stroke $h = 0.02$ m
Total cam angle $\beta = 90°$
Follower mass $m = 50$ kg
Drive train spring stiffness $k_s = 10,000$ N-m/rad
Cam moment of inertia $I = 0.005$ kg-m^2
Return spring coefficient (the ratio between the maximum spring force and the maximum nominal follower inertia force) $a = 1.5$.

Initially, let us assume that the design is based on a cycloidal cam, which gives

$$x'_{max} = \frac{2h}{\beta} = \frac{2(0.02)}{\dfrac{\pi}{2}} = 0.0255$$

$$x''_{max} = \frac{2\pi h}{\beta^2} = \frac{2\pi(0.02)}{\left(\dfrac{\pi}{2}\right)^2} = 0.051 \;.$$

Thus the return spring rate, the linear frequency ratio, and the maximum reflected inertia ratio are

$$k_r = \frac{am}{h} x''_{max} \dot{\theta}_i^{\,2} = \frac{1.5(50)}{0.02}(0.051)(36.65)^2 = 0.257 \times 10^6 \; N/m$$

$$\eta = \frac{\omega\ell}{\omega_b}\frac{\beta}{2\pi\dot{\theta}_i}\sqrt{\frac{k_s}{I}} = \frac{\beta^2}{(2\pi\dot{\theta}_i)^2}\frac{k_s}{I}$$

$$= \frac{\left(\dfrac{\pi}{2}\right)^2}{(2\pi \times 36.65)^2}\frac{10,000}{0.005} = 9.31$$

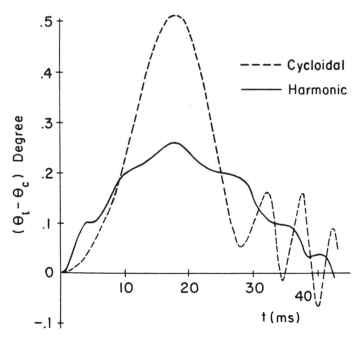

Fig. 16-19. Comparison of shaft–windup between harmonic cam and cycloidal cam.

$$Q_m = \frac{m}{I} (x'_{max})^2 = \frac{50}{0.005} (0.0255)^2 = 6.50 .$$

From Fig. 16-17 we obtain $\beta_m = 0.006$. The corresponding maximum drive shaft windup is

$$\theta_i - \theta_c = 0.006 \left(\frac{\pi}{2} \right) = 0.0094 \text{ rad } (0.54°) ,$$

and the associated dynamic windup torque is

$$T_m = k_s \beta_m \beta = 10,000 \times 0.006 \times \frac{\pi}{2} = 94.2 \text{ N-m.}$$

Graphical plots of windup versus time and of radial contact force versus time are given as the dashed curves in Figs. 16-19 and 16-20, respectively.

If this design is unacceptable, we may replace the cycloidal cam curve with a simple harmonic curve, keeping the other condition intact. By so doing we can calculate

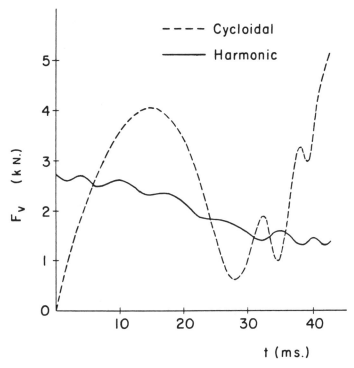

Fig. 16-20. Comparison of contact force between harmonic cam and cycloidal cam.

$$x'_{max} = \frac{h\pi}{2\beta} = 0.02$$

$$x''_{max} = \frac{h\pi^2}{2\beta^2} = 0.04 .$$

η will remain unchanged, but k_r becomes equal to 0.2×10^6 N/m, and Q_m becomes equal to approximately 4.0.

From Fig. 16-17 we obtain $\beta_m = 0.0025$. Thus $\theta_i - \theta_c = 0.25°$, and its corresponding peak windup torque is $T_m = 45$ N-m. Therefore, a change from a cycloidal rise to a harmonic rise reduces the forcing function by about 50 percent. Charts of windup versus time and of radial contact force versus time for this harmonic cam system are given as the solid curves in Figs. 16-19 and 16-20, respectively.

Finally, we consider the third model with its formulation given in Eqs. (15-37), (15-38), and (15-39). This is an eleven-degrees-of-freedom dynamic model of a cam-follower-drive shaft system. The dynamic response of the system, taking all sources of error into account including the stochastic nature of manufacturing tolerances, can be obtained by computer simulation.

Kim and Newcombe (124) have developed a computer program using the modified Runge–Kutta scheme (246) to simulate the response of the cam mechanism so that the effects of system flexibility and of profile errors can be investigated separately as well as in combination. The following example is used to demonstrate this.

Example 16-3

A cam–follower–drive shaft system is to be simulated according to the following specifications:

Motor power P_m = 1457 watts

Camshaft speed   800 rpm

Motion program: Dwell–rise–dwell–return

Cam Rotation	Follower Motion
$\theta°$ ~ 30°	Dwell
30° ~ 180°	Rise 0.381 m with modified trapezoidal motion
180° ~ 210°	Dwell
210° ~ 360°	Return 0.381 m with 4–5–6–7 polynomial motion

Cam base circle radius	= 0.381 m
Follower roller radius	= 0.09525 m
Spring length δ_{rs}	= 0.127 m
Tolerance on cam profile	= ± 1.27 × 10^{-5} m
Tolerance on follower roller	= ± 0.254 × 10^{-5} m .

The properties of the passive parameters of the system are given in Table 16-2.
Fig. 16-21 shows the follower displacement curve. The roughness and flexibility effects are included, but they cannot be discerned because of scale. The cam is shown running in the third revolution so that any transient effects are minimized. Substantial fluctuation in cam torque can be noted.

Table 16-2. Properties of Passive Elements of Example 16-3

Masses (kg)	Moments of Inertia (kg·m²)	Spring Stiffnesses		Damping Coefficients	
		Translational (N/m)	Torsional (N·m/rad)	Translational (N-sec/m)	Tortional (N-m-sec/rad)
$M_1 = 1.36$	$I_m = 0.00329$	$k_{rs} = 1.05 \times 10^4$	$k_{s1} = 2.26 \times 10^4$	$c_{vs} = 753.86$	$c_{mb} = 0.0904$
$M_{cs} = 5.096$	$I_{cp} = 0.113$	$k_{rb} = 2.627 \times 10^8$	$k_{s2} = 2.26 \times 10^4$	c_f^*	$c_{s1} = 0.01354$
$M_r = 0.023$	$I_c = 0.00115$	$k_{vs} = 2.592 \times 10^8$		c_{fl}^*	$c_{s2} = 0.01356$
M_f^*		k_f^*			$c_{cc} = 0.113$
M_{fc}^*		k_{vc}^*			
		k_h^{**}			

*Internally computed according to the position of follower
**Internally computed in accordance with contact point

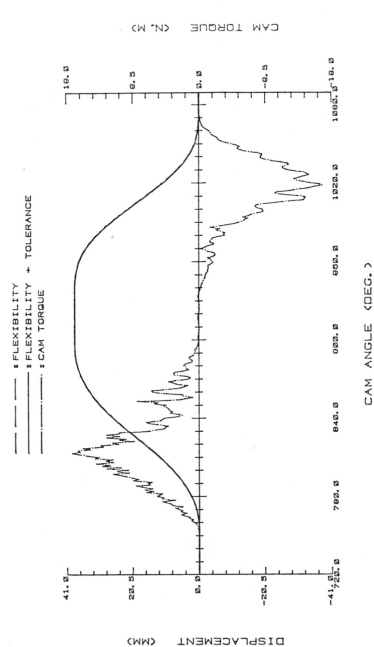

Fig. 16-21. Flexibility and tolerance effects on displacement and cam torque for example 16-3.

456

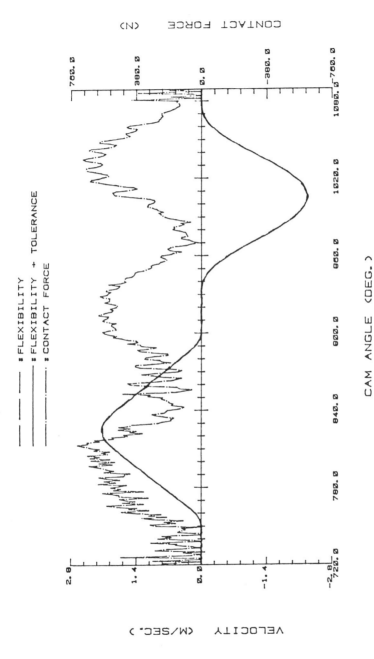

Fig. 16-22. Flexibility and tolerance effects on velocity for example 16-3.

457

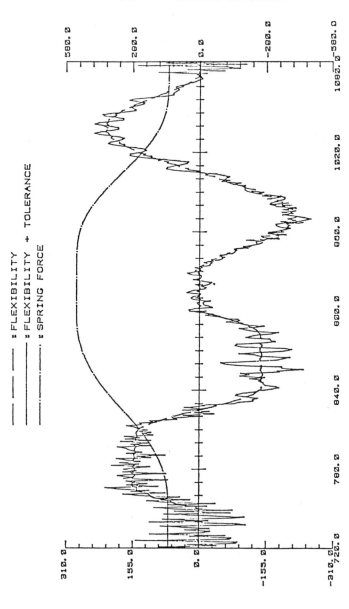

Fig. 16.23 Flexibility and tolerance effect on acceleration for example 16.3.

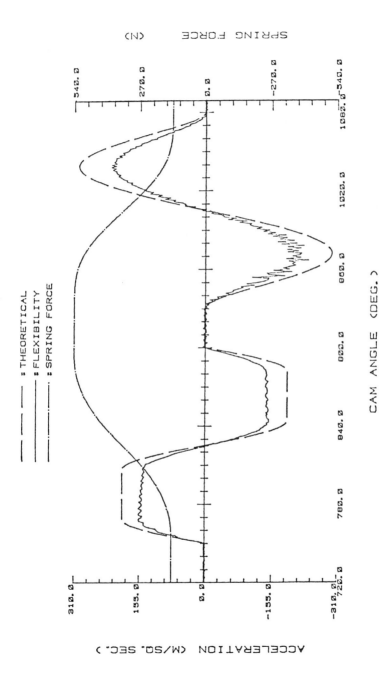

Fig. 16-24. Effect of flexibility alone on acceleration for example 16-3.

459

Fig. 16-22 shows the separate and the combined effects of the flexibility in the system and of the tolerances of the cam and the follower on the velocity. Although not illustrated here, the peak follower velocity has been reduced somewhat from the theoretical value because of the system flexibility. By examining the curve for the contact force, it can be seen that the follower is almost at the point of jumping in several locations.

In Fig. 16-23 the effect of tolerance on the acceleration is seen to be appreciable. The effect of flexibility alone, which is to reduce the peak acceleration, can be seen in Fig. 16-24. Tolerances produce appreciable variations in the acceleration of the follower, especially in the trapezoidal rise motion and in the transition from the dwells.

A simulation is the representation of a system by mathematical relationships and the manipulation of those relationships for the purpose of envisioning the system's performance. With today's simulation techniques, detailed design questions can be answered without having to build a prototype.

Digital simulation has come on strong during the last few years because of the rapid development of digital computers, data terminals, and easy-to-use programming languages. For more discussion on some of the available programming languages for the design of cam mechanisms, the reader is to refer to Chapter 17.

17
Optimal Synthesis and Computer-Aided Design of Cam-And-Follower Systems: An Overview

17-1. INTRODUCTION

Recently much can be heard about design synthesis, design optimization, and computer-aided design. At one extreme these turn out to be little more than the systemization of a trial-and-error process in which a few open parameters are identified by means of mathematical programming techniques. At the other extreme, however, serious claims of automating major aspects of the design process are being made. Generally speaking, the essential elements of the design process include:

- generating alternative solutions, and recognizing those that are acceptable, and
- identifying the optimal solution among the acceptable solutions based on a criterion and conditions of constraints.

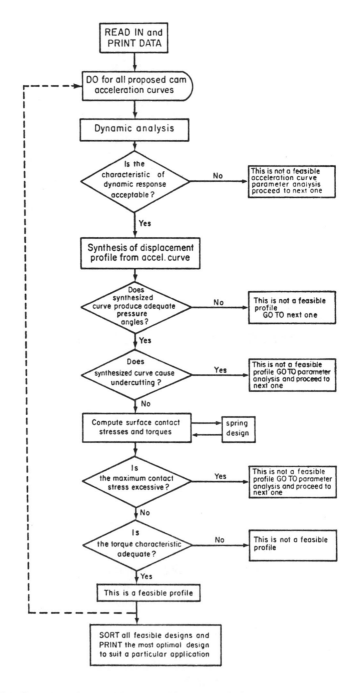

Fig. 17-1. Flow chart of a closed–loop cam–driven system design.

This chapter gives an overview of these aspects associated with the design of cam–and–follower systems. In addition, a brief account of the status of the current development of program languages for use in the design of cam mechanisms is also given.

17-2. GENERATING ALTERNATIVE SOLUTIONS AND RECOGNIZING ACCEPTABLE DESIGNS

With the aid of a computer, the design of a cam–driven mechanical system can be considered in its entirety rather than as an assemblage of fragmented and uncollated specific entities. When viewed in its entirety, a design is essentially composed of two major phases linked together by a kinematic synthesis of cam profiles. The two phases are the analysis of system dynamics and the interpretation of interrelated system parameters. Typical computations involved in the overall process are, for example, the dynamic analysis of response amplitudes, the velocities and the accelerations of the various follower masses, the kinematic computations of profile curvatures and pressure angles, checking for surface contact stresses, the determination of spring rates and damping constants, checking for the follower jump condition, the evaluation of loading variation and camshaft torque fluctuation, etc. Although the design system can be arranged and stated in many different ways, the underlying logic basically involves the procedures shown in Fig. 17-1. In this figure many of the analysis steps involve computations using existing methods, which are more or less established routines and have been covered in the text of the previous chapters. Also note that the path in connection with the outer loop of Fig. 17-1 represents a feedback path associated with redesign.

If the simulated performance is not what the designer wants, he must change a parameter or a group of parameters, based on the knowledge gained from parametric study. The designer must acquaint himself with the advantages and the limitations of each typical shape that might be considered for a base excitation curve. By trying various patterns in a systematic way, he can gain insight into the nature of the system response characteristics, he is able to identify those variables and parameters that are most critical at certain ranges of frequency values, and he can even estimate the order of magnitude of the trade–off relationships among the key parameters of the system. The complete success of this preliminary stage of design depends largely upon the knowledge of parameter adjustment. It is possible in this way to move steadily in the direction of an optimal or a near optimal design (but there is no guarantee this will happen) through a series of progressive profile and parameter revisions. The criterion of total performance can be applied in a systematic way to assist in finding the most desirable cam profile and the dynamic parameters of the follower linkage through trial and error to insure compatibility between the evolved design and its intended application.

17-3. OPTIMAL SYNTHESIS

Over the past two decades, a large body of mathematical techniques has been developed to address the problem of producing an optimal or a best solution to a design problem. Several disciplines have contributed to this development, which has generally been lumped under the title of optimization by mathematical programming. Basically, these techniques assume some criterion function (CF) that is to be optimized (minimized or maximized) subject to a set of constraining conditions. When the optimization method is applied to cam–driven mechanisms, some property of the cam–follower system is chosen as the objective or criterion function. This is then optimized by varying the cam parameters (including parameters that change the cam profile), while making sure that a given set of constraint (equality or inequality) functions is met. The constraints are expressed as bounded functions, which are said to be satisfied when the value of the constraint function is within the bounds. The parameters that are varied to obtain the optimal design are called "design variables" and are finite in number. The problem may be formally formulated as follows:

Minimize $f(X)$

subject to $\bar{\phi}_i(X, \tau) \geq 0 \qquad i = 1, 2, \ldots m'$

$\phi_i(X) \geq 0, \qquad i = m' + 1, \ldots, m,$

where f is called the objective or criterion function, and $\bar{\phi}$ and ϕ are constraints. The term $X = (x_1, x_2, \ldots x_n)^T$ represents the n–dimensional vector of design variables, where the superscript T is used to denote the transpose of the vector. The constraints ϕ, called ordinary constraints, depend on the design variables only. The constraints $\bar{\phi}$, called parametric constraints, not only depend on X, but also depend on some other variables τ (for example time or the cam angle). The essential difference between the two types of constraints is that while the maximum of an ordinary constraint can be computed readily, the maximum value of a parametric constraint as well as the value of τ at which it occurs are either not known or are very difficult to calculate. For example, the residual vibration amplitude depends on the cam speed, and the magnitude of the maximum and the speed at which it occurs usually vary as the design variables are changed. In general, no closed–form solution for the maximum is available.

Most of the cam properties that are of interest to the cam designer are parametric. The residual vibration and the actual forces on the follower mass depend on time (or the cam angle), as well as on cam speed. The pressure angle and the radius of curvature are also dependent on the cam angle.

Sometimes, it is difficult to identify one measure of a design problem that accurately describes the worth of a proposed solution. Often, two or more independent criteria will be necessary to satisfactorily accomplish this task. Much of the work in this area involves optimizing each of the criteria in turn and then producing some type of trade-off relations among the various criteria.

Kwakernaak and Smit (139) have proposed a method of finding cam profiles with limited follower velocity, acceleration, and jerk and minimal residual vibrations over a prescribed range of cam speeds. Based on an undamped single-degree-of-freedom system model, they formulated the problem as one of mathematical optimization and obtained the solutions by using both the quadratic optimization method and the linear programming method. Kanzaki and Itao (121) have suggested a cam design method for typehead positioning in high-speed teleprinters. In this method the cam-follower mechanism is modeled as a single-degree-of-freedom system, and the Laplace transform method is used for finding solutions. Residual vibrations are reduced over a wide range of the cam rise time, and are extinguished at certain plural multiplicity of rise times. However, the effects of this specification on the overall characteristics of the system, i.e., peak velocity, acceleration, and jerk of the input or output motion, are not included. Even though limitation of the residual vibrations is important, singling out this phenomenon to the exclusion of other characteristics is not always desirable.

In a recent study by Berzak (21), a cam-follower system was optimally synthesized by the polydyne cam-design method. In this method the desired output motion of the cam follower is described by a polynomial function. To accommodate the inertia forces and the flexibility of the system in the design, the system is again approximated by a single-degree-of-freedom model. The formulated equation is solved by means of the Laplace transformation method. The constraints specified for the output motions are the vanishing velocities and accelerations at the terminals and the constraints on the displacements. A new representation of the output motion, with the characteristics of the system expressed as a function of the independent parameters, permits the development of the optimization procedure. This process represents a balance among the various system performance coefficients. Berzak applied two methods of optimization. In the first, the objective function is defined as a weighted sum of the characteristics of the system and is minimized over the feasible range of the independent parameters. The second method matches the acceleration of the entire output motion with the acceleration of a reference motion by a least-square approximation using a trigonometric series. Berzak concluded that the algebraic properties of polynomials satisfying prescribed conditions provide certain inherent bounds on achievable performance. The design was shown to consist of trade-offs between the various characteristics of the system.

By controlling the harmonic content of the imposed motion through the use of finite trigonometric series, Wiederrich and Roth (229) synthesized cam profiles based on the assumptions that the homogeneous uncoupled equation of the multiple-degree-of-freedom coincides with the homogeneous equation for the single–degree–of–freedom system, that the input force is representable by a trigonometric series whose harmonic content is below resonance, and that the first and the second modes of the series approximation are predominant. The relative vibrational response of a simple spring–mass system model was obtained with the aid of a Duhamel integral. In the results of their study the authors reached the following conclusions:

(1) The highest harmonic spectrum of the input force of a cam–and–follower system must be substantially less than the natural frequency of the model to avoid vibrational buildup. This conclusion confirms the results obtained by Freudenstein (84), which we discussed in Chapter 16.

(2) High–speed cam designs should not be based upon the overly generalized rule of thumb that states that motions with discontinuous accelerations or high values of jerk always have bad vibrational responses.

Other studies of the optimal design of cam–follower systems include the work by Sermon and Liniecki (206). They have devised a scheme for designing a minimum–volume cam subjected to the constraints of the pressure angle and the maximum value of surface contact stress. On the basis of a linear system model, Sandler (199) suggested the use of the spectral theory of random processes for optimal synthesis of a cam–driven system. Chen and Shah (35) have demonstrated the optimal design of geometric parameters using a sequential random vector technique. It is felt that interest in the optimization of cam–driven mechanisms will continue.

17-4. PROGRAMMING LANGUAGES

A number of computer programs for designing cam–and–follower systems have become available during recent years. Most of these software packages aim at the mechanization of essentially well–known aspects of kinematic and static force analysis of cam mechanisms. In terms of dynamic synthesis and optimization, and on–line design manipulations of such mechanisms, these programs are rather limited.

The purpose of this section is to give a brief description of the various program languages available for use in the analysis and the design of cam mechanisms with appropriate references so the reader can investigate any or all of them more thoroughly.

COMMEND (COMputer–aided Mechanical Engineering Design System)

The cam design program in COMMEND was developed by Lafuente (140) of the IBM Corporation for the IBM–7090 computer. The program described was developed to study the application of graphic display devices to mechanical design problems and to explore programming techniques for communicating graphically with a computer while solving such problems. The cam design program presents five display "panels" described as follows.

The cam design panel is displayed first and redisplayed at appropriate times during the problem solution. Depending on his progress in solving the problem, the designer uses the cam design panel to request any one of three functions. He can select the section of input data to be initially described and subsequently modified (by selecting the word LINKAGE, DIMENSIONS, or MOTION); he can select the computation program that computes and displays the results on the screen (by selecting the word CALCULATIONS); or he can request the results in final printed form (by selecting HARD–COPY OUTPUT). Neither CALCULATIONS nor HARD–COPY OUTPUT can be selected until all input parameters have been specified. Selecting CALCULATIONS on the cam design panel causes the display of the calculations panel, which, in turn, shows the results of the computations on the screen.

The linkage panel enables the designer to describe the type of cam–follower mechanism desired. He specifies the desired linkage characteristics by making the proper selections in subsequent subpanels that display the types of follower arm, the follower types, and the follower linkage types available for use.

The dimensions panel is used by the designer to specify the parameters of the input data pertaining to the physical characteristics of the cam–follower mechanism.

The motion panel is used by the designer to describe the desired motion of the point of interest. The designer can specify the duration angle, the displacement, and the curve type for each section. As he proceeds from section to section, the motion diagram is automatically generated on the display screen.

The calculations panel, which is displayed during the design computations, shows the displacement, the velocity, and the acceleration curves for the point of interest being plotted as the program computes the results. The outline of the cam is traced along with the output curves.

Warning messages concerning certain design problems are displayed in this panel. For example, if the pressure angle at any time exceeds 40°, the message PRESSURE ANGLE EXCEEDS MAXIMUM is displayed to signal the designer that a redesign may be necessary. If the radius of curvature of the follower path at any point is less than the radius of the follower, a warning message is displayed to alert the user that the phenomenon of undercut is present.

Selection of the RETURN option on the lower part of the display causes the initial cam design panel to be redisplayed. All input data are saved after completion of the design, and the operator can change any input parameter and repeat the calculations, or he can proceed to an entirely different problem. If a design is satisfactory, the designer may use HARD–COPY OUTPUT after using RETURN from the calculations panel.

Choosing the HARD-COPY OUTPUT option causes the design results to be printed on the system on-line printer. Output information consists of tables of the displacement, the velocity, and the acceleration of the point of interest, the pressure angle, and the radius of curvature of the follower path at specified degree intervals over the cam profile. Manufacturing information is also available in a cutting schedule at specified intervals. The output may be directed to a plotting device or to a film recorder. It is possible to produce the output on tape for a numerically controlled cutting machine by pressing a function key.

The cam profile determination in this program is based on the envelope theory (49). The program does not include the analysis of dynamic response.

Minimum Weight Cam Program

A FORTRAN program for minimum weight cam design using mathematical programming to determine the design parameters for a specified follower motion has been made available by Fenton and Lo (80) for the IBM-370 digital computer.

The objective function in this program is the weight, the volume, or the size of the cam. The search for the optimum of the objective function is conducted within the feasible region of the typical design variables: cam base circle radius, cam thickness, follower offset, follower roller radius, and spring constant, bounded by the constraints. As indicated previously, the constraint on stress is difficult to evaluate. The normal stress between the cam and its follower is dependent upon the load acting on the follower, the pressure angle, and the radii of curvature of the cam and the follower roller. The load, the pressure angle, and the cam curvature are variable quantities, their values being dependent on the cam position. The pressure angle and the cam curvature are also functions of the follower offset and the cam base circle radius. For each combination of these design variables, suboptimization is performed to find the maximum value of the contact stress on the cam surface. After obtaining the optimum parameters, a complete kinematic, dynamic, and stress analysis is performed on the selected cam-mechanism. The polar coordinates of the cam profile are also computed. Results can be numerically displayed or graphically plotted on a CRT. The program can also be interfaced with an APT-compiler to prepare the types necessary to manufacture the cam on a numerically controlled machine.

CAM, KAVM, and NCCAM

CAM (Computer-Aided Design of Cams), KAVM (Computer-Aided Design of Mechanisms), and NCCAM (Computer-Aided Manufacturing) are integrated computer programs developed by De Fraine and his colleagues (56) at the Catholic University of Louvain in Belgium. Each program can run indivi-

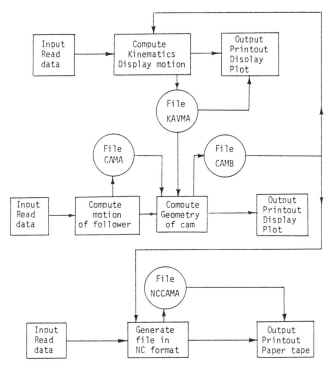

Fig. 17-2. Structure of the integrated programs of CAM, KAVM, and NCCAM.

dually, but the full power of the integrated program system lies in the close interaction among the three programs. The structure of these three programs is shown in Fig. 17-2.

The program CAM is composed of four segments: input, computation of the law of motion, computation of geometrical characteristics, and output. In the input segment, the data describing the cam (e.g., the diameters of the follower, the cutter, and the base circle, and the length of the swing arm for oscillating follower, etc.) are read from the keyboard. In the second segment, the law of motion (the lift, the velocity, and the acceleration of the follower) is computed and written in a file CAMA. Each record of this file contains the position (angular for rotating and linear for translating cams), the lift, the velocity, and the acceleration of the follower. A special value of the position that is physically meaningless is used as a flag to indicate the presence of a dwell. This file is used as an input for the computation of the geometrical characteristics (the path of the follower and the cutter in X–Y and polar coordinates, the pressure angle, the curvature, etc.). Those results are written in file CAMB that is structured in the same way as file CAMA. Finally, the output segment uses the data of the file CAMB to generate printed output on the teletype and the line printer and the graphic output on the screen and the plotter. The graphical representation of the different results (e.g., pressure angle versus cam position) is essential for the immediate understanding of the cam behavior.

The program KAVM is composed of three segments: input, computation, and output. With the input segment, the data describing the mechanism (length of bars, position of slides, sequence of the elements forming a loop, etc.) are read from the keyboard. The kinematic computation (the position, the velocity, and the acceleration of each element of the mechanism) is performed in the second segment; during this process the successive positions of the mechanism are displayed on the screen, and the user sees the mechanism in motion. If in some position the mechanism is locked, the display of this position allows the user to detect easily the origin of the problem and to solve it. The position, the velocity, and the acceleration of each element of the mechanism are written in file KAVMA. Finally, the output segment uses this file to generate printed and graphic output in the same way as does the program CAM.

The program NCCAM is composed of three segments: input, computation, and output. This program reads the coordinates of the successive positions of the cutter from file CAMB and translates them into the format requested by the NC–machine. The information describing the NC–machine (e.g., the format for circular interpolation if provided, the format of the coordinates with or without leading and/or trailing zeros, etc.) is stored in the machine data file. This file need be established only the first time that a cam is manufactured on the machine. In the input segment the user gives the name of the file with the data of his machine; he also has the possibility of manual input of NC–blocks preceding the blocks for automatic cam machining. These blocks are used to machine reference holes, key seats, etc. In the second segment NCCAM generates file NCCAMA containing the blocks in NC–format. The output segment punches the tape (in EIA, ISO, or ASCII format) and prints the listing of the tape on the line–printer.

For more detailed instructions on the use of these programs the reader is referred to the paper by De Fraine (56).

Other available computer programs for the analysis and the design of cam mechanisms include CAMPAK, developed by Matthew (213) at the University of Florida, and DYCAM and CAMCHK for use in the analysis of automotive valve gear mechanisms, developed by Valland (219) at the Technical University of Norway, Trondheim. In addition, cam manufacturers in industry must have some sort of computer–aided cam design programs developed by themselves for internal use. We do not attempt to describe them here.

The advent of conversational digital computer languages and sophisticated software packages has established the necessary grounds for meaningful man–machine dialogues. This raises the possibility of powerful design processes with promising and immediate practicality. For this to be realized, further computer software improvements must be encouraged to provide programming and language characteristics that are oriented toward block– and table-based information, and that can be implemented for easy and natural problem-oriented designer-model conversations. Future progress in the computer-aided design of cam mechanisms should have the capacity not to be confined to simple studies of limited scope concerning the sensitivity of a given design to variations in parameters and operational bounds. It should permit the extensive use of data tables and lists of structural and parametric information concerning the design, the model building, the evaluations, and the design synthesis. All this is at the finger tips of the designer, enabling him to use alternate modules or subsystems, and to play on different combinations of structural and parametric sequences. The design process may thus become even more complex in the future and may require deeper immersion in advanced and sophisticated computer-aided design techniques. With the advent of numerical control, it is becoming more common to deliver the machining data directly in NC format. The end result of the computer-aided design thus emerges as a piece of hardware, the cam itself.

References

1. Allais, D.C. 1963. Cycloidal vs. modified trapezoidal cams. *Mach. Des.* Jan. 31: 92-96.
2. Alt, H. 1963. Der Ruck. *Reuleaux-Mitteilungen* 4: 581-582.
3. Anderson, D.G. 1953. Cam dynamics. *Prod. Eng.* 24: Oct., 170-176.
4. Ardayfio, D.D. 1980. Kinetothermoelasto dynamic (kited) synthesis of cam profiles. *Mech. Mach. Theory.* 15 (1): 1-4.
5. Arnold, R.N. 1952. The limiting speeds of operation on simple cam system. In *Proc. Eighth International Congress on Theoretical and Appl. Mechanics,* pp. 403-404. Istanbul, Turkey.
6. Ayres, V. 1951. Valve lash, automatic tappets, and instrumentation. Paper read at SAE National Passenger-Car, Body, and Materials Meeting, March 1951, at Detroit, Michigan.
7. Bagci, S. 1974. Stop designing and testing cam-follower systems using the rise portion of the displacement program only. In *The Third World Congress for the Theory of Machines and Mechanisms,* Yugoslavia, G. Paper 25, pp. 347-364.
8. Bakonyi, S.M. 1968. The advantages of over-head crankshafts — what are they? *SAE Pap.* 680028.
9. Baranyi, S.J. 1970. Multiple-harmonic cam profiles. *ASME Pap.* 70-MECH-59.
10. Baratta, F.J., and Bluhm, J.I. 1954. When will a cam follower jump? *Prod. Eng.* 25: July, 156-159.
11. Barkan, P. 1953. Calculation of high-speed valve motion with a flexible overhead linkage. *SAE Trans.* 61: 687-700.
12. Barkan, P., and McGarrity, R.V. 1965. A spring-actuated, cam-follower system: Design theory and experimental results, *J. Eng. Ind., Trans. ASME* 87B (3): 279-286.
13. Baumgarten, J.R. 1962. Preload force necessary to prevent separation of follower from cam. Paper read at Trans. 7th Conference on Mechanisms, October 1962, at Purdue University, Lafayette, Indiana.
14. _____. 1962. Preventing cam-follower separation, *Mach. Des.* 34 (27): 179-180. Nov.
15. Baxter, M.L., Jr. 1948. Curvature-acceleration relations for plane cams. *Trans. ASME* 70: 483-489.
16. _____. 1956. Discussion on determination of radius of curvature by Kloomok and Muffley. *Trans. ASME:* 801-802.
17. Beard, C.A., and Hempson, J.G.G. 1963. Problems in valve gear design and instrumentation. SAE Progress in Technology, 5.

18. Benedict, C.E., and Tesar, D. 1973. Dynamic responses of a mechanical system containing a coulomb friction force. Paper read at Proc. Third Appl. Mechanism Conference, Oklahoma State University, Stillwater, Oklahoma, Paper 44.
19. Berry, W.R. 1944. Practical problems in spring design. *Proc. Inst. Mech. Eng.* 139: 431.
20. Berzak, N., and Freudenstein, F. 1979. Optimization criteria in polydyne cam design. In *Proceedings of the 5th World Congress on Theory of Machines and Mechanisms,* pp. 1303-1306.
21. Berzak, N. 1979. Optimization of cam follower systems in polydyne cam design. Doctoral thesis, Columbia University. 239 pp.
22. _____. 1980. Optimization of cam follower systems with kinematic and dynamic constraints. *ASME Pap.* 80-DET-11.
23. Bialkowicz, B.; Klimowicz, J.; and Oledzki, A. 1979. Changes of the dynamic properties of the real cam profile during its wear. In *Proceedings of the 5th World Congress on Theory of Machines and Mechanisms,* pp. 584-587.
24. Bishop, J.L.H. 1950-1951. An analytical approach to automobile valve gear design. *Proc. Automobil. Div. Inst. Mech. Eng.* 4: 150-160.
25. Bloom, F., and Radcliffe, C.W. 1964. The effect of cam shaft elasticity on the responses of cam drive systems. Douglas Missile and Space Systems Division, Pap. 3040.
26. Brat, V. 1975. On the dynamic optimization of mechanical system. In *4th World Congress on the Theory of Machines and Mechanisms,* pp. 483-487. London: Mechanical Engineering Publ.
27. Brittain, H.H.C., and Horsnell, R. 1967-68. Prediction of some causes and effects of cam profile errors. *Proc. Inst. Mech. Eng.* 182, (3L): 145-151.
28. Broeke, H. 1965. Improving the performance of dynamically loaded cam mechanisms. Maschinenbautechnik 14: 157-163.
29. Buhayar, E.S. 1966. Computerized cam design and plate cam manufacture. *ASME Pap.* 66-MECH-2.
30. Carlson, J.A. 1958. Principles and practice of constant-loaded cam design for high speed operation. *Mach. Des.* Jan. 10: 121-128.
31. Carver, W.B., and Quinn, B.E. 1945. An analytical method of cam design. *Mech. Eng.* 67 (8): Aug., 523-526.
32. Chakraborty, J., and Dhande, S.G. 1977. *Kinematics and geometry of planar and spatial cam mechanisms.* New York: J. Wiley.
33. Chen, F.Y. 1969. An algorithm for computing the contour of a slow-speed cam. *J. Mech.* 4 (2): 171-175.
34. _____. 1972. A refined algorithm for finite-difference synthesis of cam profiles. *J. Mech.* 7 (4): 453-460.
35. Chen, F.Y., and Shah, A.M. 1972. Optimal design of the geometric parameters of a cam mechanism using a sequential random vectors technique. *ASME Pap.* 72-MECH-73.
36. _____. 1973b. Kinematic synthesis of cam profiles for prescribed acceleration by a finite intergratiom method. *Trans. ASME, J. Eng. Ind.* 95B (2): 519-524.
37. _____. 1973a. Analysis and design of cam-driven mechanisms with nonlinearities. *Trans. ASME, J. Eng. Ind.* 95B (3): 685-694.
38. Chen, F.Y., and Polvanich, N. 1975a. Dynamics of high speed cam-driven mechanisms: Part I — Linear system models. *Trans. ASME, J. Eng. Ind.* 97E (3): 769-776.
39. _____. 1975b. Dynamics of high speed cam-driven mechanisms: Part II— Nonlinear system models. *Trans. ASME, J. Eng. Ind.* 97B (3): 777-784.
40. _____. 1977b. Dynamic responses of a cam-actuated mechanism with pneumatic coupling. *Trans. ASME, J. Eng. Ind.* 99B (2): 300-306.
41. _____. 1977a. A survey of the state of the art of cam system dynamics. *Mech. Mach. Theory.* 12 (3): 201-224.
42. _____. 1978b. Stororidal motion—a new class of cam profile. *ASME Pap.* 78-DET-20. 8 pp.

43. _____. 1978a. Discrete modeling of mechanical systems. *ASME Pap.* 78-DET-80. 8 pp.

44. _____. 1980b. Numerical scheme for determining the pressure angle and radius of curvature of cams. *ASME Pap.* 80-DET-70. 8 pp.

45. _____. 1980a. Assessment of the dynamic quality of a class of dwell–rise–dwell cams. *ASME Pap.* 80-DET-83. 14 pp.

46. Chironis, N.P. 1965. German methods simplify layout of tailored cycloidal cams. *Prod. Eng.* Nov. 8: 108-111.

47. Choubey, M., and Rao, A.C. 1980. Optimum sensitivity synthesis of a cam system incorporating manufacturing tolerances. *ASME Pap.* 80-DET-31.

48. Church, J.A., and Soni, A.H. 1971. On Harrisberger's adjustable trapezoidal motion program for cam design. Paper read at Proc. of the Applied Mechanisms Conference, October 1971 at Oklahoma State University, Stillwater, Oklahoma. Paper 41.

49. Churchill, F.T., and Hansen, R.S. 1962. Theory of envelopes provides new cam design equations. *Prod. Eng.* 35: 45-55.

50. Clenshaw, C.W., and Hayes, J.G. 1963. Curve and surface fitting. *J. Inst. Math. & Appl.* 1.

51. Cowie, A. 1961. Kinematics and design of mechanisms. Scranton, Pennsylvania: International.

52. Cram, W.D. 1956. Practical approach to cam design. *Mach. Des.:* Nov. 1: 92-103.

53. Crossley, F.R.E. 1960. How to modify positioning cams. *Mach. Des.:* Mar. 3: 121-126.

54. Crossley, F.R.E.; Oledzki, A.; and Szydlowski, W. 1969. On the modeling of impacts of two elastic bodies having flat and cylindrical surface with application to cam mechanisms. *Proceedings of the 5th World Congress on Theory of Machines and Mechanisms,* pp. 1090-1092.

55. Davidson, J.K. 1978. Calculating cam profiles quickly. *Mach. Des.:* Dec. 7: 151-156.

56. DeFraine, J. 1969. Integration of computer aided design and computer aided manufacturing for cam–driving mechanisms. In *Proceedings of the 5th World Congress on Theory of Machines and Mechanisms,* pp. 122-125.

57. Dejuhasz, K.J. 1938. Graphical analysis of surges in mechanical springs. *J. Franklin Inst.* 226: Oct., 505-532.

58. Den Hartog, J.P. 1956. *Mechanical vibrations.* 4th ed. New York: McGraw–Hill.

59. Dennis, R.C., and Neuser, C.J. 1972. Computer–assisted valve train design and development. *SAE Pap.* 660348. See also Part II, *SAE Pap.* 720213.

60. Dhande, S.G.; Bhadoria, B.S.; and Chakraborty, J. 1975. A unified approach to the analytical design of three–dimensional cam mechanisms. *Trans. ASME J. Eng. Ind.* 97B (1): 327-333.

61. Dhande, S.G., and Chakraborty, J. 1975. Mechanical error analysis of cam–follower systems — A stochastic approach. In *4th World Congress on the Theory of Machines and Mechanisms,* pp. 957-962. London: Mechanical Engineering Publ.

62. _____. 1976a. Curvature analysis of surfaces in higher pair contact, Part I: An analytical investigation. *Trans. ASME, J. Eng. Ind.* 96B (2): 397-402.

63. _____. 1976b. Curvature analysis of surfaces in higher pair contact, Part II: Application to spatial cam mechanism. *Trans. ASME, J. Eng. Ind.* 96B (2): 403-409.

64. Di Benedetto A., and Papa, L. 1974. Sintesi cinematica di profile di camme per assegnato andamento del jerk. In *II Congresso Nazionale Aimeta,* pp. 95-106.

65. _____. 1975. Some methods of kinematic synthesis of cam profiles for prescribed jerk pattern. In *Fourth World Congress on the Theory of Machines and Mechanisms,* pp. 936-968. London: Mechanical Engineering Publ.

66. Di Benedetto, A. 1972. Profile di camme per cedenti translanti assegnato andamento del jerk. Disegno Di Machine 1: 25-40.

67. Di Benedetto, A., and Vinciguerra, A. 1969. A new algorithm of kinematic synthesis of plate cam profiles for prescribed follower acceleration. In *Proceedings of the 5th World Congress on Theory of Machines and Mechanisms,* pp. 549-552.

68. _____. 1980. Kinematic analysis of plate cam profiles not analytically defined. *ASME Pap.* 80-DET-12.
69. Dittrich, G., and Zakel, H. 1969. Classification and design of three dimensional cam mechanisms. In *Proceedings of the 5th World Congress on Theory of Machines and Mechanisms,* pp. 1086-1089.
70. Dixon, M.W., and Ting, K.L. 1969. Generalized design technique for a spatial cam-link function generator. In *Proceedings of the 5th World Congress on Theory of Machines and Mechanisms,* pp. 1307-1310.
71. Donkin, W.T., and Clark, H.H. 1929. Electric telemeter and valve-spring surge. *SAE J.* 24: 315-326.
72. Dudley, W.M. 1948. New methods in valve cam design. *SAE Q. Trans.* 2 (7): 19-33.
73. Eiss, N.S., Jr. 1964. Vibration of cams having two degrees of freedom. *Trans. ASME, J. Eng. Ind.* 86B (4): 343-350.
74. Erisman, R.J. 1967. Automotive cam profile synthesis and valve gear dynamics from dimensionless analysis. *SAE Trans.* 75 (1): 128-147.
75. Fanella, R.J. 1959. Dynamic analysis of cylindrical cams. *ASME Pap.* 59-SA-3.
76. Fawcett, G.F., and Fawcett, J.N. 1974a. Comparison of polydyne and non-polydyne cams. Paper read at Proc. of Conference on Mechanisms — Cams and Cam Mechanisms, September 1974, at Liverpool Polytechnic, England.
77. _____. 1974b. Synthesis of complex cam mechanisms. *Proc. Inst. Mech. Eng.* 188 (58/74): 647-656.
78. Fenton, R.G. 1966. Determining minimum cam size. *Mach. Des.:* Jan. 20: 155-158.
79. _____. 1967. Cam design-determining of the minimum base radius for disc cams with reciprocating flat faced followers. *Automobil. Eng.:* May, 184-187.
80. Fenton, R.G., and Lo, C-H. 1976. Computer aided design of disc cams. *ASME Pap.* 76-DET-62. 8 pp.
81. Forsythe, G.E. 1957. Generation and use of orthogonal polynomials for data-fitting with a digital computer. *J. Soc. Ind. Appl. Math.* 5: 74.
82. Fox, F.W. 1961. Cam profile synthesis by finite differences. Technical Report, Continental Can Co.
83. Fox, J.G., and Mahanty, J. 1970. The effective mass of an oscillating spring. *Am. J. Phys.* 38 (1): 98-100.
84. Freudenstein, F. 1960. On the dynamics of high-speed cam profiles. *Int. J. Mech. Sci.* 1: 342-349.
85. Gagne, A.F., Jr. 1953. Design high speed cams. *Mach. Des.:* Jan., 121-135.
86. Ganter, M.A., and Uicker, J.J., Jr. 1979. Design charts for disk cams with reciprocating radial roller followers. *Trans. ASME, J. Mech. Des.* 101B (3): 465-470.
87. Garrett, R.E. 1962. Froce cams. *Mach. Des.:* Aug. 16: 174-176.
88. Giordana, F.; Rognonl, V.; and Ruggierd, G. 1980. The influence of construction errors in the law of motion of cam mechanisms. *Mech. Mach. Theory.* 15 (1): 29-45.
89. Grant, B., and Soni, A.H. 1974. *Cam design survey. Design technology,* transfer-ed. A.H. Soni, pp. 177-219. ASME Publication, Oct.
90. Gutman, A.S. 1961. To avoid vibration — try this new cam profile. *Prod. Eng.* Dec. 25: 42-48.
91. Hain, K. 1960. Systematik mehrpliedriger kurvengetr und ihre anwendungsmog-lichkeiten. *Maschinenbautechnik* 9: 641-649.
92. _____. 1967. *Applied kinematics.* 2nd ed. New York: McGraw-Hill. Bibliography Section, pp. 639-704. 2348 references on general mechanism topics including cams.
93. _____. 1971. Optimization of a cam mechanism to give good transmissibility, maximal output angle of swing and minimal acceleration. *J. Mech.* 6, (4): 419-434.
94. _____. 1974. Kurvengetriebe mit umlaufender doppelkurve zur erzeugung von baknkurven mit vorgeschriebener geschwindigkeit. *Mech. Mach. Theory.* 9 (1): 7-26.

95. Hanaoka, M., and Fukumura, S. A study of valve train noises and a method of cam design to reduce the noises. *SAE Pap.* 730247.
96. Hart, F.D., and Zorowski, C.F. 1964. Coupled effects of preloads and damping on dynamic cam–follower separation. *ASME Pap.* 64-MECH-18.
97. Hayes, J.G., and Vickers, J. 1951. The fitting of polynomials to unequally spaced data. *Philos. Mag.* 7: 42.
98. Hebeler, C.B. 1961. Design equations and graphs for finding the dynamic response of cycloidal-motion cam systems. *Mach. Des.* Feb. 2: 102-107.
99. Hildebrand, F. 1956. *Introduction to numerical analysis.* New York: McGraw–Hill.
100. Hirschhorn, J. Disc–cam curvature. *Mach. Des.* Feb. 5: 121-129.
101. _____. 1962. Pressure angle and minimum base radius. *Mach. Des.* 34 (21): 191-193.
102. Holowenko, A.R., and Hall, A.S. 1953. Cam curvature. *Mach. Des.* Aug., 170-177, Sept., 162-169, Nov., 148-156.
103. Horan, R.P. 1953. Overhead valve gear problems. *SAE Trans.* 61: 678-686.
104. Hrones, J.A. 1948. Analysis of dynamic force in a cam–driven system. *Trans. ASME* 70: 473-482.
105. Hoschek, J. 1978. Paare kongrunter kurvenscheiben. *Mech. Mach. Theory.* 13 (3): 281-292.
106. Hundal, M.S. 1963. Aid of digital computer in the analysis of rigid spring loaded valve mechanisms. SAE Progress in Technology, 5, Application of Computers in Valve Gear Design.
107. Hussmann, A.W. 1938a. Rechnerische verfahren zur harmonischen analyze und synthese. Berline, Germany: Julius Springer Verlag.
108. _____. 1938b. Schwingungen in schraubenformigen ventilfedern. Jahrbuch der Deutschen Luftfahrtforschugn, Part II, pp. 119-133.
109. Janssen, B. 1969. Dynamik der kurvengetriebe. *VDI–Berichte.* 127: 73-78.
110. Jehle, F., and Spiller, W.R. 1929. Idiosyncrasies of valve mechanisms and their causes. *SAE J.* 24: 133-143.
111. Jennings, J. 1941. Calculating springs for cams. *Machinery (London)* 57: 433.
112. Jensen, P.W. 1965b. Your guide to mechanisms for generating cam curves. *Prod. Eng.* Mar. 1: 41-47.
113. _____. 1965a. *Cam design and manufacture.* New York: Industrial Press.
114. Jhala, P.B., and Venkataramanan, C.G. 1969. Optimization of picking cam design through dynamic studies. In *Proceedings of the 5th World Congress on Theory of Machines and Mechanisms,* pp. 992-995.
115. Johnson, A.R. 1965. Motion control for a series system of n–degrees of freedom using numerically derived and evaluated equations. *Trans. ASME, J. Eng. Ind.* 87B (2): 191-204.
116. Johnson, R.C. 1955. Method of finite differences provides simple but flexible arithmatical techniques for cam design. *Mach. Des.* Nov., 195-204.
117. _____. 1956. A rapid method for developing cam profiles having desired acceleration characteristics. *Mach. Des.* Dec., 129-132.
118. _____. 1959. The dynamic analysis and design of relatively flexible cam mechanisms having more than one degree of freedom. *Trans. ASME, J. Eng. Ind.* 81B (4): 323-331.
119. Johnson, G.I. 1963. *Studying valve dynamics with electronic computers.* SAE Progress in Technology, vol. 5, Application of Computers in Valve Gear Design.
120. Kanago, R., and Patnaik, N. 1969. Improving dynamic characteristic of a cam–follower mechanism through finite-difference techniques. In *Proceedings of the 5th World Congress on Theory of Machines and Mechanisms,* pp. 591-594.
121. Kanzaki, K., and Itao, K. 1972. Polydyne cam mechanisms for typehead positioning. *Trans. ASME, J. Eng. Ind.* 94B (1): 250-254.
122. Kass, R.C., and Chase, M.A. 1975. An approach to the simulation of two dimensional higher pair contacts. In Fourth World Congress on the Theory of Machines and Mechanisms, pp. 1057-1062. London: Mechanical Engineering Publ.
123. Kim, H.R. 1978. Stochastic error analysis in cam mechanisms. *Mech. Mach. Theory.* 13 (6): 631-641.

124. Kim, H.R., and Newcombe, W.R. 1981. The effect of cam profile errors and system flexibility on cam mechanism output. *Mech. Mach. Theory.* 16: 4.
125. Kloomok, M., and Muffley, R.V. 1955a. Plate cam design–pressure angle analysis. *Prod. Eng.* May, 155-171.
126. _____. 1955b. Plate cam design–radius of curvature. *Prod. Eng.* Sept., 186-187.
127. _____. 1956c. Plate cam design — evaluating dynamic loads. *Prod. Eng.* Jan., 178-182.
128. _____. 1956a. Determination of radius of curvature for radial and swinging-follower cam system. *Trans. ASME* 78 May, 795-802.
129. _____. 1956b. Determining of pressure angles for swinging-follower cam system. *Trans. ASME.* 78 May, 803-806.
130. Knight, B.A., and Johnson, H.L. 1966. Motion analysis of flexible cam-follower systems. *ASME Pap.* 66-*MECH*-3.
131. Kobrinskiy, A.Y. 1948. *Effect of elasticity of components on the kinematics of certain cam mechanisms.* Defense Press.
132. _____. 1950. On selection of the law of motion of a pusher. Trudy Seminara Po Teorii Mashin Mekhanizmor, 35, Izd, ANSSSR.
133. Koster, M.P. 1970. *Vibration of cam mechanisms.* London: Macmillan.
134. _____. 1975b. Effect of flexibility of driving shaft on the dynamic behavior of a cam mechanism. *Trans. ASME* 97B (2): 595-602.
135. _____. 1975a. Digital simulation of the dynamics of cam follower and camshafts. In *Fourth World Congress of the Theory of Machine and Mechanisms,* pp. 969-974. London: Mechanical Engineering Publ.
136. Koumans, P.W. 1978. The calculation of the maximum pressure angle and the minimum radius of curvature of a cam using special graphs. In *Cam and Cam Mechanisms,* ed. J.R. Jones, London: Mechanical Engineering Publ.
137. Kozhevnikov, S.N., and Autonyuk, E.Y. 1974. Synthesis of a cam–differential mechanism with periodic dwell of the output link. *Mech. Mach. Theor.* 9 (2): 219-229.
138. Krasnikov, V.F. 1978. An analytical method of determining the radii of curvature of automatic machine cams. *Russ. Eng. J.* 58 (4): 32-33.
139. Kwakernaak, H., and Smit, J. 1968. Minimum vibration cam profile. *J. Mech. Eng. Sci.* 10 (3): 219-227.
140. Lafuente, J.M. 1968. Interactive graphics in data processing cam design on graphics console. *IBM Syst. J.* 3-4: 365-343.
141. Lenz, R. 1957. A graphical method of modifying cam acceleration. *Mach. Des.* Sept. 19: 168-170.
142. Levitskii, N.I. *Cam mechanisms.* Moscow: Machine Technology Publ., (in Russian).
143. Liniecki, A.G. 1975. Optimum design of disk cams by nonlinear programming. Paper read at Proc. of the Fourth Applied Mechanism Conference, November 1975, at Chicago, Illinois, Paper 6.
144. Liou, M.L. 1966. Time and frequency domain analysis of linear time-invariant systems. In *System Analysis by Digital Computer,* eds. F.F. Kuo and J.F. Kaiser, pp. 99-112. New York: Wiley.
145. Lipson, C. 1967. *Wear considerations in design.* Englewood Cliffs, New Jersey: Prentice-Hall.
146. Lundberg, G., and Odqvist, F.K.G. 1932. Studies on stress distributions in the vicinity of the contact region between bodies, with applications. *Ing. Venskaps Akad. Handl.* 116.
147. Mabie, H.H., and Qcvirk, F.W. 1979. *Mechanisms and dynamics of machinery.* New York: Wiley.
148. Makino, H. 1969. Basic analysis and optimal design of in-line transfer indexing cam. *Proceedings of the 5th World Congress on Theory of Machines and Mechanisms,* pp. 875-878.
149. Marti, W. 1936. Vibrations in valve springs for internal combustion engines. *Sulzer Tech. Rev.* 2.

150. Martin, R.B. 1975. Measuring the moment of inertia of irregular cross sections. *Rev. Sci. Instrum.* 46 (7): 838-839.
151. Matthew, G.K., and Tesar, D. 1971. Formalized matrix method for nth derivative trapezoidal motion specifications for cams. In *Comm. of the Third World Congress for the Theory of Machines and Mechanisms,* pp. 247-260. Yugoslavia, H. Paper 19.
152. _____. 1975b. The design of modeled cam systems — Part I: Dynamic synthesis and chart design for the two-degree-of-freedom model. *Trans. ASME, J. Eng. Ind.* 95B (4): 1175-1180.
153. _____. 1975a. The design of model cam systems — Part II: Minimization of motion distortion due to modeling errors. *Trans. ASME, J. Eng. Ind.* 95B (4): 1181-1189.
154. _____. 1976. Cam system design: The dynamic synthesis and analysis of the one degree of freedom model. *Mech. Mach. Theor.* 11 (4): 247-257.
155. Matthew, G.K. 1979. The modified polynomial specification for cams. In *Proceedings of the 5th World Congress on Theory of Machines and Mechanisms,* pp. 1299-1302.
156. Mckellar, M.R. 1966. Overhead camshaft stirs new tempest. *SAE J.* 74 (11): 69-73.
157. Meneghetti, U., and Andrisano, A.O. 1969. On the geometry of cyclindrial cams. In *Proceedings of the 5th World Congress on Theory of Machines and Mechanisms,* pp. 595-598.
158. Mercer, S., and Holowenko, A.R. 1958. Dynamic characteristics of cam forms calculated by the digital computer. *Trans. ASME* 80 (8): 1695-1705.
159. Midha, A.; Badlani, M.L.; and Erdman, A.G. 1979. Periodic response of high-speed cam mechanism with flexible follower and camshaft using a closed-form numerical algorithm. In *Proceedings of the 5th World Congress on Theory of Machines and Mechanisms,* pp. 1311-1314.
160. Mischke, C. 1970. Optimal offset on translating follower plate cams. *Trans. ASME, J. Eng. Ind.* 92B (1): 172-176.
161. Mitchell, D.B. 1950. Tests on dynamic response of cam follower systems. *Mech. Eng.* 72: 467-471.
162. Molian, S. 1963. Use of algebraic polynomials in design of cams. Engineer 22.
163. _____.1968b. *The design of cam mechanisms and linkages.* New York: American Elsevier.
164. _____. 1968a. *The design of cam mechanisms and linkages.* London: Comstable.
165. Moon, C.H. 1961. A simplified universal procedure for designing cam profiles. *Mach. Des.* Apr. 13: 179-187.
166. Moon, C.H. 1962. Simplified method for determining cam radius of curvature. *Mach. Des.:* 123-125.
167. Morrison, R.A. 1968. Load/life curves for gear and cam materials. *Mach. Des.* Aug. 1: 102-108.
168. Nakanishi, F. 1941. On cam forms which induce no surging in valve springs. Report of the Aeronautical Research Institute, Tokyo Imperial University, 220, Nov. pp. 271-280.
169. _____. 1944. Report of the Aeronautical Research Institute of the Tokyo Imperial University, 300, July, pp. 1-9.
170. Neklutin, C.N. 1952. Designing cams for controlled inertia and vibration. *Mach. Des.* June, 143-160.
171. _____. 1954. Vibration analysis of cams. In *Trans. of Second Conference on Mechanisms,* pp. 6-14. Cleveland: Penton Publ.
172. _____. 1959. Tring-type cam profiles. *Mach. Des.* Oct. 15: 175-187.
173. _____. 1969. *Mechanisms and cams for automatic machines.* New York: American Elsevier.
174. Nourse, J.H. 1965. Recent developments in cam profile measurements and evaluation. *SAE Pap.* 964A.
175. Nourse, J.H.; Dennis, R.C.; and Wood, W.M. 1963. Recent developments in cam design. *SAE Tech. Prog. Ser.* 5: 29-57. See also *SAE Pap.* 202A.

176. Okcuoglu, S.A. 1960. An application of polydyne cam design. In *Trans., Sixth Conference on Mechanism*, pp. 44-47. Cleveland: Penton Publ.
177. Olmstead, E.H. 1939. Poppet valve dynamics. *J. E.S. Taylor Aeronautical Sci.* 6 July, 370-375.
178. Pagel, P.A. 1978a. Custom cams from building blocks. *Mach. Des.* May 11: 86-90.
179. _____. 1978b. Sizing cams for long life. *Mach. Des.:* Sept. 7: 104-109.
180. Pasin, F. 1974. Uber die berechnung der eigenfreguenzen vonschwingungen bei kurven-mechanismen. *Mech. Mach. Theor.* 9 (2): 231-238.
181. Peisakh, E.E. 1966. Improving the polydyne cam design method. *Russ. Eng. J.* XLVI (12): 25-27.
182. Radcliffe, C.W. 1980. Matrix methods for plate cam geometry. *ASME Pap.* 80-DET-111.
183. Raghavacharyulu, E., and Rao, J.S. 1976. Jump phenomena in cam–follower systems, a continuous–mass–model approach. *ASME Pap.* 76-WA/DE-26, 8 pp.
184. Ragsdell, K.M., and Gilkey, H.E. 1969. Optimal cam design using the skewed modified trapezoidal profile. Paper read at Proc. of the Applied Mechanism Conference, at Oklahoma State University, Stillwater, Oklahoma. Paper 28.
185. Rahman, Z.V., and Bussell, W.H. 1971. An iterative method analyzing oscillating cam follower motion. *Trans. ASME, J. Eng. Ind.* 93B (1): 149-156.
186. Rao, A.C. 1976. Minimum flexibility error and optimum sensitivity synthesis of cam mechanisms. *Mech. Mach. Theor.* 14 (3): 209-214.
187. Rao, J.S., and Raghavacharyulu, E. 1975. Experimental determination of jump characteristics in cam–follower systems. In *Fourth World Congress on the Theory of Machines and Mechanisms*, pp. 951-956. London: Mechanical Engineering Publ.
188. Raven, F.H. 1959. Analytical design of disk cams and their three–dimensional cams by independent position equations. *ASME Trans.* 26E (1): 18-24.
189. Reeve, J., and Rees–Jones, J. 1974. The dynamic response of cam curves based on sinusoidal segments. Paper read at Proc., Conference on Mechanisms-Cams and Cam Mechanisms, September 1974 at Liverpool Polytechnic, England.
190. Reid, N.E. 1964. Two methods for determining the minimum radius of curvature of disk cams. *ASME Pap.* 64-MECH-20.
191. Roggenbuck, R.A. 1953. Designing the cam profile for low vibration at high speeds. *SAE Trans.* 61: 701-705.
192. Root, R.R., and Ragsdell, K.M. 1975. A survey of optimization methods applied to the design of mechanisms. *ASME Pap.* 75-DET-95.
193. Rothbart, H.A. 1956. *Cams–design, dynamics, and accuracy.* New York: Wiley.
194. _____. 1957. Limitations on cam pressure angles. *Prod. Eng.:* 193-195.
195. _____. 1958. Cam torque curves. In *Trans. of 5th Conference on Mechanisms*, pp. 36-41. Cleveland: Penton Publ.
196. _____. 1964. Mechanical design and systems handbook. In *Cam mechanisms*, Chapter 5, pp. 5.1-5.14. McGraw–Hill.
197. Sandler, B.Z. 1974b. Suboptimal mechanism synthesis. *Isr. J. Technol.* 12: 160-168.
198. Sanchez, M.N., and Dejalon, J.G. 1980. Application of b–spline function to the motion specification of cams. *ASME Pap.* 80-DET-28.
199. Sandler, B.Z. 1974a. Suboptimal dynamic synthesis of linearized mechanical system. *ASME Pap.* 74-DET-27.
200. _____. 1974. The influence of cam profile errors in follower motion. Paper read at IFTOMM International Symposium, 12–13 September 1974 in England.
201. Sarsten, A., and Valland, H. 1974. Computer assistance in valve design — a university approach. In *ASME Design Technology Transfer Conference*, pp. 167-176. New York.
202. Schmidt, E. 1960. Continuous cam curves. *Mach. Des.* 32 (1): 127-132.
203. Sergeev, P.V. 1966a. A synthesis of sliding cam mechanisms. *Russ. Eng. J.* XLVI (5): 43-45.
204. _____. 1966b. A synthesis of sliding cam mechanisms. *Russ. Eng. J.* XLVI (12): 23-25.

205. _____. 1968. Synthesis of cam mechanisms by using the criterion of permissible wear. *Russ. Eng. J.* XLVIII. (12): 30-32.
206. Sermon, C.F., and Liniecki, A. 1972. Search for optimum solution of a single disk cam mechanism with an oscillating roller follower. *ASME Pap.* 72-MECH-61.
207. Shoup, T.E., and Berk, J. 1976. The kinetothermal analysis and synthesis of cam systems. *Mech. Mach. Theor.* 11 (5): 321-329.
208. Singh, Y.P., and Kohli, D. 1979. Synthesis of cam–link mechanism for exact path generation. In *Proc. 6th, Applied Mechanism Conference,* 13 pp. Denver, Colorado. Paper 35.
209. Stoddart, D.A. 1953. Polydyne cam design. *Mach. Des.* 25 (1): 121-135; 25, 2, 146-154; 25, 3, 149-164.
210. Szakallas, L.E., and Savage M. 1980. The characterization of cam drive system windup. *Trans. ASME, J. Mech. Des.* 102 (2): 278-285.
211. Takno, M., and Toyama, S. 1969. Dynamics of indexing cam mechanism and speed–up of its motion. In *Proceedings of the 5th World Congress on Theory of Machines and Mechanisms,* pp. 1408-1411.
212. Talbourdet, G.J. A progress report on the surface endurance limits of materials. *ASME Pap.* 54-LUB-14.
213. _____. 1976b. *The dynamic synthesis, analysis, and design of modeled cam systems.* Lexington, Massachusetts: Lexington Books.
214. Tesar, D., and Matthew, G.K. 1976a. Dynamic distortion in cam systems. *Mach. Des.* Mar. 25: 186-191.
215. Thoren, T.R.; Engemann, H.H.; and Stoddart, D.A. 1952. Cam design as related to valve train dynamics. *SAE Q. Trans.,* Jan. 6, 1: 1-14.
216. Turkish, M.C. 1946. Valve gear problems. Dumont Oscillographer 8.
217. _____. 1950. Inspection of cam contours by the electronic method. Eaton Forum, Mar.
218. _____. 1953. Relationship of valve–spring design to valve gear dynamics and hydraulic lifter pump–up. *SAE Trans.* (61): 706-716.
219. Valland, H. 1969. Computer programs for analysis of valve train dynamics and cam profile evaluation. The Inst. of Internal Combustion Engines Bulletin No. IF-N:5, Trondheim, Norway.
220. Veldkamp, G.R. 1972. On mating profiles in three–link rolling cam drives. *Inst. Mech. Eng.* C110: 140-142.
221. Van Der Hoek, W. 1966. Das voraussagfu des dynamischen verhaltens bei kurvenge trieben. Vdi Ausschub Getriebetechnik, Goslar, Februar 1966.
222. _____. 1967a. Het voorspellen van dynamisch gedrag en positioneringsnauw keurigheid van coustructies en mechanismen. De Ingenieur, 10, Febr. P. W 19.
223. _____. 1967b. Het voorspellen van dynamisch gedrag en positioneringsnauw keurigheid van coustructies en mechanismen. *Polytech. Tidschr.* 22 (16): 671; (17): 734; (18): 763.
224. Wagstaff, P.R. 1967-1968. Analysis of valve gear dynamics with a digital computer. In *Proc. Institution of Mechanical Engineers,* Pt. 3L, 182, pp. 137-144.
225. Warming, T. 1949. Vibrations in valve mechanisms. Paper read at Proc. of the National Oil and Gas Power Conference, ASME.
226. Weber, T., Jr. 1960. Cam dynamics via filter theory. *Mach. Des.* Oct. 13: 160-165.
227. _____. 1979. Simplifying complex cam design. *Mach. Des.* Mar. 22: 115-120.
228. Weiderrich, J.L. 1973. Design of cam profiles for systems with high inertial loadings. Ph.D. Thesis, Standford University.
229. Wiederrich, J.L., and Roth, B. 1974. Dynamic synthesis of cams using finite trigonometric series. *Trans. ASME* 96B (1): 287-293.
230. _____. 1978. Design of low vibration cam profiles. In *Cam and cam mechanisms,* ed. J.R. Jones, London: Mechanical Engineering Publ.

231. _____. 1980. Residual vibration criteria applied to multiple degree of freedom cam followers. *ASME Pap.* 80-*DET*-3.

232. Wildt, P. 1953. Zwanglaufige triebkurvenherstellung. Dusseldorf; VDI-Trgungsheft 1. pp.11-20.

233. Winfrey, R.C.; Anderson, R.V.; and Gnilka, C.W. 1973. Analysis of elastic machinery with clearances. *Trans. ASME, J. Eng. Ind.* 95B (3): 695-703.

234. Wolford, J.C., and Kersten, L. 1975. On the optimum b valve for a modified trapezoidal indexing cam. Paper read at Proc. of the Fourth Appl. Mechanism Conference, Chicago, Illinois. Paper No. 30.

235. Young, D.S., and Shoup, T.E. 1980. The sensitivity analysis of cam mechanism dynamics. *ASME Pap.* 80-*DET*-93.

236. Young, V.C. 1974. Considerations in valve gear design. *SAE Q. Trans.* 1: 359-365.

237. Zigo, M. 1967. A general numerical procedure for the calculation of cam profiles from arbitrarily specified acceleration curves. *J. Mech.* 2 (4): 407-413.

238. Buckingham, E., and Talbourdet, G.J. 1950. Recent roll tests on endurance limits of materials. In *ASM Conference on Mechanical Wear*, pp. 289. MIT.

239. Falk, S. 1963. Das verfahren von Rayleigh-Ritz mit hermiteschen interpolations polynomen. *ZAMM.*

240. Hertz, H. Über die Beruhrüng fester elastischer Körper (1881); Über die Berubrüng fester elastischer Körper ünd über die Harte (1882).

241. Kepler, H.B. 1960. *Basic graphical kinematics,* New York: McGraw–Hill.

242. Lundberg, G., and Odgvist, F.K.G. 1932. Studies on stress distributions in the vicinity of the contact region between bodies with applications. *Ing. Vetensk. Akad. Handl.* 116.

243. Schimmel, W.B. 1962. Evaluation of symmetric polynomial coefficients. In *Trans. of the 7th Conference on Mechanisms,* pp. 186-189. Purdue University. Lafayette, Indiana.

244. Shigley, I.E. 1961. *Theory of machines,* McGraw-Hill. New York Eq. 16-3(c), Chapter 6, p. 117.

245. Thomas, H.R., and Hoersch. 1930 Stresses due to the pressure of one elastic solid upon another. *Univ. Ill. Eng. Exp. St. Bull.* 212.

246. Vandergraft, J.S. 1978. *Introduction to numerical computations.* New York: Academic Press.

247. Varnum, E.C. 1951. Circular nomogram theory and construction technique. *Prod. Eng.* Aug., 152-156.

APPENDIX A
TABLES OF CAM CURVES

Table A1. Harmonic Factors

Table A2. Cycloidal Factors

Table A3. Modified Trapezoid Factors

Table A4. Modified Sine Factors

Table A1. Harmonic Factors

Pt.	K	Cv	Ca	Pt.	K	Cv	Ca	Pt.	K	Cv	Ca	Pt.	K	Cv	Ca
0	0.00000	0.0000	4.9348	30	0.14644	1.1107	3.4895	60	0.50000	1.5708	0.0000	90	0.85356	1.1107	-3.4895
1	0.00017	0.0411	4.9331	31	0.15582	1.1394	3.3969	61	0.51309	1.5703	-0.1292	91	0.86269	1.0813	-3.5796
2	0.00069	0.0822	4.9281	32	0.16543	1.1673	3.3020	62	0.52617	1.5686	-0.2582	92	0.87157	1.0511	-3.6673
3	0.00154	0.1232	4.9196	33	0.17527	1.1945	3.2049	63	0.53923	1.5660	-0.3872	93	0.88021	1.0202	-3.7525
4	0.00274	0.1642	4.9078	34	0.18543	1.2207	3.1056	64	0.55227	1.5622	-0.5158	94	0.88858	0.9985	-3.8351
5	0.00428	0.2050	4.8926	35	0.19562	1.2462	3.0041	65	0.56527	1.5574	-0.6441	95	0.89668	0.9562	-3.9150
6	0.00615	0.2457	4.8741	36	0.20611	1.2865	2.9006	66	0.57822	1.5515	-0.7719	96	0.90451	0.9233	-3.9924
7	0.00837	0.2862	4.8522	37	0.21679	1.2945	2.7951	67	0.59112	1.5469	-0.8993	97	0.91207	0.8897	-4.0669
8	0.01092	0.3266	4.8270	38	0.22768	1.3174	2.6877	68	0.60396	1.5365	-1.0260	98	0.91934	0.8555	-4.1387
9	0.01381	0.3667	4.7985	39	0.23875	1.3393	2.5784	69	0.61672	1.5274	-1.1520	99	0.92632	0.8207	-4.2076
10	0.01704	0.4066	4.7666	40	0.25000	1.3604	2.4674	70	0.62941	1.5173	-1.2772	100	0.93302	0.7854	-4.2737
11	0.02059	0.4461	4.7316	41	0.26142	1.3804	2.3547	71	0.64201	1.5061	-1.4015	101	0.93941	0.7495	-4.3368
12	0.02447	0.4854	4.6933	42	0.27300	1.3996	2.2404	72	0.65451	1.4939	-1.5250	102	0.94550	0.7131	-4.3970
13	0.02868	0.5243	4.6518	43	0.28474	1.4178	2.1245	73	0.66691	1.4807	-1.6473	103	0.95129	0.6762	-4.4541
14	0.03321	0.5629	4.6071	44	0.29663	1.4350	2.0072	74	0.67919	1.4665	-1.7685	104	0.95677	0.6389	-4.5082
15	0.03806	0.6011	4.5592	45	0.30866	1.4564	1.8884	75	0.69134	1.4564	-1.8884	105	0.96194	0.6011	-4.5592
16	0.04323	0.6389	4.5082	46	0.32081	1.4665	1.7685	76	0.70337	1.4350	-2.0072	106	0.96679	0.5629	-4.6071
17	0.04871	0.6762	4.4541	47	0.33309	1.4807	1.6473	77	0.71526	1.4178	-2.1245	107	0.97132	0.5243	-4.6518
18	0.05450	0.7131	4.3970	48	0.34549	1.4939	1.5250	78	0.72700	1.3996	-2.2404	108	0.97553	0.4854	-4.6933
19	0.06059	0.7495	4.3368	49	0.35799	1.5061	1.4015	79	0.73858	1.3804	-2.3547	109	0.97941	0.4461	-4.7316
20	0.06698	0.7854	4.2737	50	0.37059	1.5173	1.2772	80	0.75000	1.3604	-2.4674	110	0.98296	0.4066	-4.7666
21	0.07368	0.8207	4.2076	51	0.38328	1.5274	1.1520	81	0.76125	1.3393	-2.5784	111	0.98619	0.3667	-4.7985
22	0.08066	0.8555	4.1387	52	0.39604	1.5365	1.0260	82	0.77232	1.3174	-2.6877	112	0.98908	0.3266	-4.8270
23	0.08793	0.8897	4.0669	53	0.40888	1.5469	0.8993	83	0.78321	1.2945	-2.7951	113	0.99163	0.2862	-4.8522
24	0.09549	0.9233	3.9924	54	0.42178	1.5515	0.7719	84	0.79389	1.2865	-2.9006	114	0.99385	0.2457	-4.8741
25	0.10332	0.9562	3.9150	55	0.43478	1.5574	0.6441	85	0.80438	1.2462	-3.0041	115	0.99572	0.2050	-4.8926
26	0.11142	0.9985	3.8351	56	0.44773	1.5622	0.5158	86	0.81466	1.2207	-3.1056	116	0.99726	0.1642	-4.9078
27	0.11979	1.0202	3.7525	57	0.46077	1.5660	0.3872	87	0.82473	1.1945	-3.2049	117	0.99846	0.1232	-4.9196
28	0.12843	1.0511	3.6673	58	0.47383	1.5686	0.2583	88	0.83457	1.1673	-3.3020	118	0.99931	0.0822	-4.9281
29	0.13731	1.0813	3.5796	59	0.48691	1.5703	0.1292	89	0.84418	1.1394	-3.3969	119	0.99983	0.0411	-4.9331
30	0.14644	1.1107	3.4895	60	0.50000	1.5708	0.0000	90	0.85356	1.1107	-3.4895	120	1.00000	0.0000	-4.9348

484

Table A2. Cycloidal Factors

Pt.	K	Cv	Ca	Pt.	K	Cv	Ca	Pt.	K	Cv	Ca	Pt.	K	Cv	Ca
0	0.000000	0.0000	0.0000	30	0.09085	1.0000	6.2832	60	0.50000	2.0000	0.0000	90	0.90915	1.0000	-6.2832
1	0.00001	0.0014	0.3289	31	0.09940	1.0523	6.2746	61	0.51666	1.9986	-0.3289	91	0.91726	0.9477	-6.2746
2	0.00003	0.0055	0.6568	32	0.10839	1.1045	6.2488	62	0.53331	1.9945	-0.6568	92	0.92495	0.8955	-6.2488
3	0.00010	0.0123	0.9829	33	0.11781	1.1564	6.2059	63	0.54990	1.9877	-0.9829	93	0.93219	0.8436	-6.2059
4	0.00024	0.0218	1.3063	34	0.12766	1.2079	6.1459	64	0.56642	1.9782	-1.3063	94	0.93900	0.7921	-6.1459
5	0.00048	0.0341	1.6262	35	0.13794	1.2588	6.0691	65	0.58286	1.9659	-1.6262	95	0.94540	0.7412	-6.0691
6	0.00082	0.0489	1.9416	36	0.14864	1.3090	5.9757	66	0.59918	1.9511	-1.9416	96	0.95136	0.6910	-5.9757
7	0.00130	0.0664	2.2517	37	0.15975	1.3584	5.8659	67	0.61536	1.9336	-2.2517	97	0.95691	0.6416	-5.8659
8	0.00194	0.0865	2.5556	38	0.17128	1.4067	5.7400	68	0.63140	1.9135	-2.5556	98	0.96206	0.5933	-5.7400
9	0.00275	0.1090	2.8525	39	0.18320	1.4540	5.5984	69	0.64725	1.8910	-2.8525	99	0.96680	0.5460	-5.5984
10	0.00375	0.1340	3.1416	40	0.19550	1.5000	5.4414	70	0.66291	1.8660	-3.1416	100	0.97116	0.5000	-5.4414
11	0.00499	0.1613	3.4221	41	0.20820	1.5446	5.2695	71	0.67835	1.8387	-3.4221	101	0.97514	0.4554	-5.2695
12	0.00645	0.1910	3.6931	42	0.22124	1.5878	5.0832	72	0.69355	1.8090	-3.6931	102	0.97876	0.4122	-5.0832
13	0.00817	0.2228	3.9541	43	0.23465	1.6293	4.8830	73	0.70849	1.7772	-3.9541	103	0.98201	0.3707	-4.8830
14	0.01018	0.2569	4.2043	44	0.24840	1.6691	4.6693	74	0.72316	1.7431	-4.2043	104	0.98494	0.3309	-4.6693
15	0.01246	0.2929	4.4429	45	0.26246	1.7071	4.4429	75	0.73754	1.7071	-4.4429	105	0.98754	0.2929	-4.4429
16	0.01506	0.3309	4.6693	46	0.27684	1.7431	4.2043	76	0.75160	1.6691	-4.6693	106	0.98982	0.2569	-4.2043
17	0.01799	0.3707	4.8830	47	0.29151	1.7772	3.9541	77	0.76535	1.6293	-4.8830	107	0.99183	0.2228	-3.9541
18	0.02124	0.4122	5.0832	48	0.30645	1.8090	3.6931	78	0.77876	1.5878	-5.0832	108	0.99355	0.1910	-3.6931
19	0.02486	0.4554	5.2695	49	0.32165	1.8387	3.4221	79	0.79180	1.5446	-5.2695	109	0.99501	0.1613	-3.4221
20	0.02884	0.5000	5.4414	50	0.33709	1.8660	3.1416	80	0.80450	1.5000	-5.4414	110	0.99625	0.1340	-3.1416
21	0.03320	0.5460	5.5984	51	0.35275	1.8910	2.8525	81	0.81680	1.4540	-5.5984	111	0.99725	0.1090	-2.8525
22	0.03794	0.5933	5.7400	52	0.36860	1.9135	2.5556	82	0.82872	1.4067	-5.7400	112	0.99806	0.0865	-2.5556
23	0.04309	0.6416	5.8659	53	0.38464	1.9336	2.2517	83	0.84025	1.3584	-5.8659	113	0.99870	0.0664	-2.2517
24	0.04864	0.6910	5.9757	54	0.40082	1.9511	1.9416	84	0.85136	1.3090	-5.9757	114	0.99918	0.0489	-1.9416
25	0.05460	0.7412	6.0691	55	0.41714	1.9659	1.6262	85	0.86206	1.2588	-6.0691	115	0.99952	0.0341	-1.6262
26	0.06100	0.7921	6.1459	56	0.43358	1.9782	1.3063	86	0.87234	1.2079	-6.1459	116	0.99976	0.0218	-1.3063
27	0.06781	0.8436	6.2059	57	0.45010	1.9877	0.9829	87	0.88219	1.1564	-6.2059	117	0.99990	0.0123	-0.9829
28	0.07505	0.8955	6.2488	58	0.46669	1.9945	0.6568	88	0.89161	1.1045	-6.2488	118	0.99997	0.0055	-0.6568
29	0.08274	0.9477	6.2746	59	0.48334	1.9986	0.3289	89	0.90060	1.0523	-6.2746	119	0.99999	0.0014	-0.3289
30	0.09085	1.0000	6.2832	60	0.50000	2.0000	0.0000	90	0.90915	1.0000	-6.2832	120	1.00000	0.0000	0.0000

485

Table A3. Modified Trapezoid Factors

Pt.	K	Cv	Ca	Pt.	K	Cv	Ca	Pt.	K	Cv	Ca	Pt.	K	Cv	Ca
0	0.00000	0.0000	0.0000	30	0.10451	1.0000	4.8881	60	0.50000	2.0000	0.0000	90	0.89549	1.0000	-4.8881
1	0.00001	0.0021	0.5110	31	0.11300	1.0407	4.8881	61	0.51667	1.9979	-0.5110	91	0.90370	0.9593	-4.8881
2	0.00005	0.0085	1.0163	32	0.12181	1.0815	4.8881	62	0.53328	1.9915	-1.0163	92	0.91153	0.9185	-4.8881
3	0.00016	0.0190	1.5105	33	0.13100	1.1222	4.8881	63	0.54985	1.9810	-1.5105	93	0.91900	0.8778	-4.8881
4	0.00037	0.0336	1.9882	34	0.14053	1.1629	4.8881	64	0.56623	1.9664	-1.9882	94	0.92614	0.8371	-4.8881
5	0.00073	0.0521	2.4440	35	0.15036	1.2037	4.8881	65	0.58255	1.9479	-2.4440	95	0.93294	0.7963	-4.8881
6	0.00120	0.0743	2.8731	36	0.16057	1.2444	4.8881	66	0.59873	1.9257	-2.8731	96	0.93939	0.7556	-4.8881
7	0.00198	0.0999	3.2708	37	0.17113	1.2851	4.8881	67	0.61467	1.9001	-3.2708	97	0.94555	0.7149	-4.8881
8	0.00293	0.1287	3.6326	38	0.18203	1.3259	4.8881	68	0.63036	1.8713	-3.6326	98	0.95136	0.6741	-4.8881
9	0.00413	0.1604	3.9546	39	0.19323	1.3666	4.8881	69	0.64586	1.8396	-3.9546	99	0.95679	0.6334	-4.8881
10	0.00561	0.1945	4.2333	40	0.20471	1.4073	4.8881	70	0.66101	1.8055	-4.2333	100	0.96187	0.5927	-4.2333
11	0.00738	0.2308	4.4655	41	0.21669	1.4481	4.8881	71	0.67592	1.7693	-4.4655	101	0.96666	0.5519	-4.4655
12	0.00946	0.2688	4.6489	42	0.22891	1.4888	4.8881	72	0.69053	1.7312	-4.6489	102	0.97106	0.5112	-4.6489
13	0.01186	0.3081	4.7813	43	0.24147	1.5295	4.8881	73	0.70476	1.6919	-4.7813	103	0.97517	0.4705	-4.7813
14	0.01460	0.3483	4.8613	44	0.25443	1.5703	4.8881	74	0.71873	1.6517	-4.8613	104	0.97894	0.4297	-4.8613
15	0.01767	0.3890	4.8881	45	0.26767	1.6110	4.8881	75	0.73233	1.6110	-4.8881	105	0.98233	0.3890	-4.8881
16	0.02106	0.4297	4.8881	46	0.28126	1.6517	4.8613	76	0.74557	1.5703	-4.8881	106	0.98540	0.3483	-4.8613
17	0.02483	0.4705	4.8881	47	0.29524	1.6919	4.7813	77	0.75853	1.5295	-4.8881	107	0.98814	0.3081	-4.7813
18	0.02894	0.5112	4.8881	48	0.30947	1.7312	4.6489	78	0.77109	1.4888	-4.8881	108	0.99054	0.2688	-4.6489
19	0.03334	0.5519	4.8881	49	0.32408	1.7693	4.4655	79	0.78331	1.4481	-4.8881	109	0.99262	0.2308	-4.4655
20	0.03813	0.5927	4.8881	50	0.33899	1.8055	4.2333	80	0.79529	1.4073	-4.8881	110	0.99439	0.1945	-4.2333
21	0.04321	0.6334	4.8881	51	0.35414	1.8396	3.9546	81	0.80677	1.3666	-4.8881	111	0.99587	0.1604	-3.9546
22	0.04864	0.6741	4.8881	52	0.36964	1.8713	3.6326	82	0.81797	1.3259	-4.8881	112	0.99707	0.1287	-3.6326
23	0.05445	0.7149	4.8881	53	0.38533	1.9001	3.2708	83	0.82887	1.2851	-4.8881	113	0.99802	0.0999	-3.2708
24	0.06061	0.7556	4.8881	54	0.40127	1.9257	2.8731	84	0.83943	1.2444	-4.8881	114	0.99874	0.0743	-2.8731
25	0.06706	0.7963	4.8881	55	0.41745	1.9479	2.4440	85	0.84964	1.2037	-4.8881	115	0.99927	0.0521	-2.4440
26	0.07386	0.8371	4.8881	56	0.43377	1.9664	1.9882	86	0.85947	1.1629	-4.8881	116	0.99963	0.0336	-1.9882
27	0.08100	0.8778	4.8881	57	0.45015	1.9810	1.5105	87	0.86900	1.1222	-4.8881	117	0.99984	0.0190	-1.5105
28	0.08847	0.9185	4.8881	58	0.46672	1.9915	1.0163	88	0.87819	1.0815	-4.8881	118	0.99995	0.0085	-1.0163
29	0.09630	0.9593	4.8881	59	0.48333	1.9979	0.5110	89	0.88700	1.0407	-4.8881	119	0.99999	0.0021	-0.5110
30	0.10451	1.0000	4.8881	60	0.50000	2.0000	0.0000	90	0.89549	1.0000	-4.8881	120	1.00000	0.0000	0.0000

Table A4. Modified Sine Factors

Pt.	K	Cv	Ca	Pt.	K	Cv	Ca	Pt.	K	Cv	Ca	Pt.	K	Cv	Ca
0	0.00000	0.0000	0.0000	30	0.11718	1.0997	4.7874	60	0.50000	1.7596	0.0000	90	0.88282	1.0997	-4.7874
1	0.00000	0.0024	0.5778	31	0.12650	1.1392	4.6380	61	0.51466	1.7588	-0.1929	91	0.89182	1.0594	-4.8809
2	0.00005	0.0096	1.1493	32	0.13616	1.1778	4.5829	62	0.52931	1.7564	-0.3856	92	0.90048	1.0184	-4.9685
3	0.00018	0.0215	1.7082	33	0.14613	1.2156	4.4722	63	0.54393	1.7523	-0.5778	93	0.90880	0.9767	-5.0501
4	0.00042	0.0380	2.2484	34	0.15642	1.2524	4.3561	64	0.55851	1.7467	-0.7693	94	0.91676	0.9343	-5.1255
5	0.00083	0.0589	2.7640	35	0.16701	1.2882	4.2347	65	0.57304	1.7395	-0.9599	95	0.92436	0.8912	-5.1946
6	0.00142	0.0840	3.2493	36	0.17788	1.3229	4.1081	66	0.58750	1.7307	-1.1493	96	0.93161	0.8477	-5.2574
7	0.00224	0.1130	3.6989	37	0.18905	1.3566	3.9765	67	0.60178	1.7204	-1.3373	97	0.93849	0.8036	-5.3138
8	0.00331	0.1455	4.1081	38	0.20049	1.3892	3.8401	68	0.61617	1.7084	-1.5237	98	0.94500	0.7592	-5.3638
9	0.00467	0.1813	4.4723	39	0.21220	1.4206	3.6989	69	0.63035	1.6950	-1.7082	99	0.95114	0.7143	-5.4072
10	0.00634	0.2199	4.7874	40	0.22417	1.4508	3.5553	70	0.64442	1.6800	-1.8907	100	0.95690	0.6691	-5.4440
11	0.00834	0.2610	5.0501	41	0.23638	1.4798	3.4034	71	0.65835	1.6635	-2.0708	101	0.96229	0.6236	-5.4742
12	0.01069	0.3040	5.2574	42	0.24883	1.5075	3.2493	72	0.67214	1.6455	-2.2484	102	0.96730	0.5778	-5.4977
13	0.01341	0.3484	5.4072	43	0.26150	1.5340	3.0912	73	0.68577	1.6260	-2.4233	103	0.97192	0.5320	-5.5145
14	0.01650	0.3939	5.4977	44	0.27439	1.5590	2.9294	74	0.69924	1.6051	-2.5952	104	0.97611	0.4860	-5.5246
15	0.01998	0.4399	5.5280	45	0.28748	1.5828	2.7640	75	0.71252	1.5828	-2.7640	105	0.98002	0.4399	-5.5280
16	0.02389	0.4860	5.5246	46	0.30076	1.6051	2.5952	76	0.72561	1.5590	-2.9294	106	0.98350	0.3939	-5.4977
17	0.02808	0.5320	5.5145	47	0.31423	1.6260	2.4233	77	0.73850	1.5340	-3.0912	107	0.98659	0.3484	-5.4072
18	0.03270	0.5778	5.4977	48	0.32786	1.6455	2.2484	78	0.75117	1.5075	-3.2493	108	0.98931	0.3040	-5.2574
19	0.03771	0.6236	5.4742	49	0.34165	1.6635	2.0708	79	0.76362	1.4798	-3.403	109	0.99166	0.2610	-5.0501
20	0.04310	0.6691	5.4440	50	0.35558	1.6800	1.8907	80	0.77583	1.4508	-3.5553	110	0.99366	0.2199	-4.7874
21	0.04886	0.7143	5.4072	51	0.36965	1.6950	1.7082	81	0.78780	1.4206	-3.6989	111	0.99533	0.1813	-4.4722
22	0.05500	0.7592	5.3638	52	0.38383	1.7084	1.5237	82	0.79951	1.3892	-3.8401	112	0.99669	0.1455	-4.1081
23	0.06151	0.8036	5.3138	53	0.39812	1.7204	1.3373	83	0.81095	1.3566	-3.9765	113	0.99776	0.1130	-3.6989
24	0.06839	0.8477	5.2574	54	0.41250	1.7307	1.1493	84	0.82212	1.3229	-4.1081	114	0.99858	0.0840	-3.2493
25	0.07564	0.8912	5.1946	55	0.42696	1.7395	0.9599	85	0.83299	1.2882	-4.2347	115	0.99917	0.0589	-2.7640
26	0.08324	0.9343	5.1255	56	0.44149	1.7467	0.7693	86	0.84358	1.2524	-4.3561	116	0.99958	0.0380	-2.2484
27	0.09120	0.9767	5.0501	57	0.45607	1.7523	0.5778	87	0.85387	1.2156	-4.4722	117	0.99982	0.0215	-1.7082
28	0.09952	1.0184	4.9685	58	0.47069	1.7564	0.3856	88	0.86384	1.1778	-4.5829	118	0.99995	0.0096	-1.1493
29	0.10818	1.0594	4.8809	59	0.48534	1.7588	0.1929	89	0.87350	1.1392	-4.6680	119	1.00000	0.0024	-0.5778
30	0.11718	1.0997	4.7874	60	0.50000	1.7596	0.0000	90	0.88282	1.0997	-4.7874	120	1.00000	0.0000	0.0000

APPENDIX B
LISTING OF FORTRAN PROGRAMS

The following FORTRAN programs are developed and fully listed in this appendix

FDSYN1   (Finite-Difference SYNthesis 1)

FDSYN2   (Finite-Difference SYNthesis 2)

FINTG   (Finite-INTeGration)

PARAD   (Pressure Angle and RADius of curvature)

CAMPA   (CAM Pressure Angle)

RAD1   (RADius of curvature 1)

RAD2   (RADius of curvature 2)

TRESP   (Time RESPonse)

SPEC1   (SPECtra 1)

SPEC2   (SPECtra 2)

SPEC3   (SPECtra 3)

The essential ingredients of the above listed programs (method of solution, input, output, and subroutines used) are contained in the individual program.

```
C
C
C          PROGRAM FDSYN1
C
C
C          BY F. Y. CHEN
C
C
C              NUMERICAL SYNTHESIS OF CAM DISPLACEMENT FROM A PRESCRIBED
C          ACCELERATION PATTERN USING FINITE-DIFFERENCE MATHEMATICAL
C          INDUCTION FORMULA.
C
C              IN THIS PROGRAM, SIMPLE-HARMONIC MOTION IS TESTED BY THIS
C          NUMERICAL SYNTHESIS METHOD AND THEN COMPARED THE RESULTS OBTAINED
C          WITH THE EXACT SOLUTION. THE EXACT MOTION CALLS FOR KNOWING THE
C          KINEMATIC EQUATIONS OF SIMPLE-HARMONIC MOTION.
C
C              THE OUTPUTS TABULATE THE GIVEN VALUES OF CAM ACCELERATION AND
C          THE SYNTHESIZED VALUES OF CAM DISPLACEMENT AS A FUNCTION OF CAM
C          ROTATIONAL ANGLE THETA.
C
C              INPUT DATA CONTAIN THE INITIAL VALUE OF CAM DISPLACEMENT YO
C          FINAL VALUE OF CAM DISPLACEMENT YN, TOTAL ANGULAR DISPLACEMENT OF
C          CAMSHAFT BETA IN DEGREES, ANGULAR VELOCITY OF THE CAMSHAFT IN RPM,
C          AND THE ANGULAR INCREMENT INCR IN DEGREES, WITH (5F10.5) FORMAT.
C
           REAL INCR,INCRE
           DIMENSION YI(200),YID(200),YIDD(200),YIPP(200)
           DIMENSION Y(200),THETA(200),ERROR(200)
           READ(5,5)MM
         5 FORMAT(I2)
           DO 110 M=1,MM
C
C          READ INPUT DATA
C
           READ(5,10)YO,YN,BETA,THAD,INCR
        10 FORMAT(5F10.5)
C
C          PRINTOUT GIVEN DATA
C
           WRITE(6,21)
        21 FORMAT(1H1,/////,'THE GIVEN DATA ARE')
           WRITE(6,20)YO
        20 FORMAT(/,5X,'INITIAL READING OF THE ORDINATE',6X,'YO=',F10.6,1X,'I
          1NCHES')
           WRITE(6,22)YN
        22 FORMAT(/,5X,'FINAL READING OF THE ORDINATE',4X,'YN=',F10.6,1X,'INC
          1HES')
           WRITE(6,23)BETA
        23 FORMAT(/,5X,'TOTAL ANG. DISPL. OF CAMSHAFT',9X,'BETA=',F10.6,1X,'D
          1EGREES')
           WRITE(6,24)THAD
        24 FORMAT(/,5X,'ANG. VELOCITY OF THE CAMSHAFT',9X,'THAD=',F7.2,1X,'RP
          1M')
           WRITE(6,25)INCR
        25 FORMAT(/,5X,'THE ANGULAR INCREMENT',6X,'INCREMENT=',F5.2,1X,'DEGRE
          1ES')
C
C          COMPUTE THE CAM DISPLACEMENT PROFILES BY USING
```

```
C       INDUCTION FORMULA FINITE DIFFERENCE
C
        PI=3.14159265
        CF1=0.01745329
        DELX=INCR/(6.*THAD)
        BETAR=BETA*CF1
        INCRE=INCR*CF1
        THET=THAD*PI/30.
        DELTA=YN-YO
        N=(BETA/INCR)+.01
        PARMA=PI/BETAR
        THETA(1)=INCRE
        THEO=0.
        ACCEL=DELTA*((PARMA*THET)**2.)/2.
        VEL=0.
        ACCEL=0.
        DISP=YO
        DISPR=YO
        ERRO=0.
        DO 30 I=1,N
        ARG=PARMA*THETA(I)
        YI(I)=0.5*DELTA*(1.-COS(ARG))
        YID(I)=(0.5*DELTA*PI*THET/BETAR)*SIN(ARG)
        YIDD(I)=((0.5*DELTA*PI*PI*THET*THET)/(BETAR*BETAR))*COS(ARG)
        YIPP(I)=YIDD(I)*(DELX**2)
        III=I+1
        THETA(III)=THETA(I)+INCRE
30      CONTINUE
        PARMB=((N*YO)+DELTA)/N
        TOTAL=0.
        DO 40 JJ=1,N
        SUM=(N-JJ)*YIPP(JJ)
        TOTAL=TOTAL+SUM
40      CONTINUE
        Y(1)=PARMB-(TOTAL/N)
        DO 50 KK=2,N
        L=KK-1
        TOTA = 0.
        DO 60 K=1,L
        SUMA=(KK-K)*YIPP(K)
        TOTA=TOTA+SUMA
60      CONTINUE
        Y(KK)=((1-KK)*YO)+(KK*Y(1))+TOTA
50      CONTINUE
        DO 70 II=1,N
        ERROR(II)=YI(II)-Y(II)
70      CONTINUE
C
C       PRINTOUT THE SYNTHESISED PROFILES
C
        WRITE(6,80)
80      FORMAT(////,7X,'CAM',7X,'ACCEL.',3X,'VELOCITY',3X,'DISPL.',5X,'DIS
       1PL.',6X,'ERROR',/,6X,'ANGLE',35X,'(EXACT)',1X,'(SYNTHESIZED)',//,7
       2X,'DEG',5X,'IN/SEC**2',2X,'IN/SEC',4X,'INCH',7X,'INCH',7X,'INCH',/
       3,6X,61(1H-))
        WRITE(6,90)THEO,ACCEL,VEL,DISP,DISPR,ERRO
90      FORMAT(/,6X,F5.2,2X,F11.4,2X,F7.4,3(3X,F8.6))
        DO 110 I=1,N
        THETA(I)=THETA(I)*180./PI
        WRITE(6,90)THETA(I),YIDD(I),YID(I),YI(I),Y(I),ERROR(I)
110     CONTINUE
        STOP
        END
```

```
C
C      PROGRAM FDSYN2
C
C
C      BY F. Y. CHEN
C
C
C      NUMERICAL SYNTHESIS OF CAM PROFILE FOR A PRESCRIBED
C      ACCELERATION PATTERN BASED ON A REFINED FINITE-DIFFERENCE
C      ALGORITHM. THE SCHEME IS BASED ON DIFFERENTIATION OF STIRLING
C      INTERPOLATION FORMULA, THEREBY REFINING THE PRESCRIBED INITIAL
C      ACCELERATION DATA SO THAT THEY WILL BE CORRECT TO DIFFERENCE OF
C      HIGH ORDER.
C
C         IN THIS PROGRAM, CYCLOIDAL MOTION IS TESTED BY THE METHOD AND
C      THEN COMPARED THE RESULTS OBTAINED WITH THE MATHEMATICALLY EXACT
C      CYCLOIDAL SOLUTION.
C
C         THE OUTPUTS INCLUDE (1) A CENTRAL-DIFFERENCE TABLE, (2) A
C      TABLE OF MODIFIED VALUES OF INITIAL ACCELERATION DATA AND (3)
C      SYNTHESIZED VALUES OF CAM PROFILE AS A FUNCTION OF CAM ROTATIONAL
C      ANGLE THETA
C
C         INPUT THE NUMBER OF DATA POINT N AND THE VALUE OF THE
C      ACCELERATION WITH (I5/(4F10.0)) FORMAT.
C
       DIMENSION F(20,20),G(20,20)
       DIMENSION SUM(20),GM(20,20)
C
C      READ THE INPUT ACCELERATION PATTERN
C
       READ(5,99) N,(F(1,I),I=1,N)
   99  FORMAT(I5/(4F10.6))
       WRITE(6,133)
  133  FORMAT(1H1,48X,'DIFFERENCE TABLE',///)
       WRITE(6,130)
  130  FORMAT(10X,'Y',8X,'DY',7X,'(D**2)Y',3X,'(D**3)Y',3X,'(D**4)Y',3X,'
      1(D**5)Y',3X,'(D**6)Y',3X,'(D**7)Y',3X,'(D**8)Y',3X,'(D**9)Y',3X,'(
      2D**10)Y',/,6X,110(1H-),//)
C
C      COMPUTE THE COEFFICIENTS OF THE MODIFIED ACCELERATION
C      PATTERN  BASED ON NEWTON:S INTERPOLATION
C
       DO 10 K=2,N
       M=N+1-K
       DO 10 I=1,M
       F(K,I)=F(K-1,I+1)-F(K-1,I)
       G(1,I)=F(1,I)
       G(3,I)=F(3,I)/12.
       G(5,I)=F(5,I)/(-240.)
       G(7,I)=F(7,I)*31./60480.
       G(9,I)=F(9,I)*(-289./3628800.)
   10  G(11,I)=F(11,I)*6657./479001600.
C
C      COMPUTE AND PRINT TABLE OF DIFFERENCES
C
       DO 20 I=1,N
       L=I-1
       M=N+1-I
   20  WRITE(6,104) (F(K,I),K=1,M)
  104  FORMAT(5X,11F10.6)
C
C      PRINT THE MODIFIED ACCELERATION PATTERN. THE
C      :SUM: COLUMN REPRESENTS THE MODIFIED ACCEL.
C
       WRITE(6,132)
  132  FORMAT(////,45X,'MODIFIED DIFFERENCE TABLE',///)
       WRITE(6,131)
  131  FORMAT(9X,'SUM',14X,'Y',9X,'+1/12(D**2)Y',3X,'-1/240(D**2)Y',2X,'+
      162/3.8I(D**6)Y',2X,'-289/10I(D**8)Y',2X,'+6657/12I(D**10)Y',/,6X,1
      210(1H-),//)
       LAA=0
       MAA=N
       JKA=1
       DO 118 JJA=1,11,2
       DO 119 KKA=1,MAA
       KMA=KKA+LAA
```

```
119 GM(JJA,KMA)=G(JJA,KKA)
    MAA=MAA-2
118 LAA=LAA+1
    KM=1
    DO 125 II=1,6
    SUMA=0.
    DO 127 JI=1,KM,2
127 SUMA=SUMA+GM(JI,II)
    KM=KM+2
125 SUM(II)=SUMA
    JII=9
    DO 124 II=7,11
    SUMA=0.
    DO 128 JI=1,JII,2
128 SUMA=SUMA+GM(JI,II)
    SUM(II)=SUMA
124 JII=JII-2
    NP=1
    DO 120 KAA=1,6
    WRITE(6,141) SUM(KAA),(GM(JAA,KAA),JAA=1,NP,2)
141 FORMAT(3(5X,F10.6),4(7X,F10.6))
120 NP=NP+2
    NPP=9
    DO 123 KAA=7,11
    WRITE(6,141) SUM(KAA),(GM(JAA,KAA),JAA=1,NPP,2)
123 NPP=NPP-2
    STOP
    END
```

```
C
C       PROGRAM FINTG
C
C
C       BY F. Y. CHEN
C
C
C           SYNTHESIS OF CAM PROFILES FOR PRESCRIBED ACCELERATION BY
C       FINITE INTEGRATION.
C
C           IN THIS METHOD, EVALUATION OF INTEGRAL EQUATION IS REDUCED TO
C       SUCCESSIVE MULTIPLICATIONS OF A SPECIALLY DERIVED INTEGRATING
C       MATRIX ON THE BASIS OF ONE-SIDED QUADRATURE FORMULAS. THE PROGRAM
C       AUTOMATICALLY GENERATES THIS INTEGRATING MATRIX.
C
C           IN THIS PROGRAM, THE DWELL-RISE-DWELL PORTION OF A CAM
C       PROFILE GOVERNED BY AN EIGHTH DEGREE POLYNOMIAL IS TESTED BY THE
C       SCHEME.
C
C           THE OUTPUTS TABULATE THE GIVEN VALUES OF CAM ACCELERATION AND
C       THE SYNTHESIZED VALUES OF CAM DISPLACEMENT AS A FUNCTION OF CAM
C       ANGLE THETA.
C
C           INPUT THE NUMBER OF DATA POINT N, GRID SIZE H AND THE VALUES
C       OF THE ACCELERATION WITH 8F10.6 FORMAT.
C
        DIMENSION A(20,20),AA(400),AN(20),X(20),B(20,20)
        EQUIVALENCE (A(1,1),AA(1))
        READ (5,200) N,H
    200 FORMAT(1I2,F10.6)
        READ(5,100) (AN(I),I=1,N)
    100 FORMAT(8F10.6)
C
C       GENERATION OF THE NUMERICAL INTEGRATION MATRICES
C
        DO 10 I=1,N
        DO 10 J=1,N
     10 A(I,J)=0
        A(2,1)=5.
        A(2,2)=8.
        A(2,3)=-1.
        A(3,1)=4.
        A(3,2)=16.
        A(3,3)=4.
        K=3
        M=K+2
        DO 11 I=4,N,2
        DO 12 J=1,M
        IF(J-K) 20,21,21
     20 A(I,J)=A(I-1,J)
        A(I+1,J)=A(I-1,J)
        GO TO 12
     21 J1=J-K+1
        A(I,J)=A(I-1,J)+A(2,J1)
        A(I+1,J)=A(I-1,J)+A(3,J1)
     12 CONTINUE
        K=M
     11 M=K+2
        DO 33 J=1,N
        DO 33 I=1,N
        K=(J-1)*N+I
        AA(K)=A(I,J)
     33 CONTINUE
C
C       PRINT THE OUTPUT RESULTS
C
        WRITE(6,25)
     25 FORMAT('1',36H THE NUMERICAL INTEGRATION MATRIX IS  //)
        DO 44 J=1,N
        WRITE(6,120) (AA((I-1)*N+J),I=1,N)
    120 FORMAT(19F7.1)
     44 CONTINUE
        CALL GMMUT (A,A,B,N,N,N)
        CALL GMMUT (B,AN,X,N,N,1)
        WRITE(6,35)
     35 FORMAT(////1X,6H ANGLE,5X,17H CAM ACCELERATION,10X,25HSYNTHESIZED
       1DISPLACEMENT //)
```

```
      DO 15 I=1,N
      NN=I-1
      X(I)=(X(I)*H**2)/144.
      WRITE(6,110)NN,AN(I),X(I)
110   FORMAT(6X,I5,10X,F10.6,10X,F15.6)
 15   CONTINUE
      STOP
      END

      SUBROUTINE GMMUT(A,B,R,N,M,L)
      DIMENSION A(1),B(1),R(1)
      IR=0
      IK=-M
      DO 10 K=1,L
      IK=IK+M
      DO 10 J=1,N
      IR=IR+1
      JI=J-N
      IB=IK
      R(IR)=0
      DO 10 I=1,M
      JI=JI+N
      IB=IB+1
 10   R(IR)=R(IR)+A(JI)*B(IB)
      RETURN
      END
```

```
C
C      PROGRAM PARAD
C
C      BY F. Y. CHEN
C
C          FINITE-DIFFERENCE  SCHEME  OF  NUMERICAL-DIFFERENTIATION
C      FOR COMPUTING PRESSURE ANGLE AND RADIUS OF CURVATURE OF ANY TYPE
C      OF PLATE CAMS, WHEN THE CAM MOTION IS SPECIFIED IN NUMERICAL FORM.
C
C          THIS PROGRAM SHOWS A TYPICAL CASE OF A CAM WITH RECIPROCATING
C      OFFSET ROLLER FOLLOWER. CYCLOIDAL MOTION IS COMPUTED BY USING THE
C      NUMERICAL  SCHEME   AND THEN COMPARED THE RESULTS OBTAINED WITH THE
C      EXACT SOLUTION. THE EXACT MOTION CALLS FOR KNOWING THE KINEMATIC
C      EQUATIONS OF CYCLOIDAL MOTION. PROGRAM USES SUBROUTINE DIFF FOR
C      GENERATING A FINITE-DIFFERENCE TABLE.
C
C          THE  OUTPUTS TABULATE THE  FIRST  ORDER AND SECOND ORDER
C      DERIVATIVES AS WELL AS THE CAM PRESSURE ANGLE AND RADIUS OF
C      CURVATURE AS A FUNCTION OF CAM ROTATIONAL ANGLE THETA IN BOTH
C      EXACT VALUES AND APPROXIMATE VALUES FOR THE PURPOSE OF COMPARISON.
C
C          INPUT CAM PROFILE IN NUMERICAL FORM WITH (F10.6) FORMAT.
C
       DIMENSION S(2), DS(2), DDS(2), ROA(2), F(40,10), PA(2)
C      READ CAM PROFILE
C
       DO 41 J=1,10
       DO 41 I=1,40
   41  F(I,J)=0.0
       READ (5,30) N
       K=2*N
       READ (5,31) (F(I,1),I=2,K,2)
   30  FORMAT (I2)
   31  FORMAT (8F10.6)
       WRITE (6,32)
   32  FORMAT (1H1,10X,'THETA',5X,'S',8X,'DS',7X,'(D**2)S',3X,
      <'(D**3)S',3X,'(D**4)S',3X,'(D**5)S',3X,'(D**6)S',3X,
      <'(D**7)S',3X,'(D**8)S',/,10X,100(1H-),//)
C
C      READ PRIME CIRCLE RADIUS R ,FOLLOWER OFFSET E, AND LIFT H
C
       READ (5,33) R,E,H
   33  FORMAT (3F10.6)
       BETA=N-1
C
C      CALL DIFF SUBROUTINE AND PRINT DEFFERENCE TABLE
C
       CALL DIFF (F,N)
       F(1,2)=-F(3,2)
       F(2*N+1,2)=-F(2*N-1,2)
       PI=6.283185
       WRITE (6,36)
   36  FORMAT ('1',27X,'HALF FACE WIDTH OF',26X,'RADIUS OF CURVATURE',
      <4X,'PRESSURE-ANGLE',/,33X,'FOLLOWER')
       WRITE (6,38)
   38  FORMAT (/,9X,'THETA',3X,'S',11X,2HS',8X,2HS',10X,
      <2HS",8X,2HS",9X,'ROA',7X,'ROA',10X,'PA',8X,'PA',//,
      <27X,'EXACT',5X,'APPROX',6X,'EXACT',5X,'APPRO',7X,'EXACT',
      <5X,'APPROX',6X,'EXACT',5X,'APPROX',//)
   40  FORMAT (/,9X,I3,F10.6,2X,4(2F10.6,2X))
       DO 35 J=1,N
       I=2*J
       L=J-1
       S(1)=F(I,1)
       ARG=PI*L/BETA
       DS(1)=((F(I-1,2)+F(I+1,2))/2.0-(F(I-1,4)+F(I+1,4))/12.0
      <     +(F(I-1,6)+F(I+1,6))/60.0)/H
       DDS(1)=(F(I,3)-F(I,5)/12.0+F(I,7)/90.0)/H**2
       S(2)=H/PI*(ARG-SIN(ARG))
       DS(2)=H/BETA*(1-COS(ARG))
       DDS(2)=PI*H/BETA/BETA*SIN(ARG)
       PA(1)=FCT1(S(1),DS(1),R,E)
       PA(2)=FCT1(S(2),DS(2),R,E)
       ROA(1)=FCT2(PA(1),S(1),DS(1),DDS(1),R,E)
       ROA(2)=FCT2(PA(2),S(2),DS(2),DDS(2),R,E)
       WRITE (6,40) L,S(1),DS(2),DS(1),DDS(2),DDS(1),ROA(2),ROA(1),
```

```
          <PA(2),PA(1)
       35 CONTINUE
          STOP
          END



          SUBROUTINE DIFF(F,N)
          DIMENSION F(40,10)
C
C         COMPUTE AND PRINT TABLE OF DIFFERENCES
C
          J=N
          IF(N .GT. 9) J=9
          DO 16 K=2,J
          KX=K+1
          M=2*N-K+1
          DO 16 I=KX,M,2
       16 F(I,K)=F(I+1,K-1)-F(I-1,K-1)
        1 FORMAT (25X,4(F10.6,10X))
        2 FORMAT (10X,I2,3X,5(F10.6,10X))
          M=2*N
          DO 44 I=2,M
          L=(I-2)/2
          II=I-1
          IF (II .GT. 9) II=9
          IF (((I-1).GT. N) .AND. (N .LE. 9)) II=2*N-I+1
          IF (((I-1).GT. (2*N-8)) .AND. (N .GT. 9)) II=2*N-I+1
          JJ=I/2
          KK=I-JJ*2
          IF (KK) 4,4,3
        4 WRITE (6,2) L, (F(I,K),K=1,II,2)
          GO TO 44
        3 WRITE (6,1) (F(I,K),K=2,II,2)
       44 CONTINUE
          RETURN
          END



          FUNCTION FCT1(X,X1,R,E)
C
C         CALCULATE PRESSURE   ANGLE
C
          A=X1-E
          B=X+SQRT(R*R-E*E)
          FCT1=ATAN(A/B)
          RETURN
          END
          FUNCTION FCT2(Y,X,X1,X2,R,E)
C
C         CALCULATE RADIUS OF CURVATURE
C
          B=X+SQRT(R*R-E*E)
          TAU=COS(Y)/B
          A=TAU*(1+TAU*(X1*SIN(Y)-X2*COS(Y)))
          FCT2=1/A
          RETURN
          END
```

```
C
C      PROGRAM CAMPA
C
C      BY F. Y. CHEN
C
C         THIS PROGRAM GENERATES THE PRESSURE ANGLE DESIGN CURVES
C      FOR CAMS WITH OSCILLATING ROLLER FOLLOWER SUITABLE FOR ANY INPUT
C      CAM PROFILE.
C
C         USE OF CALCOMP FOR AUTOMATIC PLOT. THE OUTPUT REPRESENTS THE
C      MAXIMUM PRESSURE ANGLE VERSUS TOTAL CAM ROTATIONAL RANGE.
C
C         PROGRAM SHOWS A TYPICAL CASE OF CYCLOIDAL MOTION WITH INPUT
C      PARAMETERS L/RO=1.5 FOR BOTH TAU=2 AND TAU=30.
C
       REAL L,LRO
       DIMENSION T(2),X(52),Y(52),BUF(5000)
       ARSIN(X)=ATAN(X/SQRT(1.-X**2))
       ARCOS(X)=(3.1415926/2.)-ATAN(X/SQRT(1.-X**2))
C
C
C      PRESSURE ANGLE ANALYSIS
C
C
       CALL PLOTS(BUF,20000,7)
       CALL PLOT(0.6,1.0,-3)
       T(1)=2.
       T(2)=30.
       PI=6.28315
       N=2
       L=0.5
       LRO=1.5
       RO=L/LRO
       CRO=LRO+.25
       X(52)=1.0
       X(51)=0.0
       Y(52)=10.0
       Y(51)=0.0
       DO 300 I=1,3
       C=CRO*RO
       DO 250 JJ=1,N
       BT=0.2
       TAUXX=T(JJ)/57.29578
       WRITE(6,395)
  395  FORMAT('1',1X,'THE CYCLOIDAL PRES ANGLE ANALYSIS')
       WRITE(6,10)LRO,CRO,T(JJ)
   10  FORMAT('0',1X,'FOR L/RO = ',F6.2/1X,'FOR C/RO = ',F6.2/1X,'TAU = '
      *,F6.2,' DEGREES'//8X,'B/T', 7X,'ALPHA'/)
       DO 200 J=1,50
       BETA=BT*TAUXX
       THETB=0.001
       AMAX=0.
   15  CONTINUE
C
C      CYCLOIDAL EQUATIONS
C
       S=TAUXX*(THETB-SIN(PI**THETB)/PI)
       V=TAUXX/BETA*(1-COS(PI*THETB))
```

```
C
C    END OF SPECIFIC MOTION EQUATIONS
C
400 GAMMA=S
    DDELT=V
    DELTO=ARCOS(((L**2)+(C**2)-(RO**2))/(2.*L*C))
    DELTA=DELTO+GAMMA
    R=SQRT((L**2)+(C**2)-(2.0*L*C*COS(DELTA)))
    SI=ARCOS(((C**2)+(R**2)-(L**2))/(2.0*R*C))
    A=ARSIN((C/R)*SIN(DELTA))
    G=(R**2)/(L*C*SIN(DELTA)*DDELT)
    D=((C**2)-(R**2)-(L**2))/(2.0*R*C*SIN(SI))
    B=ATAN(1./(G+D))
    ALPHA=-3.1415926/2.+A+B
    ALPHA=SQRT((ALPHA**2))
    IF(ALPHA-AMAX)25,25,20
 20 AMAX=ALPHA
 25 IF(1.-THETB)35,35,30
 30 THETB=THETB+.1
    GO TO 15
 35 AMAX=AMAX*57.29578
    WRITE(6,40)BT,AMAX
 40 FORMAT(1X,F10.3,1X,F10.3)
    IF(AMAX-80.0)155,150,150
150 AMAX=80.0
155 CONTINUE
    X(J)=BT
    Y(J)=AMAX
    BT=BT+.2
200 CONTINUE
    CALL PLOT(0.0,0.0,-3)
    CALL LINE(X,Y,50,1,0,0)
    CALL PLOT(0.0,0.0,3)
250 CONTINUE
    CRO=CRO+.25
300 CONTINUE
    CALL AXIS(0.0,0.0,'BETA/TAU (ROTATION TOWARD FROM PIVOT)',-35,5.0,
   <  0.0,X(51),X(52))
    CALL AXIS(0.0,0.0,'MAXIMUM PRESSURE ANGLE',22,8.0,90.0,Y(51),Y(52)
   <)
    CALL SYMBOL(0.8,-1.0,0.14,'CYCLOIDAL MOTION',0.0,16)
    STOP
    END
```

```
C
C
C       PROGRAM RAD1
C
C
C       BY F. Y. CHEN
C
C
C          GENERATE MINIMUM RADIUS OF CURVATURE DESIGN CURVES FOR CAMS
C       WITH RECIPROCATING ROLLER FOLLOWER AND FOR ANY CAM MOTION PROFILE.
C       PROGRAM SHOWS THE TYPICAL CASE OF SIMPLE-HARMONIC MOTION.
C
C          USE OF SUBROUTINE MMPLOT FOR PLOT. OUTPUT REPRESENTS A PLOT
C       DIMENSIONLESS RATIO BETWEEN BASE-CIRCLE RADIUS AND THE MINIMUM
C       RADIUS OF CURVATURE VERSUS TOTAL CAM ROTATIONAL RANGE.
C
C          INPUT TITLE IS WITH (12A1, 12A1) FORMAT AND BASE RADIUS WITH
C       (F10.4) FORMAT.
C
        DIMENSION X(85),Y(85),XL(12),YL(12)
        READ (5,10) XL,YL
   10   FORMAT(12A1,12A1)
        DO 1 J=1,2
        WRITE (6,33)
   33   FORMAT( '1')
        READ (5,5) R
    5   FORMAT(F10.4)
        K=0
        RAD=3.14159/180.
        DO 3 IBETA=5,400,5
        BETA=RAD*IBETA
        K=K+1
        RMIN=2000.
        DO 4 ITHE=1,361,5
        THETA=RAD*(ITHE-1)
        F0=(R/2.)*(1.-COS(3.14159*THETA/BETA))
        F1=((3.14159*R)/(2.*BETA))*(SIN(3.14159*THETA/BETA))
        F2=R*((3.14159**2)/(2.*(BETA**2)))*(COS(3.14159*THETA/BETA))
        RR1=((1.+F0)**2+F1**2)**1.5
        RR2=(1.+F0)**2+2.*(F1**2)-(1.+F0)*F2
        ROE=RR1/RR2
        ROE=ABS(ROE)
        IF(ROE-RMIN) 7,4,4
    7   RMIN=ROE
    4   CONTINUE
        Y(K)=RMIN
        X(K)=IBETA
    3   CONTINUE
        WRITE(6,30) (X(I),Y(I),I=1,80)
   30   FORMAT (2F15.5,10X,2F15.5)
        CALL MMPLOT(X,Y,80,1,XL,YL)
    1   CONTINUE
        STOP
        END
```

```
C
C     PROGRAM: RAD2
C
C     BY F. Y. CHEN
C
C        THIS PROGRAM GENERATES CURVES OF RADIUS OF CURVATURE FOR
C     CAMS WITH OSCILLATING ROLLER FOLLOWER SUITABLE FOR ANY INPUT CAM
C     PROFILE.
C
C        USE OF CALCOMP FOR AUTOMATIC PLOT. THE OUTPUT REPRESENTS A
C     PLOT OF DIMENSIONLESS RATIO BETWEEN THE MINIMUM RADIUS OF
C     CURVATURE AND BASE CIRCLE RADIUS VERSUS TOTAL CAM ROTATIONAL
C     RANGE.
C
C        PROGRAM SHOWS A TYPICAL CASE OF CYCLOIDAL MOTION WITH INPUT
C     PARAMETERS L/RO=1.5 FOR TAU=2, TAU=10, AND TAU=30.
C
      REAL L,LRO
      DIMENSION T(3),BUF(5000), X(52),Y(52)
      CALL PLOTS(BUF,20000,10,0)
      T(1)=2.
      T(2)=10.
      T(3)=30.
      X(51)=0.0
      Y(51)=0.0
      X(52)=1.0
      Y(52)=0.1
      N=3
      L=1.0
      LRO=1.5
      RO=L/LRO
      CRO=LRO+.25
      DO 200 J=1,2
      C=RO*CRO
      DO 300 KK=1,N
      TAUXX=T(KK)/57.29578
      BT=0.2
      WRITE(6,15)
15    FORMAT(1H1,10X,'L/RO',20X,'C/RO',20X,'TAU',/)
      WRITE(6,6) LRO,CRO,T(KK)
6     FORMAT(9X,F5.1,20X,F5.2,17X,F6.1)
      WRITE (6,7)
7     FORMAT(/,18X,'ROWMIN/RO',16X,'BETA/TAU',/)
      DO 400 JJ=1,50
      B=TAUXX*BT
      ROWM=1000.
      THETB=0.001
      DO 500 II=1,11
C
C     CYCLOIDAL MOTION
C
      GAM=TAUXX*(THETB-SIN(6.28315*THETB)/6.28315)
      DGDT=TAUXX/B*(1-COS(6.28315*THETB))
      DG2DT=6.28315*SIN(6.28315*THETB)/B/B*TAUXX
C
C
C     END OF SPECIFIC EQUATIONS
C
```

```
C   EQUATIONS FOR ROTATION AWAY FROM PIVOT
C
    DELTO=ARCOS((((L**2)+(C**2)-(RO**2))/(2.*L*C))
    DELT=DELTO+GAM
    R=SQRT((L**2)+(C**2)-(2.0*L*C*COS(DELT)))
    FPTH=(L*C/R)*DGDT*SIN(DELT)
    FDPTH=((L*C*SIN(DELT)*DG2DT)+(L*C*COS(DELT)*(DGDT**2))-(FPTH**2))/
   $R
    SI=ARCOS((((R**2)+(C**2)-(L**2))/(2.0*R*C))
    DSDR=((C**2)-(R**2)-(L**2))/(2.*(R**2)*C*SIN(SI))
    DSDTH=FPTH*DSDR
    GPTH=1.0-DSDTH
    AA=-(R**2)*SIN(SI)
    BB=C**2-R**2-L**2
    CC=(R/2.)*COS(SI)*DSDTH+SIN(SI)*FPTH
    DD=AA-BB*CC
    DSDRT=DD/((R**3)*C*(SIN(SI))**2)
    GDPTH=-((DSDR*FDPTH)+(FPTH*DSDRT))
    DRDPH=FPTH/GPTH
    D2RDP  =((GPTH*FDPTH)-(FPTH*GDPTH))/(GPTH**3)
    ROW=(((R**2)+(DRDPH**2))**1.5)/((R**2)+(2.0*(DRDPH**2))-(R*D2RDP))
    ROWAB=ABS(ROW)
C
C   TESTING FOR ROWMIN
C
    IF(ROWM-ROWAB) 10,10,20
20  ROWM=ROWAB
10  CONTINUE
    THETB=THETB+.1
500 CONTINUE
    ROWRO=ROWM/RO
    X(JJ)=BT
    Y(JJ)=ROWRO
    WRITE(6,9) ROWRO,BT
9   FORMAT(15X,F10.4,15X,F10.4)
    BT=BT+.2
400 CONTINUE
    CALL PLOT(0.0,0.0,-3)
    CALL LINE(X,Y,50,1,0,0)
    CALL PLOT(0.0,0.0,3)
300 CONTINUE
    CRO=CRO+.5000
200 CONTINUE
    CALL AXIS(0.0,0.0,'BETA/TAU (ROTATION AWAY FROM PIVOT)',-35,5.0,
   <  0.0,X(51),X(52))
    CALL AXIS(0.0,0.0,'ROWMIN/RO',9,8.0,90.0,Y(51),Y(52))
    CALL SYMBOL(0.8,-1.0,0.14,'CYCLOIDAL MOTION',0.0,16)
    STOP
    END
```

```
C
C
C      PROGRAM TRESP
C
C      BY F. Y. CHEN
C
C              DISPL, VEL AND ACCEL TIME RESPONSES OF SYSTEM USING STATE-
C      VARIABLE SOLUTION APPROACH DUE TO ARBITRARY MOTION EXCITATION
C      AND INITIAL CONDITIONS OF THE SYSTEM. TIME RESPONSES ARE GIVEN
C      BOTH IN NUMERICAL AND GRAPHICAL FORMS. THE PROGRAM CALLS
C      SUBROUTINES CALCU, RUNGE, TRESP, YDOT AND MMPLOT.
C
C      INPUT ITEMS ARE AS FOLLOWS
C
C      PROBLEM TITLE AND SYSTEM ORDER    5A4, I2 FORMAT
C      COEFFICIENT MATRIX                8F10.3
C      CONTROL VECTOR                    8F10.3
C      OUTPUT VECTOR                     8F10.3
C      FEEDBACK COEFFICIENTS             8F10.3
C      CONTROLLER GAIN                   8F10.3
C      INITIAL CONDITIONS                8F10.3
C      INITIAL TIME, FINAL TIME,
C      TIME STEP, AND FREQUENCY OF
C      OUTPUT                            8F10.3
C      VARIABLES TO BE PLOTTED           8A2
C
       INTEGER CHAR(15)
       COMMON IPLOT,IVAR(10)
       DIMENSION A(10,10),C(10),B(10),AK(10),X(10),NAME(5)
       DATA CHAR(1),CHAR(2),CHAR(3),CHAR(4),CHAR(5),
      *CHAR(6),CHAR(7),CHAR(8),CHAR(9),CHAR(10),CHAR(11),
      *CHAR(12),CHAR(13),CHAR(14),CHAR(15)/2H 1,2H 2,2H 3,2H 4,
      *2H 5,2H 6,2H 7,2H 8,2H 9,2H10,2H E,2H U,2H Y,2H R,2H  /
3      FORMAT (8F10.3)
1000   FORMAT (1H0, 10X, 8HTZERO = , F10.6,10X, 5HTF = ,F10.6/
      * 11X,5HDT = ,F10.6,13X,7HFREQ = ,I5 )
1001   FORMAT (1H0,10X,13H THE A MATRIX   /)
1002   FORMAT (6(1PE20.8))
1003   FORMAT (1H0,10X,19H INITIAL CONDITIONS   /)
1004   FORMAT (1H0,10X,13H THE B MATRIX   /)
1005   FORMAT (1H0,10X,16H FEEDBACK COEFF.   /)
1006   FORMAT (1H0,10X,8H GAIN = ,1PE20.8  )
1007   FORMAT (1H0,10X,13H THE C MATRIX   /)
1008   FORMAT (8A2)
1009   FORMAT( 5X,25HPROBLEM IDENTIFICATION - ,5A4)
1010   FORMAT(1H1,4X,23HGRAPHICAL TIME RESPONSE)
1011   FORMAT(/5X,45(1H*))
10     READ(5,1,END=20) (NAME(I),I=1,5),N
1      FORMAT (5A4,I2)
       DO 60 I=1,8
60     IVAR(I)=CHAR(15)
       WRITE(6,1010)
       WRITE(6,1009) (NAME(I),I=1,5)
       WRITE(6,1011)
       WRITE(6,1001)
       DO 2 I=1,N
       READ(5,3) (A(I,J),J=1,N)
       WRITE(6,1002) (A(I,J),J=1,N)
2      CONTINUE
       READ(5,3) (B(I),I=1,N)
       WRITE(6,1004)
       WRITE(6,1002) (B(I),I=1,N)
       READ(5,3) (C(I),I=1,N)
       WRITE(6,1007)
       WRITE(6,1002) (C(I),I=1,N)
       READ(5,3) (AK(I),I=1,N)
       WRITE(6,1005)
       WRITE(6,1002) (AK(I),I=1,N)
       READ(5,3) GAIN
       WRITE(6,1006) GAIN
       READ(5,3) (X(I),I=1,N)
       WRITE(6,1003)
       WRITE(6,1002) (X(I),I=1,N)
       READ(5,3) TZERO,TF,DT,FREQ
       IFQ=FREQ
       WRITE(6,1000) TZERO,TF,DT,IFQ
       WRITE(6,1011)
       READ(5,1008) (IVAR(I),I=1,8)
```

```
          DO 40 I=1,8
          DO 30 J=1,15
          IF(IVAR(I)-CHAR(J))30,25,30
25        IVAR(I)=J
          GO TO 40
30        CONTINUE
40        CONTINUE
          MIN=1
          MAX=8
          M=8
419       DO 42 I=MIN,MAX
          IF(IVAR(I).NE.15)GO TO 42
          M=MAX-1
          IF(I.GT.M) GO TO 42
          DO 43 J=I,M
43        IVAR(J)=IVAR(J+1)
          GO TO 431
42        CONTINUE
          GO TO 432
431       MIN=I
          MAX=M
          GO TO 419
432       IPLOT = M
          IF(IPLOT.LT.2) GO TO 50
          LIM=IPLOT-1
          DO 44 I=1,LIM
          MIN=I+1
          DO 44 J=MIN,IPLOT
          IF(IVAR(I)-IVAR(J))44,44,45
45        IHOLD=IVAR(I)
          IVAR(I)=IVAR(J)
          IVAR(J)=IHOLD
44        CONTINUE
50        CALL TRESP(A,X,B,AK,TZERO,TF,DT,IFQ,N,GAIN,C)
          GO TO 10
20        STOP
          END


          SUBROUTINE TRESP(A,Y,B,AK,X,XMAX,H,IFREQ,N,GAIN,C)
C         THIS SUBROUTINE COMPUTES AND PLOTS TIME RESPONSE
C         USING CALU,RUNGE,YDOT AND  Y8VSX
          INTEGER CHAR(15)
          COMMON IPLOT,IVAR(10)
          DIMENSION SKJ(101,9),C(10)
          DIMENSION PX(909),PY(909),XL(12),YL(12)
          EQUIVALENCE (SKJ(1,1),PY(1))
          DIMENSION FN(10),Y(10),A(10,10),B(10),AK(10)
          DATA CHAR(1),CHAR(2),CHAR(3),CHAR(4),CHAR(5),
         *CHAR(6),CHAR(7),CHAR(8),CHAR(9),CHAR(10),CHAR(11),
         *CHAR(12),CHAR(13),CHAR(14),CHAR(15)/1H1,1H2,1H3,1H4,
         *1H5,1H6,1H7,1H8,1H9,1HA,1HE,1HU,1HY,1HR,1H /
24        FORMAT (2F10.0,2I10)
25        FORMAT (8F10.0)
          WRITE (6,45)
45        FORMAT('1')
28        FORMAT(//,8X,1HT,12X,4HY(T),10X,4HU(T),4X,
         *  7(5X,1HX,I1,4H(T)  , 3X))
29        FORMAT(10(1PE14.6))
1000      FORMAT(/,5X,33HMAXIMUM NUMBER OF POINTS EXCEEDED /)
          NN=N+1
          WRITE(6,28) (J,J=1,NN)
          II=0
          J=0
          KOUNT=IFREQ
300       CALL CALCU(Y,U,X,N,AK,GAIN,R)
          KOUNT=KOUNT+1
          IF(KOUNT-IFREQ)50,350,350
350       KOUNT=0
450       P1=0.0
          Y(N+1)=0.0
          DO 451 I=1,N
          Y(N+1)=Y(N+1)+A(N,I)*Y(I)
451       P1=P1+C(I)*Y(I)
          Y(N+1)=Y(N+1)+B(N)*U
          WRITE(6,29)X,P1,U,(Y(M),M=1,NN)
          IF(IPLOT.EQ.0)GO TO 21
```

```
            J=J+1
            IF(J.GT.101)GO TO 222
            SKJ(J,1)=X
            DO 40 I=1,IPLOT
            MM=IVAR(I)
            IF(MM.EQ.0) GO TO 40
            IF(MM.GT.10) GO TO 35
            SKJ(J,I+1)=Y(MM)
            GO TO 40
   35       KNOW=MM-10
            GO TO (36,37,38,39),KNOW
   36       SKJ(J,I+1)=R-P1
            GO TO 40
   37       SKJ(J,I+1)=U
            GO TO 40
   38       SKJ(J,I+1)=P1
            GO TO 40
   39       SKJ(J,I+1)=R
   40       CONTINUE
   21       CONTINUE
   50       CALL RUNGE (N, FN, H, X, Y, L,II)
            IF(L-1) 100,200,100
  200       CALL CALCU(Y,U,X,N,AK,GAIN,R)
            CALL YDOT(A,Y,FN,B,U,N)
  550       GO TO 50
  222       WRITE(6,1000)
            GO TO 400
  100       IF(X-XMAX) 300,300,400
  400       IF(IPLOT.EQ.0) GO TO 403
            WRITE(6,600)
  600       FORMAT(1H1,50X,15HSYSTEM RESPONSE//)
            WRITE(6,601)
  601       FORMAT(48X,8HVARIABLE,8X,6HSYMBOL//)
            DO 608 I=1,IPLOT
            MM=IVAR(I)
            IF(MM.GT.10) GO TO 603
            WRITE(6,602)IVAR(I),CHAR(I)
  602       FORMAT(51X,1HX,I2,13X,A1)
            GO TO 608
  603       KK=IVAR(I)-10
            GO TO(604,605,606,607),KK
  604       WRITE(6,610)CHAR(I)
            GO TO 608
  605       WRITE(6,611)CHAR(I)
            GO TO  608
  606       WRITE(6,612)CHAR(I)
            GO TO 608
  607       WRITE(6,613)CHAR(I)
  608       CONTINUE
  610       FORMAT(50X,5HERROR,12X,A1)
  611       FORMAT(49X,7HCONTROL,11X,A1)
  612       FORMAT(50X,6HOUTPUT,11X,A1)
  613       FORMAT(50X,5HINPUT,12X,A1)
            NPLOT=IPLOT+1
            DO 44 II=2,NPLOT
            DO 44 JJ=1,J
            LL=(II-2)*J+JJ
            PY(LL)=SKJ(JJ,II)
            PX(LL)=(JJ-1)*H*IFREQ
   44       CONTINUE
            CALL MMPLOT (PX,PY,J,IPLOT,XL,YL)
  403       RETURN
            END



            SUBROUTINE CALCU(X,U,T,N,AK,GAIN,R)
  C         THIS SUBROUTINE COMPUTES THE REFERENCE AND CONTROL INPUTS
            DIMENSION X(10),AK(10)
  C         THE CARDS BETWEEN HERE AND THE NEXT COMMENT CART
  C         ARE SUPPLIED BY THE USER TO DEFINE R(T)
            WN=6.283/0.4
            PHI=0.0
            IF(T.GT.1.0)GO TO 1001
            R=1.0*T-1.0/6.283*SIN(6.283*T)
            DR=(1-COS(6.283*T))
            GO TO 1002
```

```
1001 R=1.0
1002 CONTINUE
C     END OF ROUTINE TO DIFINE R(T)
      U=WN*WN*R+2.0*PHI*DR*WN
      DO 1 I=1,N
1     U=U-AK(I)*X(I)
      U=U*GAIN
      RETURN
      END



      SUBROUTINE RUNGE (N,FN, H, X, Y, L,I)
C     FOURTH ORDER RUNGE KUTTA INTEGRATION ROUTINE
      DIMENSION Y(600),SAVEY(600),PHI(600),FN(10)
      I=I+1
      GO TO   (1,2,3,4,5),I
1     L=1
      RETURN
2     DO 600 J=1,N
      SAVEY(J)=Y(J)
      PHI(J)=FN(J)
600   Y(J)=SAVEY(J)+.5*H*FN(J)
      X=X+.5*H
      L=1
      RETURN
3     DO 700 J=1,N
      PHI(J)=PHI(J)+2.*FN(J)
700   Y(J)=SAVEY(J)+.5*H*FN(J)
      L=1
      RETURN
4     DO 800 J=1,N
      PHI(J)=PHI(J)+2.*FN(J)
800   Y(J)=SAVEY(J)+H*FN(J)
      X=X+.5*H
      L=1
      RETURN
5     DO 900 J=1,N
900   Y(J)=SAVEY(J)+(H/6.)*(PHI(J)+FN(J))
      L=2
      I=0
      RETURN
      END



      SUBROUTINE YDOT(A,Y,XDOT,B,U,N)
C     THIS SUBROUTINE IS USED TO COMPUTE DERIVATIVES FOR RUNGE
      DIMENSION Y(10),A(10,10),B(10),XDOT(10)
      DO 2 I=1,N
      XDOT(I)=0.0
      DO 1 J=1,N
      XDOT(I)=XDOT(I)+A(I,J)*Y(J)
1     CONTINUE
      XDOT(I)=XDOT(I)+B(I)*U
2     CONTINUE
      RETURN
      END
```

```
C
C      PROGRAM SPEC1
C
C
C      BY F. Y. CHEN
C
C
C         THIS PROGRAM GENERATES THE PRIMARY AND RESIDUAL DYNAMIC
C      RESPONSE SPECTRA BASED ON RUNGE-KUTTA NUMERICAL SCHEME FOR SOLUTION
C      OF THE SYSTEM EQUATION.
C
C         SUBROUTINE FCT IS USED TO INPUT THE CAM EXITATIONAL FUNCTION.
C
C         INPUT DATA CARD CONTAINING DAMP, H, XK1, XM IS IN 4F10.5
C      FORMAT.
C
C         OUTPUT IS BOTH PRINTED AND CARD PUNCHED IN 10F8.5 FORMAT FOR
C      A TOTAL OF 300 POINTS FOR THE PRIMARY RESPONSE SPECTRUM AND RESIDUAL
C      RESPONSE SPECTRUM RESPECTIVELY.
C
       REAL K0,K1,K2,K3,M0,M1,M2,M3
       DIMENSION PRI(300),RES(300),Y(2),DATA(2,2000)
       COMMON DAMP,WN,H,PI,TRK,T1,T,DLTAT
       READ(5,900) DAMP,H,XK1,XM
       NUMB = 300
       WN = SQRT(XK1/XM)
       PI = 3.1415926
       DLTAT = .0001
       TN = 2.*PI/WN
       DO 140 N = 1,NUMB
       INT = 1
       TR = .1 + (N-1)*.05
       T1 = TR*TN
       XST = 1.0
       TLAST = 2.*T1
       COUNT = 2.*T1/DLTAT
       ICT = COUNT
       MCT = ICT/2 + 1
       NCT = MCT + 1
       DO 10 I = 1,2
       DO 10 IJ = 1,2000
       DATA(I,IJ) = 0.0
   10  Y(I) = 0.0
       T = 0.0
   20  M0 = Y(2)
       TRK = T
       CALL FCT(Y(1),Y(2),K0)
       M1 = Y(2) + K0*DLTAT/2.
       X1 = Y(1) + M0*DLTAT/2.
       X2 = Y(2) + K0*DLTAT/2.
       TRK = T + DLTAT/2.
       CALL FCT(X1,X2,K1)
       M2 = Y(2) + K1*DLTAT/2.
       X1 = Y(1) + M1*DLTAT/2.
       X2 = Y(2) + K1*DLTAT/2.
       TRK = T + DLTAT/2.
       CALL FCT(X1,X2,K2)
       M3 = Y(2) + K2*DLTAT
       X1 = Y(1) + M2*DLTAT
       X2 = Y(2) + K2*DLTAT
       TRK = T + DLTAT
       CALL FCT(X1,X2,K3)
       Y(1) = Y(1) + (M0+2.*M1+2.*M2+M3)/6.*DLTAT
       Y(2) = Y(2) + (K0+2.*K1+2.*K2+K3)/6.*DLTAT
       IF(INT-MCT) 80,80,90
   80  DATA(1,INT) = ABS(Y(1)/XST)
       GO TO 100
   90  DATA(2,INT) = ABS(Y(1)/XST)
  100  CONTINUE
       INT = INT + 1
       T = T + DLTAT
       IF(T-TLAST) 20,20,70
   70  CONTINUE
       PRI(N) = DATA(1,1)
       DO 110 I = 1,MCT
       IF(PRI(N)-DATA(1,I)) 120,110,110
  120  PRI(N) = DATA(1,I)
```

```
110 CONTINUE
    RES(N) = DATA(2,NCT)
    DO 140 I = NCT,ICT
    IF(RES(N)-DATA(2,I)) 130,140,140
130 RES(N) = DATA(2,I)
140 CONTINUE
    ML = NUMB/10
    DO 150 M = 1,ML
    K = 10*M
    L = K-9
    WRITE(6,910) (PRI(J),J=L,K)
    WRITE(7,930) (PRI(J),J=L,K)
150 CONTINUE
    DO 160 M = 1,ML
    K = 10*M
    L = K-9
    WRITE(6,910) (RES(J),J=L,K)
    WRITE(7,930) (RES(J),J=L,K)
160 CONTINUE
    STOP
900 FORMAT(4F10.5)
910 FORMAT(10E12.5)
930 FORMAT(10F8.5)
    END

    SUBROUTINE FCT(X1,X2,S)
    COMMON DAMP,WN,H,PI,T,T1,TIME,DLTAT
    A=-2.*DAMP*WN*X2-X1*WN**2
    ZZ=4.888124*H/(T1**2)
    FP=4.*PI
    IF(T-T1) 130,130,140
140 S=A
    GO TO 10
130 IF(T-7.*T1/8.) 110,110,120
120 S=A-ZZ*SIN(FP*T/T1-3.*PI)
    GO TO 10
110 IF(T-5.*T1/8.) 90,90,100
100 S=A-ZZ
    GO TO 10
 90 IF(T-T1/2.) 70,70,80
 80 S=A-ZZ*SIN(FP*T/T1-2.*PI)
    GO TO 10
 70 IF(T-3.*T1/8.) 50,50,60
 60 S=A+ZZ*SIN(FP*T/T1-PI)
    GO TO 10
 50 IF(T-T1/8.) 30,30,40
 40 S=A+ZZ
    GO TO 10
 30 S=A+ZZ*SIN(FP*T/T1)
 10 RETURN
    END
```

```
C
C      SPEC 2
C
C
C      BY F. Y. CHEN
C
C
C
C          THIS PROGRAM GENERATES LINER PLOTS FOR THE PRIMARY AND RESIDUAL
C      SHOCK SPECTRA FOR DISP, VELOCITY AND ACCELERATION. DATA INPUT IS
C      AS FOLLOWS:
C
C          CARD 1 CONTAIN NCURV, MODE, H, XK1, XM, VMAX, AND AMAX IN
C      FORMAT 2I1, 8X, 5F10.5, WHERE NCURV IS THE NUMBER OF PLOTED
C      CURVES CORRESPONDING TO DAMPING VALUE; MODE = 1 FOR DISP, = 2 FOR
C      VELOCITY, =3 FOR ACCEL. VMAX IS THE MAX VELOCITY FACTOR, AMAX IS
C      THE MAX ACCEL FACTOR.
C
C          CARD 2 CONTAINS THE TITLE IN 30A2 FORMAT.
C
C          CARDS FOR PRIMARY OR RESIDUAL SPECTRA IN FORMAT 10F8.5, 30
C      CARDS FOR EACH CURVE.
C
       INTEGER LABEX(3),TIT1(20),TIT2(20),TIT3(20),L1(2),L2(2),L3(3)
       DIMENSION Y(302),T(302)
       DIMENSION IBUF(5000)
       DATA LABEX/'T1','/T','N '/
       DATA L1/'SN','D '/
       DATA L2/'SN','V '/
       DATA L3/'SN','A '/
       CALL PLOTS(IBUF(1),20000,10)
       READ(5,940) NCURV,MODE,H,XK1,XM,VMAX,AMAX
       READ(5,910) (TIT1(J),J=1,10),(TIT2(J),J=1,10),(TIT3(J),J=1,10)
       PI = 3.1415926
       WN = SQRT(XK1/XM)
       TN = 2.0*PI/WN
       DO 204 NC = 1,NCURV
       ISCAL = 1
       CALL PLOT(0.0,0.0,-3)
       Y(301) = 0.0
       T(301) = 0.0
       T(302) = 2.0
       DO 40 N = 1,300
   40  T(N) = .1 + (N-1)*.05
       DO 500 M = 1,30
       K = 10*M
       L = K - 9
  500  READ(5,900) (Y(J),J=L,K)
       DO 104 N = 1,300
       IF(Y(N)) 700,701,701
  700  Y(N) = 0.0
  701  CONTINUE
       T1 = TN*T(N)
       GO TO (101,102,103), MODE
  101  CONTINUE
       Y(N) = Y(N)/H
       GO TO 104
  102  CONTINUE
       Y(N) = Y(N)*WN*T1/H/VMAX
       GO TO 104
  103  CONTINUE
       Y(N) = Y(N)*WN*WN*T1*T1/H/AMAX
  104  CONTINUE
       GO TO (105,106),ISCAL
  105  YMAX = Y(1)
       DO 107 I = 1,300
       IF(YMAX-Y(I)) 108,108,107
  108  YMAX = Y(I)
  107  CONTINUE
       Y(302) = YMAX/6.0
       ISCAL = 2
  106  CALL LINE(T,Y,300,1,0,0)
       CALL PLOT(0.0,0.0,3)
  204  CONTINUE
       CALL AXIS(0.0,0.0,LABEX,-3006,8.0,0.0,0.0,2.0)
       GO TO (301,302,303), MODE
  301  CALL AXIS(0.0,0.0,L1,3004,6.0,90.0,Y(301),Y(302))
```

```
      GO TO 304
302 CALL AXIS(0.0,0.0,L2,3004,6.0,90.0,Y(301),Y(302))
      GO TO 304
303 CALL AXIS(0.0,0.0,L3,3004,6.0,90.0,Y(301),Y(302))
304 CONTINUE
      CALL SYMBOL(4.0,6.0,.14,TIT1,0.0,20)
      CALL SYMBOL(4.0,5.72,.14,TIT2,0.0,20)
      CALL SYMBOL(4.0,5.44,.14,TIT3,0.0,20)
      CALL PLOT(0.0,0.0,3)
110 CONTINUE
400 STOP
900 FORMAT(10F8.5)
910 FORMAT(3(10A2))
940 FORMAT(2I1,8X,5F10.5)
      END
```

```
C
C      SPEC 3
C
C      BY F. Y. CHEN
C
C          THIS PROGRAM PRODUCES A 4-GRID LOG PLOT FOR DYNAMICS RESPONSE
C      SPECTRA OF CAMS. DATA INPUT IS AS FOLLOWS:
C
C          CARD 1 CONTAINS TITLE IN 30A2 FORMAT.
C
C          CARD 2 CONTAIN H, XK1, XM, VMAX, AMAX IN 5F10.5 FORMAT.
C
C          NEXT 30 CARDS CONTAIN 300 PRIMARY POINTS, NEXT 30 CARDS CONTAIN
C      300 RESIDUAL POINTS, IN 10F8.6 FORMAT.
C
C          ACCEL AND DISP GRIDS ARE SCALED AUTOMATICALLY, VELOCITY GRID
C      IS CONFINED TO .01 TO 1.0.
C
C
       INTEGER LABEX(4),LABEY(4),LABA(3),LABD(2),ITLE(30)
       REAL T(302),PRI(300),RES(300),PVEL(302),RVEL(302),ALINE(302),
     5     XG(8),YG(8),G(8)
       DIMENSION IBUF(5000)
       DATA LABA/'AC','CE','L '/, LABD/'DI','SP'/
       DATA LABEY/'VE','LO','CI','TY'/
       DATA LABEX/'T1','OV','ER','TN'/
       CALL PLOTS(IBUF(1),20000,10,0)
C
C      READ INPUT DATA
C
 155   READ(5,910) (ITLE(J),J=1,30)
       READ(5,920) H,XK1,XM,VMAX,AMAX
       DO 10 N = 1,30
       K = 10*N
       L = K - 9
 10    READ(5,900) (PRI(J),J=L,K)
       DO 20 N = 1,30
       K = 10*N
       L = K - 9
 20    READ(5,900) (RES(J),J=L,K)
       PI = 3.1415926
       WN = SQRT(XK1/XM)
       TN = 2.*PI/WN
       ALINE(301) = 0.0
       ALINE(302) = 1.0
       T(301) = 0.0
       PVEL(301) = 0.0
       RVEL(301) = 0.0
       T(302) = 1.0
       PVEL(302) = 1.0
       RVEL(302) = 1.0
C
C      CALCULATE PRIMAY AND RESIDUAL VELOCITY, GENERATE TIME AXIS
C
       DO 30 N = 1,300
       T(N) = .1 + (N-1)*.05
       T1 = TN*T(N)
       PVEL(N) = PRI(N)*WN*T1/H/VMAX
       RVEL(N) = RES(N)*WN*T1/H/VMAX
 30    CONTINUE
       PACC = PRI(1)*WN*WN*T1*T1/H/AMAX
       PDIS = PRI(1)/H
       FAC = PVEL(1)/PACC
       FAC2 = PVEL(1)/PDIS
       B = ALOG(10.0)
       DO 40 N = 1,300
       IF(PVEL(N)) 50,60,50
 50    PVEL(N) = 3.*((ALOG(PVEL(N))/B)+2.)
 60    IF(RVEL(N)) 70,40,70
 70    RVEL(N) = 3.*((ALOG(RVEL(N))/B)+2.)
 40    T(N) = (ALOG(T(N))/B + 1.0)*3.67632
       DO 150 N = 1,300
       IF(RVEL(N)) 200,210,210
 200   RVEL(N) = 0.0
 210   CONTINUE
       T(N) = ABS(T(N))
       PVEL(N) = ABS(PVEL(N))
```

```
         RVEL(N) = ABS(RVEL(N))
         IF(PRI(N)) 31,31,32
      31 PVEL(N) = 0.0
      32 IF(RES(N)) 33,33,150
      33 RVEL(N) = 0.0
     150 CONTINUE
         CALL PLOT(0.0,0.0,-3)
C
C        GENERATE GRID LINE POSITIONS
C
         G(1) = .1
         G(2) = .2
         G(3) = .5
         G(4) = 1.0
         G(5) = 2.0
         G(6) = 5.0
         G(7) = 10.0
         G(8) = 15.0
         DO 80 I = 1,8
         XG(I) = 3.67632*(1.0 + ALOG(G(I))/B)
      80 YG(I) = 3.0*(1.0 + ALOG(G(I))/B)
C
C        DRAW VERTICAL GRID LINES
C
         DO 90 I = 1,7,2
         CALL PLOT(XG(I),0.0,2)
         CALL PLOT(XG(I),6.0,2)
         J = I + 1
         CALL PLOT(XG(J),6.0,2)
      90 CALL PLOT(XG(J),0.0,2)
C
C        DRAW HORIZONTAL GRID LINES
C
         CALL PLOT(8.0,6.0,2)
         CALL PLOT(0.0,6.0,2)
         CALL PLOT(0.0,0.0,2)
         DO 100 I = 1,5,2
         CALL PLOT(0.0,YG(I),2)
         CALL PLOT(8.0,YG(I),2)
         J = I + 1
         CALL PLOT(8.0,YG(J),2)
     100 CALL PLOT(0.0,YG(J),2)
         CALL PLOT(0.0,0.0,3)
C
C        LABEL X AND Y NUMBERS AND TITLES
C
         DO 110 I = 1,8
         XNUM = XG(I) - .14
     110 CALL NUMBER(XNUM,-.16,.07,G(I),0.0,1)
         CALL SYMBOL(3.664, -.6,.14,LABEX,0.0,6)
         CALL PLOT(0.0,0.0,3)
         DO 120 I = 1,3
         YNUM = YG(I) - .02
         YNUMB = G(I)/10.0
     120 CALL NUMBER(-.33,YNUM,.07,YNUMB,0.0,2)
         DO 130 I = 4,7
         YNUM = YG(I) - .02
         YNUMB = G(I)/10.0
     130 CALL NUMBER(-.26,YNUM,.07,YNUMB,0.0,1)
         CALL SYMBOL(-.6,2.44,.14,LABEY,90.0,8)
         CALL PLOT(0.0,0.0,3)
         CALL SYMBOL(.25,6.28,.14,ITLE,0.0,60)
         CALL PLOT(0.0,0.0,3)
C
C        CALCULATE AND DRAW POSITION OF DISPLACEMENT GRID
C
C
C        CALCULATE Y-INTERCEPT AND FIND NEXT LOWEST TENS VALUE
C
         JA = 0
         IY = IFIX(ALOG(PDIS)/B)
         IF(IY) 690,690,695
     690 IY = IY - 1
     695 Y = 10.**IY
         DO 704 KM = 1,3
         K = 1
         Z = Y
```

```
650 CONTINUE
    Z = Z*FAC2
    YA = 3.*((ALOG(Z)/B) + 2.)
    DO 630 N = 1,300
    ALINE(N) = .75*T(N) + YA
    IF(ALINE(N)) 610,610,600
610 ALINE(N) = 0.0
600 CONTINUE
    IF(ALINE(N) - 6.0) 630,630,640
640 ALINE(N) = 6.0
630 CONTINUE
    CALL LINE(T,ALINE,300,1,0,0)
    IF(KM-2) 675,680,675
680 W1 = ALINE(3) + .014
    W2 = Y
    W3 = ALINE(6) + .014
    IF(JA) 660,670,660
670 CALL NUMBER(T(3),W1,.07,W2,38.,2)
    TX = T(3) + .4
    CALL SYMBOL(TX,W3,.07,LABD,38.,4)
660 JA = 1
675 CONTINUE
    GO TO (701,702,703),K
701 Z = Y/2.
    K = 2
    GO TO 650
702 Z = Y/5.
    K = 3
    GO TO 650
703 Y = Y/10.
704 CONTINUE
C
C       CALCULATE AND DRAW POSITION OF ACCEL GRID
C
C       CALCULATE Y-INTERCEPT AND FIND NEXT LOWEST TENS VALUE
C
    JA = 0
    IY = IFIX(ALOG(PACC)/B)
    IF(IY) 490,490,495
490 IY = IY - 1
495 Y = 10.**IY
    DO 604 KM = 1,3
    K = 1
    Z = Y
550 CONTINUE
    Z = Z*FAC
    YA = 3.*((ALOG(Z)/B) + 2.)
C       CALCULATE POINTS ON GRID LINE
    DO 530 N = 1,300
    ALINE(N) = -.75*T(N) + YA
C       TEST FOR Y LESS THAN 0
    IF(ALINE(N)) 510,510,500
510 ALINE(N) = 0.0
500 CONTINUE
C       TEST FOR Y GREATER THAN 6
    IF(ALINE(N)-6.) 530,530,540
540 ALINE(N) = 6.0
530 CONTINUE
    CALL LINE(T,ALINE,300,1,0,0)
    W1 = ALINE(1) + .014
    W2 = 1.0/Y
    W3 = ALINE(1) + .014
    TX = T(1) + .4
    IF(JA) 560,570,560
570 CALL NUMBER(T(1),W1,.07,E2,-38.,2)
    CALL SYMBOL(TX,W3,.07,LABA,-38.,5)
560 JA = 1
    GO TO (601,602,603),K
601 Z = Y*2.
    K = 2
    GO TO 550
602 Z = Y*5.
    K = 3
    GO TO 550
603 Y = Y*10.
604 CONTINUE
    CALL PLOT(0.0,0.0,3)
```

```
C       PLOT CURVES
C
        CALL  LINE(T,PVEL,300,1,0,0)
        CALL  PLOT(0.0,0.0,3)
        CALL  LINE(T,RVEL,300,1,0,0)
  900 FORMAT(10F8.5)
  910 FORMAT(30A2)
  920 FORMAT(5F10.5)
  151 STOP
        END
```

Index

ABOUT THE AUTHOR

Fan Y. Chen had been on the faculty of the Department of Mechanical Engineering at Ohio University since 1959. He received his B.S. degree from National Taiwan University in 1953, M.S. degree from the University of Illinois in 1959, and Ph.D. degree from Purdue University in 1972. A member of several professional societies, Professor Chen had written over 70 technical papers published in learned journals. His other writing includes five chapters in *Linkage Design Monographs* and "A Survey of Computer use in Mechanism Analysis and Synthesis in *Design Technology Transfer* in 1976, and 1974 respectively (both edited by A. H. Soni).

He was selected as a Research Institute Fellow by Ohio University in 1974, and received the Procter and Gamble Award on applied mechanism papers in 1969. He was listed in *Who's Who in Science and Technology, Who's Who in the Midwest,* and *Dictionary of International Biography.*

Professor Chen died December 1981.

ACKNOWLEDGMENTS

I am grateful to the listed authors for permission to reprint from previously published material:

Dr. P. Barkan, "Calculation of High-Speed Valve Motion with a Flexible Overhead Linkage," *SAE Trans.,* Vol. 61, 1953.

M.A. Ganter and J.J. Uicker, Jr., Design Charts for Disk Cams with Reciprocating Radial Roller Follower, Trans., *ASME,* 101B, 3, 1979, pp. 465-470.

H.R. Kim and W.R. Newcombe, The Effect of Cam Profile Errors and System Flexibility on Cam Mechanism Output.

M. Kloomok, "Plate cam design: radius of curvature," *Product Engineering,* 26, No. 9, 1955, pp. 186-201.

M.P. Koster, Effect of Flexibility of Driving Shaft on the Dynamic Behavior of a Cam Mechanism, Trans., *ASME,* 97B, 2, pp. 595-602.

P.W. Koumans, The Calculation of the Max. Pressure Angle and the Min. Radius of Curvature of a Cam Using Special Graphs.

J.W. Rao and E. Raghavacharyulu, Experimental Determination of Jump Characteristics in Cam-Follower System, *IME Proc.,* 1975, pp. 951-956.

L.E. Szakallas and M. Savage, The Characterization of Cam Drive System Windup, J. of Mech. Design, Trans., *ASME,* 102, 2, pp. 278-285.